# AN ESSAY

concerning

# Human Understanding

by

# JOHN LOCKE

*Abridged and Edited*

by

A. S. PRINGLE-PATTISON

OXFORD
AT THE CLARENDON PRESS

*Oxford University Press, Amen House, London E.C.4*
GLASGOW NEW YORK TORONTO MELBOURNE WELLINGTON
BOMBAY CALCUTTA MADRAS KARACHI LAHORE DACCA
CAPE TOWN SALISBURY NAIROBI IBADAN ACCRA
KUALA LUMPUR HONG KONG

FIRST EDITION 1924
REPRINTED 1928, 1934, 1941, 1947, 1950, 1956, 1960, 1964

PRINTED IN GREAT BRITAIN

# PREFACE

In his 'Epistle to the Reader' Locke refers to the way in which the Essay was written—'by catches and many long intervals of interruption'—as being 'apt to cause some repetitions'. 'I will not deny,' he says, 'but possibly it might be reduced to a narrower compass than it is. But, to confess the truth, I am now too lazy or too busy to make it shorter.' If the length of the Essay and its endless repetitions called for some apology, even on its first appearance, when the 'new way of ideas' might be deemed unfamiliar to its first readers, these qualities tell with tenfold force against it to-day. Partly owing to the extraordinary extent to which the *Essay* permeated popular thought in the succeeding century, many of the ideas which Locke considered 'new and out of the ordinary way', have become accepted commonplaces. Doctrines, on the other hand, which he is never weary of returning to demolish have only a languid historical interest for the present generation. It is to be feared that the natural impatience produced in the modern reader by Locke's prolixity and the apparent triteness of much of his matter have already had the effect of discouraging the first-hand study of the Essay by students of philosophy. But, in spite of its defects, Locke's work is a philosophical classic in the best sense of the term, and its doctrines fill far too large a space in modern thought to be learned from the colourless abstracts in Histories of Philosophy. Locke gives us the first characteristically modern statement of the questions about human knowledge which meet us again in Hume and

Kant, and which to a certain extent are still with us to-day. It is impossible to understand either Berkeley or Hume or Kant without reference to Locke; and Locke's own analysis and philosophical conclusions possess a freshness, an independence, and a transparent honesty of purpose which make them well worthy of independent study. The more carefully they are studied, the more suggestive will they appear, and the more relevant to our modern questions. The more also will the reader learn to hold their author in affection and to relish his robust and often racy, on occasion even eloquent, English style.

The object of the present edition is to promote the independent study of the *Essay* by doing for the text what Locke had not the leisure or the patience to do himself. In the first instance, by the omission of unnecessary repetitions it has been reduced to almost exactly half its original length, and in the second place an attempt has been made by means of an Introduction and Notes to keep before the modern reader the main trend of Locke's conclusions, to direct attention to his most significant recurring ideas, and in general to guide the student to the philosophically important sections of the work. It is not possible to do this service for Locke simply by picking out a few of the more obviously important chapters and publishing them separately. For these chapters themselves contain many repetitions, as well as much matter that is merely distracting to the modern student. And, what is more important, a true appreciation of Locke's meaning in such chapters can only be reached through a knowledge of the scheme of the *Essay* as a whole. It is only in the light of the First Book, for example, antiquated and superfluous as much of the discussion now seems, that the analysis of the Second Book can be fully understood and fairly interpreted. And,

## *Preface*

again, owing to Locke's 'discontinued way of writing', his dominant ideas are apt to recur in different settings. From different starting-points the discussion winds round into some familiar train of thought which never fails to warm Locke's style with a touch of enthusiasm or of honest indignation. So it happens that a pointed statement of his general position or one of his happiest passages may often be found embedded in disquisitions which, as a whole, may be neglected with impunity. The present volume is, in its idea, not so much a series of selections from the *Essay* as an 'edition with omissions'. The external framework of the *Essay* is retained, even to the extent of supplying the titles of chapters from which no extracts are given. The aim has been to leave out nothing that was in any way characteristic of Locke's thinking, and for that reason there will still be found repetitions and re-inculcations of favourite ideas. Without such recurrences Locke would be unrecognizable. Moreover their rigorous excision would falsify our impression of Locke's scheme by obscuring the relative importance of his various positions in his own mind. In a question of omitting and retaining no two editors are likely to agree in every detail. Some students may miss an occasional passage on which they have been accustomed to lay stress. But if so, I am reasonably confident that they will find in the text of this edition equally characteristic expressions with an entirely identical sense. Other readers may think that the process of compression might have been carried farther with advantage; but each teacher can suggest to his pupils such further omissions as the time at their disposal or his sense of the importance of the subject suggests. The present version has been made with the needs of university teachers and students in view, and the editor's aim has been, while pruning the text somewhat severely of its redundancies, to leave with the reader an authentic picture of the *Essay* as it shaped itself in its author's mind, and so to retain in academic use one of the classical documents of English philosophy.

I will only add that the text was adjusted and arrangements made for publication as far back as 1909, but pressure of other work caused the project to be temporarily laid aside. The text has been repeatedly revised in the interval and is now as near my idea as I can hope to make it. Locke's own summaries have been retained at the head of the sections, except where they are merely repetitions of the text, and the italics of the original editions, although unusual in modern books of the kind, have been occasionally reproduced where they seemed to be a guide to the emphasis in Locke's mind as he wrote.

In the proof-reading and collation with the original editions and in the preparation of the Index I have been greatly indebted to my friend, Mr. H. F. Hallett, to whom I desire to express my warm thanks.

A. SETH PRINGLE-PATTISON.

EDINBURGH, *January* 1924.

# CONTENTS

|  | PAGE |
|---|---|
| PREFACE | iii |
| EDITOR'S INTRODUCTION | ix |

## AN ESSAY CONCERNING HUMAN UNDERSTANDING

THE EPISTLE TO THE READER . . . . . . 3

### BOOK I
#### OF INNATE NOTIONS

CHAP.
- I. Introduction . . . . . . . . 9
- II. No Innate speculative Principles . . . . 16
- III. No Innate practical Principles . . . . . 28
- IV. Other Considerations concerning innate Principles, both speculative and practical . . . . . 36

### BOOK II
#### OF IDEAS

- I. Of Ideas in general, and their Original . . . 42
- II. Of simple Ideas . . . . . . . 53
- III. Of Ideas of one Sense . . . . . . 55
- IV. Of Solidity . . . . . . . . 57
- V. Of simple Ideas of more than one Sense. . . 60
- VI. Of simple Ideas of Reflection . . . . 61
- VII. Of simple Ideas of both Sensation and Reflection . 61
- VIII. Some farther Considerations concerning our simple Ideas 64
- IX. Of Perception . . . . . . . 73
- X. Of Retention . . . . . . . . 79
- XI. Of Discerning, and other Operations of the Mind . 85
- XII. Of complex Ideas . . . . . . . 92
- XIII. Of Space, and its simple Modes . . . . 95
- XIV. Of Duration, and its simple Modes . . . 106
- XV. Of Duration and Expansion considered together . 115
- XVI. Of Number . . . . . . . . 121
- XVII. Of Infinity . . . . . . . . 124
- [XVIII. Of other simple Modes]
- XIX. Of the Modes of Thinking . . . . . 133
- [XX. Of the Modes of Pleasure and Pain]
- XXI. Of Power . . . . . . . . 135
- XXII. Of mixed Modes . . . . . . . 150
- XXIII. Of our complex Ideas of Substances . . . 154
- XXIV. Of collective Ideas of Substances . . . . 175
- XXV. Of Relation . . . . . . . . 175

| CHAP. | | PAGE |
|---|---|---|
| XXVI. | Of Cause and Effect, and other Relations | 180 |
| XXVII. | Of Identity and Diversity | 182 |
| XXVIII. | Of other Relations | 201 |
| XXIX. | Of clear and obscure, distinct and confused Ideas | 204 |
| XXX. | Of real and fantastical Ideas | 208 |
| XXXI. | Of adequate and inadequate Ideas | 209 |
| XXXII. | Of true and false Ideas | 215 |
| XXXIII. | Of the Association of Ideas | 217 |

# BOOK III

## OF WORDS

| I. | Of Words or Language in general | 223 |
|---|---|---|
| II. | Of the Signification of Words | 225 |
| III. | Of general Terms | 226 |
| IV. | Of the Names of simple Ideas | 237 |
| V. | Of the Names of mixed Modes and Relations | 240 |
| VI. | Of the Names of Substances | 242 |
| [VII. | Of Particles] | |
| VIII. | Of abstract and concrete Terms | 253 |
| [IX. | Of the Imperfection of Words | |
| X. | Of the Abuse of Words | |
| XI. | Of the Remedies of the foregoing Imperfections and Abuses] | |

# BOOK IV

## OF KNOWLEDGE AND OPINION

| I. | Of Knowledge in general | 255 |
|---|---|---|
| II. | Of the Degrees of our Knowledge | 261 |
| III. | Of the Extent of Human Knowledge | 267 |
| IV. | Of the Reality of our Knowledge | 287 |
| V. | Of Truth in general | 291 |
| VI. | Of Universal Propositions, their Truth and Certainty | 293 |
| VII. | Of Maxims | 299 |
| VIII. | Of trifling Propositions | 306 |
| IX. | Of our Knowledge of Existence | 309 |
| X. | Of our Knowledge of the Existence of a God | 310 |
| XI. | Of our Knowledge of the Existence of other Things | 321 |
| XII. | Of the Improvement of our Knowledge | 329 |
| [XIII. | Some farther Considerations concerning our Knowledge] | |
| XIV. | Of Judgement | 333 |
| XV. | Of Probability | 334 |
| XVI. | Of the Degrees of Assent | 337 |
| XVII. | Of Reason | 344 |
| XVIII. | Of Faith and Reason, and their distinct Provinces | 355 |
| XIX. | Of Enthusiasm | 359 |
| XX. | Of wrong Assent, or Error | 363 |
| XXI. | Of the Division of the Sciences | 369 |

INDEX . . . . . . . . . . 373

# EDITOR'S INTRODUCTION

BORN in 1632, in the same year as Spinoza and five years before the publication of Descartes's *Discourse on Method*, Locke suffered at Oxford as an undergraduate from the scholastic Aristotelianism which still survived at that university. It seemed to him 'perplexed with obscure terms and useless questions', and its logical disputations invented for 'wrangling and ostentation rather than to discover truth'. Hence, although he gave his own philosophy to the world only towards the close of a long life—the first edition of the *Essay* appeared in 1690—we still meet in his pages the attitude of mind familiar to us in Bacon and other pioneers of modern philosophy, the same disparaging criticism of scholastic philosophy and the Aristotelian logic, the same revolt against tradition and authority in all its forms. He returns again and again in the *Essay* to emphasize the mischief wrought by the indolent acceptance of traditional dogmas and unverified assumptions. 'So much as we ourselves consider and comprehend of truth and reason, so much we possess of real and true knowledge. The floating of other men's opinions in our brains makes us not one jot the more knowing, though they happen to be true.'[1] The very word 'principle' has evil associations for him, for it seems to him to mean a doctrine upon which other doctrines are founded, but which is regarded as itself withdrawn from the criticism of reason. His whole polemic against 'innate principles' in Book I reveals itself in the closing paragraphs as a protest in the modern spirit against the tendency ' to take men off from the use of their own reason and judgement and put them upon believing and taking upon trust without further examination'.[2] In the same spirit he

[1] I. 4. 23.  [2] I. 4. 24.

protests in Book III against the tyranny of empty words. The first step in philosophy is to use no word without an idea, that is to say, without a clear and determinate meaning. However he may differ from Descartes in other respects, he accepts unreservedly the Cartesian criticism of truth as consisting in the possession of clear and distinct ideas and the apprehension of their necessary connexion. Every philosophical doctrine must justify itself in this fashion to the self-conscious reason of the individual thinker. Reason, as he finely says, is ' the candle of the Lord set up by himself in men's minds ',[1] and to put out that candle would be to plunge us into Egyptian darkness. ' Reason must be our last judge and guide in everything.'[2] This attitude or temper of mind, while it carries us back to the fundamental principle of modern thought, helps also to explain how the *Essay* became, in England and France at least, ' the philosophical Bible ' of the eighteenth century, the age of Enlightenment, the century *par excellence* of European rationalism.

Locke's recorded statements, as well as the internal evidence of his writings, establish sufficiently the closeness of the historical relation between his own thought and the philosophy of Descartes. Although he was preceded in England by two thinkers of the first rank—Bacon and Hobbes—Locke derived little that is specific from either. Bacon's theory of scientific method and his classification and organization of the sciences have little in common with Locke's critical inquiry into the powers of the human mind. Locke may even be said to be a philosopher in a sense in which Bacon was none ; for in regard to knowledge Bacon occupies the standpoint of ordinary scientific thought, assuming its competency, and leaving unraised those questions as to the ultimate nature of Knowing and Being, and the relation of the two, which have been the peculiar business of modern philosophy. Locke's question thus goes deeper than Bacon's. Hobbes wrote systematically,

[1] IV. 3. 20.            [2] IV. 19. 14.

## Relation to Descartes

both on psychology and (in his own words) on 'such premises as appertain to the nature of philosophy in general'.[1] But the questions about knowledge which occupy Locke, and most modern philosophers after him, are not raised by Hobbes, and consequently he has no theory of knowledge in the modern sense. Philosophy, defined by him as the knowledge of bodies, is simply the systematization of science, that is to say, of the theory of mechanical motion which was the great scientific discovery of his age. He has been called 'the founder of empirical psychology', but his psychology is presented by him as an application of the same fundamental doctrine of movement, and its interest for him lies in the basis it furnishes for his ethical and political theories. It was not unnatural, therefore, that his acute psychological work should be almost lost sight of in the storm of obloquy which these theories excited. For a long time the influence of Hobbes upon English thought was confined to ethics and political philosophy, and was powerful there chiefly through the reaction it provoked. Locke refers, in controversy with the Bishop of Worcester, to the 'justly decried names' of Hobbes and Spinoza, as authors with whom he has but a slender acquaintance. In the *Essay* itself the ethical doctrines of the 'Hobbists' are incidentally referred to,[2] and it may be that in some other passages Locke has these doctrines and Hobbes's notorious materialism in view. But at the points where influence might have been most naturally looked for there is no trace of it, and Locke was of too sincere a nature, and too modest about his own place as 'an under-labourer'[3] in the cause of knowledge, to disguise his obligations, had they existed, to a predecessor, however unpopular. The internal evidence of his writings confirms therefore his own repeated statements to Lady Masham that 'the first books which gave him a relish of philosophical things were those of Descartes'.

[1] *Concerning Body*, Part I, ch. 1. 9.   [2] I. 3. 5.
[3] Epistle to the Reader, p. 7.

But although he thus traced his philosophic awakening to Descartes, Locke was far from adopting an attitude of discipleship towards his predecessor. Not infrequently it is through explicit criticism of Cartesian doctrines that he works out his own conclusions; and, as he proceeded, he may well have been more conscious of difference than of agreement with Descartes's philosophy. The sweeping metaphysical claims of the system were alien to his more modest estimate of human capacity, and the semi-mystical developments of Cartesianism, when he was brought face to face with them in Malebranche and others, seemed hardly intelligible to his practical, and in the main unspeculative, habit of mind. Nevertheless the influence of Descartes was deeper and more pervasive than Locke consciously realized. It is seen not so much in specific doctrines taken over by the younger thinker—for example, the restriction of 'knowledge' to the sphere of necessary truth—as in supplying the silent presuppositions on which the whole inquiry proceeds. Descartes's start from the certainty of the subjective life—the known certainty of his own existence and of the 'ideas' or internal objects which formed the contents of his individual mind—determined the whole subsequent course of modern philosophy by the dualism thus created between the knower and the real world of objects commonly supposed to be revealed in sense-perception. Whether the dualism is the result of starting with the immediate certainty of our own internal experiences, or that start is to be regarded merely as a methodic device, itself the result of the previous dogmatic assumption of mind and matter as two independent substances,[1] does not affect the situation. The gulf between the subject and the object has once for all been fixed, and it becomes the immediate task of philosophy to find a means of passing from the one to the other. The theory of Representa-

[1] As Professor Kemp Smith maintains, *Studies in the Cartesian Philosophy*, pp. 13-14. Cf. also Professor Gibson's *Locke's Theory of Knowledge*, p. 223.

## Cartesian Dualism

tive Perception in one form or another is the first device; and we find this both in Descartes and Locke as the historical starting-point of further developments. It was accordingly with a true sense of historic perspective that Reid, in the following century, confronted by the bankruptcy of British philosophy in the absolute scepticism of Hume, and reviewing the steps which led to that conclusion, declared the theories of Malebranche, Locke, Berkeley, and Hume, to be, all of them, modifications of a common 'system of the human understanding', which, after all the improvements made upon it by these thinkers, 'may still be called the Cartesian system'.[1] As regards Locke it is sufficient to quote the words of his latest and most luminous interpreter: 'The whole conception of "ideas" as the proper objects of knowledge is Cartesian in origin. Without the influence of the Cartesian view of knowledge and the Cartesian conception of self-consciousness, it is not too much to say that the *Essay*, as we know it, would never have been written.'[2]

In spite of this affiliation, however, the two thinkers differ profoundly in their conception of the task of philosophy and in their mode of procedure. It is not too much to say that Locke's account of his own undertaking involved a new departure which was to give a permanent direction to subsequent philosophy. Descartes, after his provisional or methodic doubt has yielded him a criterion of truth as consisting in clear and distinct ideas, assumes the competence of human reason to deal with any problem that presents itself. He seeks, in point of fact, to elaborate a comprehensive system of metaphysics by a mathematically rigorous deduction from a few 'simple notions' or ultimate conceptions. He is thus, in Kant's sense of the term, a Dogmatist, inasmuch as he employs traditional and current philosophical conceptions without investigating their competence for the task to which he puts them. He confidently uses the ideas of Substance and Cause,

[1] *Inquiry into the Human Mind*, ch. 7.   [2] Gibson, *op. cit.*, p. 207.

for example, to determine the nature and activity of God and of the human mind. His metaphysics is, in fact, largely a development of the implications of these abstract conceptions, without considering whether they are appropriate or valid in such a sphere, or whether the human mind possesses any resources which would enable it to deal with such a subject-matter. Now the *Essay concerning Human Understanding* is expressly announced by its author as an attempt ' to examine our own abilities and see what objects our understandings were or were not fitted to deal with '.[1] The understanding itself is the object investigated, or, as he puts it in another place,[2] the subject of his inquiry is ' the certainty, evidence, and extent ' of human knowledge. By this formulation of the question, Locke impressed upon philosophy the epistemological character which it has retained during most of the modern period. He has thus some right to be considered the second founder of modern philosophy. For Hume and Kant, as well as for most of the thinkers of the nineteenth century, philosophy has been primarily a theory of knowledge; and, as anticipating in his own way the Kantian demand for a systematic criticism of reason, Locke has sometimes been enrolled as the first critical philosopher.[3] There is, indeed, a striking similarity between the language in which Locke describes the motives and occasion of his inquiry, and the description afterwards given by Kant, in the *Critique of Pure Reason* and in the *Prolegomena*, of his own investigation. The presentation of philosophy as a doctrine of the *limits* of human reason, with the sharp distinction between the knowable and the unknowable, is common to both, and the similarity extends even to the metaphors in which they clothe their thesis.

Locke's account of his purpose in writing explains the structure of the *Essay* as it eventually took shape. It is divided into four Books, the last of which, ' Of Knowledge and

[1] Epistle to the Reader, p. 4.  [2] I. 1. 3.
[3] By Riehl, for example, in his *Philosophischer Kriticismus*.

## Second Founder of Modern Philosophy

Opinion', contains the execution of Locke's original design, giving us the conclusions he arrived at about the nature and extent of our Knowledge as distinguished from the Probability (Opinion, Faith, Belief, Judgement, are used by him as equivalent terms) with which we have to content ourselves ' in the greatest part of our concernment '.[1] It has been suggested that this Book, which contains few references to what precedes, and which really depends little on the special investigations of the earlier Books, may have been the first written. But the opening definition of knowledge, as consisting in ' the perception of the agreement or disagreement of any of our ideas ',[2] naturally suggests some preliminary elucidation of what we mean by these ' ideas ', which are declared in the context to be the only ' immediate object ' of the mind, and which Locke habitually refers to as ' the instruments or materials of our knowledge '.[3] The Second Book ('Of Ideas') gives us, accordingly, an account of ' the original of our ideas ' and ' a view of their several sorts '.[4] It contains Locke's celebrated theory of the way in which the mind ' comes to be furnished ' with simple ideas of sensation and reflection which it subsequently manipulates so as to form complex ideas of modes, substances, and relations. It is here that Locke applies what he calls his ' historical plain method ',[5] and he claims to have given ' a short but true history of the first beginnings of human knowledge '.[6] Ideas are not in themselves knowledge but only ' the materials of thinking ' ;[7] being in themselves ' nothing but bare appearances, or perceptions in our own minds ',[8] they are neither true nor false. Truth or falsehood always supposes affirmation or negation, and it is only ' when the mind refers any of its ideas to anything extraneous to them '[9] that they may intelligibly be spoken of as the one or the other. In the concluding paragraph of the Second Book he reminds

---

[1] IV. 14. 2.   [2] IV. 1. 2.   [3] II. 33. 19. Cf. II. 1. 2.
[4] II. 29. 1.   [5] I. 1. 2.    [6] II. 11. 15.
[7] II. 1. 2.    [8] II. 32. 1.  [9] II. 32. 4.

us, therefore, that, after all that has been said about ideas, we have still in front of us the question 'what use the understanding makes of them, and what knowledge we have by them '.[1] This, as already explained, is the subject of Book IV. The standpoint of the Second Book is thus professedly psychological in the modern sense of the term, although Locke does not consistently maintain himself at that point of view. Ideas are treated as mental facts or occurrences, to be analysed into their elements and referred to their causes. In the Fourth Book, on the contrary, ideas are treated as they occur in propositions or judgements, that is to say, as vehicles of 'meaning', as giving us information, true or false, about reality. The standpoint of the Fourth Book is therefore epistemological. To employ a familiar distinction, Book II deals with the question of origin, Book IV with the question of validity. The latter question was the one which Locke set out to solve; it is the properly philosophical question. But Book IV has been overshadowed in the historical sequel by the reputation of Book II with its famous thesis of Experience as the source of all our knowledge. And in view of the acuteness and sagacity of Locke's introspective analysis this reputation is not undeserved; even to-day Book II remains the most attractive and stimulating section of the *Essay*. Book I (' Of Innate Notions') and Book III ('Of Words ') may be regarded respectively as an Introduction and an Appendix to Book II. ' The established opinion among some men that there are in the understanding certain innate principles, some primary notions ... which the soul brings into the world with it ',[2] must first be demolished before he proceeds to show, by positive appeal to facts and the actual analysis of our ideas, that the whole fabric of our knowledge may be sufficiently explained from experience alone. And when his analysis of our main ideas is completed, the close connexion between ideas and words induces him to interpolate his Third Book on the various imperfections of

[1] II. 33. 19.     [2] I. 2. 1.

# *Plan of the Essay*

language as an instrument of exact thinking, along with some suggestions for remedying these defects. This Book, although it contains some of Locke's characteristic doctrines, is in the main a practical treatise on the improvement of the understanding, recalling and perhaps suggested by similar chapters in the Port Royal Logic, the Cartesian manual on *The Art of Thinking*, published in 1662, which circulated widely during the remainder of the seventeenth century.

There are two main issues prominent in the *Essay*, in regard to which it is important to define Locke's exact position. In their ultimate consequences and in the various forms they assume, the two issues may have significant relations to one another, but in an initial statement at least they can be clearly enough distinguished. The first is the controversy between Empiricism and Rationalism (or, in its modern form, Transcendentalism) as regards the origin or source of our knowledge, or at least of its constitutive concepts; the second is that between Realism and Idealism or Mentalism, concerning the immediate object of perception or the nature of our knowledge of the external world. In both cases Locke's individual position has been seriously misrepresented in consequence of the historical perspective in which he is regarded. His statements have been read in the light of later developments. And as he almost boasts that he is 'not nice about phrases', it is not always easy to determine what a particular doctrine precisely meant for Locke himself. That is a problem of interpretation which can only be solved by a careful comparison of his different utterances, a consideration of the setting in which the doctrines in question occur, and an appreciation of the counter-doctrines in opposition to which they are propounded. This is particularly the case with the Empiricism usually attributed to him.

By the famous opening sections of the Second Book Locke has written himself down as the founder of the English Philosophy of Experience. 'Whence has [the mind] all the materials of reason and knowledge ? To this I answer, in one word, from experience: in that all our knowledge is founded, and from that it ultimately derives itself.' In virtue of this statement and many others like it, Locke stands irrevocably in the historic succession that leads through Berkeley to Hume. His doctrine was also developed by Condillac in France into a pure Sensationalism. Empiricism, when it is pure and consistent, reduces itself, in fact, necessarily to Sensationalism; and Association, as we find it in Hume or in James Mill, becomes the sole cohesive force by which it is sought to explain our apparent knowledge of a world of reality. But on the strength of this historic affiliation it has been too common for critics and historians to visit upon Locke the sins of his latest descendants and to read into his phrases about 'experience' a meaning intelligible only in the light of the sharper distinctions due to the subsequent development. Thus Cousin, in his course of lectures on Locke, criticizes him exclusively as the progenitor of the 'École sensualiste', and Sir William Hamilton regards 'Locke and Gassendi as exactly upon a par', and declares that 'Condillac must be viewed as having simplified the doctrine of his master, without doing the smallest violence to its spirit '.[1] So again, T. H. Green, in his massive Introduction to Hume (published in 1874), although he devotes no fewer than 130 pages to the discussion of Locke's philosophy, would certainly have been accused by its author of 'sticking in the incidents' and ignoring the main design. Viewing Locke's theory simply as the first step on the road to the sensationalistic scepticism of Hume, Green seizes upon the passages which admit, in the light of the sequel, of being interpreted in terms of pure sensationalism. He isolates certain ideas which he thinks he finds in Locke—often, it must be confessed, by putting a forced sense on Locke's expressions—and, after developing them mercilessly into their consequences, proceeds to demonstrate their inadequacy in the

[1] *Lectures on Metaphysics*, ii. 198.

## *The Philosophy of Experience* xix

light of principles derived from Kant's transcendental analysis of experience. Valuable as this may be, regarded as a chapter in the history of thought, it applies to Locke's work conceptions and standards which were quite foreign to his purpose, and so much outside the circle of his ideas that he could scarcely have understood what his critic found amiss and what he desiderated. More recently the historic lineaments of Locke's ' way of ideas ' were sympathetically restored by Professor Campbell Fraser in his article on Locke in the ninth edition of the *Encyclopaedia Britannica* (1882), in his volume on Locke in the series of Philosophical Classics for English Readers (1890), and in the Prolegomena to the Clarendon Press edition of the *Essay* in 1894. More recently still, Professor Gibson has given a masterly presentation of Locke's doctrines in their historical setting and their true proportions in his scholarly volume on *Locke's Theory of Knowledge* (1917).[1]

English philosophy is distinctively the Philosophy of Experience, and the advance of English Philosophy in its successive representatives consists in the more precise definition of what experience means. Locke, as we shall immediately see, uses the term so vaguely that he supposes much to be derived from experience which cannot possibly have its source there when the ' given ' is limited, as it is by Hume, to

[1] An earlier attempt to do justice to neglected elements in Locke's philosophy was made in T. E. Webb's *Intellectualism of Locke* (Dublin, 1837). Directed against the criticisms of Cousin and Hamilton, this treatise professes, in the author's words, ' to establish that Locke, as recognizing Ideas of which Intellect is properly the source and cognition of which intellect is exclusively the guarantee, is an intellectualist in the sense of Reid and Kant'. Directed against Cousin and Hamilton, the book is too much steeped in obsolete controversies, but the author writes acutely and adduces many relevant passages from Locke in support of his contention. He rushes, however, to the opposite extreme and often strains, and even distorts, Locke's phrases in giving them a Kantian meaning. The issues which shaped Kant's system were not, and could not be, present to Locke's mind, and if it is an error to read him in terms of Hume, it is just as serious an error to put an explicitly Kantian sense upon any of his statements.

momentary impressions. When experience is so conceived, Empiricism, as a philosophy of experience, becomes bankrupt, because it cannot explain the actual fabric of knowledge. The Transcendental philosophy of Kant is simply a fresh analysis of ordinary experience with a view to detect those elements which Empiricism had overlooked, but whose presence can be shown to be indispensable, if knowledge is to exist at all. Locke begins by offering us simple ideas of sensation and reflection as 'the original of all knowledge';[1] and of these 'the ideas got by sensation' (or, as Locke is equally ready to express himself, 'the impressions made on our senses by external objects') are first in order of time, ideas of reflection being such as the mind gets when it 'comes to reflect on its own operations about the ideas got by sensation'. These operations, he tells us, proceed 'from powers intrinsical and proper to itself',[2] but the ideas of the 'different actings'[3] of the mind are ideas of empirically observed facts just as much as the ideas of sensation. The word 'operation', therefore, in no way suggests the conception of the mind as the source of *a priori* principles or truths, a conception quite foreign to Locke's conscious habits of thinking. Looking at sensation and reflection as both modes of observation, only directed upon different objects, Locke speaks of reflection metaphorically as 'internal sense', and declares these two to be 'the only passages of knowledge to the understanding'.[4] 'The senses', he says again, 'at first let in particular ideas and furnish the yet empty cabinet.'[5]

This start with sensations, atomistically conceived as simple or particular ideas—detached and unrelated psychical events —is a presupposition of the older psychology, common to Locke, Berkeley, and Hume; and it was because Kant inherited the same presupposition as regards the data of sense that he was driven to treat space and time and the categories as functions of continuity and connexion introduced by the mind in the act

[1] II. 1. 24.     [2] II. 1. 24.     [3] II. 1. 4.
[4] II. 11. 17.     [5] I. 2. 15.

## The Start with Simple Ideas

of perception. Locke's simple idea is best exemplified in the secondary qualities, such as (to take his own examples) the coldness and hardness which a man feels in a piece of ice or the smell and whiteness of a lily. Though the qualities 'are in the things themselves so united and blended that there is no separation, no distance between them, yet it is plain the ideas they produce in the mind enter by the senses simple and unmixed'.[1] This physiological attitude, it has been pointed out, leads Locke to interpret all our experience in the light of the secondary qualities.[2] But among simple ideas Locke includes ideas of 'space or extension, figure, rest and motion', as being 'perceivable impressions both on the eyes and touch'; and he adds certain ideas which, he says, 'convey themselves into the mind by all the ways of sensation and reflection.' The most significant of his instances are existence, unity, power, and succession. Such ideas as these are so obviously on a different footing from a secondary quality like 'yellow' or 'hot', that Locke has some difficulty in fitting them into his classification. This is shown by the variety of the phraseology in which he refers to them. He tells us that they 'convey themselves into the mind'[3]—the phrase he employs throughout in speaking of the origin of our simple ideas—or again, more vaguely, that they 'make themselves way, and are suggested to the mind'.[4] He speaks of existence and unity as 'ideas which we *receive* from sensation and reflection', but also describes them as 'ideas that are *suggested* to the understanding by every object without and every idea within. When ideas are in our minds, we *consider* them as being actually there, as well as we consider things to be actually without us: which is, that they exist or have existence. And whatever we can consider as one thing, whether a real being or idea,

---

[1] II. 2. 1.
[2] Cf. Professor Kemp Smith's *Studies in the Cartesian Philosophy*, pp. 181–4.
[3] II. 7. 1.   [4] II. 3. 1.

suggests to the understanding the idea of unity.'[1] In a later connexion he speaks of ' unity ' as an idea ' constantly joined to all others ', and ' inseparable from them ', ' for there is not any object of sensation or reflection which does not *carry with it* the idea of one'.[2] It is worth noting that Berkeley, who in his youthful philosophy was much more of a consistent sensationalist than Locke, attacked the latter's account of the idea of unity, and declared roundly that ' there is not any such idea ',[3] while Hume dealt similarly with the idea of existence. After presenting his familiar demand to produce the distinct impression from which the idea is derived, Hume concludes from our inability to do so, that ' the idea of existence is the very same with the idea of what we conceive to be existent '.[4]

Because Locke uses in this connexion the term ' suggested ', the very term afterwards employed by Reid in his account of those primary notions and beliefs which he calls Principles of Common Sense and traces to 'the constitution of the mind itself ', it would be quite unwarrantable to conclude[5] that Locke has in his mind any view like that of Reid or Kant. He uses the terms ' suggested ' and ' furnished ' in various passages quite indiscriminately, and employs them in the same context in which he reiterates that all our simple ideas are ' received ' from the two sources of sensation and reflection. All that the variation of phraseology justifies us in saying is that Locke assumed as given in his 'materials' much more than a consistent Empiricism finds there. When he makes the ideas of unity and existence due to the ' consideration ' of the mind, his language

[1] II. 7. 7.   [2] II. 13. 26.

[3] *Principles of Human Knowledge*, sections 13 and 120. Berkeley, in his early philosophy, limited the possible contents of mind to particular ideas of sense and their images. This is the basis of his attack on ' abstract ideas ' in the Introduction to the *Principles of Human Knowledge*, which Hume pronounced to be 'one of the greatest and most valuable discoveries that has been made of late years in the republic of letters ' (*Treatise of Human Nature*, Bk. I, Part 1, section 7).

[4] *Treatise of Human Nature*, Bk. I, Part 2, section 6.

[5] As is done, for example, by T. E. Webb.

## Ambiguous Phraseology

is specially significant in this respect, and if he had followed up this clue, it might have modified his whole position. But although he was led to the brink of the same discovery in his treatment of certain complex ideas, all that we get is, again, a significant variation in terminology without any clear apprehension on Locke's part of what important philosophical issues hang upon the adoption of the one alternative or the other. Locke passes from the one set of terms to the other almost unconsciously and continues to use both indifferently.

This is specially observable in his treatment of the ideas of Power and Substance. Power is included, as we have seen, among those simple ideas which are suggested by every other idea, but Locke devotes a special chapter[1] to it later, after his account of 'simple modes'. The idea of power, we there learn, is got in connexion with the fact of change. ' The mind ', he says, ' being every day informed, by the senses, of the alteration of those simple ideas it observes in things without; and taking notice how one comes to an end and ceases to be, and another begins to exist which was not before ; reflecting also on what passes within itself, and observing a constant change of its ideas, sometimes by the impression of outward objects on the senses, and sometimes by the determination of its own choice ; and concluding from what it has so constantly observed to have been, that the like changes will for the future be made in the same things by like agents, and by the like ways ; *considers* in one thing the possibility of having any of its simple ideas changed, and in another the possibility of making that change ; and *so comes by* that idea which we call *power*.' In other words, what is given to the mind, what is actually seen or observed, is just the fact of change, one thing after another. The idea of power or of causation cannot be given in sensation as a phenomenon, and on that account Hume, as we know, declared the idea of causal relation between two facts to be no true idea, but only a habit of transition

[1] Chapter 21.

produced in the mind by the frequency of the particular sequence. That is consistent Empiricism, but Locke is very far from taking up such a position. In a later section of the same chapter,[1] he says, 'whatever change is observed, *the mind must collect a power somewhere,* able to make that change, as well as a possibility in the thing itself to receive it'. That is to say, we see sequence, but mere sequence does not satisfy us, especially when the sequence is repeated. We proceed to convert sequence into consequence by means of the idea of power or cause or necessary connexion. That is the mind's interpretation of the sensuous facts presented to it; and, by the language he uses, Locke acknowledges this interpretation to be an intellectual necessity, and the asserted relation between the facts to be objectively true.

His more celebrated account of the idea of substance, in chapter 23, proceeds on the same lines. ' The mind being . . . furnished with a great number of the simple ideas conveyed in by the senses . . . takes notice also, that a certain number of these simple ideas go constantly together ; which being presumed to belong to one thing . . . are called, so united in one subject, by one name . . . because, not imagining how these simple ideas can subsist by themselves, we accustom ourselves to suppose some *substratum* wherein they do subsist, and from which they do result, which therefore we call *substance*.'[2] In answer to Stillingfleet's challenge, ' Is that custom grounded upon true reason or not ? ' Locke emphasizes the intellectual necessity of the supposition. ' All the ideas of all the sensible qualities of a cherry come into my mind by sensation. . . . The ideas of these qualities are perceived by the mind to be by

[1] Section 4.

[2] Edward Stillingfleet, Bishop of Worcester, in a *Discourse in Vindication of the Doctrine of the Trinity* (1696), had referred to Locke as 'one of the gentlemen of this new way of reasoning that have almost discarded substance out of the reasonable part of the world'. Locke replied in a *Letter* (1697), to which the Bishop wrote an answer, and the controversy was continued in a series of Replies and Answers till 1699.

## Ideas of Substance and Cause

themselves inconsistent with existence, i. e. that they cannot exist or subsist of themselves. . . . Hence the mind perceives the necessary connexion with inherence or being supported, which being a relative idea superadded to the red colour in a cherry . . . the mind frames the correlative idea of a support.' If the terminology of the first passage seems to anticipate the dissolution of material substance which was presently witnessed in Berkeley, the language of the second is more suggestive of a Kantian category.[1] Locke admits, or rather he is anxious to impress upon us, that we have no other ' clear ' idea of any particular substance ' farther than of certain simple ideas coexisting together'; but he is equally emphatic in pointing out that ' our complex ideas of substances, besides all these simple ideas they are made up of, have always the confused idea of something to which they belong and in which they subsist: and therefore, when we speak of any sort of substance, we say it is a thing having such or such qualities'.[2] The idea of substance, he says in the First Book, being one 'which we neither have nor can have by sensation or reflection', is frequently supposed to be innate, but, just because we cannot have it by these channels, we find that ' we have no such clear idea at all '; the word means only ' an uncertain supposition of we know not what, which we take to be the *substratum* or support of those ideas we do know '.[3] Locke's reply to the Bishop of Worcester on this point throws an instructive light on the latitude with which he uses the phrase derived from experience; for although he has told us, as we have just seen, that the idea does not come by way of sensation

---

[1] So again, in the *Third Letter* to Stillingfleet, Locke says: 'I never denied that the mind could form for itself ideas of relation, *and that it is obliged to do so*. . . . Sensible qualities carry the supposition of substance along with them, but not intromitted by the senses with them. . . . By carrying with them a supposition, I mean that sensible qualities *imply* a substratum to exist in' (quoted by Fraser in the Clarendon Press edition of the *Essay*, vol. i, p. 108).

[2] II. 23. 3.   [3] I. 4. 18.

or reflection, but, on the contrary, is a relative idea framed by the mind, he goes on to argue that because it is *relative* to the collection by simple ideas, we are entitled to regard it as, ' by the abstraction of the mind, derived also from the simple ideas of sensation and reflection ', inasmuch as 'without these simple positive ideas, it would never have ' the general relative idea. Hence he concludes that there is nothing in the Bishop's strictures at variance with what he has himself said, namely that the idea ' is founded on simple ideas of sensation and reflection and that it is a very obscure idea '.

The change of phraseology into which he so easily slips—taking ' derived from ' and ' founded on ' as equivalent expressions—is further illustrated in his interesting account of the ideas of Immensity, Eternity, and Infinity, in the chapters on Simple Modes (Book II. 13-17). Simple modes are the complex ideas which result from the repetition of a single simple idea, as is the case with the ideas of duration, number, and space in all their varieties. Duration leads through successive periods of time to the idea of eternity, number through successive finite numbers to the idea of infinity, and space, through successive measures of space, to what Locke calls the idea of immensity, that is, boundless or infinite space. Locke's analysis of these ideas is sound and suggestive. Infinity he describes not as a number actually counted, but as ' a growing and fugitive idea, still in a boundless progression, that can stop nowhere '. The addition of finite units one to another ' suggests the idea of infinite only by a power we find we have of still increasing the sum, and adding more of the same kind, without ever coming one jot nearer the end of such progression '.[1] Similarly with the ideas of eternity and immensity; in each case, what we have is ' an endless, growing idea '. He distinguishes, as Kant afterwards did, between ' the idea of the infinity of space and the idea of a space infinite '.[2] The latter, he points out, ' carries in it

[1] II. 17. 12-13.  [2] II. 17. 7.

a plain contradiction'; we can no more have a positive or realized idea of infinite space than we can have 'a positive idea of an actual infinite number'.[1] The main feature of this suggestive analysis is the intellectual necessity which forbids a stop with any finite number, time, or space—a mysterious and baffling aspect of our experience which, with the antinomies to which it leads, was to form one of the main factors in the development of Kant's Critical Philosophy. Locke frankly acknowledges the necessity, without seeking further to explain it. 'I pretend not', he says, 'to treat of [these ideas] in their full latitude. It suffices to my design to show how the mind receives them, such as they are, from sensation and reflection, and how even the idea we have of infinity, how remote soever it may seem to be from any object of sense or operation of our mind, has nevertheless, as all our other ideas, its original there.'[2] Thus the whole analysis has been undertaken, it turns out, to prove his well-worn thesis about the origin of our ideas. But it is peculiarly awkward to speak of these ideas as 'received' from sensation, seeing that they are essentially based, as Kant pointed out, on the inadequacy of the sensuous understanding to the demands of the reason. What meaning can we attach to the statement that the ideas of infinity and eternity are given in sensation like the ideas of hard or yellow? Locke once more, therefore, varies his phrase: they are not really 'received' from sensation and reflection, but at least they may be said to have their origin there, inasmuch as it is in a process which starts from the facts of sense that they reveal themselves.

If we ask how Locke failed to realize the important difference between his various forms of statement, the reply must be that he had never formulated to himself a pure and thoroughgoing empiricism, such as is exemplified in the 'sensualism' of Condillac or the scepticism of Hume. Consequently he never contemplated an analysis of knowledge such as Kant

[1] II. 17. 16.  [2] II. 17. 22.

afterwards undertook, in order to exhibit its necessary conditions. Locke may be said to have included so much in his data that such an analysis could have no urgency for him. Ideas are for him not independent facts from which he starts; they are *ab initio* the objects of a permanent self, whose existence is intuitively or directly known, which possesses 'powers intrinsical and proper to itself'[1] and is capable, consequently, of various 'actions about its ideas',[2] the effects of which are for him as legitimate elements in the concrete tissue of knowledge as the sense-data which we can more strictly be said to 'receive'. In a way, therefore, he assumes the function of reason in experience; but the effects of its operations (such as 'considering', 'collecting', 'framing relative ideas', and in general 'comparing' and 'abstracting') are so fused in the concrete result that, as we have just seen, he fails to perceive their significance, and even suggests by his language that they are already contained in the mere sense-data as such. His real interest in the Second Book in tracing the history or origin of our ideas is not, it must be repeated, the transcendental problem of a later age, but the much more simple demonstration that all our knowledge begins with sense-experience, is rooted in such experience, and that without such experience we should have no knowledge at all. But so far is he from equating experience with passively received sensations, that the principle of Association (which in that case becomes, as we find it in Hume, the one cohesive force relating and combining the otherwise loose and separate ideas) was introduced by Locke only as an afterthought in a short chapter[3] in the fourth edition of the *Essay*, and is treated by him there as an explanation of 'wrong and unnatural combinations of ideas', producing superstitious beliefs, unreasonable antipathies, and the blind acceptance of party or sectarian shibboleths. He distinguishes it, as a 'connexion of ideas wholly owing to chance or custom', from the 'natural correspondence and connexion [of ideas] one

[1] II. 1. 24.   [2] II. 1. 4.   [3] II. 33.

'*Ideas coeval with Sensation*' xxix

with another ... which is founded in their peculiar beings', and which ' it is the office and excellence of our reason to trace '.

The truth is that in the scheme of the *Essay*, and in Locke's mind, the whole argument of Book II is the positive complement of the denial of innate principles and ideas with which he starts. In Book I Locke asks to be shown any such principles, and, as none can be produced, he feels justified in discarding the 'received doctrine, that men have native ideas and original characters stamped upon their mind in their very first being '.[1] In Book II he proceeds to show ' how men, barely by the use of their natural faculties, may attain to all the knowledge they have, without the help of any innate impressions, and may arrive at certainty, without any such original notions or principles '.[2] And if we refer to the various passages in which he reviews or summarizes his argument and conclusions, e. g. at the close of the general argument about ' sensation and reflection ' (II. 1. 20–4), we find that what he is concerned to prove is that ' ideas in the understanding are *coeval* with sensation '. ' I see no reason to believe that the soul thinks *before the senses have furnished it with ideas to think on.*' ' All those sublime thoughts which tower above the clouds, and reach as high as heaven itself, *take their rise and footing here:* in all that great extent wherein the mind wanders in those remote speculations it may seem to be elevated with, it stirs not one jot beyond those ideas which *sense* or *reflection* have offered for its contemplation.' But how much may be involved in the ' contemplation ' by the mind we have already partly seen. So again, at the close of chapter 11, when he has completed his survey of our simple ideas, he claims to have given ' a true history of the first beginnings of human knowledge ',

[1] II. 1. 1.
[2] I. 2. 1. The latter part of this sentence—the reference to certainty —may be said to point on to Book IV. The polemic there against ' Maxims ' (chapter 7) is a further proof of the importance of Book I. for a proper interpretation of the *Essay*.

and betrays the real preoccupation of his mind by the added remark, 'If other men have either innate ideas or infused principles, they have reason to enjoy them ... I can speak but of what I find in myself.'

'That all our knowledge begins with experience there can be no doubt.' The sentence with which Kant opens the *Critique of Pure Reason* obviously points back to Locke's famous dictum in the opening sections of his Second Book. Locke's contention, in the sense explained, is so obviously true that it is difficult to believe that any thinker of repute ever held an opposite view. 'For how otherwise', Kant proceeds, 'should the faculty of knowledge be awakened to exercise but by objects which, acting upon our senses, partly of themselves produce ideas in us, and partly set our faculty of understanding in motion to compare these ideas with one another, to combine or separate them, and so to convert the raw material of sensible impressions into a knowledge of objects which is called experience. In order of time, therefore, no knowledge of ours is prior to experience, and with experience all our knowledge begins.' The whole passage is reminiscent of Locke's phraseology.[1] 'But,' Kant continues in his second paragraph, 'although all our knowledge *begins with* experience, it by no means follows that it is all *derived from* experience. For it might quite well be the case that our experience is itself a compound of what we received through impressions of sense, and what is supplied from itself by our faculty of knowledge on occasion of these impressions.' In these words Kant adumbrates the theory which he goes on to work out in the *Critique*. I am far from suggesting that Kant's theory is to be accepted, in the form which he has given it, as a definitive settlement of the question. But his wider conception of Experience (in the larger sense in which he uses the term), as involving its rational implicates as well as its empirical data, at least opens the way for a more satisfactory theory of knowledge than

[1] Cf. his account of complex ideas, II. 12. 1.

was possible either to Rationalist or Empiricist in the pre-Kantian era.

In view of the importance which the refutation of the doctrine of innate notions possessed for Locke himself, it is a question of some interest to determine against whom the arguments of Book I are directed. There has been considerable discussion on this point. The only writer to whom Locke refers by name is Lord Herbert of Cherbury; but as he had not heard of Lord Herbert's book till his own argument was fully under way,[1] he must have had others in view when he undertook the controversy. The five sections devoted to Lord Herbert of Cherbury are, in fact, entirely episodic, and there is no further reference to him in the course of the *Essay*. It has been very generally supposed that Locke's polemic was directed against the Cartesians, for Descartes places a theory of innate ideas in the very forefront of his philosophy. His chief argument for the existence of God is the innateness of the idea of a Perfect Being. Locke refers to this argument when he is dealing himself with the existence of God, in Book IV, and, as Professor Gibson points out,[2] the repeated use, in Book I, of Descartes's term 'adventitious' (as opposed to innate) shows that the Cartesian doctrines were present to his mind as he wrote. But, from the form which Locke's polemic assumes, it was clearly not the Cartesian position which he had primarily in view. The argument is throughout against 'innate principles' and only secondarily or inferentially against innate ideas.[3] Moreover, the appeal to 'universal consent'

[1] I. 3. 15.         [2] *Op. cit.*, p. 43.
[3] Professor Gibson refers to Locke's statement (I. 4. 1), that if the upholders of 'innate principles' had but realized that the innateness of a proposition implies the innateness of the ideas which make it up, ' they would not perhaps have been so forward to believe ' in the doctrine of innate truths or principles. This remark by itself, Professor Gibson adds, 'is sufficient to refute the supposition that the polemic is primarily directed against the Cartesians'. *Op. cit.*, p. 230.

which Locke associates so prominently with the doctrine he is attacking forms no part of the theory of innate ideas as we find it in Descartes. Professor Gibson has conclusively shown that Locke's real antagonists were the 'scholastic men'[1] whose theory of reasoning from 'maxims' he attacks in the seventh chapter of Book IV. The 'magnified maxims' which he denies in Book IV to be ' the foundations of all our other knowledge ', ' the principles from which we deduce all other truths ', are the same principles whose innateness he denies in Book I. He takes the same instances, those magnified principles of demonstration, 'Whatsoever is, is', and 'It is impossible for the same thing to be, and not to be', and the line of argument is in both cases the same. For innateness, as constituting 'a distinct sort of truth',[2] Locke substitutes self-evidence, which men may perceive barely by the use of their natural faculties, and which is perceived as clearly in individual instances as in these general maxims of the Schools. It is impossible to read the two chapters together (Bk. I, ch. 2, and Bk. IV, ch. 7) without being convinced that they form part of a single argument, and that in both Locke has in view the same opponents. The theory which Locke is attacking regarded all reasoning as a process of subsumption, in which any particular truth is proved by being deduced from certain ultimate premisses or so-called ' principles ', which are, therefore, ' the foundations of all other knowledge '. These principles are not themselves susceptible of proof, but must be accepted on their own evidence and are supposed to be guaranteed by the ' universal assent ' accorded to them. But self-evidence limited in this way to a specific number of propositions easily assumes a mystical quality. The propositions in question tend to be treated as ' a distinct sort of truth ', and their certainty is regarded as due, not to the simple insight of reason, but to the action of nature or of God, imprinting them upon the mind in its first being. And this in turn is taken to explain

---

[1] IV. 7. 11.  [2] I. 2. 5.

## Scholastic Men and Maxims

the universal agreement of mankind about them.[1] The phrase κοιναὶ ἔννοιαι, which Locke quotes as the equivalent of innate principles, and the stress laid upon universal assent indicate the influence of Stoic conceptions. In other respects the theory of reasoning is that which Locke found current in ' those places which brought the Peripatetic philosophy into their Schools, where it continued many ages, without teaching the world anything but the art of wrangling '.[2] It is the depraved Aristotelianism from which he suffered in his own youth in Oxford. Locke denies the fact of universal assent; but even if it could be shown to exist, he repudiates the attempt to explain such assent, and the self-evidence on which it is based, by the psychological fact of innateness. He who assents to a ' self-evident ' truth does so, ' not because it was innate, but because the consideration of the nature of the things contained in those words would not suffer him to think otherwise, how or whensoever he is brought to reflect on them '.[3] ' Intuitive knowledge neither requires nor admits any proof, one part of it more than another. He that will suppose it does, takes away the foundation of all knowledge and certainty.'[4] Knowledge, in short, consists, in all its parts, in the perception of the agreement or disagreement of ideas; and the advance of knowledge depends on ' finding out intermediate ideas ',[5] by means of which we may discover the agreement or disagreement of those which we cannot immediately compare. This is the Cartesian criterion of truth, as consisting in the apprehension of necessary connexion between ideas, which Locke holds in some respects more firmly than Descartes himself.

It must be confessed, however, that Locke's actual method of argument in Book I is bound to appear tedious and trifling.

---

[1] So Glanville speaks of ' those inbred fundamental notices that God hath implanted in our souls . . . independent upon other principles or deductions, commanding a sudden assent, and acknowledged by all sober mankind ' (quoted by Professor Gibson, *op. cit.*, p. 31).

[2] IV. 7. 11.   [3] I. 2. 21.   [4] IV. 7. 19.   [5] IV. 7. 11.

## Introduction

The modern reader has never felt any temptation to believe that babies come into the world with abstract principles ready formulated, which they proceed to apply syllogistically to the particular cases of the nurse and the blackamoor, the apple or the sugar. He calls the controversy quite rightly 'a dead issue'. But was it ever a live one? It is difficult, says Professor Campbell Fraser, to find any one who would have denied Locke's thesis.[1] His argument has been attacked accordingly as a glaring case of *ignoratio elenchi*. ' Innate', said his pupil, the third Lord Shaftesbury, ' is a word Mr. Locke poorly plays on. For what has birth, or the progress of the foetus, to do in this case?' The true question is ' whether the constitution of man be such, that being adult and grown up', such and such ideas ' will not infallibly and necessarily spring up in consciousness '.[2] But Locke himself in the very context in which he denies their innateness emphasizes the self-evidence of the principles or maxims which he is discussing. Both in Book I and in Book IV his argument is that, just because they carry their ' own light and evidence ' with them,[3] it is superfluous to suppose them innate. But the vaunted maxims, he contends, do but put in an abstract form the same self-evidence on which the mind relies in particular instances. ' Many a one knows that one and two are equal to three ... and knows it as certainly as any other man knows that the whole is equal to all its parts.'[4] And he quite truly points out, in pursuance of his ' historical plain method ', that ' it was in those particular instances that the first discoverer found the truth, without the help of the general maxims '.... ' For in particulars our knowledge begins, and

---

[1] Locke's method of argument, however, it might be suggested in exculpation, is really the familiar philosophical *reductio ad absurdum*. He does not so much accuse his opponents of holding their doctrine in the form in which he states it ; he argues that such is the absurd conclusion to which their vaguely held doctrine commits them.

[2] See Fraser, Prolegomena to his edition of the *Essay*, vol. i, p. 72.

[3] I. 3. 4.

[4] IV. 7. 10.

## *Defect of Locke's Argument*

so spreads itself, by degrees, to generals.'[1] This statement, in Locke's mouth, has nothing in common, it should be observed, with the subsequent attempt of Empiricism to deny necessity of connexion altogether—to recognize only the spurious universality constituted by a summation of observed instances, and to substitute therefore for logical implication the ingrained association of ideas produced by uniform *de facto* conjunction in the past. For Locke, as for Aristotle, the universal is revealed in the particular cases, and the necessity which is present from the first depends on the intrinsic nature of the ideas, or (as he said in a passage quoted above) on 'the nature of the things contained in those words', which 'would not suffer him to think otherwise.'

Leibniz made it one of the main points of his criticism of Locke that to deny innate ideas was to obliterate the distinction between 'truths of reason' and 'truths of fact', thus reducing necessary truths to the level of inductive generalizations. But Locke, although he may not have realized all its consequences, was fully awake to the distinction in question: It forms the basis of the sharp distinction he draws in Book IV between the 'general certainty' attainable in 'knowledge'—a certainty which 'lies only in our own thoughts, and consists barely in the contemplation of our own abstract ideas'[2]—and the 'probability' with which we have to content ourselves in the natural sciences, where we are exclusively dependent on 'experience and history'. In the latter case, we find 'upon trial' certain coexistences and sequences occurring between nature's facts; but such experience, 'which way ever it prove in that particular body I examine, makes me not certain that it is so in all or in any other bodies but that which I have tried'.[3] The distinction between 'universal knowledge' (or necessary truth) and what he calls on occasion, by courtesy, 'experimental knowledge'[4] is drawn by Locke almost in the same words as

[1] IV. 7. 11.  [2] IV. 6. 13 and 16.
[3] IV. 12. 9.  [4] IV. 6. 7.

xxxvi　　　　　*Introduction*

by his critic. But he would not have understood Leibniz's assertion that 'all arithmetic and all geometry are innate and are in us virtually', seeing that 'all truths which can be drawn from primitive innate knowledge can still be called innate, because the mind can draw them from its own depths'.[1] He would have retorted that to describe all demonstrative truth as innate is, to say the least, a misleading form of expression. It deliberately perpetuates that confusion between logical implication and temporal pre-existence in the individual mind against which Locke's argument was directed.[2] And, as a matter of history, since Locke's time, and largely as a result of his polemic, the terminology has been abandoned. Instead of discussing innate ideas or principles, philosophers have mostly talked of self-evident or intuitive truths, necessary truths, or, in the language of Kant[3] and his followers, transcendental principles, principles involved in the very possibility of knowledge or experience. It is not surprising, therefore, as Professor Alexander remarks, that 'the attack upon innate ideas should have come to be that part of Locke's teaching which the public connected habitually with his name'.[4]

The second main issue mentioned as prominent in the *Essay* concerns the nature of the object of knowledge, more particu-

[1] *New Essays*, Bk. I, ch. 1, Langley's translation, pp. 78-9. Still less would he have understood the intimation that, in strictness of language and according to Leibniz's own system, '*all* the thoughts and actions and acts of our soul come from its own depths, with no possibility of their being given to it by the senses', any apparent concession to the contrary being simply an accommodation to received expressions, ' as the Copernicans speak like other men of the movement of the sun'. If *all* our knowledge is innate, Locke might have replied, the dispute is certainly at an end; but he would hardly have taken seriously the Leibnizian theory of 'windowless' monads.

[2] Cf. Gibson, *op. cit.*, p. 285.

[3] Although Kant himself is not free from the old confusion between logical apriority and psychological pre-existence.

[4] *Locke*, p. 57, in the series 'Philosophies Ancient and Modern'.

## Perception: Locke's Assumptions xxxvii

larly the nature of our knowledge in sense-perception. This is connected, as we have already seen, with Locke's use of the term ' idea ', and with the fundamental dualism between mind and matter which he inherited from the Cartesian system. Locke gives us his practical assumptions in the eighth chapter of Book II, the ' little excursion into natural philosophy' which he finds it convenient to append to his account of our simple ideas. He takes for granted a system of independently existing material substances, on the one hand, and, on the other, a number of separate minds, conceived as immaterial substances with the power of thinking. He further assumes the interaction of these two sorts of substances ; in perception the material substance communicates a knowledge of itself to the perceiving mind by a species of impact or mechanical impression. 'Bodies produce ideas in us ... manifestly by impulse, the only way which we can conceive bodies operate in.'[1] Through the ' ideas ' thus produced we gain a knowledge of the ' qualities ' of the things. These two terms are, in fact, correlative ; ' the power to produce any *idea* in our mind, I call *quality* of the subject wherein that power is.'[2] The ideas represent, or correspond to, the qualities—sometimes, as in the primary qualities, in the sense of exactly resembling those ' modifications of matter in the bodies which cause such perceptions in us'; at other times, in the case of the secondary qualities, corresponding only as effect to cause. ' The ideas of primary qualities of bodies are resemblances of them, and their patterns do really exist in the bodies themselves', but our ideas of the secondary qualities ' are, in the bodies we denominate from them, only a power to produce those sensations in us: and what is sweet, blue, or warm in idea, is but the certain bulk, figure, and motion of the insensible parts in the bodies themselves, which we call so '.[3] In the case of the primary qualities of body—' original ', ' real ', and ' inseparable ' qualities, as he

---

[1] Section 11.     [2] Section 8.     [3] Section 15.

xxxviii *Introduction*

also designates them—Locke frequently [1] speaks of us as 'perceiving' the qualities, and it is to be noted that he begins his exposition of 'the nature of our ideas' in this chapter by saying that 'it will be convenient to distinguish them, as they are ideas or perceptions in our minds, and as they are modifications of matter in the bodies that cause such perceptions in us'.[2] According to both these forms of expression, the duality of idea and quality tends to disappear. According to the one form, we seem to perceive the qualities directly or immediately; according to the other, the ideas seem to be actually in the things. But Locke expressly apologizes for this loose way of speaking. In strictness idea is to be taken to mean 'whatsoever the mind perceives *in itself*, or is the immediate object of perception, thought, or understanding, . . . which ideas, if I speak of sometimes as in the things themselves, I would be understood to mean those qualities in the objects which produce them in us'.[3] He extends therefore to our whole experience the physiological attitude which science has popularized in regard to the secondary qualities; all our perceptions are to be regarded as effects 'produced in us' by external causes, ideas or sensations 'produced in the mind'.[4]

The variation in phraseology just alluded to may help to explain how Locke failed to perceive the difficulties of his own theory, but inwoven with the foregoing account there is the inherited presupposition with which Locke formally opens Book IV, that 'the mind hath no other immediate object but its own ideas, which it alone does or can contemplate'.[5] 'All our knowledge', he says again, consists 'in the view the mind has of its own ideas'.[6] He states the position perhaps most explicitly in his concluding chapter: 'Since the things the mind contemplates are none of them, besides itself, present to the understanding, it is necessary that something else, as a sign or representation of the thing it considers, should be

---

[1] e. g. sections 12, 22, 23.   [2] Section 7.   [3] Section 8.
[4] Sections 18, 22, 23.   [5] IV. 1. 1.   [6] IV. 2. 1.

present to it : and these are ideas.'[1] This is the full-blown theory of Representative Perception, common to Locke with Descartes, and based on a metaphysical dualism between mind and matter, as two independent and disparate substances. Mind, on this theory, can know only what is mental; hence all knowledge of non-mental things must be mediate or indirect, ' by the intervention ', as he says, ' of the ideas it has of them '.[2] Locke contended, in reply to Stillingfleet, that his ' new way of knowing by means of ideas' was ' the same with the old way of speaking intelligibly '; and it may well be supposed that to have an idea of a thing meant at the outset no more than to know the thing. But, according to his own carefully repeated formula, ideas have themselves become the *objects* of knowledge, eclipsing the actual things which we set out to know. These immediate objects are said to be *in* the mind, but to think of them as mental states or processes would hardly be an accurate representation of Locke's position. He speaks of the mind as confined to a knowledge of its own ideas, but he would feel it decidedly unnatural to speak of it as confined to a knowledge of its own states. Ideas seem to possess for him a quasi-substantive existence between the knower and the real things.[3]

The difficulties of a theory so stated are obvious, and they were immediately fastened on by Berkeley and subsequently exploited by Hume. For if ideas are the only objects directly present to the mind, how can we compare our ideas with their originals, so as to be assured of that ' conformity between our ideas and the reality of things '[4] which the theory practically assumes ? What grounds have we, indeed, for assuming such an independent world of things at all ? As Hume afterwards put it, ' the mind has never anything present to it but the

[1] IV. 21. 4.   [2] IV. 4. 3.
[3] ' A twilight existence between the things they represent and the mind which understands them' (Alexander, *op. cit.*, p. 32).
[4] IV. 4. 3.

## Introduction

perceptions and cannot possibly reach any experience of their connexion with objects'.[1] 'We never really advance a step beyond ourselves, nor can conceive any kind of existence but those perceptions which have appeared in that narrow compass.'[2]

These difficulties force themselves upon our notice in Locke's own account of knowledge in Book IV. He begins, as we have seen, by describing ideas as the immediate objects of the mind, which it alone does or can contemplate; hence 'it is evident that our knowledge is only conversant about them'. Knowledge is then expressly defined as 'nothing but the perception of the connexion and agreement or disagreement and repugnancy of any of our ideas', and he goes on to distinguish four sorts of this agreement or disagreement: (1) Identity or diversity; (2) Relation, by which he understands the necessary implication exemplified in geometrical propositions; (3) Coexistence, by which he means the empirical connexions of fact which are investigated by physical science; (4) Real existence, or, as he expresses it more fully, 'actual real existence agreeing to any idea'. The definition applies most naturally to those intuitive and demonstrative truths to which Locke tends to restrict the term knowledge, and from a consideration of the procedure of the demonstrative sciences it was probably derived.[3] But, with a phraseology like Locke's, which is apt, as we have seen, to interchange 'idea' and 'quality', it may be intelligibly taken as including those coexistences and sequences of natural fact which constitute the third 'sort' in the above subdivision. The fourth sort, however, is not a relation between different ideas at all; it is a relation between any or all of our ideas, as such, and the real world to which they are tacitly assumed to refer. It falls therefore entirely outside of the definition, being a

[1] Hume, *Enquiry*, section 12.
[2] Hume, *Treatise*, Bk. I, Part II, section 6.
[3] Cf. Gibson, *op. cit.*, p. 176.

## Our Knowledge of Real Existence     xli

species of agreement or disagreement impossible to determine by the method of comparison which the definition contemplates.

This is borne out by Locke's results when he tries to handle the question of 'real existence' or 'the reality of human knowledge'.[1] 'The having the idea of anything in our mind', he tells us roundly, ' no more proves the existence of that thing than the picture of a man evidences his being in the world, or the visions of a dream make thereby a true history.'[2] There was one point at which Descartes and some of the Scholastics had held that the transition from idea to real existence might legitimately be made; and from the example Locke gives of his fourth sort, 'God is', it might perhaps be supposed that he had the ontological argument in view. As a matter of fact, the validity of that argument was left an open question in the *Essay*,[3] but it is alien to his whole temper of mind, and, when challenged by Stillingfleet, he expressly rejected it. Professor Gibson has called attention to an emphatic statement on the subject in a paper dated 1696. 'Real existence', he there concludes, 'can be proved only by real existence; and, therefore, the real existence of a God can only be proved by the real existence of other things.'[4] That is the course of argument followed in the *Essay*. The existence of God is treated as a demonstrative certainty, the real existence by which it is proved being that of the individual conscious subject. The latter Locke regards as an immediate certainty, and the language in which he states his position recalls that of Descartes about the *Cogito ergo sum*: 'If I doubt of all other things, that very doubt makes me perceive my own existence.' 'Experience', Locke concludes, 'convinces us that we have an *intuitive* knowledge of our own existence, and an internal infallible perception that we are. In every act of sensation, reasoning, or thinking, we are conscious to ourselves of our own being; and in this matter, come not short of the highest degree

---

[1] In chapters 9, 10, 11 of Book IV.     [2] IV. 11. 1.
[3] IV. 10. 7.     [4] *Op. cit.*, p. 169.

of *certainty.*'[1] Although Locke here and elsewhere describes our knowledge of our own existence as 'intuitive', it is clear that the knowledge in question has nothing in common with the intuitive knowledge of the agreement or disagreement of two ideas, except that both possess, as he says, the highest degree of certainty. Locke's alternative phrase, ' an internal infallible perception that we are', describes more accurately the nature of the experience. It is a certainty reached by reflective analysis, and therefore it must be allowed that the fact analysed involves ideas as an objective content ; but the certainty does not refer to relations in that content, but to the consciousness of our own existence as the condition of ' every act of sensation, reasoning or thinking '. Locke's introduction of the word ' act ' here, as a term coextensive with our whole conscious experience, is significant, and suggests the emphasis afterwards laid by Berkeley on ' activity ' as the distinctive nature of spirit.[2] It is the active functioning of the self as an element in all experience that he has in view. He is too apt, doubtless, like Descartes before him, to assume that the existence of the individual self as a ' thing that thinks ', an ' immaterial substance ', is given or disclosed in any single instance of conscious experience, whereas the permanence or self-identity which we mean to assert by such terms is clearly dependent on memory. Locke's statement, therefore, calls for further analysis in the light of Hume and Kant and of more recent philosophy and psychology ; but the necessary restatement would not seriously affect the place which this primal certainty holds in his argument.

From the real existence of the self Locke argues, as we have seen, to the real existence of God—an eternal Being, possessing ' at least all the perfections that can ever after exist '.[3] These

[1] IV. 9. 3.

[2] Locke himself had said, ' It is worth our consideration, whether active power be not the proper attribute of spirits, and passive power of matter ' (II. 23. 28). [3] IV. 10. 10.

## Sensitive Knowledge

two certainties, the one intuitive, the other demonstrative, exhaust our 'knowledge' of existence. Locke adds, indeed, a third ' degree ', which he calls at times ' sensitive knowledge ' ; but he expressly tells us that, though it 'passes under the name of knowledge ', it is not on the same level as the other two. It is a practical certainty, ' as great as our happiness or misery ', something which we cannot in earnest be so sceptical as to doubt, and in that sense, and as it were by courtesy, we may treat it as ' an assurance that deserves the name of knowledge '.[1] On this somewhat precarious footing Locke places the existence of the whole material world, as well as that of other human spirits, these being known to us only through their bodily manifestation. We are dependent for this kind of knowledge upon ' sensation '. Now the fact that we have sense-experiences from time to time is of course beyond the possibility of doubt ; these are bound up with the existence of the self, and Locke applies in their case the same term, intuitive certainty. ' But whether there be anything more than barely that idea in our minds, whether we can thence certainly infer the existence of anything without us which corresponds to that idea, is that whereof some men think there may be a question made.'[2] Locke's investigation of this difficulty leads him to the conclusion that ' when our senses do actually convey into our understandings any idea, we cannot but be satisfied that there doth something at that time really exist without us, which doth affect our senses, and by them give notice of itself to our apprehensive faculties, and actually produce that idea which we then perceive '. This assurance extends only ' as far as the present testimony of our senses, employed about particular objects that do affect them, and no farther ', except that through memory we have a similar assurance as to the causation of particular sense-affections in the past. ' But this knowledge also reaches no farther than our senses have formerly assured us ', so that this sensitive

[1] IV. 2. 14 and 11. 3.    [2] IV. 2. 14.

knowledge throughout is 'only of particulars'.[1] This is a somewhat meagre result. Instead of the precise correspondence of ideas and qualities presupposed in Book II, we are reduced to the practical conviction, in any sense-experience, that 'something really exists that causes that sensation in me'.[2] When the relation between ideas or sensations 'in us' (or 'in the mind') and the realities they represent is so conceived that the only passage from the one to the other is by a causal inference, there ceases to be any reason to suppose a resemblance between them—to invent a second set of perceptions, as Hume says, behind the first, and dub them objects. Berkeley's theory of the universal agency of God, or Hume's careless admission that the impressions of sense 'arise in the soul originally from unknown causes',[3] will equally suit the situation.

But although Locke's formal definitions and conclusions appear hardly distinguishable from the subjectivism of these two thinkers, his general attitude was too much determined by the 'presuppositions' of a common-sense realism to permit him to anticipate such an interpretation of his phrases. Representationism, as we find it in Descartes and Locke, has been illustrated by the figure of two concentric circles with the subject or knower in the centre. The outer circle stands in the figure for the external world of real things, the inner circle for the ideas, the mental or immediate objects. According to this illustration, what Berkeley did was to wipe out Locke's outer circle of material things (as purely supposititious and ultimately unintelligible) and to offer us the inner circle of ideas or subjective experiences as sufficient for all the needs of life. 'It is indeed an opinion strangely prevailing amongst men, that houses, mountains, rivers, and in a word all sensible objects, have an existence, natural or real, distinct from their being perceived by the understanding. Yet whoever shall find in his heart to call it in question may, if I mistake not, perceive

[1] IV. 11. 9–13.     [2] IV. 11. 2.     [3] *Treatise*, Bk. I, Part I, section 2.

## Sequel in Berkeley and Hume

it to involve a manifest contradiction. For what are the forementioned objects but the things we perceive by sense? and what do we perceive besides our own ideas or sensations? ... In truth the object and the sensation are the same thing.'[1] But although Locke is undoubtedly a Representationist in his terminology, he never contemplated the complete severance between the internal and the external—between idea and thing—which is implied in Berkeley's attempt to make the one do duty for the other. In Locke's usage idea and thing are correlative terms, each of which becomes unmeaning out of that mutual reference. This is true at any rate as regards the constantly implied reference of ideas to things. Green has pointed out that for Locke's 'idea of a thing' Berkeley substitutes 'idea' simply.[2] But for Locke an idea is essentially a meaning, a sign, and without this objective reference it has no function in knowledge at all. To treat ideas simply as psychical states, sufficient unto themselves, is to deprive them of cognitive value altogether; and the impossibility of such a procedure is shown by the fact that Berkeley is immediately obliged to retract his sheer identification of the object and the sensation. By treating sensations as signs of a divine Agent and as signs of other sensations, that is to say, of a permanent order of nature, he reinstates in a more roundabout fashion the objective reference which it had been his first inspiration to discard.

Because Locke assumes a reference to reality to be inherent in ideas as such, he gives himself little trouble, as Professor Campbell Fraser says, over the difficulty, pressed by Reid and other critics, ' how we can determine agreement of " ideas " with " reality ", without first having the real existence presented to us *apart from all ideas of it* '.[3] His use of the term

---

[1] *Principles of Human Knowledge*, sections 4–5. The last sentence was withdrawn in the second edition, which belongs to Berkeley's middle life (1734). [2] *Introduction to Hume*, section 173.
[3] Prolegomena to the Clarendon Press edition, vol. i, p. 83.

idea resembles somewhat closely the modern use of the term phenomenon and shares, it may be added, its ambiguity. To Locke the idea of a thing was simply the way in which the thing appeared to us; and that things do appear and manifest themselves in consciousness, he assumed as the essential prerequisite of knowledge. Hence, although he acknowledges that the question 'how shall the mind, when it perceives nothing but its own ideas, know that they agree with things themselves?' is one which 'seems not to want difficulty',[1] he is content to attack it in detail, and to point out that, in the case of our 'simple ideas' at least, this conformity exists, 'not because they are all of them images or representations' of what exists, but because, 'whether they be only constant effects or else exact resemblances of something in the things themselves', they are in either case ' the effects of powers in things without us, ordained by our Maker to produce in us such sensations '.[2] This is 'all the conformity which is intended, or which our state requires; for they represent to us things under those appearances which they are fitted to produce in us '.[3]

Locke had the instinct of the practical man and a constitutional impatience with fine-spun distinctions which seemed to him to smack too much of ' the Schools ' and their endless controversies. But this attitude of mind constitutes one of his weaknesses as a thinker. The subsequent course of European philosophy consists largely of a series of attempts to clear up the ambiguities of Locke's terminology and to surmount the difficulties created for him by his presuppositions. We have seen how his theory of Representative Perception was immediately followed by the subjective idealism of Berkeley's youthful philosophy, and that in turn by the pure idea-ism (as it might conveniently be termed) of Hume. Although neglecting important elements in Locke's construction, Hume's results were, in their way, a legitimate deduction from the exclusive Empiricism which stands in the

[1] IV. 4. 3.  [2] II. 30. 2.  [3] IV. 4. 4.

## Locke and Recent Discussion xlvii

forefront of the *Essay*, and from the ostensible start there made with simple unrelated ideas. They called forth accordingly Reid's emphatic protest against the initial presupposition common to Descartes and Locke—the supposed limitation of the mind in knowledge to its own ideas, whether regarded as its own states or as mental entities of some sort, internally present to it as a result of organic processes in the body. The Natural Realism of Reid and his followers may have been often crude and uncritical in its statements; but its fundamental contention that knowledge is essentially a judgement about reality, and that such judgement is present *ab initio* in the simplest sensation, remains of permanent philosophical importance.

Kant's celebrated reply to Hume proceeded upon other lines. So far from asserting with Reid a direct knowledge of reality, Kant in effect denies that we have such knowledge at all. We know only phenomena, and he frequently tells us that our phenomenal objects are ' mere ideas ', that they are ' real only in perception ' and ' have no existence beyond our mind '. Yet in other contexts Kant draws a sharp distinction between the phenomenal world, as a permanent object in space, and our intermittent perceptions of it. But the more he clothes it with permanence and independence, the more it tends to usurp the place of the real world of things of which it is supposed to be the appearance or the effect. The thing-in-itself was, in fact, promptly dropped by Kant's idealistic successors as an excrescence on the Critical scheme. But Kant himself maintained to the end a peculiar variety of the theory of Representative Perception, into which the double sense of the term ' object ' introduced a fundamental confusion—a confusion which we find accentuated in his latest, posthumously published writings.

The status of the external world and the nature of our knowledge of it have never been more keenly debated than during the last twenty years under the stimulus of the New

Realism and with the resources of an improved psychology. New terms have been introduced, and old ones which have proved to be ambiguous have been more strictly defined. Sensation, it has been proposed, should be restricted to the mental act or process of sensing, and a term such as 'sense-datum', 'sensible appearance' or, most concisely, 'sensum', appropriated to designate the 'object' sensed. But this undoubtedly useful distinction has unfortunately revived in some of the writers the old tendency to substantiate the sensum as a *tertium quid* between the knower and the physical reality he seeks to know. We find it seriously debated whether sensa can exist unsensed. This is not the place to attempt to clear up the fresh confusions which the discussion has brought to light, but at all events they show that the problem with which Locke deals in his Fourth Book still awaits its perfect solution. And in following the curious windings of the controversy it is difficult to resist the feeling that much superfluous debate might have been avoided by a closer acquaintance with the earlier history of the question. In this respect no modern thinker is more representative than Locke. However defective his own conclusions may be, his treatment of the subject introduces us, as nothing else can, to the whole course of subsequent discussion.

# AN ESSAY

concerning

# Human Understanding

# THE EPISTLE TO THE READER

READER,
I HERE put into thy hands what has been the diversion of some of my idle and heavy hours : if it has the good luck to prove so of any of thine, and thou hast but half so much pleasure in reading as I had in writing it, thou wilt as little think thy money, as I do my pains, ill bestowed. Mistake not this for a commendation of my work ; nor conclude, because I was pleased with the doing of it, that therefore I am fondly taken with it now it is done. He that hawks at larks and sparrows, has no less sport, though a much less considerable quarry, than he that flies at nobler game : and he is little acquainted with the subject of this treatise, the UNDER-STANDING,[1] who does not know that, as it is the most elevated faculty of the soul, so it is employed with a greater and more constant delight than any of the other. Its searches after truth are a sort of hawking and hunting, wherein the very pursuit makes a great part of the pleasure. Every step the mind takes in its progress towards knowledge, makes some discovery, which is not only new, but the best too, for the time at least.

For the understanding, like the eye, judging of objects only by its own sight, cannot but be pleased with what it discovers, having less regret for what has escaped it, because it is unknown. Thus he who has raised himself above the almsbasket, and not content to live lazily on scraps of begged opinions, sets his own thoughts on work, to find and follow truth, will (whatever he lights on) not miss the hunter's satisfaction ; every moment of his pursuit will reward his pains with some delight, and he will have reason to think his time not ill spent, even when he cannot much boast of any great acquisition.

[1] This term is used by Locke to include the whole range of human intelligence.

This, reader, is the entertainment of those who let loose their own thoughts, and follow them in writing; which thou oughtest not to envy them, since they afford thee an opportunity of the like diversion, if thou wilt make use of thy own thoughts in reading. It is to them, if they are thy own, that I refer myself; but if they are taken upon trust from others, it is no great matter what they are, they not following truth, but some meaner consideration; and it is not worth while to be concerned what he says or thinks, who says or thinks only as he is directed by another. If thou judgest for thyself, I know thou wilt judge candidly; and then I shall not be harmed or offended, whatever be thy censure. For though it be certain that there is nothing in this treatise of the truth whereof I am not fully persuaded, yet I consider myself as liable to mistakes as I can think thee; and know that this book must stand or fall with thee, not by any opinion I have of it, but thy own. If thou findest little in it new or instructive to thee, thou art not to blame me for it. It was not meant for those that had already mastered this subject, and made a thorough acquaintance with their own understandings, but for my own information, and the satisfaction of a few friends, who acknowledged themselves not to have sufficiently considered it. Were it fit to trouble thee with the history of this Essay, I should tell thee that five or six friends meeting at my chamber, and discoursing on a subject very remote from this, found themselves quickly at a stand by the difficulties that rose on every side.[1] After we had a while puzzled ourselves, without coming any nearer a resolution of those doubts which perplexed us, it came into my thoughts, that we took a wrong course; and that, before we set ourselves upon enquiries of that nature, it was necessary to examine our own abilities, and see what objects our understandings were or were not fitted to deal with.[2] This I proposed to the company, who all readily assented; and thereupon it was agreed, that this should be our first enquiry. Some hasty and undigested thoughts, on a subject I had never before considered, which I set down against our next meeting, gave the first entrance into this

[1] According to a manuscript note in a copy of the *Essay* which belonged to James Tyrrell, one of the friends present at the meeting, the difficulties arose in discussing the 'principles of morality and revealed religion'. The meeting probably took place in the winter of 1670-1.

[2] Cf. Bk. I, ch. 1, sections 4 and 7.

## *The Epistle to the Reader*

discourse, which having been thus begun by chance, was continued by entreaty; written by incoherent parcels; and, after long intervals of neglect, resumed again, as my humour or occasions permitted; and at last, in a retirement, where an attendance on my health gave me leisure, it was brought into that order thou now seest it.[1]

This discontinued way of writing may have occasioned, besides others, two contrary faults, viz., that too little and too much may be said in it. If thou findest anything wanting, I shall be glad, that what I have writ gives thee any desire that I should have gone farther: if it seems too much to thee, thou must blame the subject; for when I first put pen to paper, I thought all I should have to say on this matter would have been contained in one sheet of paper; but the farther I went, the larger prospect I had: new discoveries led me still on, and so it grew insensibly to the bulk it now appears in. I will not deny but possibly it might be reduced to a narrower compass than it is; and that some parts of it might be contracted: the way it has been writ in, by catches, and many long intervals of interruption, being apt to cause some repetitions. But to confess the truth, I am now too lazy or too busy to make it shorter.

I am not ignorant how little I herein consult my own reputation when I knowingly let it go with a fault so apt to disgust the most judicious. But I pretend not to publish this Essay for the information of men of large thoughts and quick apprehensions; to such masters of knowledge, I profess myself a scholar, and therefore warn them beforehand not to expect anything here but what, being spun out of my own coarse thoughts, is fitted to men of my own size, to whom, perhaps, it will not be unacceptable, that I have taken some pains to make plain and familiar to their thoughts some truths, which established prejudice, or the abstractness of the ideas themselves, might render difficult. Some objects had need be turned on every side; and when the notion is new, as I confess

---

[1] Locke speaks of his book as 'completed' in June 1679, at the close of nearly four years spent in France, but the 'retirement' here referred to is his residence, for political reasons, in Holland from 1683 to 1689. An epitome of the *Essay* in French appeared in January 1688 in Le Clerc's *Bibliothèque Universelle*. The first edition of the *Essay* was published in March 1690, a few months after his return to England. Locke was then in his fifty-eighth year, and it was the first work published under his own name.

some of these are to me, or out of the ordinary road, as I suspect they will appear to others, it is not one simple view of it that will gain it admittance into every understanding, or fix it there with a clear and lasting impression. There are few, I believe, who have not observed in themselves or others, that what in one way of proposing was very obscure, another way of expressing it has made very clear and intelligible ; though afterward the mind found little difference in the phrases, and wondered why one failed to be understood more than the other. But everything does not hit alike upon every man's imagination. We have our understandings no less different than our palates. I have so little affectation to be in print, that if I were not flattered this Essay might be of some use to others, as I think it has been to me, I should have confined it to the view of some friends, who gave the first occasion to it. My appearing therefore in print being on purpose to be as useful as I may, I think it necessary to make what I have to say as easy and intelligible to all sorts of readers as I can. And I had much rather the speculative and quick-sighted should complain of my being in some parts tedious, than that any one not accustomed to abstract speculations, or prepossessed with different notions, should mistake or not comprehend my meaning.

It will possibly be censured as a great piece of vanity or insolence in me to pretend to instruct this our knowing age, it amounting to little less when I own that I publish this Essay with hopes it may be useful to others. If I have not the good luck to please, yet nobody ought to be offended with me. I plainly tell all my readers, except half a dozen, this treatise was not at first intended for them ; and therefore they need not be at the trouble to be of that number. But yet if any one thinks fit to be angry and rail at it, he may do it securely; for I shall find some better way of spending my time than in such kind of conversation. I shall always have the satisfaction to have aimed sincerely at truth and usefulness, though in one of the meanest ways. The commonwealth of learning is not at this time without master-builders, whose mighty designs in advancing the sciences will leave lasting monuments to the admiration of posterity ; but every one must not hope to be a Boyle or a Sydenham ; and in an age that produces such masters as the great Huvgenius, and the incomparable Mr. Newton, with some other

## The Epistle to the Reader

of that strain,[1] it is ambition enough to be employed as an under-labourer in clearing the ground a little, and removing some of the rubbish that lies in the way to knowledge; which certainly had been very much more advanced in the world, if the endeavours of ingenious and industrious men had not been much cumbered with the learned but frivolous use of uncouth, affected, or unintelligible terms, introduced into the sciences, and there made an art of to that degree, that philosophy, which is nothing but the true knowledge of things,[2] was thought unfit or uncapable to be brought into well-bred company and polite conversation. Vague and insignificant forms of speech, and abuse of language, have so long passed for mysteries of science; and hard or misapplied words, with little or no meaning, have, by prescription, such a right to be mistaken for deep learning and height of speculation, that it will not be easy to persuade either those who speak or those who hear them, that they are but the covers of ignorance, and hindrance of true knowledge. To break in upon this sanctuary of vanity and ignorance, will be, I suppose, some service to human understanding: though so few are apt to think they deceive or are deceived in the use of words, or that the language of the sect they are of has any faults in it which ought to be examined or corrected, that I hope I shall be pardoned if I have in the Third Book dwelt long on this subject; and endeavoured to make it so plain, that neither the inveterateness of the mischief, nor the prevalency of the fashion, shall be any excuse for those who will not take care about the meaning of their own words, and will not suffer the significancy of their expressions to be enquired into.

I have been told that a short epitome of this treatise, which was printed 1688, was by some condemned without reading, because innate ideas were denied in it; they too hastily concluding, that if innate ideas were not supposed, there would be little left either of the notion or proof of spirits. If any one take the like offence at the entrance of this treatise, I shall desire him to read it through; and then I hope he will be

---

[1] The names cited recall Locke's lifelong interest in the scientific movement of his time and the friendships he formed with a number of its leaders.

[2] Compare William James's definition of metaphysics: 'metaphysics means only an unusually obstinate attempt to think clearly and consistently' (*Textbook of Psychology*, p. 461).

convinced, that the taking away false foundations is not to the prejudice, but advantage of truth, which is never injured or endangered so much as when mixed with or built on falsehood.[1]

[1] A second edition of the *Essay* was published in 1694 with an additional chapter on ' Identity and Diversity ' (Bk. II, ch. 27), and considerable alterations in the discussion of Liberty and the Will in the chapter on Power (II. 21). A third edition, which was only a reprint of the second, appeared in 1695. The fourth edition, the last in Locke's lifetime, was published in the end of 1699, dated 1700. It contained two new chapters, one on the Association of Ideas (Bk. II, ch. 33), and the other on Enthusiasm (Bk. IV, ch. 19). What Locke had originally intended to form a third additional chapter, but withheld on account of its length, was published separately among his posthumous works under the title, *Conduct of the Understanding*. Some slight farther additions and changes occur in the fifth edition issued in 1706, two years after Locke's death. Most of them had already appeared in the French version of the *Essay*, prepared at Oates under Locke's eye by Coste, his amanuensis, and published in 1700.

# OF HUMAN UNDERSTANDING

## BOOK I

### CHAPTER I[1]

#### INTRODUCTION

1. *An enquiry into the understanding pleasant and useful.*[2] Since it is the *understanding* that sets man above the rest of sensible beings, and gives him all the advantage and dominion which he has over them, it is certainly a subject, even for its nobleness, worth our labour to enquire into. The understanding, like the eye, whilst it makes us see and perceive all other things, takes no notice of itself ; and it requires art and pains to set it at a distance, and make it its own object. But whatever be the difficulties that lie in the way of this enquiry ; whatever it be that keeps us so much in the dark to ourselves ; sure I am that all the light we can let in upon our own minds, all the acquaintance we can make with our own understandings, will not only be very pleasant, but bring us great advantage in directing our thoughts in the search of other things.

2. *Design.*—This, therefore, being my purpose, to enquire into the original, certainty, and extent of human Knowledge,[3] together with the grounds and degrees of Belief, Opinion, and Assent, I shall not at present meddle with the physical

---

[1] This chapter constitutes an Introduction to the *Essay* as a whole, and is not specially connected with the subject-matter of Bk. I. It was separated from Bk. I in the French version, the latest form of the *Essay* supervised by Locke himself, and that arrangement is followed in the Clarendon Press edition by Professor Campbell Fraser ; but, for convenience of reference in the numbering of the chapters, the usual English arrangement is here retained.

[2] The summaries of the successive sections are by Locke himself. They were printed in the first edition as a detailed Table of Contents at the end of the volume, and in subsequent editions they appeared in the margin of the text as well.

[3] By knowledge, when he uses the term strictly, Locke means what is absolutely certain, as opposed to what is merely probable, however strong the probability may be. He here indicates the subjects of Bk. II and Bk. IV.

consideration of the mind,[1] or trouble myself to examine wherein its essence consists, or by what motions of our spirits,[2] or alterations of our bodies, we come to have any sensation by our organs, or any ideas in our understandings; and whether those ideas do, in their formation, any or all of them, depend on matter or no. These are speculations which, however curious and entertaining, I shall decline, as lying out of my way in the design I am now upon. It shall suffice to my present purpose, to consider the discerning faculties of a man as they are employed about the objects [3] which they have to do with: and I shall imagine I have not wholly misemployed myself in the thoughts I shall have on this occasion, if, in this historical, plain method,[4] I can give any account of the ways

[1] By 'physical consideration of the mind' and 'to examine wherein its essence consists' Locke means the same thing. In his 'division of the sciences' in the closing chapter of the *Essay* (IV. 21) he defines Physica or natural philosophy, 'in a little more enlarged sense of the word', as 'the knowledge of things as they are in their own proper beings, their constitutions, properties and operations, whereby I mean not only matter and body, but spirits also, which have their proper natures, constitutions, and operations, as well as bodies.' From such a science he distinguishes his own investigation as 'a doctrine of signs' to which the name 'logic' might be given, 'the nature whereof is to consider the nature of signs the mind makes use of for the understanding of things or conveying its knowledge to others'. Ideas are the signs of things and words are the signs of ideas, so that Locke describes his undertaking as 'the consideration of ideas and words as the great instruments of knowledge'. But, as Professor Gibson remarks, 'it is notoriously easier to propose such absolute divisions than to carry them through, and Locke's account of the doctrine of signs clearly bristles with metaphysical assumptions'. Cf. *Locke's Theory of Knowledge*, pp. 11–13.

[2] By 'spirits' here Locke means the 'animal spirits' of the old physiology, corresponding to the modern conception of nerve currents or nervous energy. It is to be taken in close connexion with the other phrase he uses, 'alteration of our bodies'. He is declining to deal with the relation of mental facts to bodily processes as that is treated in physiological psychology.

[3] 'Objects' is a fatally ambiguous word in philosophical discussion, as it may signify either the real things whose nature we desire to know or the 'signs' of these, the 'ideas' which, according to Locke and many others, are the only 'immediate' objects of the mind.

[4] 'Experience and history' are contrasted by Locke (IV. 12. 10) with the deductive or demonstrative method of mathematical science which Descartes had sought to apply in the philosophical sphere. Kant subsequently contrasted Locke's method, as 'psychological', with his own transcendental analytic, and commented on its inadequacy to solve the problem of knowledge (*Critique of Pure Reason*, Transcendental

whereby our understandings come to attain those notions of things we have, and can set down any measures of the certainty of our knowledge, or the grounds of those persuasions which are to be found amongst men, so various, different, and wholly contradictory; and yet asserted somewhere or other with such assurance, and confidence, that he that shall take a view of the opinions of mankind, observe their opposition, and at the same time consider the fondness and devotion wherewith they are embraced, the resolution and eagerness wherewith they are maintained, may perhaps have reason to suspect that either there is no such thing as truth at all, or that mankind hath no sufficient means to attain a certain knowledge of it.

3. *Method.*—It is therefore worth while to search out the *bounds* between Opinion and Knowledge, and examine by what measures, in things whereof we have no certain knowledge, we ought to regulate our assent, and moderate our persuasions. In order whereunto, I shall pursue this following method:—

First, I shall enquire into the *original* of those *ideas*, notions, or whatever else you please to call them, which a man observes, and is conscious to himself he has in his mind; and the ways whereby the understanding comes to be furnished with them.[1]

Secondly, I shall endeavour to show what *knowledge* the understanding hath by those *ideas*, and the certainty, evidence, and extent of it.[2]

Thirdly, I shall make some enquiry into the nature and grounds of Faith or Opinion; whereby I mean that assent which we give to any proposition as true, of whose truth yet we have no certain knowledge: and here we shall have occasion to examine the reasons and degrees of *Assent*.[3]

4. *Useful to know the extent of our comprehension.*—If by this enquiry into the nature of the understanding, I can discover the powers thereof, *how far* they reach, to what things they

---

Analytic, ch. ii, section 1). Locke certainly fails to distinguish clearly between the psychological question of the origin and development of ideas in the individual consciousness and the epistemological question of their place and function in the constitution of knowledge; but the epistemological interest is throughout predominant, and he thought of his work as calculated to yield us ' another sort of logic and critic than what we have hitherto been accustomed to' (IV. 21. 4). So far as the words go, the anticipation of Kant's descriptions of his own achievement could hardly be more exact. [1] This is the subject of Bk. II.
[2] Bk. IV, chs. 1-13.  [3] Bk. IV, chs. 14-20.

are in any degree proportionate, and where they fail us, I suppose it may be of use, to prevail with the busy mind of man to be more cautious in meddling with things exceeding its comprehension, to stop when it is at the utmost extent of its tether, and to sit down in a quiet ignorance of those things which, upon examination, are found to be beyond the reach of our capacities. We should not then perhaps be so forward, out of an affectation of an universal knowledge, to raise questions, and perplex ourselves and others with disputes about things to which our understandings are not suited, and of which we cannot frame in our minds any clear or distinct perceptions, or whereof (as it has, perhaps, too often happened) we have not any notions at all. If we can find out how far the understanding can extend its view, how far it has faculties to attain certainty, and in what cases it can only judge[1] and guess, we may learn to content ourselves with what is attainable by us in this state.

5. *Our capacity suited to our state and concerns.*—For though the comprehension of our understandings comes exceeding short of the vast extent of things, yet we shall have cause enough to magnify the bountiful Author of our being for that portion and degree of knowledge he has bestowed on us, so far above all the rest of the inhabitants of this our mansion. Men have reason to be well satisfied with what God hath thought fit for them, since he has given them, as St. Peter says, πάντα πρὸς ζωὴν καὶ εὐσέβειαν, 'whatsoever is necessary for the conveniences of life, and information of virtue'; and has put within the reach of their discovery the comfortable provision for this life, and the way that leads to a better. How short soever their knowledge may come of an universal or perfect comprehension of whatsoever is, it yet secures their great concernments that they have light enough to lead them to the knowledge of their Maker, and the sight of their own duties. Men may find matter sufficient to busy their heads and employ their hands with variety, delight, and satisfaction, if they will not boldly quarrel with their own constitution, and throw away the blessings their hands are filled with, because they are not big enough to grasp everything. We shall not have much reason to complain of the narrowness of our minds, if we will but employ them about what may be of

[1] For Locke's peculiar use of 'judgement', as equivalent to 'opinion', and contrasted with 'knowledge and certainty', compare Bk. IV, ch. 14.

use to us; for of that they are very capable; and it will be an unpardonable as well as childish peevishness, if we undervalue the advantages of our knowledge, and neglect to improve it to the ends for which it was given us, because there are some things that are set out of the reach of it. It will be no excuse to an idle and untoward servant, who would not attend his business by candlelight, to plead that he had not broad sunshine. The candle that is set up in us[1] shines bright enough for all our purposes. The discoveries we can make with this ought to satisfy us; and we shall then use our understandings right, when we entertain all objects in that way and proportion that they are suited to our faculties, and upon those grounds they are capable of being proposed to us; and not peremptorily or intemperately require demonstration, and demand certainty, where probability only is to be had, and which is sufficient to govern all our concernments. If we will disbelieve everything because we cannot certainly know all things, we shall do much-what as wisely as he who would not use his legs, but sit still and perish, because he had no wings to fly.

6. *Knowledge of our capacity a cure of scepticism and idleness.*—When we know our own strength, we shall the better know what to undertake with hopes of success: and when we have well surveyed the *powers* of our own minds, and made some estimate what we may expect from them, we shall not be inclined either to sit still, and not set our thoughts on work at all, in despair of knowing anything; nor on the other side question everything, and disclaim all knowledge, because some things are not to be understood. It is of great use to the sailor to know the length of his line, though he cannot with it fathom all the depths of the ocean. It is well he knows that it is long enough to reach the bottom at such places as are necessary to direct his voyage, and caution him against running upon shoals that may ruin him. Our business here is not to know all things, but those which concern our conduct. If we can find out those measures whereby a rational creature, put in that state which man is in in this world, may and ought to govern his opinions, and actions depending thereon, we need not be troubled that some other things escape our knowledge.

[1] 'The spirit of man is the candle of the Lord' (Prov. xx. 27). This metaphor for the light of reason is used by Whichcote, Locke's favourite preacher. It occurs again, IV. 3. 20.

7. *Occasion of this Essay.*[1]—This was that which gave the first rise to this Essay concerning the Understanding. For I thought that the first step towards satisfying several enquiries the mind of man was very apt to run into, was, to take a survey of our own understandings, examine our own powers, and see to what things they were adapted. Till that was done, I suspected we began at the wrong end, and in vain sought for satisfaction in a quiet and secure possession of truths that most concerned us, whilst we let loose our thoughts into the vast ocean of Being ; as if all that boundless extent were the natural and undoubted possession of our understandings, wherein there was nothing exempt from its decisions, or that escaped its comprehension. Thus men, extending their enquiries beyond their capacities, and letting their thoughts wander into those depths where they can find no sure footing, it is no wonder that they raise questions and multiply disputes, which, never coming to any clear resolution, are proper only to continue and increase their doubts, and to confirm them at last in perfect scepticism. Whereas, were the capacities of our understandings well considered, the extent of our knowledge once discovered, and the horizon found which sets the bounds between the enlightened and dark parts of things ; between what is and what is not comprehensible by us, men would perhaps with less scruple acquiesce in the avowed ignorance of the one, and employ their thoughts and discourse with more advantage and satisfaction in the other.[1]

8. *What ' idea ' stands for.*—Thus much I thought necessary

---

[1] This section, along with certain passages in the Epistle to the Reader, is the clearest statement of the scope and intention of the *Essay*. Its phraseology, especially the metaphor of ' the horizon which sets bounds between what is and what is not comprehensible by us ', forms a striking parallel to Kant's language when he expounds his doctrine of the extent and limits of human knowledge. Kant makes it a reproach to Hume that ' he merely declares the understanding to be limited, instead of showing what its limits were, thus creating a general mistrust in the power of our faculties, without giving us any determinate knowledge of the bounds of our necessary and unavoidable ignorance. Whereas a complete review of the powers of reason, and the conviction thence arising that we are in possession of a limited field of action, while we must admit the vanity of higher claims, puts an end to all doubt and dispute, and induces reason to rest satisfied with the undisturbed possession of its limited domain ' (*Critique of Pure Reason,* Transcendental Doctrine of Method, ch. i, section 2, *ad finem*). Of course Locke and Kant do not find the horizon exactly in the same place.

to say concerning the occasion of this enquiry into human understanding. But, before I proceed on to what I have thought on this subject, I must here, in the entrance, beg pardon of my reader for the frequent use of the word *idea* which he will find in the following treatise. It being that term which, I think, serves best to stand for whatsoever is the object of the understanding when a man thinks,[1] I have used it to express

[1] Endless controversy has gathered round this definition and round Locke's actual use of the term ' idea '. It is important to remember, in the first place, the distinction signalized by Descartes between an idea as a mental state, a psychical occurrence, and the same idea as functioning in knowledge and conveying a certain meaning. The former he called the *esse formale seu proprium* of an idea, and in this respect all ideas stand upon the same footing. (' If ideas are taken in so far only as they are certain modes of consciousness, I do not remark any difference between them, and they all seem in the same manner to proceed from myself.' Third Meditation.) The treatment of ideas so regarded belongs to psychology. But ideas not only exist as facts in the mental history of this or that individual ; they have also, in the modern phrase, a ' content ' or meaning; they signify something other than themselves. We regard them, in Descartes's words, ' as images, of which one represents one thing and another a different thing ', and this is the important aspect of ideas for us. He calls it their *esse obiectivum seu vicarium*. So regarded, ideas are the subject-matter of epistemology or theory of knowledge, and it is in this light that Locke appears to contemplate them in the definition. That certainly is his fundamental interest in ideas throughout. The ' historical plain method ', however, adopted in the first and second Books, is appropriate only to ideas in their psychological aspect, so that much confusion results.

Even if we confine ourselves to ideas in their cognitive aspect, a farther ambiguity exists in connexion with the word ' object ', used by Locke in this definition and constantly recurring throughout the *Essay*. Ideas, we are told, are ' the immediate objects ' of the mind, ' which it alone does or can contemplate '; and object here (as well as in the Cartesian phrase) means a mental or subjective content, not the real object or thing apprehended through the medium of that content. Are ideas, then, to be regarded as quasi-independent entities ' contemplated ' by the mind, or are they only another name for the mental act of apprehension ? This question led to an acute divergence of opinion within the Cartesian school. Descartes himself regarded ideas as mental modifications : ' I hold that there is no other difference between the mind and its ideas than between a piece of wax and the diverse figures which it can receive. And since the receiving diverse figures is not properly an action in the wax, but a passion, so it seems to me to be also a passion in the mind that it receives this or that idea, and that its volitions alone are actions ' (Epistle cccxlvii, *Œuvres* (Adam et Tannery), vol. iv, p. 113). But the passive rôle assigned to the mind in knowing led naturally to Malebranche's doctrine of seeing all things in God ; and for Malebranche the intelligible world thus contemplated had certainly an existence independent of the individual mind. Arnauld, on

whatever is meant by *phantasm, notion, species,* or whatever it is which the mind can be employed about in thinking; and I could not avoid frequently using it.

I presume it will be easily granted me, that there are such *ideas* in men's minds; every one is conscious of them in himself, and men's words and actions will satisfy him that they are in others.

Our first enquiry then shall be, how they come into the mind.

## CHAPTER II

### NO INNATE PRINCIPLES IN THE MIND

1. *The way shown how we come by any knowledge, sufficient to prove it not innate.*—It is an established opinion amongst some men,[1] that there are in the understanding certain *innate principles*; some primary notions, κοιναὶ ἔννοιαι, characters, as it were stamped upon the mind of man, which the soul receives in its very first being, and brings into the world with it. It would be sufficient to convince unprejudiced readers of the falseness of this supposition, if I should only show (as I hope I shall in the following parts of this discourse) how men, barely by the use of their natural faculties, may attain to all the knowledge they have, without the help of any innate impressions; and may arrive at certainty, without any such original notions or principles. For I imagine any one will easily grant, that it would be impertinent to suppose the ideas of colours innate in a creature to whom God hath given sight, and a power to receive them by the eyes from external objects:

the contrary, insisted that the idea is in no way distinct from the act of perception. Locke's usage is by no means clear. If challenged, he would no doubt, especially with Malebranche's theory in his mind, disclaim the attribution of anything like an independent existence to ideas; he says, indeed, in that connexion that 'ideas are nothing but perceptions of the mind' (*Examination of Malebranche,* section 15). But 'perception' itself is an ambiguous word, both in Descartes and in Locke. It may mean either the act of perceiving or the object perceived, and Locke habitually uses language which seems to imply, in Professor Alexander's phrase, a twilight existence of the ideas between the things they represent and the mind which understands them. Cf. Professor Gibson, *op. cit.,* pp. 13–21; Adamson's *Development of Modern Philosophy,* chs. 1 and 2; and the Appendix to Veitch's translation of Descartes's *Method and Meditations.*

[1] For a discussion of the question who the men were whom Locke had in view, see Introduction, pp. xxxi–xxxiii.

and no less unreasonable would it be to attribute several truths to the impressions of nature and innate characters, when we may observe in ourselves faculties fit to attain as easy and certain knowledge of them as if they were originally imprinted on the mind.

But because a man is not permitted without censure to follow his own thoughts in the search of truth, when they lead him ever so little out of the common road, I shall set down the reasons that made me doubt of the truth of that opinion, as an excuse for my mistake, if I be in one; which I leave to be considered by those who, with me, dispose themselves to embrace truth wherever they find it.

2. *General assent the great argument.*—There is nothing more commonly taken for granted, than that there are certain principles, both *speculative* and *practical* (for they speak of both), universally agreed upon by all mankind; which therefore, they argue, must needs be the constant impressions which the souls of men receive in their first beings, and which they bring into the world with them, as necessarily and really as they do any of their inherent faculties.

3. *Universal consent proves nothing innate.*—This argument, drawn from universal consent, has this misfortune in it, that if it were true in matter of fact, that there were certain truths wherein all mankind agreed, it would not prove them innate, if there can be any other way shown, how men may come to that universal agreement in the things they do consent in; which I presume may be done.

4. *' What is, is,' and ' It is impossible for the same thing to be, and not to be,' not universally assented to.*—But, which is worse, this argument of universal consent, which is made use of to prove innate principles, seems to me a demonstration that there are none such; because there are none to which all mankind give an universal assent. I shall begin with the speculative, and instance in those magnified principles of demonstration: 'Whatsoever is, is,' and 'It is impossible for the same thing to be, and not to be,' which, of all others, I think, have the most allowed title to innate. These have so settled a reputation of maxims universally received, that it will, no doubt, be thought strange if any one should seem to question it. But yet I take liberty to say, that these propositions are so far from having an universal assent, that there are a great part of mankind to whom they are not so much as known.

5. *Not on the mind naturally imprinted, because not known to children, idiots, &c.*—For, first, it is evident, that all children and idiots have not the least apprehension or thought of them : and the want of that is enough to destroy that universal assent, which must needs be the necessary concomitant of all innate truths : it seeming to me near a contradiction to say, that there are truths imprinted on the soul which it perceives or understands not ; imprinting, if it signify anything, being nothing else but the making certain truths to be perceived. No proposition can be said to be in the mind which it never yet knew, which it was never yet conscious of.[1] For if any one may, then, by the same reason, all propositions that are true, and the mind is capable ever of assenting to, may be said to be in the mind, and to be imprinted ; since if any one can be said to be in the mind, which it never yet knew, it must be only because it is capable of knowing it ; and so the mind is of all truths it ever shall know. Nay, thus truths may be imprinted on the mind which it never did, nor ever shall know : for a man may live long, and die at last in ignorance of many truths which his mind was capable of knowing, and that with certainty. So that if the capacity of knowing be the natural impression contended for, all the truths a man ever comes to know will, by this account, be every one of them innate : and this great point will amount to no more, but only to a very improper way of speaking. But then, to what end such contest for certain innate maxims ? If truths can be imprinted

[1] This is the presupposition of Locke's whole argument in the First Book—nothing can be said to be in the mind of which we are not clearly and explicitly conscious. Locke, that is to say, follows Descartes in equating mental process with self-conscious thought. Leibniz in his criticism of Locke introduced into modern philosophy the important conception of the sub-conscious. Distinguishing between ' apperception ' or self-conscious knowledge, and mere ' perception ', he lays stress on the ' minute ' or ' insensible perceptions ' (*perceptions petites*) which are present as the vague background of our explicit consciousness, perceived only in the mass or by their total effect. Much, he argues, may be present in the mind at this level, ' not strong enough to attract our attention and our memory '. The process of our experience may therefore consist, in part at least, of bringing into the full light of consciousness what was thus dimly present in our mental organization from the first. Leibniz, indeed, in accordance with his theory of ' windowless ' or self-contained monads, considers the whole life-history of any individual to be simply the unfolding of what is preformed in this way in the germ. In this sense, *all* our ideas would be innate. Cf. *New Essays on the Human Understanding*, Preface and Bk. I.

on the understanding without being perceived, I can see no difference there can be between any truths the mind is capable of knowing in respect of their original : they must all be innate, or all adventitious ;[1] in vain shall a man go about to distinguish them. He therefore that talks of innate notions in the understanding, cannot (if he intend thereby any distinct sort of truths) mean such truths to be in the understanding as it never perceived, and is yet wholly ignorant of. For if these words ' to be in the understanding ' have any propriety, they signify to be understood. If therefore these two propositions : ' Whatsoever is, is,' and, ' It is impossible for the same thing to be, and not to be,' are by nature imprinted, children cannot be ignorant of them ; infants, and all that have souls, must necessarily have them in their understandings, know the truth of them, and assent to it.[2]

6. *That men know them when they come to the use of reason, answered.*—To avoid this, it is usually answered, that all men know and *assent* to them, *when they come to the use of reason*, and this is enough to prove them innate. [7.] To apply this answer with any tolerable sense to our present purpose, it must signify one of these two things ; either, that as soon as men come to the use of reason, these supposed native inscriptions come to be known and observed by them ; or else, that the use and exercise of men's reasons assists them in the discovery of these principles, and certainly makes them known to them.

---

[1] The consistency of Leibniz's theory involves the view that all are innate, and he states this view in various places, but in defending innateness against Locke's attack he usually gives the term a more restricted application to ' distinct sorts of truths ', e. g. to necessary truths or ' truths of the reason ', as distinguished from ' truths of fact ', or to certain fundamental conceptions present in all knowledge. Descartes began by distinguishing innate as a ' distinct sort ' of idea or truth, but the dualism which he set up between thought and extension eventually drove him to speak of all ideas as innate, seeing that no ideas can be given to mind by anything distinct in nature from itself. In his own words, ' the ideas of no things, such as we form them by thought, can be presented to us by the things ; so that there is nothing in our ideas which is not innate in the mind or faculty of thought, with the exception of those circumstances, for example, which gave to mind the occasion to form the ideas at that rather than at some other time ' (*Œuvres*, x. 96. Cf. Adamson's *Development of Modern Philosophy*, i. 38).

[2] ' Knowledge ' and ' assent ', here used convertibly, are technically distinguished in Bk. IV, self-evidence or demonstration being required to constitute knowledge, while assent is determined by weighing probabilities.

8. *If reason discovered them, that would not prove them innate.*—If they mean that by the *use of reason* men may discover these principles, and that this is sufficient to prove them innate, their way of arguing will stand thus: viz. That whatever truths reason can certainly discover to us, and make us firmly assent to, those are all naturally imprinted on the mind; and by this means there will be no difference between the maxims of the mathematicians and theorems they deduce from them: all must be equally allowed innate, they being all discoveries made by the use of reason, and truths that a rational creature may certainly come to know, if he apply his thoughts rightly that way.[1]

9. *It is false that reason discovers them.*—But how can these men think the use of reason necessary to discover principles that are supposed innate, when reason (if we may believe them) is nothing else but the faculty of deducing unknown truths from principles or propositions that are already known? That certainly can never be thought innate which we have need of reason to discover, unless, as I have said, we will have all the certain truths that reason ever teaches us, to be innate. We may as well think the use of reason necessary to make our eyes discover visible objects, as that there should be need of reason, or the exercise thereof, to make the understanding see what is originally engraven in it. [10.] And I think those who give this answer will not be forward to affirm, that the knowledge of

[1] This is expressly claimed by Leibniz as a characteristic of necessary truths. 'In this sense it must be said that all arithmetic and all geometry are innate, and are in us virtually, so that we can find them there if we consider attentively and set in order what we already have in the mind, without making use of any truths learned through experience or through tradition from others.' And he goes on to refer to the procedure of Socrates in the *Meno*, eliciting from the slave-boy the knowledge of a geometrical theorem by a series of questions without giving him any information. 'I cannot admit this proposition: all that one learns is not innate.' 'All truths which can be drawn from primitive innate knowledge can still be called innate, because the mind can draw them from its own depths, although often that may not be an easy matter' (*New Essays*, Bk. I, ch. 1). Similarly, it was just the 'immutable natures' of geometrical ideas and the possibility of deducing from these natures properties which we had not previously thought of in connexion with the figures that impressed Descartes with their innateness. 'When I now discover them, I do not so much appear to learn anything new, as to call to remembrance what I before knew, or for the first time to remark what was before in my mind, but to which I had not hitherto directed my attention' (*Meditations*, v).

this maxim, ' That it is impossible for the same thing to be, and not to be,' is a deduction of our reason.[1] For this would be to destroy that bounty of nature they seem so fond of, whilst they make the knowledge of those principles to depend on the labour of our thoughts. For all reasoning [1] is search and casting about, and requires pains and application. And how can it with any tolerable sense be supposed, that what was imprinted by nature, as the foundation and guide of our reason, should need the use of reason to discover it ?

11. Those who will take the pains to reflect with a little attention on the operations of the understanding, will find that this ready assent of the mind to some truths, depends not either on native inscription, or the use of reason, but on a faculty of the mind quite distinct from both of them,[2] as we shall see hereafter.

12. *The coming to the use of reason, not the time we come to know these maxims.*—If by knowing and assenting to them ' when we come to the use of reason ', be meant, that as soon as children come to the use of reason, they come also to know and assent to these maxims ; this also is false and frivolous. How many instances of the use of reason may we observe in children, a long time before they have any knowledge of this maxim, ' That it is impossible for the same thing to be, and not to be ! ' And a great part of illiterate people and savages pass many years, even of their rational age, without ever thinking on this and the like general propositions. I grant, men come not to the knowledge of these general and more abstract truths, which are thought innate, till they come to the use of reason ; and I add, nor then neither. Which is so, because till after they come to the use of reason, those general

[1] ' Reason ' is used in these sections, as frequently by Locke, as equivalent to ' reasoning '—the deductive faculty, as he calls it here ; the discursive faculty, as he calls it in section 15. He interchanges reason and reasoning in the present section.

[2] Locke's appeal is to self-evidence or ' intuitive knowledge ', which ' neither requires nor admits any proof, one part of it any more than another ' (IV. 7. 19). ' In this the mind is at no pains of proving or examining, but perceives the truth as the eye doth light, only by being directed towards it. Thus the mind perceives that white is not black, that a circle is not a triangle, that three are more than two, and equal to one and two. . . . It is on this intuition that depends all the certainty and evidence of all our knowledge ' (IV. 2. 1. Cf. the whole section, also IV. 17. 14).

abstract ideas are not framed in the mind, about which those general maxims are.

15. *The steps by which the mind attains several truths.*—The senses at first let in particular ideas, and furnish the yet empty cabinet :[1] and the mind by degrees growing familiar with some of them, they are lodged in the memory, and names got to them. Afterwards the mind proceeding farther, abstracts them, and by degrees learns the use of general names. In this manner the mind comes to be furnished with ideas and language, the materials about which to exercise its discursive faculty ; and the use of reason becomes daily more visible, as these materials, that give it employment, increase. But though the having of general ideas, and the use of general words and reason, usually grow together, yet I see not how this any way proves them innate. The knowledge of some truths, I confess, is very early in the mind ; but in a way that shows them not to be innate. For, if we will observe, we shall find it still to be about ideas not innate, but acquired ; it being about those first, which are imprinted by external things, with which infants have earliest to do, which make the most frequent impressions on their senses. In ideas thus got, the mind discovers that some agree, and others differ, probably as soon as it has any use of memory, as soon as it is able to retain and receive distinct ideas. But whether it be then or no, this is certain, it does so long before it has the use of words, or comes to that which we commonly call ' the use of reason '. For a child knows as certainly, before it can speak, the difference between the ideas of sweet and bitter (i. e., that sweet is not bitter), as it knows afterwards (when it comes to speak) that wormwood and sugar-plums are not the same thing.

16. A child knows not that three and four are equal to seven till he comes to be able to count to seven, and has got the name and idea of equality ; and then, upon explaining those words, he presently assents to, or rather perceives the truth of that proposition. But neither does he then readily assent because it is an innate truth, nor was his assent wanting till then because he wanted the use of reason ; but the truth of it

---

[1] Locke here anticipates his account, in Bk. II, of the origin and elaboration of ideas. The metaphor of the ' empty cabinet ' recurs II. 11. 17 : ' Methinks the understanding is not much unlike a closet wholly shut from light, with only some little openings left, to let in external visible resemblances, or ideas of things without.'

appears to him as soon as he has settled in his mind the clear and distinct ideas that these names stand for; and then he knows the truth of that proposition upon the same grounds, and by the same means, that he knew before, that a rod and cherry are not the same thing; and upon the same grounds also, that he may come to know afterwards, ' that it is impossible for the same thing to be, and not to be ', as we shall more fully show hereafter.[1] So that the later it is before any one comes to have those general ideas about which those maxims are, or to know the signification of those general terms that stand for them, or to put together in his mind the ideas they stand for; the later also will it be before he comes to assent to those maxims, whose terms, with the ideas they stand for, being no more innate than those of a cat or a weasel, he must stay till time and observation have acquainted him with them.

17. *Assenting as soon as proposed and understood, proves them not innate.*—This evasion therefore of general assent when men come to the use of reason, failing as it does, and leaving no difference between those supposed innate, and other truths that are afterwards acquired and learnt, men have endeavoured to secure an universal assent to those they call maxims, by saying, they are generally *assented to as soon as proposed* and the terms they are proposed in understood. [18.] But if such an assent be a mark of innate, they must then allow all such propositions to be innate which are generally assented to as soon as heard; whereby they will find themselves plentifully stored with innate principles. That ' one and two are equal to three ', that ' two and two are equal to four ', and a multitude of other the like propositions in numbers that everybody assents to at first hearing and understanding the terms, must have a place amongst these innate axioms. Nor is this the prerogative of numbers alone. That ' two bodies cannot be in the same place ', that ' white is not black ', that ' a square is not a circle ', that ' yellowness is not sweetness ' : these, and a million of other such propositions, as many at least as we have distinct ideas, every man in his wits at first hearing, and knowing what the names stand for, must necessarily assent to. But since no proposition can be innate, unless the ideas about which it is be innate, this will be to suppose all our ideas of colours, sounds, tastes, figure, &c., innate : than which there

[1] Cf. note to section 11, *supra*.

cannot be anything more opposite to reason and experience. Universal and ready assent upon hearing and understanding the terms, is, I grant, a mark of self-evidence: but self-evidence, depending not on innate impressions, but on something else (as we shall show hereafter[1]), belongs to several propositions, which nobody was yet so extravagant as to pretend to be innate.

19. *Such less general propositions known before these universal maxims.*—Nor let it be said, that those more particular self-evident propositions which are assented to at first hearing, as, that ' one and two are equal to three ', that ' green is not red ', &c., are received as the consequences of those more universal propositions, which are looked on as innate principles; since any one who will but take the pains to observe what passes in the understanding will certainly find that these and the like less general propositions are certainly known and firmly assented to by those who are utterly ignorant of those more general maxims; and so, being earlier in the mind than those (as they are called) first [2] principles, cannot owe to them the assent wherewith they are received at first hearing. [20.] And as to the usefulness of these magnified maxims, that perhaps will not be found so great as is generally conceived, when it comes in its due place to be more fully considered.[3]

21. This cannot be denied, that men grow first acquainted with many of these self-evident truths, upon their being proposed; but it is clear that whosoever does so, finds in himself that he then begins to know a proposition which he knew not before; and which from thenceforth he never questions; not because it was innate, but because the consideration of the nature of the things contained in those words would not suffer

[1] Cf. note to section 11, *supra*.

[2] ' But they are not " first " because *soonest* apprehended by the individual mind, but because presupposed in the nature of things, or in reason, and so *first in logical order* ' (Fraser). Cf. Aristotle's distinction between πρότερον τῇ φύσει καὶ πρὸς ἡμᾶς πρότερον (*Posterior Analytics*, I. 2. 71$^b$. 33). Locke, throughout his discussion, ignores the fact that although the universal propositions, which he calls maxims, are not apprehended in their abstract form till long after the apprehension of a great variety of particular propositions, which are accepted as self-evident, the recognition of the self-evidence of each particular proposition involves, and in that sense depends upon, the acceptance of the universal principle (e. g. of non-contradiction).

[3] Bk. IV, ch. 7, ' Of Maxims '.

him to think otherwise, how or whensoever he is brought to reflect on them.

22. *Implicitly known before proposing, signifies that the mind is capable of understanding them, or else signifies nothing.*—If it be said, 'The understanding hath an *implicit knowledge* of these principles, but not an explicit, before this first hearing', (as they must who will say that they are in the understanding before they are known,) it will be hard to conceive what is meant by a principle imprinted on the understanding implicitly; unless it be this, that the mind is capable of understanding and assenting firmly to such propositions. And thus all mathematical demonstrations, as well as first principles, must be received as native impressions on the mind.

25. *These maxims not the first known.*—But that I may not be accused to argue from the thoughts of infants, which are unknown to us, and to conclude from what passes in their understandings, before they express it, I say next, that these two general propositions are not the truths that first possess the minds of children, nor are antecedent to all acquired and adventitious notions; which, if they were innate, they must needs be. Whether we can determine it or no, it matters not; there is certainly a time when children begin to think, and their words and actions do assure us that they do so. When therefore they are capable of thought, of knowledge, of assent, can it rationally be supposed they can be ignorant of those notions that nature has imprinted were there any such? Can it be imagined, with any appearance of reason, that they perceive the impressions from things without, and be at the same time ignorant of those characters which nature itself has taken care to stamp within? Can they receive and assent to adventitious notions, and be ignorant of those which are supposed woven into the very principles of their being, and imprinted there in indelible characters, to be the foundation and guide of all their acquired knowledge and future reasonings? This would be to make nature take pains to no purpose, or, at least, to write very ill; since its characters could not be read by those eyes which saw other things very well: and those are very ill supposed the clearest parts of truth and the foundations of all our knowledge, which are not first known, and without which the undoubted knowledge of several other things may be had. The child certainly knows that the nurse that feeds it, is neither the cat it plays with,

nor the Blackmoor it is afraid of; that the wormseed or mustard it refuses is not the apple or sugar it cries for; this it is certainly and undoubtedly assured of: but will any one say, it is by virtue of this principle, that 'it is impossible for the same thing to be and not to be', that it so firmly assents to these and other parts of its knowledge? [1] or that the child has any notion or apprehension of that proposition at an age wherein yet, it is plain, it knows a great many other truths? He that will say, 'Children join these general abstract speculations with their sucking-bottles and their rattles', may, perhaps, with justice be thought to have more passion and zeal for his opinion, but less sincerity and truth, than one of that age.

26. *And so not innate.*—Though therefore there be several general propositions that meet with constant and ready assent as soon as proposed to men grown up, who have attained the use of more general and abstract ideas, and names standing for them; yet they not being to be found in those of tender years, who nevertheless know other things, they cannot pretend to universal assent of intelligent persons, and so by no means can be supposed innate: [2] it being impossible that any truth which is innate (if there were any such) should be unknown,

---

[1] ' It is true ', says Leibniz, ' that we commence sooner to perceive particular truths, as we commence with ideas more complex and rude; but that does not prevent the order of nature from beginning with the simpler, or the proof of the particular truths from depending on the more general, of which they are only examples. And when we wish to consider what is in us virtually and before all *apperception*, we are right in beginning with the simpler. For general principles enter into our thoughts, of which they form the soul and the connecting bond. They are as necessary thereto as the muscles and sinews are for walking, although we do not think of them. The mind leans upon these principles every moment, but it does not come so easily to disengage them and to consider them distinctly and separately, because that demands great attention to its acts, of which most people, little accustomed to reflection, are scarcely capable.' ' We build on these maxims,' he says in the same context, ' as we build upon the suppressed majors when we reason by enthymemes. . . . The force of this conclusion always consists in part of that which is suppressed and could not come from any other source, as will be found when we wish to justify it.' As regards ' the two great speculative principles ', ' at bottom everybody knows them, and makes use at every moment of the principle of contradiction, for example, without considering it distinctly'.

[2] ' Whatsoever is innate must be universal in the strictest sense; one exception is a sufficient proof against it' (*Third Letter* to Stillingfleet, p. 447).

at least to any one who knows anything else. Since, if they are innate truths, they must be innate thoughts; there being nothing a truth in the mind that it has never thought on. Whereby it is evident if there be any innate truths, they must necessarily be the first of any thought on, the first that appear.

27. *Not innate, because they appear least where what is innate shows itself clearest.*—There is this farther argument against their being innate: that these characters, if they were native and original impressions, should appear fairest and clearest in those persons in whom yet we find no footsteps of them. Children, idiots, savages, and illiterate people, being of all others the least corrupted by custom or borrowed opinions, one might reasonably imagine, that in their minds these innate notions should lie open fairly to every one's view, as it is certain the thoughts of children do. But, alas! amongst children, idiots, savages, and the grossly illiterate, what general maxims are to be found? What universal principles of knowledge? A child knows his nurse and his cradle, and, by degrees, the playthings of a little more advanced age; and a young savage has perhaps his head filled with love and hunting, according to the fashion of his tribe. But he that from a child untaught, or a wild inhabitant of the woods, will expect these abstract maxims and reputed principles of sciences, will, I fear, find himself mistaken. Such kind of general propositions are seldom mentioned in the huts of Indians; much less are they to be found in the thoughts of children, or any impressions of them on the minds of naturals. They are the language and business of the schools and academies of learned nations, accustomed to that sort of conversation or learning where disputes are frequent: these maxims being suited to artificial argumentation and useful for conviction; but not much conducing to the discovery of truth or advancement of knowledge. But of their small use for the improvement of knowledge I shall have occasion to speak more at large, Bk. IV, ch. 7.[1]

[1] The repeated references forward to this chapter on 'Maxims' confirm the conclusion arrived at by Professor Gibson that it is the Scholastic Aristotelianism which Locke is attacking in Bk. I.

## CHAPTER III

### NO INNATE PRACTICAL PRINCIPLES

1. *No moral principles so clear and so generally received as the fore-mentioned speculative maxims.*—If those speculative maxims whereof we discoursed in the foregoing chapter have not an actual universal assent from all mankind, as we there proved, it is much more visible concerning *practical principles,* that they come short of an universal reception.

2. *Faith and justice not owned as principles by all men.*—Whether there be any such moral principles wherein all men do agree, I appeal to any who have been but moderately conversant in the history of mankind, and looked abroad beyond the smoke of their own chimneys. Where is that practical truth that is universally received without doubt or question, as it must be if innate ? Justice, and keeping of contracts, is that which most men seem to agree in. This is a principle which is thought to extend itself to the dens of thieves, and the confederacies of the greatest villains ; and they who have gone farthest towards the putting off of humanity itself, keep faith and rules of justice one with another. I grant that outlaws themselves do this one amongst another ; but it is without receiving these as the innate laws of nature. They practise them as rules of convenience within their own communities : but it is impossible to conceive that he embraces justice as a practical principle who acts fairly with his fellow-highwayman, and at the same time plunders or kills the next honest man he meets with.

3. *Objection. ' Though men deny them in their practice, yet they admit them in their thoughts,' answered.*—Perhaps it will be urged, that the tacit assent of their minds agrees to what their practice contradicts. I answer, First, I have always thought the actions of men the best interpreters of their thoughts. Secondly, It is very strange and unreasonable to suppose innate practical principles that terminate only in contemplation. Practical principles derived from nature are there for operation, and must produce conformity of action, not barely speculative assent to their truth, or else they are in vain distinguished from speculative maxims. Nature, I confess, has put into man a desire of happiness, and an aversion to misery ;

these, indeed, are innate practical principles, which (as practical principles ought) do continue constantly to operate and influence all our actions without ceasing: these may be observed in all persons and all ages, steady and universal; but these are inclinations of the appetite to good, not impressions of truth on the understanding.

4. *Moral rules need a proof; ergo, not innate.*—Another reason that makes me doubt of any innate practical principles, is, that I think *there cannot any one moral rule be proposed whereof a man may not justly demand a reason*: which would be perfectly ridiculous and absurd, if they were innate, or so much as self-evident; which every innate principle must needs be. He would be thought void of common sense who asked on the one side, or on the other side, went about to give a reason, why it is impossible for the same thing to be, and not to be. It carries its own light and evidence with it, and needs no other proof; he that understands the terms assents to it for its own sake, or else nothing will ever be able to prevail with him to do it. But should that most unshaken rule of morality, and foundation of all social virtue, ' That one should do as he would be done unto ', be proposed to one who never heard it before, but yet is of capacity to understand its meaning; might he not without any absurdity ask a reason why? And were not he that proposed it, bound to make out the truth and reasonableness of it to him?

5. *Instance in keeping compacts.*—That men should keep their compacts, is certainly a great and undeniable rule in morality; but yet, if a Christian, who has the view of happiness and misery in another life, be asked why a man must keep his word, he will give this as a reason: ' Because God, who has the power of eternal life and death, requires it of us.' But if an Hobbist [1] be asked why, he will answer, ' Because the public requires it, and the Leviathan will punish you if you do not '. And if one of the old heathen philosophers had been asked, he would have answered, ' Because it was dishonest, below the dignity of a man, and opposite to virtue, the highest perfection of human nature, to do otherwise '.

6. *Virtue generally approved, not because innate, but because profitable.*—Hence naturally flows the great variety of opinions concerning moral rules, which are to be found among men

[1] This is the only express mention of Hobbes in the *Essay*.

according to the different sorts of happiness they have a prospect of, or propose to themselves. I grant the existence of God in so many ways manifest, and the obedience we owe him so congruous to the light of reason, that a great part of mankind give testimony to the law of nature: but yet I think it must be allowed, that several moral rules may receive from mankind a very general approbation, without either knowing or admitting the true ground of morality; which can only be the will and law of a God, who sees men in the dark, has in his hand rewards and punishments, and power enough to call to account the proudest offender. For God having, by an inseparable connexion, joined virtue and public happiness together, and made the practice thereof necessary to the preservation of society, and visibly beneficial to all with whom the virtuous man has to do; it is no wonder that every one should not only allow, but recommend and magnify those rules to others, from whose observance of them he is sure to reap advantage to himself.

7. Perhaps *conscience* will be urged as checking us for breaches [of morality], and so the internal obligation and establishment of the rule be preserved. [8.] To which I answer, that I doubt not but, without being written on their hearts, many men may, by the same way that they come to the knowledge of other things, come to assent to several moral rules, and be convinced of their obligation. Others also may come to be of the same mind, from their education, company, and customs of their country; which persuasion, however got, will serve to set conscience on work, which is nothing else but our own opinion or judgement of the moral rectitude or pravity of our own actions. And if conscience be a proof of innate principles, contraries may be innate principles; since some men with the same bent of conscience prosecute what others avoid. [9.] Have there not been whole nations, and those of the most civilized people, amongst whom the exposing their children, and leaving them in the fields, to perish by want or wild beasts, has been the practice, as little condemned or scrupled as the begetting them? Do they not still, in some countries, put them into the same graves with their mothers, if they die in childbirth; or dispatch them if a pretended astrologer declares them to have unhappy stars? And are there not places where, at a certain age, they kill or expose their parents without any remorse at all? In a part of Asia, the sick, when their case comes to be

thought desperate, are carried out and laid on the earth before they are dead, and left there, exposed to wind and weather, to perish without assistance or pity.... The virtues whereby the Tououpinambos believed they merited Paradise, were revenge, and eating abundance of their enemies. The saints who are canonized amongst the Turks, lead lives which one cannot with modesty relate.

12. If any can be thought to be naturally imprinted, none, I think, can have a fairer pretence to be innate than this: 'It is the duty of parents to preserve their children.' But what duty is, cannot be understood without a law; nor a law be known, or supposed, without a law-maker, or without reward and punishment. So that it is impossible that this or any other practical principle should be innate (that is, be imprinted on the mind as a duty), without supposing the ideas of God, of law, of obligation, of punishment, of a life after this, innate. [13.] Without such a knowledge as this, a man can never be certain that anything is his duty. But let any one see the fault, and the rod by it, and with the transgression, a fire ready to punish it; a pleasure tempting, and the hand of the Almighty visibly held up and prepared to take vengeance (for this must be the case where any duty is imprinted on the mind), and then tell me, whether it be possible for people with such a prospect, such a certain knowledge as this, wantonly, and without scruple, to offend against a law which they carry about them in indelible characters, and that stares them in the face whilst they are breaking it. I would not be here mistaken, as if, because I deny an innate law, I thought there were none but positive laws. There is a great deal of difference between an innate law and a law of nature;[1] between something

---

[1] 'Truth and keeping of faith belong to men as men, and not merely as members of society,' Locke says in his *Treatise of Government*, II. 14. As a political thinker Locke was influenced by Hugo Grotius's conception of a *ius naturale* based on man's nature as a social being, a system of natural rights determinable by reason, independent of the *ius civile* of any particular nation, and in a sense more fundamental. Hooker also, whom Locke greatly admired, speaks of 'that law which, as laid up in the bosom of God, they call eternal' (*Ecclesiastical History*, i. 3). The laws of nature, he says, 'bind men absolutely, even as they are men, though they have never any settled fellowship, never any solemn agreement among themselves'. Hooker's view of natural law was largely drawn from Aquinas. A similar doctrine was propounded by Culverwell in his *Discourse of the Light of Nature* (1652): 'All the moral law is founded in natural and common light, in the light of reason ';

imprinted on our minds in their very original, and something that we, being ignorant of, may attain to the knowledge of, by the use and due application of our natural faculties. And I think they equally forsake the truth, who running into the contrary extremes, either affirm an innate law, or deny that there is a law knowable by the light of nature ; i. e., without the help of positive revelation.

14. *Those who maintain innate practical principles, tell us not what they are.*—It is enough to make one suspect that the supposition of such innate principles is but an opinion taken up at pleasure, since those who talk so confidently of them are so sparing to tell us which they are. Since nobody that I know has ventured yet to give a catalogue of them, they cannot blame those who doubt of these innate principles. . . .

15. *Lord Herbert's innate principles examined.*—When I had writ this, being informed that my Lord Herbert had, in his book *De Veritate*,[1] assigned these innate principles, I presently consulted him, hoping to find, in a man of so great parts, something that might satisfy me in this point, and put an end to my enquiry. In his chapter *De Instinctu Naturali*, p. 76, edit. 1656, I met with these six marks of his *Notitiae Communes* : ' 1. Prioritas. 2. Independentia. 3. Universalitas. 4. Certitudo. 5. Necessitas,' i. e. as he explains it, ' faciunt ad hominis

its obligation and binding virtue rest ' partly in the excellence and equity of the commands themselves, but they principally depend upon the sovereignty and authority of God himself, thus commanding and contriving the welfare of his creature and advancing a rational nature to the just perfection of its being '. For Locke's own somewhat vacillating theory compare his account of ideas of ' moral relations ' (II. 28. 4-16) and his speculations on the possibility of a demonstrative science of ethics (IV. 3. 18-20).

[1] Lord Herbert of Cherbury (1581-1648), elder brother of George Herbert the poet, published his *De Veritate* in 1624, and the 'little treatise' *De Religione Laici* was added to the third edition (London, 1645). By making universal consent ' the highest criterion of truth ', he is in some ways a precursor of the philosophy of Common Sense. He derives from what he calls ' natural instinct ' certain ' common notions ' which belong to the nature of intelligence itself. His own investigation is limited to the common notions of religion. The five quoted in this paragraph constitute, according to him, the whole doctrine of the religion of reason, which was in his view the primitive religion before men ' gave ear to the covetous and crafty sacerdotal order '. He thus laid the foundation of English Deism of the eighteenth century. Locke's reference to him is retained in the text for its historical interest, but it is quite unimportant for the general argument.

conservationem. 6. Modus conformationis, i. e. Assensus nulla interposita mora.' And at the latter end of his little treatise *De Religione Laici*, he says this of these innate principles: 'Adeo ut non uniuscuiusvis religionis confinio arctentur quae ubique vigent veritates. Sunt enim in ipsa mente coelitus descriptae, nullisque traditionibus, sive scriptis sive non scriptis, obnoxiae,' p. 3; and ' Veritates nostrae catholicae, quae tanquam indubia Dei effata in foro interiori descripta '. Thus having given the marks of the innate principles, or common notions, and asserted their being imprinted on the minds of men by the hand of God, he proceeds to set them down, and they are these : ' 1. Esse aliquod supremum numen. 2. Numen illud coli debere. 3. Virtutem cum pietate coniunctam optimam esse rationem cultus divini. 4. Resipiscendum esse a peccatis. 5. Dari praemium vel poenam post hanc vitam transactam.' Though I allow these to be clear truths, and such as, if rightly explained, a rational creature can hardly avoid giving his assent to ; yet I think he is far from proving them innate impressions 'in foro interiori descriptae'. For I must take leave to observe,

16. First, That these five propositions are either not all, or more than all, those common notions writ on our minds by the finger of God, if it were reasonable to believe any at all to be so written. Since there are other propositions, which, even by his own rules, have as just a pretence to such an original, and may be as well admitted for innate principles, as, at least, some of these five he enumerates, viz. ' Do as thou wouldst be done unto ', and, perhaps, some hundreds of others, when well considered.

17. Secondly, That all his marks are not to be found in each of his five propositions, viz. his first, second, and third marks, agree perfectly to neither of them ; and the first, second, third, fourth, and sixth marks, agree but ill to his third, fourth, and fifth propositions. For, besides that we are assured from history of many men, nay, whole nations, who doubt or disbelieve some or all of them, I cannot see how the third, viz. ' That virtue, joined with piety, is the best worship of God ', can be an innate principle, when the name, or sound, virtue, is so hard to be understood ; liable to so much uncertainty in its signification ; and the thing it stands for, so much contended about, and difficult to be known. [18.] If virtue be taken, as most commonly it is, for those actions which,

according to the different opinions of several countries, are accounted laudable, [it] will be a proposition so far from being certain, that it will not be true. If virtue be taken for actions conformable to God's will, or to the rule prescribed by God, which is the true and only measure of virtue, when virtue is used to signify what is in its own nature right and good, then this proposition, ' That virtue is the best worship of God ', will be most true and certain, but of very little use in human life, since it will amount to no more than this, viz. ' That God is pleased with the doing of what he commands '; which a man may certainly know to be true, without knowing what it is that God doth command ; and so be as far from any rule or principle of his actions as he was before. [19.] Nor is the fourth proposition (viz. ' Men must repent of their sins ') much more instructive, till what those actions are, that are meant by sins, be set down. And therefore, I imagine, it will scarce seem possible, that God should engrave principles in men's minds, in words of uncertain signification, such as are *virtues* and *sins*, which, amongst different men, stand for different things.

21. *Contrary principles in the world.*—I easily grant that there are great numbers of opinions which, by men of different countries, educations, and tempers, are received and embraced as first and unquestionable principles ; many whereof, both for their absurdity as well as oppositions one to another, it is impossible should be true. But yet all those propositions, how remote soever from reason, are so sacred somewhere or other, that men even of good understanding in other matters will sooner part with their lives, and whatever is dearest to them, than suffer themselves to doubt, or others to question, the truth of them.

22. *How men commonly come by their principles.* This, however strange it may seem, is that which every day's experience confirms : and will not, perhaps, appear so wonderful if we consider the ways and steps by which it is brought about, and how really it may come to pass, that doctrines that have been derived from no better original than the superstition of a nurse, or the authority of an old woman, may, by length of time and consent of neighbours, grow up to the dignity of principles in religion or morality. For such who are careful (as they call it) to principle children well, instil into the unwary, and as yet unprejudiced, understanding (for white paper [1] receives any

[1] Cf. II. 1. 2.

## Ch. 3    *No Innate Practical Principles*    35

characters) those doctrines they would have them retain and profess. These being taught them as soon as they have any apprehension, and still as they grow up confirmed to them, either by the open profession or tacit consent of all they have to do with; or at least by those of whose wisdom, knowledge, and piety they have an opinion, who never suffer those propositions to be otherwise mentioned but as the basis and foundation on which they build either their religion or manners, come, by these means, to have the reputation of unquestionable, self-evident, and innate truths.

24. This will appear very likely, and almost unavoidable to come to pass, if we consider the nature of mankind and the constitution of human affairs : wherein most men cannot live without employing their time in the daily labours of their callings, nor be at quiet in their minds without some foundation or principles to rest their thoughts on. There is scarce any one so floating and superficial in his understanding who hath not some reverenced propositions, which are to him the principles on which he bottoms his reasonings, and by which he judgeth of truth and falsehood, right and wrong ; which some wanting skill and leisure, and others the inclination, and some being taught that they ought not, to examine; there are few to be found who are not exposed, by their ignorance, laziness, education, or precipitancy, to *take them upon trust.*

25. This is evidently the case of all children and young folk ; and custom, a greater power than nature, seldom failing to make them worship for divine what she hath inured them to bow their minds and submit their understandings to, it is no wonder that grown men, either perplexed in the necessary affairs of life, or hot in the pursuit of pleasures, should not seriously sit down to examine their own tenets ; especially when one of their principles is, that principles ought not to be questioned. And, had men leisure, parts, and will, who is there almost that dare shake the foundations of all his past thoughts and actions, and endure to bring upon himself the shame of having been a long time wholly in mistake and error ? Who is there hardy enough to contend with the reproach which is everywhere prepared for those who dare venture to dissent from the received opinions of their country or party ? And where is the man to be found that can patiently prepare himself to bear the name of whimsical, sceptical, or atheist, which he is sure to meet with, who does in the least scruple any of the

common opinions? And he will be much more afraid to question those principles when he shall think them, as most men do, the standards set up by God in his mind to be the rule and touchstone of all other opinions.

## CHAPTER IV

### OTHER CONSIDERATIONS CONCERNING INNATE PRINCIPLES BOTH SPECULATIVE AND PRACTICAL

1. *Principles not innate, unless their ideas be innate.*—Had those who would persuade us that there are innate principles, not taken them together in gross, but considered separately the parts out of which those propositions are made, they would not, perhaps, have been so forward to believe they were innate ; since, if the ideas which made up those truths were not, it was impossible that the propositions made up of them should be innate.

2. *Ideas, especially those belonging to principles, not born with children.*—If we will attentively consider new-born children, we shall have little reason to think that they bring many ideas into the world with them. For, bating perhaps some faint ideas of hunger, and thirst, and warmth, and some pains which they may have felt in the womb, there is not the least appearance of any settled ideas at all in them ; especially of ideas answering the terms which make up those universal propositions that are esteemed innate principles.

4. *Identity, an idea not innate.*—If identity (to instance in that alone) be a native impression, and, consequently, so clear and obvious to us that we must needs know it even from our cradles, I would gladly be resolved, by one of seven or seventy years old, whether a man being a creature consisting of soul and body, be the same man when his body is changed? Whether Euphorbus and Pythagoras, having had the same soul, were the same man, though they lived several ages asunder? Nay, whether the cock, too, which had the same soul, were not the same with both of them? Whereby, perhaps, it will appear, that our *idea of sameness* is not so settled and clear as to deserve to be thought innate in us.[1]

[1] Hence Locke added a chapter on the subject in his second edition (II. 27, ' Of Identity and Diversity '). The difficulties attaching to the theory of transmigration reappear there.

5. Nor let any one think that the questions I have here proposed, about the identity of man, are bare, empty speculations. He that shall, with a little attention, reflect on the resurrection, and consider that divine justice shall bring to judgement, at the last day, the very same persons, to be happy or miserable in the other, who did well or ill in this life, will find it, perhaps, not easy to resolve with himself what makes the same man, or wherein identity consists ; and will not be forward to think he and every one, even children themselves, have naturally a clear idea of it.

8. *Idea of God not innate.*—If any idea can be imagined innate, the *idea of God* may, of all others, for many reasons, be thought so ; since it is hard to conceive how there should be innate moral principles without an innate idea of a Deity : without a notion of a law-maker, it is impossible to have a notion of a law, and an obligation to observe it. Besides the atheists taken notice of amongst the ancients, and left branded upon the records of history, hath not navigation discovered, in these latter ages, whole nations, at the Bay of Soldania, in Brazil, in Boranday, and the Caribbee Islands, &c., amongst whom there was to be found no notion of a God, no religion ? And perhaps, if we should with attention mind the lives and discourses of people not so far off, we should have too much reason to fear that many, in more civilized countries, have no very strong and clear impressions of a Deity upon their minds ; and that the complaints of atheism made from the pulpit are not without reason.

9. But had all mankind everywhere a notion of a God (whereof yet history tells us the contrary), it would not from thence follow that the idea of him was innate, especially if it be such an idea as is agreeable to the common light of reason,[1] and naturally deducible from every part of our knowledge, as that of a God is. For the visible marks of extraordinary wisdom

---

[1] ' The common light of reason ' is the same as ' the light of nature ' mentioned in ch. 3, section 13, and there distinguished from ' the help of positive revelation '. ' Reason ', Locke says (IV. 19. 4), ' is natural revelation, whereby the eternal Father of Light and Fountain of all Knowledge communicates to mankind that portion of truth which he has laid within the reach of their natural faculties.' The *lumen naturale* is a phrase frequently used by Descartes to designate what Locke calls intuition, the faculty by which we apprehend self-evident truths, such as the *cogito ergo sum* and other ultimate propositions which we apprehend with the same necessity.

and power appear so plainly in all the works of the creation, that a rational creature who will but seriously reflect on them, cannot miss the discovery of a Deity ; and the influence that the discovery of such a Being must necessarily have on the minds of all that have but once heard of it, is so great, and carries such a weight of thought and communication with it, that it seems stranger to me that a whole nation of men should be anywhere found so brutish as to want the notion of a God, than that they should be without any notion of numbers, or fire.

12. *'Suitable to God's goodness that all men should have an idea of Him, therefore naturally imprinted by him', answered.*—This argument, if it be of any force, will prove much more than those who use it in this case expect from it. For if we may conclude that God hath done for men all that men shall judge is best for them, because it is suitable to his goodness so to do, it will prove not only that God has imprinted on the minds of men an idea of himself, but that he hath plainly stamped there, in fair characters, all that men ought to know or believe of him, all that they ought to do in obedience to his will ; and that he hath given them a will and affections conformable to it. This, no doubt, every one will think it better for men, than that they should, in the dark, grope after knowledge, as St. Paul tells us all nations did after God (*Acts* xvii. 27), than that their wills should clash with their understandings, and their appetites cross their duty. I think it a very good argument to say, ' The infinitely wise God hath made it so, and therefore it is best '. But it seems to me a little too much confidence of our own wisdom to say, ' I think it best, and therefore God hath made it so ' ; and in the matter in hand, it will be in vain to argue from such a topic that God hath done so, when certain experience shows us that he hath not. But the goodness of God hath not been wanting to men without such original impressions of knowledge, or ideas stamped on the mind ; since he hath furnished man with those faculties which will serve for the sufficient discovery of all things requisite to the end of such a being ; and I doubt not but to show that a man, by the right use of his natural abilities, may, without any innate principles, attain the knowledge of a God, and other things that concern him. God, having endued man with those faculties of knowing which he hath, was no more obliged by his goodness to implant those innate notions in his mind, than

Ch. 4    *Considerations on Innate Principles*    39

that, having given him reason, hands, and materials, he should build him bridges or houses.

19. *Ideas of substance not innate.*—I confess there is another idea which would be of general use for mankind to have, as it is of general talk as if they had it; and that is the *idea of substance,* which we neither have nor can have by sensation or reflection.[1] If nature took care to provide us any ideas, we might well expect it should be such as by our own faculties we cannot procure to ourselves: but we see, on the contrary, that, since by those ways whereby other ideas are brought into our minds this is not, we have no such *clear* idea at all, and therefore signify nothing by the word *substance,* but only an uncertain supposition[2] of we know not what, i.e., of something whereof we have no [particular, distinct, positive[3]] idea, which we take to be the *substratum,* or support of those ideas we do know.

24. *Men must think and know for themselves.*[4]—What censure

---

[1] For Locke's account of the idea of substance cf. II. 13. 17–20 and II. 23, 'Of our complex Ideas of Substances'. The explicit statement here that the idea is not derivable from sensation or reflection is important in view of Locke's general doctrine that 'these two are the fountains of knowledge from which all the ideas we have, or can naturally have, do spring' (II. 1. 2).

[2] Cf. II. 23. 1 (' we accustom ourselves to suppose some substratum wherein they do subsist '), and relative note on Stillingfleet's criticism of the expression and Locke's reply.

[3] ' particular, distinct, positive '. These words were added in the fourth edition to guard the statement against Stillingfleet's objections.

[4] It has been well pointed out by Professor Campbell Fraser that in this and the following section we get the key to ' the really moral purpose of Locke's persistent war against innateness '. ' The argument against innate principles and ideas is expressly put by him as a protest of reason against the tyranny of traditional assumptions and empty words shielded by their assumed innateness from the need of verification by our mental experience. ... Locke believed that by insisting on "experienced" ideas and principles, he was helping to put self-evidence and demonstration and well-calculated probabilities in the room of blind repose upon authority' (*Locke* (Philosophical Classics), p. 113).

Taken in any stricter sense, as a contribution to a theory of knowledge, Locke's argument in Bk. I is vitiated by the peculiar sense which he puts upon the word 'innate'. This was sufficiently emphasized by a contemporary critic (Lee, *Anti-Scepticism,* Preface): 'Herein surely he has no adversary, for no one does, or at least can reasonably, assert that the minds of embryos, in the first moment after their creation or union to their organized bodies, are ready furnished with ideas or have any propositions or principles implanted in them or stamped upon them; that is an idle supposition. Such expressions are to be understood

doubting thus of innate principles may deserve from men who will be apt to call it ' pulling up the old foundations of knowledge and certainty ', I cannot tell: I persuade myself, at least, that the way I have pursued, being conformable to truth, lays those foundations surer. This I am certain, I have not made it my business either to quit or follow any authority in the ensuing discourse : truth has been my only aim ; and wherever that has appeared to lead, my thoughts have impartially followed, without minding whether the footsteps of any other lay that way or no. Not that I want a due respect to other men's opinions ; but, after all, the greatest reverence is due to truth ; and I hope it will not be thought arrogance to say, that perhaps we should make greater progress in the discovery of rational and contemplative knowledge, if we sought it in the fountain, *in the consideration of things themselves*, and made use rather of our own thoughts than other men's to find it. For, I think, we may as rationally hope to see with other men's eyes as to know by other men's understandings. So much as we ourselves consider and comprehend of truth and reason, so much we possess of real and true knowledge. The floating of other men's opinions in our brains makes us not one jot the more knowing, though they happen to be true. What in them was science is in us but opiniatrety,[1] whilst we give up our assent only to reverend names, and do not, as they did, employ our own reason to understand those truths which gave them reputation. Aristotle was certainly a knowing man, but nobody ever thought him so because he blindly embraced and confidently vented the opinions of another. And if the taking up of another's principles without examining them made not him a philosopher, I suppose it will hardly make anybody else so. In the sciences, every one has so much as he really knows and comprehends : what he believes only, and takes upon trust, are but shreds ; which, however well in the whole piece, make no considerable addition to his stock who gathers them. Such borrowed wealth, like fairy money, though it were gold in the hand from which

figuratively, to signify that the ideas owe their origin to the constitution of human nature, as it stands necessarily related to other parts of the universe.' Locke himself says elsewhere, ' we are born free, as we are born rational, not that we have the actual exercise of either (*Treatise on Government*, II, section 61).

[1] Obstinate adherence to opinion.

he received it, will be but leaves and dust when it comes to use.

25. *Whence the opinion of innate principles.*—When men have found some general propositions that could not be doubted of as soon as understood, it was, I know, a short and easy way to conclude them innate. This being once received, it eased the lazy from the pains of search, and stopped the enquiry of the doubtful, concerning all that was once styled innate : and it was of no small advantage to those who affected to be masters and teachers, to make this the principle of principles,—that principles must not be questioned ; for, having once established this tenet, that there are innate principles, it put their followers upon a necessity of receiving some doctrines as such ; which was to take them off from the use of their own reason and judgement, and put them upon believing and taking them upon trust, without farther examination ; in which posture of blind credulity, they might be more easily governed by, and made useful to some sort of men who had the skill and office to principle and guide them. Whereas had they examined the ways whereby men came to the knowledge of many universal truths, they would have found them to result in the minds of men from the being of things themselves, when duly considered ; and that they were discovered by the application of those faculties that were fitted by nature to receive and judge of them, when duly employed about them.

26. To show how the understanding proceeds herein, is the design of the following discourse.[1]

---

[1] The sections here numbered 19, 24, 25, 26 appear in most editions as 18, 23, 24, 25, owing to the fact that Locke has, apparently by inadvertence, two sections numbered 15. The numeration is corrected in the Clarendon Press edition.

# BOOK II

## CHAPTER I

### OF IDEAS IN GENERAL AND THEIR ORIGINAL

1. *Idea is the object of thinking.*—Every man being conscious to himself that he thinks, and that which his mind is applied about whilst thinking being the ideas that are there, it is past doubt that men have in their minds several ideas, such as are those expressed by the words, 'whiteness, hardness, sweetness, thinking, motion, man, elephant, army, drunkenness', and others. It is in the first place then to be enquired, How he comes by them? I know it is a received doctrine, that men have native ideas and original characters stamped upon their minds in their very first being. This opinion I have at large examined already; and, I suppose, what I have said in the foregoing Book will be much more easily admitted, when I have shown whence the understanding may get all the ideas it has, and by what ways and degrees they may come into the mind; for which I shall appeal to every one's own observation and experience.

2. *All ideas come from sensation or reflection.*—Let us then suppose the mind to be, as we say, white paper, void of all characters, without any ideas; how comes it to be furnished? Whence comes it by that vast store, which the busy and boundless fancy of man has painted on it with an almost endless variety? Whence has it all the materials of reason and knowledge? To this I answer, in one word, from EXPERIENCE; in that all our knowledge is founded, and from that it ultimately derives itself.[1] Our observation, employed either about

[1] In virtue of this statement and the polemic against innate notions with which it is associated, Locke has been acclaimed, on the one hand, or condemned on the other, as the father of the characteristically English Philosophy of Experience, in contrast to the Continental Rationalism of Descartes and Leibniz, the Transcendentalism of Kant, and Intuitionism of every variety. But the ambiguity of the term 'experience' is one of the main difficulties in the way of arriving at a correct interpretation of this *Essay*. Locke is far from being a consistent Empiricist (that is, a pure Sensationalist), of the type of Hume, Condillac, or James Mill. See Introduction, pp. xix–xxx.

external sensible objects, or about the internal operations of our minds, perceived and reflected on by ourselves, is that which supplies our understandings with all the materials[1] of thinking. These two are the fountains of knowledge, from whence all the ideas we have, or can naturally have, do spring.

3. *The objects of sensation one source of ideas.*—First, our senses, conversant about particular sensible objects, do convey into the mind several distinct perceptions of things, according to those various ways wherein those objects do affect them; and thus we come by those *ideas* we have of yellow, white, heat, cold, soft, hard, bitter, sweet, and all those which we call sensible qualities; which when I say the senses convey into the mind, I mean, they from external objects convey into the mind what produces there those perceptions. This great source of most of the ideas we have, depending wholly upon our senses, and derived by them to the understanding, I call, SENSATION.[2]

4. *The operations of our minds the other source of them.*—Secondly, the other fountain, from which experience furnisheth the understanding with ideas, is the perception of the operations of our own minds within us, as it is employed about the ideas it has got; which operations, when the soul comes to reflect on and consider, do furnish the understanding with another set of ideas which could not be had from things without: and such are perception, thinking, doubting, believing,

[1] The word 'materials', used twice in this section, recalls attention to the fact that in Bk. II we are dealing with ideas as 'appearances' in the mind, which are, as it were, the instruments or the medium of knowledge. The nature of knowledge as such, the question 'what knowledge the understanding hath by those ideas' is, reserved for Bk. IV. But Locke applies the term more particularly to the 'simple' ideas which we can neither make nor destroy but only variously combine and manipulate.

[2] Note in this section the liberty Locke allows himself in his phraseology. The mere presence of sensations in the mind is otherwise described as a knowledge of 'sensible qualities' or as 'perceptions of things' possessing these qualities. The statement that 'the senses convey' those perceptions 'into the mind' is corrected into what he considers a more precise form of expression, 'they from external objects convey into the mind what produces there those perceptions'. In section 23 he expressly defines 'sensation' as the organic affection which somehow produces a 'perception' in the understanding. But, in ch. 19. 1, he returns to the usage which identifies the sensation with 'the perception or thought' and distinguishes it from the 'impression on the body made by an external object'.

reasoning, knowing, willing, and all the different actings of our own minds; which we being conscious of, and observing in ourselves, do from these receive into our understanding as distinct ideas, as we do from bodies affecting our senses. This source of ideas every man has wholly in himself: and though it be not sense, as having nothing to do with external objects, yet it is very like it, and might properly enough be called internal sense.[1] But as I call the other Sensation, so I call this REFLECTION, the ideas it affords being such only as the mind gets by reflecting on its own operations within itself. By Reflection, then, in the following part of this discourse, I would be understood to mean that notice which the mind takes of its own operations, and the manner of them, by reason whereof there come to be ideas of these operations in the understanding. These two, I say, viz., external material things as the objects of Sensation, and the operations of our own minds within as the objects of Reflection, are, to me, the only originals from whence all our ideas take their beginnings. The term *operations* here, I use in a large sense, as comprehending not barely the actions of the mind about its ideas, but some sort of passions arising sometimes from them, such as is the satisfaction or uneasiness arising from any thought.[2]

5. *All our ideas are of the one or the other of these.*—The understanding seems to me not to have the least glimmering of any ideas which it doth not receive from one of these two. *External objects* furnish the mind with the ideas of sensible qualities, which are all those different perceptions they produce in us; and *the mind* furnishes the understanding with ideas of its own operations.[3] These, when we have taken a full survey of

---

[1] 'Internal sense' is a somewhat misleading metaphor, which was afterwards adopted by Kant with confusing results.

[2] So he includes 'pleasure' and 'pain' among the simple ideas which convey themselves into the mind by all the ways of sensation and reflection (ch. 7).

[3] Locke's admission of Reflection as an independent source of ideas has sometimes been represented as an acknowledgement on his part of necessary or innate notions, constitutive principles of thought, furnished by the mind itself. Thus Leibniz saw in Locke's language an approximation to his own doctrine. 'Reflection is nothing else than attention to what is in us, and the senses do not give us what we already carry with us. That being so, can it be denied that there is much that is innate in our mind, since we are innate, so to speak, to ourselves?' He introduces at this point his famous addition to the maxim, '*Nihil est in intellectu quod non fuerit in sensu*'—*nisi ipse intellectus*,

them, and their several modes, combinations, and relations, we shall find to contain all our whole stock of ideas; and that we have nothing in our minds which did not come in one of these two ways. Let any one examine his own thoughts, and thoroughly search into his understanding, and then let him tell me, whether all the original ideas he has there, are any other than of the objects of his senses, or of the operations of his mind considered as objects of his reflection; and how great a mass of knowledge soever he imagines to be lodged there, he will, upon taking a strict view, see that he has not any idea in his mind but what one of these two have imprinted, though perhaps with infinite variety compounded and enlarged by the understanding, as we shall see hereafter.

6. *Observable in children.*—He that attentively considers the state of a child at his first coming into the world, will have little reason to think him stored with plenty of ideas that are to be the matter of his future knowledge. It is by degrees he comes to be furnished with them: and though the ideas of obvious and familiar qualities imprint themselves before the memory begins to keep a register of time and order, yet it is often so late before some unusual qualities come in the way, that there are few men that cannot recollect the beginning of their acquaintance with them: and if it were worth while, no doubt a child might be so ordered as to have but a very few even of the ordinary ideas till he were grown up to a man. But all that are born into the world being surrounded with bodies

and he proceeds, 'Now the soul comprises being, substance, unity, identity, cause, perception, reason, and many other notions which the senses cannot give' (*New Essays*, Preface and Bk. II. 1). So Dugald Stewart thought that Locke would not 'have hesitated for a moment to admit, with Cudworth and Price, that the Understanding is itself a source of new ideas', indeed of 'all the simple ideas which are necessarily implied in our intellectual operations' (*Dissertation*, Part II, section 1, foot-note). But clearly Locke intends no such concession to the doctrine he has just been at so much pains to refute. He certainly assumes the reality of the mind and its activity in combining and otherwise operating upon ideas—differing in that from his Sensationalist followers who resolve the mind into a series of sensations attracting one another according to the laws of association—but his ideas of reflection, the ideas of the mind's 'own operations within itself', are as much empirically observed facts as the ideas of sensible qualities and natural processes received 'from external objects'. Locke is not thinking at all of a mental furniture of necessary notions or categories.

that perpetually and diversely affect them, variety of ideas, whether care be taken about it or no, are imprinted on the minds of children. Light and colours are busy and at hand everywhere when the eye is but open; sounds and some tangible qualities fail not to solicit their proper senses, and force an entrance to the mind; but yet I think it will be granted easily, that if a child were kept in a place where he never saw any other but black and white till he were a man, he would have no more ideas of scarlet or green, than he that from his childhood never tasted an oyster or a pine-apple has of those particular relishes.

7. *Men are differently furnished with these according to the different objects they converse with.*—Men then come to be furnished with fewer or more simple ideas from without, according as the objects they converse with afford greater or less variety; and from the operations of their minds within, according as they more or less reflect on them. For, though he that contemplates the operations of his mind cannot but have plain and clear ideas of them; yet, unless he turn his thoughts that way, and considers them *attentively*, he will no more have clear and distinct ideas of all the operations of his mind, and all that may be observed therein, than he will have all the particular ideas of any landscape, or of the parts and motions of a clock, who will not turn his eyes to it, and with attention heed all the parts of it. The picture or clock may be so placed, that they may come in his way every day; but yet he will have but a confused idea of all the parts they are made up of, till he applies himself with attention to consider them each in particular.

8. *Ideas of reflection later, because they need attention.*—And hence we see the reason why it is pretty late before most children get ideas of the operations of their own minds; and some have not any very clear or perfect ideas of the greatest part of them all their lives. Because, though they pass there continually, yet, like floating visions, they make not deep impressions enough to leave in the mind clear, distinct, lasting ideas, till the understanding turns inwards upon itself, reflects on its own operations, and makes them the object of its own contemplation. Children, when they come first into it, are surrounded with a world of new things, which, by a constant solicitation of their senses, draw the mind constantly to them, forward to take notice of new, and apt to be delighted

with the variety of changing objects. Thus the first years are usually employed and diverted in looking abroad. Men's business in them is to acquaint themselves with what is to be found without ; and so, growing up in a constant attention to outward sensations, seldom make any considerable reflection on what passes within them till they come to be of riper years ; and some scarce ever at all.

9. *The soul begins to have ideas when it begins to perceive.*—To ask, at what *time* a man has first any ideas, is to ask when he begins to perceive ; having ideas, and perception, being the same thing. I know it is an opinion, that the soul always thinks ;[1] and that it has the actual perception of ideas in itself constantly, as long as it exists ; and that actual thinking is as inseparable from the soul, as actual extension is from the body : which if true, to enquire after the beginning of a man's ideas is the same as to enquire after the beginning of his soul. For by this account, soul and its ideas, as body and its extension, will begin to exist both at the same time.

10. *The soul thinks not always ; for this wants proofs.* But whether the soul be supposed to exist antecedent to, or coeval with, or some time after the first rudiments or organization, or the beginnings of life in the body, I leave to be disputed by those who have better thought of that matter. I confess

---

[1] The reference is to the Cartesian definition of the mind as a substance whose whole essence or nature consists only in thinking (*Discourse on Method*, Part IV). Sections 9-19, which discuss the question whether the mind is always consciously active, appear as a digression from the main theme of the chapter. The connexion in Locke's mind seems to be that to admit that the soul thinks always—that its existence consists in thinking—may be held to imply that it can think independently of the normal bodily channels of ideas and so may have had ideas before its union with the body, i.e. innate ideas. Hence he calls upon supporters of the theory to produce specimens of 'its pure native thoughts before it borrowed anything from the body' (section 17). Locke fears, as a contemporary critic quaintly puts it, that 'if the soul should think while the organs of the external senses cease from exercise, it should steal some ideas which it had not got in his honest way of sensation only' (Lee, *Anti-Scepticism*, p. 44). Locke's attack upon the Cartesian attempt to settle matters by a definition is characteristically forcible ; but his argument on the question of fact is largely vitiated by leaving out of account the possibility of continued activity at a subconscious level. The phenomena of subconscious or 'unconscious' mental activity have been much more carefully studied since Locke's time, especially in recent years, and the discussion in the text is out of date.

myself to have one of those dull souls that doth not perceive itself always to contemplate ideas ; nor can conceive it any more necessary for the soul always to think, than for the body always to move : the perception of ideas being, as I conceive, to the soul, what motion is to the body, not its essence, but one of its operations[1]. And, therefore, though thinking be supposed never so much the proper action of the soul, yet it is not necessary to suppose that it should be always thinking, always in action. That, perhaps, is the privilege of the infinite Author and Preserver of all things, ' who never slumbers nor sleeps'; but is not competent to any finite being, at least not to the soul of man. We know certainly by experience, that we sometimes think; and thence draw this infallible consequence—that there is something in us that has a power to think: but whether that substance perpetually thinks, or no, we can be no farther assured than experience informs us. For to say, that actual thinking is essential to the soul and inseparable from it, is to beg what is in question, and not to prove it by reason ; which is necessary to be done, if it be not a self-evident proposition. But whether this, that ' the soul always thinks', be a self-evident proposition, that everybody

[1] So Bk. II. 19. 4. 'I ask whether it be not probable that thinking is the action and not the essence of the soul, since the operations of agents will easily admit of intension and remission, but the essences of things are not conceived capable of any such variation.' But compare Leibniz's criticism of ' bare faculties ': ' Faculties without some act, in a word, the pure process of the schools, are fictions which nature knows not and which are obtained only by process of abstraction. Where will you ever find a faculty which shuts itself up in power alone without performing any act ? There is always a particular disposition to action and to one action more than another. . . Real powers are never simple possibilities. There is always tendency and action. . . A state without thought in the soul and a state of absolute rest in body appear to me equally contrary to nature and without an example in the world' (*New Essays*, II. 1). Berkeley also opposes Locke on this point, basing his objection on the ground that time is ' nothing, abstracted from the succession of ideas in our minds '. From this ' it follows that the duration of any finite spirit must be estimated by the number of ideas or actions succeeding each other in that same spirit or mind. Hence it is a plain consequence that *the soul always thinks*; and in truth whoever shall go about to divide in his thoughts, or abstract the *existence* of a spirit from its *cogitation*, will, I believe, find it no easy task ' (*Principles of Human Knowledge*, section 98). Cf. Lotze (*Metaphysic*, Bk. III, ch. v, section 307) : ' If the soul in a perfectly dreamless sleep thinks, feels, and wills nothing, *is* the soul then at all, and what is it ? How often has the answer been given, that *if* this could ever happen, the

## Of Ideas in General

assents to at first hearing, I appeal to mankind. [It is doubted whether I thought all last night, or no ; the question being about a matter of fact, it is begging it to bring as a proof for it an hypothesis which is the very thing in dispute ; which way of proving amounts to this,—that I must necessarily think all last night because another supposes I always think, though I myself cannot perceive that I always do so. But men in love with their opinions may not only suppose what is in question, but allege wrong matter of fact. How else could any one make it an inference of mine, that a thing is not, because we are not sensible of it in our sleep? I do not say, there is no soul in a man because he is not sensible of it in his sleep ; but I do say, he cannot think at any time, waking or sleeping, without being sensible of it. Our being sensible of it is not necessary to anything but to our thoughts ; and to them it is, and to them it will always be, necessary, till we can think without being conscious of it.][1]

13. Thus, methinks, every drowsy nod shakes their doctrine who teach that the soul is always thinking. Those, at least, who do at any time sleep without dreaming can never be convinced that their thoughts are sometimes for four hours busy without their knowing of it ; and if they are taken in the very act, waked in the middle of that sleeping contemplation, can give no manner of account of it.

14. *That men dream without remembering it, in vain urged.*— It will perhaps be said, that the soul thinks even in the soundest sleep, but the memory retains it not. That the soul in a sleeping man should be this moment busy a-thinking, and the next moment in a waking man not remember, nor be able to recollect one jot of all those thoughts, is very hard to be conceived, and would need some better proof than bare assertion to make it be believed. For who can without any more ado but being barely told so, imagine that the greatest part of men do, during all their lives, for several hours every day think of something which, if they were asked even in the middle of these thoughts, they could remember nothing at all of?

soul *would* have no being! Why have we not had the courage to say that, *as often as* this happens, the soul *is* not ? . . . Why should not its life be a melody with pauses ?'

[1] The passage in brackets was added in the second edition, in reply to criticism.

17. *If I think when I know it not, nobody else can know it.*—
Those who so confidently tell us that the soul always actually thinks, I would they would also tell us what those ideas are that are in the soul of a child before or just at the union with the body, before it hath received any by sensation. The dreams of sleeping men are, as I take it, all made up of the waking man's ideas, though for the most part oddly put together. It is strange, if the soul has ideas of its own that it derived not from sensation or reflection (as it must have, if it thought before it received any impressions from the body), that it should never in its private thinking (so private that the man himself perceives it not) retain any of them the very moment it wakes out of them, and then make the man glad with new discoveries. It is strange the soul should never once, in a man's whole life, recall over any of its pure native thoughts, and those ideas it had before it borrowed anything from the body ; never bring into the waking man's view any other ideas but what have a tang of the cask, and manifestly derive their original from that union.

18. *How knows any one that the soul always thinks? For if it be not a self-evident proposition, it needs proof.*—I would be glad also to learn from these men, who so confidently pronounce that the human soul, or, which is all one, that a man always thinks, how they come to know it. [19.] Consciousness is the perception of what passes in a man's own mind. Can another man perceive that I am conscious of anything, when I perceive it not myself ? No man's knowledge here can go beyond his experience. Wake a man out of a sound sleep, and ask him what he was that moment thinking on. If he himself be conscious of nothing he then thought on, he must be a notable diviner of thoughts that can assure him that he was thinking : may he not with more reason assure him he was not asleep ? This is something beyond philosophy ; and it cannot be less than revelation, that discovers to another, thoughts in my mind, when I can find none there myself : and they must needs have a penetrating sight who can certainly see that I think, when I cannot perceive it myself, and when I declare that I do not ; and yet can see that dogs or elephants do not think, when they give all the demonstration of it imaginable, except only telling us that they do so. But it is but defining the soul to be a substance that always thinks, and the business is done. If such definition be of any authority, I

know not what it can serve for, but to make many men suspect that they have no souls at all, since they find a good part of their lives pass away without thinking. For no definitions that I know, no suppositions of any sect, are of force enough to destroy constant experience; and perhaps it is the affectation of knowing beyond what we perceive that makes so much useless dispute and noise in the world.

20. *No ideas but from sensation or reflection, evident, if we observe children.*—I see no reason therefore to believe that the soul thinks before the senses have furnished it with ideas to think on; and as those are increased and retained, so it comes by exercise to improve its faculty of thinking in the several parts of it; as well as afterwards, by compounding those ideas and reflecting on its own operations, it increases its stock, as well as facility in remembering, imagining, reasoning, and other modes of thinking. [23.] If it shall be demanded, then, *when a man begins to have any ideas?* I think the true answer is, when he first has any sensation. For since there appear not to be any ideas in the mind before the senses have conveyed any in, I conceive that ideas in the understanding are coeval[1] with sensation; which is such an impression or motion made in some part of the body as produces some perception in the understanding.[2] [It is about these impressions made on our senses by outward objects, that the mind seems first to employ itself in such operations as we call perception, remembering, consideration, reasoning, &c.][3]

24. *The original of all our knowledge.*—In time the mind comes to reflect on its own operations about the ideas got by sensation, and thereby stores itself with a new set of ideas, which I call ideas of reflection. These—the impressions that are made on our senses by outward objects, that are extrinsical to the mind, and its own operations, proceeding from powers intrinsical and proper to itself, which, when reflected on by itself, become also objects of its contemplation—are, as I have said, the original of all knowledge. Thus the first capacity of human intellect is, that the mind is fitted to receive the

[1] Cf. Introduction, p. xxix.

[2] Compare this definition of sensation with section 3 and with II. 19. 1. In the first three editions the sentence ran: ' such an impression or motion, made in some part of the body, as makes it be taken notice of in the understanding.'

[3] This sentence and the first two sentences of the following sections were first introduced in the French version.

impressions[1] made on it, either through the senses by outward objects, or by its own operations when it reflects on them. This is the first step a man makes towards the discovery of anything, and the groundwork whereon to build all those notions whichever he shall have naturally in this world. All those sublime thoughts which tower above the clouds, and reach as high as heaven itself, take their rise and footing here: in all that great extent wherein the mind wanders in those remote speculations it may seem to be elevated with, it stirs not one jot beyond those ideas which *sense* or *reflection* have offered for its contemplation.

25. *In the reception of simple ideas, the understanding is most of all passive.*—In this part the understanding is merely passive;[1] and whether or no it will have these beginnings and, as it were, materials of knowledge, is not in its own power. For the objects of our senses do many of them obtrude their particular ideas upon our minds, whether we will or no; and the operations of our minds will not let us be without at least some obscure notions of them. No man can be wholly ignorant of what he does when he thinks. These simple ideas, when offered to the mind, the understanding can no more refuse to have, nor alter when they are imprinted, nor blot them out and make new ones itself, than a mirror can refuse, alter, or obliterate the images or ideas, which the objects set before it do therein produce. As the bodies that surround us do diversely affect our organs, the mind is forced to receive the impressions,[2] and cannot avoid the perception of those ideas that are annexed to them.

[1] In speaking of the mind here as merely passive, Locke does not mean to deny a certain activity even in the receiving of ideas. Perception is 'the first faculty of the mind exercised about our ideas'. The impression upon the organ of sense is not enough, being often 'not taken notice of in the understanding' when attention is directed elsewhere. What he means to emphasize is the *involuntariness* of 'bare naked perception' as contrasted with the voluntary activity involved in 'framing' complex ideas out of the simple ones received. In the case of simple ideas the mind 'cannot make one to itself', and 'what it perceives it cannot avoid perceiving'. (Cf. II. 9. 1–2, and 12. 1.) He treats this involuntariness later as a guarantee that 'our simple ideas are all real and true, because they answer and agree to those powers of things which produce them in our minds' (II. 30. 2).

[2] The 'impressions' are said to be 'made on the mind' (or, alternatively, the mind is said to 'receive' the impressions), yet the impressions are distinguished from 'the perception of those ideas that are annexed to them', as 'sensation' and 'perception' were distinguished in section 23.

## CHAPTER II

### OF SIMPLE IDEAS

1. *Uncompounded appearances.*—The better to understand the nature, manner, and extent of our knowledge, one thing is carefully to be observed concerning the ideas we have; and that is, that some of them are *simple,* and some *complex.*

Though the qualities that affect our senses are, in the things themselves, so united and blended that there is no separation, no distance between them; yet it is plain the ideas they produce in the mind enter by the senses simple and unmixed. For though the sight and touch often take in from the same object at the same time different ideas; as a man sees at once motion and colour, the hand feels softness and warmth in the same piece of wax; yet the simple ideas thus united in the same subject are as perfectly distinct as those that come in by different senses. The coldness and hardness which a man feels in a piece of ice being as distinct ideas in the mind as the smell and whiteness of a lily, or as the taste of sugar and smell of a rose: and there is nothing can be plainer to a man than the clear and distinct perception he has of those simple ideas;[1] which, being each in itself uncompounded, contains in it nothing but one uniform appearance or conception in the mind, and is not distinguishable into different ideas.

2. *The mind can neither make nor destroy them.*—These

---

[1] What Locke gives us here is an analysis of ideas into their simple (i.e. not further analysable) constituents, not an historical account of their most primitive form and subsequent development. He admits himself that the qualities are 'united and blended' in the things themselves; and for modern psychology intellectual advance consists in the progressive differentiation of what is first apprehended vaguely as a whole. The simple ideas are therefore abstractions, arrived at as the last result of a reflective analysis of the presented content. As Professor Gibson well observes: 'For thinkers of the seventeenth century, to whom all ideas of development were entirely foreign, the place which is now filled by the conception of evolution was occupied by the idea of composition, with the implied distinction between the simple and the complex.' He points out that the same theory appears in Bacon's assumption that each natural body may be resolved into a number of 'simple natures', in Descartes's division of the objects of thought into the simple natures' which constitute our innate ideas, and the complexes which result from their combination, and, again, in Leibniz's ideal of the analysis of all our notions and truths into certain primitive ones, like letters of the alphabet. Cf. *op. cit.*, pp. 47–8.

simple ideas, the materials of all our knowledge, are suggested and furnished [1] to the mind only by those two ways above mentioned, viz., sensation and reflection. When the understanding is once stored with these simple ideas, it has the power to repeat, compare, and unite them, even to an almost infinite variety, and so can make at pleasure new complex ideas. But it is not in the power of the most exalted wit or enlarged understanding, by any quickness or variety of thought, to invent or frame one new simple idea in the mind, not taken in by the ways before mentioned; nor can any force of the understanding destroy those that are there. The dominion of man in this little world of his own understanding, being much-what the same as it is in the great world of visible things, wherein his power, however managed by art and skill, reaches no farther than to compound and divide the materials that are made to his hand, but can do nothing towards the making the least particle of new matter, or destroying one atom of what is already in being. The same inability will every one find in himself, who shall go about to fashion in his understanding any simple idea not received in by his senses from external objects, or by reflection from the operations of his own mind about them. I would have any one try to fancy any taste which had never affected his palate, or frame the idea of a scent he had never smelt; and when he can do this, I will also conclude, that a blind man hath ideas of colours, and a deaf man true distinct notions of sounds.

3. This is the reason why, though we cannot believe it impossible to God to make a creature with other organs, and more ways to convey into the understanding the notice of corporeal things than those five, as they are usually counted, which he has given to man: yet I think it is *not possible* for any one *to imagine* any other qualities in bodies, howsoever constituted, whereby they can be taken notice of, besides sounds, tastes, smells, visible and tangible qualities. And had mankind been made with but four senses, the qualities then which are the object of the fifth sense, had been as far from our notice, imagination, and conception, as now any belonging to a sixth, seventh, or eighth sense, can possibly be: which, whether yet some other creatures, in some other parts of

---

[1] Note that Locke uses these two terms convertibly. The term 'suggestion' afterwards played a great part in Berkeley's philosophy and, in a different connexion, in Reid's philosophy of Common Sense.

this vast and stupendous universe, may not have, will be a great presumption to deny.[1] He that will not set himself proudly at the top of all things, but will consider the immensity of this fabric, and the great variety that is to be found in this little and inconsiderable part of it which he has to do with, may be apt to think, that in other mansions of it there may be other and different intelligible beings, of whose faculties he has as little knowledge or apprehension, as a worm shut up in one drawer of a cabinet hath of the senses or understanding of a man; such variety and excellency being suitable to the wisdom and power of the Maker. I have here followed the common opinion of man's having but five senses, though perhaps there may be justly counted more;[2] but either supposition serves equally to my present purpose.

## CHAPTER III

### OF IDEAS OF ONE SENSE

1. *Division of simple ideas.*—The better to conceive the ideas we receive from sensation,[3] it may not be amiss for us to consider them in reference to the different ways whereby they make their approaches to our minds, and make themselves perceivable by us.

First, then, There are some which come into our minds *by one sense* only.

Secondly. There are others that convey themselves into the mind *by more senses than one*.

Thirdly. Others that are had from *reflection* only.

Fourthly. There are some that make themselves way, and are suggested to the mind *by all the ways of sensation and reflection*.

We shall consider them apart under these several heads.

First, There are some ideas which have admittance only

---

[1] This speculation is elaborated by Voltaire (*Micromégas*, ch. 2)., Cf. Hamilton's *Lectures on Metaphysics*, Lect. VIII.

[2] Modern psychology usually differentiates more fully, especially in the case of tactual sensations, but the precise number is irrelevant to Locke's argument.

[3] 'From sensation' is inaccurate, as he proceeds to give a classification of all our simple ideas.

through one sense, which is peculiarly adapted to receive them. Thus light and colours, as white, red, yellow, blue, with their several degrees or shades and mixtures, as green, scarlet, purple, sea-green, and the rest, come in only by the eyes ; all kinds of noises, sounds, and tones, only by the ears ; the several tastes and smells, by the nose and palate. And if these organs, or the nerves which are the conduits to convey them from without to their audience in the brain, the mind's presence-room (as I may so call it), are, any of them, so disordered as not to perform their functions, they have no postern to be admitted by, no other way to bring themselves into view, and be perceived by the understanding.

The most considerable of those belonging to the touch are heat, and cold, and solidity ; all the rest, consisting almost wholly in the sensible configuration, as smooth and rough ; or else, more or less firm adhesion of the parts, as hard and soft, tough and brittle, are obvious enough.

2. *Few simple ideas have names.*—I think it will be needless to enumerate all the particular simple ideas belonging to each sense. Nor indeed is it possible if we would, there being a great many more of them belonging to most of the senses than we have names for. The variety of smells, which are as many almost, if not more than species of bodies in the world, do most of them want names. Sweet and stinking commonly serve our turn for these ideas, which in effect is little more than to call them pleasing or displeasing ; though the smell of a rose and violet, both sweet, are certainly very distinct ideas. Nor are the different tastes that by our palates we receive ideas of, much better provided with names. Sweet, bitter, sour, harsh, and salt, are almost all the epithets we have to denominate that numberless variety of relishes which are to be found distinct, not only in almost every sort of creatures, but in the different parts of the same plant, fruit, or animal. The same may be said of colours and sounds. I shall therefore, in the account of simple ideas I am here giving, content myself to set down only such as are most material to our present purpose, or are in themselves less apt to be taken notice of, though they are very frequently the ingredients of our complex ideas ; amongst which, I think, I may well account solidity, which therefore I shall treat of in the next chapter.

## CHAPTER IV

### OF SOLIDITY

1. *We receive this idea from touch.*—The idea of solidity we receive by our touch; and it arises from the resistance which we find in body to the entrance of any other body into the place it possesses, till it has left it. There is no idea which we receive more constantly from sensation than solidity. Whether we move or rest, in what posture soever we are, we always feel something under us that supports us, and hinders our farther sinking downwards; and the bodies which we daily handle make us perceive that whilst they remain between them, they do, by an insurmountable force, hinder the approach of the parts of our hands that press them. That which thus hinders the approach of two bodies, when they are moving one towards another, I call *solidity*. I will not dispute whether this acceptation of the word solid be nearer to its original signification than that which mathematicians use it in : it suffices that, I think, the common notion of solidity will allow, if not justify, this use of it ; but if any one think it better to call it *impenetrability*, he has my consent. Only I have thought the term solidity the more proper to express this idea, not only because of its vulgar use in that sense, but also because it carries something more of positive in it than impenetrability, which is negative, and is, perhaps, more a consequence of solidity than solidity itself. This, of all other, seems the idea most intimately connected with and essential to body, so as nowhere else to be found or imagined, but only in matter ; and though our senses take no notice of it, but in masses of matter, of a bulk sufficient to cause a sensation in us ; yet the mind, having once got this idea from such grosser sensible bodies, traces it farther, and considers it, as well as figure, in the minutest particle of matter that can exist, and finds it inseparably inherent in body, wherever or however modified.

2. *Distinct from space.*—This resistance, whereby it keeps other bodies out of the space which it possesses, is so great, that no force, how great soever, can surmount it. All the bodies in the world, pressing a drop of water on all sides, will never be able to overcome the resistance which it will make,

as soft as it is, to their approaching one another, till it be removed out of their way: whereby our idea of solidity is distinguished both from pure space, which is capable neither of resistance nor motion, and from the ordinary idea of hardness.[1] For a man may conceive two bodies at a distance so as they may approach one another without touching or displacing any solid thing till their superficies come to meet; whereby, I think, we have the clear idea of space without solidity. For (not to go so far as annihilation of any particular body) I ask, whether a man cannot have the idea of the motion of one single body alone, without any other succeeding immediately into its place? I think it is evident he can: the idea of motion in one body no more including the idea of motion in another, than the idea of a square figure in one body includes the idea of a square figure in another. I do not ask, whether bodies do so exist, that the motion of one body cannot really be without the motion of another? To determine this either way is to beg the question for or against a vacuum. But my question is, whether one cannot have the idea of one body moved, whilst others are at rest? And I think this no one will deny: if so, then the place it deserted gives us the idea of pure space without solidity, whereinto another body may enter without either resistance or protrusion of anything. When the sucker in a pump is drawn, the space it filled in the tube is certainly the same, whether any other body follows the motion of the sucker or no; nor does it imply a contradiction that upon the motion of one body, another that is only contiguous to it should not follow it. The necessity of such a motion is built only on the supposition, that the world is full, but not on the distinct ideas of space and solidity; which are as different as resistance and not-resistance, protrusion and not-protrusion. And that men have ideas of space without body, their very disputes about a vacuum plainly demonstrate, as is showed in another place.[2]

[1] It is impossible to treat this idea of impenetrability or ultimate incompressibility as if it were an immediate datum of the sense of touch, even if we include muscular sensations of resistance. The idea of 'hard' might perhaps be so treated, but 'solidity', as Locke explains it, is a scientific definition of the ultimate nature of matter; it expresses, as he says in the first section, the 'essence' of body. The senses, Leibniz says, 'do not suffice, apart from the reasoning faculty, to establish this perfect impenetrability, which I hold to be true in the order of nature, but not to be learned by sensation alone'.

[2] Ch. 13.

4. *From hardness.*—Solidity is hereby also differenced from hardness, in that solidity consists in repletion, and so an utter exclusion of other bodies out of the space it possesses ; but hardness, in a firm cohesion of the parts of matter, making up masses of a sensible bulk, so that the whole does not easily change its figure. And, indeed, hard and soft are names that we give to things only in relation to the constitutions of our own bodies ; that being generally called hard by us which will put us to pain sooner than change figure by the pressure of any part of our bodies ; and that, on the contrary, soft which changes the situation of its parts upon an easy and unpainful touch.

But this difficulty of changing the situation of the sensible parts amongst themselves, or of the figure of the whole, gives no more solidity to the hardest body in the world than to the softest ; nor is an adamant one jot more solid than water. For though the two flat sides of two pieces of marble will more easily approach each other, between which there is nothing but water or air, than if there be a diamond between them ; yet it is not that the parts of the diamond are more solid than those of water, or resist more, but because the parts of water being more easily separable from each other, they will by a side-motion be more easily removed and give way to the approach of the two pieces of marble: but if they could be kept from making place by that side-motion, they would eternally hinder the approach of these two pieces of marble as much as the diamond. The softest body in the world will as invincibly resist the coming together of any two other bodies, if it be not put out of the way, but remain between them, as the hardest that can be found or imagined. He that shall fill a yielding soft body well with air or water will quickly find its resistance : and he that thinks that nothing but bodies that are hard can keep his hands from approaching one another, may be pleased to make a trial with the air enclosed in a football. [The experiment I have been told was made at Florence, with a hollow globe of gold filled with water, and exactly closed, farther shows the solidity of so soft a body as water. For the golden globe thus filled being put into a press which was driven by the extreme force of screws, the water made itself way through the pores of that very close metal, and finding no room for a nearer approach of its particles within, got to the outside, where it rose like a dew, and so fell in drops before the sides of the globe could be made to yield to the violent compression of the engine that squeezed it.][1]

5. *On solidity depend impulse, resistance, and protrusion.*—By this idea of solidity is the extension of body distinguished from the extension of space. The extension of body being nothing but the cohesion or continuity of solid, separable, movable parts; and the extension of space, the continuity of unsolid, inseparable, and immovable parts. Upon the solidity of bodies also depend their mutual impulse, resistance, and protrusion. Of pure space then, and solidity, there are several (amongst which I confess myself one) who persuade themselves they have clear and distinct ideas; and that they can think on space without anything in it that resists or is protruded by body. This is the idea of pure space, which they think they have as clear as any idea they can have of the extension of body.[2]

6. *What it is.*—If any one asks me, *what this solidity is,* I send him to his senses to inform him: let him put a flint or a football between his hands, and then endeavour to join them, and he will know. If he thinks this not a sufficient explanation of solidity, what it is, and wherein it consists, I promise to tell him what it is, and wherein it consists, when he tells me what thinking is, or wherein it consists; or explains to me what extension or motion is, which perhaps seems much easier. The simple ideas we have are such as experience teaches them us; but if, beyond that, we endeavour by words to make them clearer in the mind, we shall succeed no better than if we went about to clear up the darkness of a blind man's mind by talking, and to discourse into him the ideas of light and colours. The reason of this I shall show in another place.[3]

## CHAPTER V

### OF SIMPLE IDEAS OF DIVERS SENSES

THE ideas we get by more than one sense are of *space* or *extension, figure, rest* and *motion*: for these make perceivable impressions both on the eyes and touch; and we can receive and convey into our minds the ideas of the extension, figure,

---

[1] Added in second edition.

[2] Locke's polemic is here against the Cartesian conception of space as a *plenum*. Cf. II. 13. 11–27, where the question is more fully debated.

[3] Bk. III, ch. 4, 'Of the Names of simple Ideas', especially section 11, which gives the instance of the 'studious blind man' who said that scarlet was 'like the sound of a trumpet'.

motion, and rest of bodies, both by seeing and feeling. But having occasion to speak more at large of these in another place,[1] I here only enumerate them.

## CHAPTER VI

### OF SIMPLE IDEAS OF REFLECTION

1. *Are the operations of the mind about its other ideas.*—The mind, receiving the ideas mentioned in the foregoing chapters from without, when it turns its view inward upon itself, and observes its own actions about those ideas it has, takes from thence other ideas, which are as capable to be the objects of its contemplation as any of those it received from foreign things.

2. *The idea of perception, and idea of willing, we have from reflection.*—The two great and principal actions of the mind, which are most frequently considered, and which are so frequent that every one that pleases may take notice of them in himself, are these two: *perception*[2] or *thinking*, and *volition* or *willing*. The power of thinking is called the *Understanding*, and the power of volition is called the *Will*; and these two powers or abilities in the mind are denominated *faculties*. Of some of the modes of these simple ideas of reflection, such as are *remembrance, discerning, reasoning, judging, knowledge, faith*, &c., I shall have occasion to speak hereafter.[3]

## CHAPTER VII

### OF SIMPLE IDEAS OF BOTH SENSATION AND REFLECTION

1. There be other simple ideas which convey themselves into the mind by all the ways of sensation and reflection; viz., *pleasure* or *delight*, and its opposite, *pain* or *uneasiness*; *power*; *existence*; *unity*.

2. *Pleasure and pain.* Delight or uneasiness, one or other of

[1] In chs. 13-15 of this Book, where he discusses the 'simple modes' of space and time.
[2] Perception as equivalent to thinking is an uncommon use of the word. Perception in its usual sense is discussed by Locke in the ninth chapter of this Book. He also uses the word for perception of the meaning of words and for the perception of the agreement or disagreement between ideas in which knowledge consists (Bk. IV, ch. 2).
[3] Bk. II, chs. 10, 11, and in the latter chapters of Bk. IV.

them, join themselves to [1] almost all our ideas both of sensation and reflection; and there is scarce any affection of our senses from without, any retired thought of our mind within, which is not able to produce in us pleasure or pain. By pleasure and pain, I would be understood to signify whatsoever delights or molests us; whether it arises from the thoughts of our minds, or anything operating on our bodies. For whether we call it satisfaction, delight, pleasure, happiness, &c., on the one side, or uneasiness, trouble, pain, torment, anguish, misery, &c., on the other, they are still but different degrees of the same thing, and belong to the ideas of pleasure and pain, delight or uneasiness; which are the names I shall most commonly use for those two sorts of ideas.

3. The infinite wise Author of our being, to excite us to these actions of thinking and motion that we are capable of, has been pleased to join to several thoughts and several sensations a perception of delight. If this were wholly separated from all our outward sensations and inward thoughts, we should have no reason to prefer one thought or action to another, negligence to attention, or motion to rest. And so we should neither stir our bodies, nor employ our minds, but let our thoughts (if I may so call it) run adrift, without any direction or design; and suffer the ideas of our minds, like unregarded shadows, to make their appearances there as it happened, without attending to them. In which state man, however furnished with the faculties of understanding and will, would be a very idle, unactive creature, and pass his time only in a lazy, lethargic dream.

4. Pain has the same efficacy and use to set us on work that pleasure has, we being as ready to employ our faculties to avoid that, as to pursue this: only this is worth our consideration, that pain is often produced by the same objects and ideas that produce pleasure in us. Thus heat, that is very agreeable to us in one degree, by a little greater increase of it proves no ordinary torment; and the most pleasant of all sensible objects, light itself, if there be too much of it, if increased beyond a due proportion to our eyes, causes a very painful sensation. Which is wisely and favourably so ordered by nature, that when any object does by the vehemency of its operation disorder the instruments of sensation, whose structures cannot

---

[1] On the variety of Locke's terminology in this chapter—'join themselves to', 'suggested by', 'received from'—cf. Introduction, pp. xx–vii.

but be very nice and delicate, we might by the pain be warned to withdraw before the organ be quite put out of order, and so be unfitted for its proper functions for the future.

7. *Existence and unity.*—Existence and unity are two other ideas that are suggested to the understanding by every object without, and every idea within. When ideas are in our minds, we consider them as being actually there, as well as we consider things to be actually without us: which is, that they exist, or have existence. And whatever we can consider [1] as one thing, whether a real being or idea, suggests to the understanding the idea of unity.

8. *Power.*—Power also is another of those simple ideas which we receive from sensation and reflection. For, observing in ourselves that we do and can think, and that we can at pleasure move several parts of our bodies which were at rest, the effects also that natural bodies are able to produce in one another occurring every moment to our senses, we both these ways get the idea of power.[2]

9. *Succession.*—Besides these there is another idea, which though suggested by our senses yet is more constantly offered us by what passes in our own minds ; and that is the idea of succession. For if we look immediately into ourselves, and reflect on what is observable there, we shall find our ideas always, whilst we are awake or have any thought, passing in train, one going and another coming without intermission.

---

[1] In attributing the ideas of ' existence ' and ' unity ' to ' consideration ' by the mind, we are going beyond the mere data of sense. Hume, who sought to restrict us to the sense datum, argues that ' the idea of existence is the very same with the idea of what we conceive to be existent'; accordingly, ' when conjoined with the idea of any object, it makes no addition to it ' (*Treatise*, Bk. I, Part II, section 6). So Berkeley says of ' unity ' (*Principles*, section 13) : ' Unity, I know, some will have to be a simple or uncompounded idea, accompanying all other ideas into the mind. That I have any such idea answering the word *unity* I do not find. To say no more, it is an abstract idea.' In other words, it is not an idea of sensation (or of reflection in Locke's sense), but a ' notion ' in Berkeley's later phraseology, a conception of reason. So Leibniz : ' The senses cannot convince us of the *existence* of sensible things without the aid of the reason. Thus I should think that the consideration of existence comes from reflection [used in a different sense from Locke's]. That of power also and unity come from the same source, and are of a wholly different nature from the perceptions of pleasure and pain.'

[2] The process is more fully described in ch. 21. 1–4, where the ' consideration ' by the mind is farther emphasized. When change is observed, 'the mind must collect a power somewhere able to make that change '.

10. *Simple ideas the materials of all our knowledge.*—These, if they are not all, are at least (as I think) the most considerable of those simple ideas which the mind has, and out of which is made all its other knowledge: all which it receives only by the two forementioned ways of sensation and reflection.

Nor let any one think these too narrow bounds for the capacious mind of man to expatiate in, which takes its flight farther than the stars, and cannot be confined by the limits of the world. I grant all this, but desire any one to assign any simple idea which is not received from one of those inlets before mentioned, or any complex idea not made out of those simple ones.

Nor will it be so strange to think these few simple ideas sufficient to employ the quickest thought or largest capacity, and to furnish the materials of all that various knowledge and more various fancies and opinions of all mankind, if we consider how many words may be made out of the various composition of twenty-four letters; or if, going one step farther, we will but reflect on the variety of combinations may be made with barely one of the above-mentioned ideas, viz., number, whose stock is inexhaustible and truly infinite: and what a large and immense field doth extension alone afford the mathematicians?

## CHAPTER VIII

### SOME FARTHER CONSIDERATIONS CONCERNING OUR SIMPLE IDEAS

1. *Positive ideas from privative causes.*—Concerning the simple ideas of sensation it is to be considered, that whatsoever is so constituted in nature as to be able by affecting our senses to cause any perception in the mind, doth thereby produce in the understanding a simple idea; which, whatever be the external cause of it, when it comes to be taken notice of by our discerning faculty, it is by the mind looked on and considered there to be a real positive idea in the understanding, as much as any other whatsoever; though perhaps the cause of it be but a privation in the subject.

2. Thus the ideas of heat and cold, light and darkness, white and black, motion and rest, are equally clear and positive ideas in the mind; though perhaps some of the causes which produce them are barely privations in those subjects from whence

our senses derive those ideas. These the understanding, in its view of them, considers all as distinct positive ideas without taking notice of the causes that produce them : which is an enquiry not belonging to the idea as it is in the understanding, but to the nature of the things existing without us. These are two very different things, and carefully to be distinguished ; it being one thing to perceive and know the idea of white or black, and quite another to examine what kind of particles they must be, and how ranged in the superficies, to make any object appear white or black.

3. A painter or dyer who never enquired into their causes, hath the ideas of white and black and other colours as clearly, perfectly, and distinctly in his understanding, and perhaps more distinctly than the philosopher [1] who hath busied himself in considering their natures, and thinks he knows how far either of them is in its cause positive or privative ; and the idea of black is no less positive in his mind than that of white, however the cause of that colour in the external object may be only a privation.

4. If it were the design of my present undertaking to enquire into the natural causes and manner of perception, I should offer this as a reason why a privative cause might, in some cases at least, produce a positive idea, viz., that all sensation being produced in us only by different degrees and modes of motion in our animal spirits, variously agitated by external objects, the abatement of any former motion must as necessarily produce a new sensation as the variation or increase of it ; and so introduce a new idea, which depends only on a different motion of the animal spirits [2] in that organ.

5. But whether this be so or no I will not here determine, but appeal to every one's own experience, whether the shadow of a man, though it consists of nothing but the absence of light (and the more the absence of light is, the more discernible is the shadow), does not, when a man looks on it, cause as clear and positive an idea in his mind as a man himself, though covered

[1] The natural philosopher or physicist. Locke describes this chapter as ' a little excursion into natural philosophy ' (section 22). It is complementary to the account of simple ideas already given, treating ideas of sensation not merely as bare appearances in the mind, but as effects produced in us by real things and as giving us a knowledge of the qualities of these bodies. It brings into view the assumptions involved in Locke's theory of knowledge. See Introduction, p. xxxvii.

[2] See note 5, p. 10.

over with clear sunshine. And the picture of a shadow is a positive thing. Indeed, we have negative names, which stand not directly for positive ideas, but for their absence, such as *insipid, silence, nihil*, &c., which words denote positive ideas, v. g., *taste, sound, being*, with a signification of their absence.

6. And thus one may truly be said to see darkness. The privative causes I have here assigned of positive ideas are according to the common opinion; but in truth it will be hard to determine whether there be really any ideas from a privative cause, till it be determined whether rest be any more a privation than motion.

7. *Ideas in the mind, qualities in bodies.*—To discover the nature of our ideas the better, and to discourse of them intelligibly, it will be convenient to distinguish them, as they are ideas or perceptions in our minds, and as they are modifications of matter in the bodies that cause such perceptions in us; that so we may not think (as perhaps usually is done) that they are exactly the images and resemblances of something inherent in the subject; [1] most of those of sensation being in the mind no more the likeness of something existing without us than the names that stand for them are the likeness of our ideas, which yet upon hearing they are apt to excite in us.

8. Whatsoever the mind perceives in itself, or is the immediate object of perception, thought, or understanding, that I call *idea*; and the power to produce any idea in our mind, I call *quality* of the subject wherein that power is.[2] Thus a snowball having the power to produce in us the ideas of white, cold, and round, the powers to produce those ideas in us as they are in the snowball, I call qualities; and as they are sensations or perceptions in our understandings, I call them ideas; which ideas, if I speak of them sometimes as in the things themselves, I would be understood to mean those qualities in the objects which produce them in us.

9. *Primary qualities of bodies.*—Qualities thus considered in bodies are, First, such as are utterly inseparable [3] from the

[1] Subject = the substance or body causing the perception.

[2] The ascription of 'power' in this sense to material things was what Berkeley called in question. Locke allows (II. 21. 4) that 'we have, from the observation of the operation of bodies by our senses, but a very imperfect obscure idea of *active* power'. The mind gets that idea 'clearer from reflection on its own operations'.

[3] 'These utterly inseparable' qualities Locke afterwards calls the 'real essence' of body.

body, in what estate soever it be ; such as, in all the alterations and changes it suffers, all the force can be used upon it, it constantly keeps ; and such as sense constantly finds in every particle of matter which has bulk enough to be perceived, and the mind finds inseparable from every particle of matter, though less than to make itself singly be perceived by our senses : v. g., take a grain of wheat, divide it into two parts, each part has still solidity, extension, figure, and mobility ; divide it again, and it retains still the same qualities : and so divide it on, till the parts become insensible ; they must retain still each of them all those qualities. [These I call *original* or *primary qualities* of body, which I think we may observe to produce simple ideas in us, viz., solidity, extension, figure, motion or rest, and number.[1]

10. *Secondary qualities of bodies.*—Secondly, Such qualities, which in truth are nothing in the objects themselves, but powers to produce various sensations in us by their primary qualities, i. e., by the bulk, figure, texture, and motion of their insensible parts, as colours, sounds, tastes, &c. ; these I call *secondary qualities*. To these might be added a third sort, which are allowed to be barely powers, though they are as much real qualities in the subject as those which I, to comply with the common way of speaking, call qualities, but, for distinction, secondary qualities. For the power in fire to produce a new colour or consistence in wax or clay by its primary qualities, is as much a quality in fire as the power it has to produce in *me* a new idea or sensation of warmth or burning, which I felt not before, by the same primary qualities, viz., the bulk, texture, and motion of its insensible parts.][2]

11. *How primary qualities produce their ideas.*—The next thing to be considered is, how bodies produce ideas in us ; and

[1] These are more summarily stated in ch. 33, section 17 : 'The primary ideas we have peculiar to body, as contradistinguished to spirit, are the cohesion of solid, and consequently separable parts, and a power of communicating motion by impulse. These, I think, are the original ideas, proper and peculiar to body ; for figure is but the consequence of finite extension.'

[2] Added in fourth edition. The distinction between primary and secondary qualities of bodies goes back in principle to Democritus, and was resuscitated by Galileo and taken over by Descartes, Gassendi, and Hobbes. The nomenclature was employed by Locke's friend Boyle in his *Origin of Forms and Qualities* (1666). Boyle's account may have suggested the somewhat elaborate treatment of the subject in this chapter.

that is manifestly by impulse, the only way which we can conceive bodies operate in.[1]

12. If, then, external objects be not united to our minds when they produce ideas in it, and yet we perceive these original qualities in such of them as singly fall under our senses, it is evident that some motion must be thence continued by our nerves or animal spirits, by some parts of our bodies, to the brains or the seat of sensation, there to produce in our minds the particular ideas we have of them. And since the extension, figure, number, and motion of bodies of an observable bigness, may be perceived at a distance by the sight, it is evident some singly imperceptible bodies must come from them to the eyes, and thereby convey to the brain some motion which produces these ideas which we have of them in us.

13. *How secondary.*—After the same manner that the ideas of these original qualities are produced in us, we may conceive that the ideas of secondary qualities are also produced, viz., by the operation of insensible particles on our senses. The different motions and figures, bulk and number of such particles, affecting the several organs of our senses, produce in us those different sensations which we have from the colours and smells of bodies; v. g., that a violet, by the impulse of such insensible particles of matter of peculiar figures and bulks, and in different degrees and modifications of their motions, causes the ideas of the blue colour and sweet scent of that flower to be produced in our minds. It being no more impossible to conceive that God should annex such ideas to such motions with which they have no similitude, than that he should annex the idea of pain to the motion of a piece of steel dividing our flesh, with which that idea hath no resemblance.

---

[1] In its original form this section continued after the word 'manifestly' as follows: ' by impulse and nothing else. It being impossible to conceive that body should operate on what it does not touch (which is all one as to imagine it can operate where it is not), or, when it does touch, operate any other way than by motion.' The change introduced in the fourth edition was due to 'the judicious Mr. Newton's incomparable book'. ' The gravitation of matter towards matter, by ways inconceivable to me,' Locke wrote, ' is not only a demonstration that God can, if he pleases, put into bodies powers and ways of operation above what can be derived from our idea of body, or can be explained by what we know of matter, but is also an unquestionable and everywhere visible instance that he has done so ' (*Reply to Second Letter*, p. 468). The words ' bodies cannot operate at a distance ' were also omitted in the first sentence of section 12.

14. What I have said concerning colours and smells may be understood also of tastes and sounds, and other the like sensible qualities ; which, whatever reality we by mistake attribute to them, are in truth nothing in the objects themselves, but powers to produce various sensations in us, and depend on those primary qualities, viz., bulk, figure, texture, and motion of parts, as I have said.

15. *Ideas of primary qualities are resemblances ; of secondary, not.*—From whence I think it is easy to draw this observation, that the ideas of primary qualities of bodies are resemblances of them,[1] and their patterns do really exist in the bodies themselves ; but the ideas produced in us by these secondary qualities have no resemblance of them at all. There is nothing like our ideas existing in the bodies themselves. They are, in the bodies we denominate from them, only a power to produce those sensations in us : and what is sweet, blue, or warm in idea, is but the certain bulk, figure, and motion of the insensible parts in the bodies themselves, which we call so.

16. Flame is denominated hot and light ; snow, white and cold ; and manna, white and sweet, from the ideas they produce in us. Which qualities are commonly thought to be the same in those bodies that those ideas are in us, the one the perfect resemblance of the other, as they are in a mirror ; and it would by most men be judged very extravagant, if one should say otherwise. And yet he that will consider that the same fire that at one distance produces in us the sensation of warmth, does at a nearer approach produce in us the far different sensation of pain, ought to bethink himself what reason he has to say, that his idea of warmth which was produced in him by the fire, is actually in the fire, and his idea of pain which the same fire produced in him the same way is not in the fire. Why is whiteness and coldness in snow, and pain not, when it produces the one and the other idea in us, and can do neither, but by the bulk, figure, number, and motion of its solid parts ?

17. The particular bulk, number, figure, and motion of the parts of fire or snow are really in them, whether any one's senses perceive them or no ; and therefore they may be called *real qualities*, because they really exist in those bodies. But light, heat, whiteness, or coldness, are no more really in them than sickness or pain is in manna. Take away the sensation

[1] This resemblance Berkeley denied : ' an idea can be like nothing but another idea ' (*Principles*, section 9).

of them; let not the eyes see light or colours, nor the ears hear sounds; let the palate not taste, nor the nose smell; and all colours, tastes, odours, and sounds, as they are such particular ideas, vanish and cease, and are reduced to their causes, i. e., bulk, figure, and motion of parts.[1]

18. A piece of manna of a sensible bulk is able to produce in us the idea of a round or square figure; and, by being removed from one place to another, the idea of motion. This idea of motion represents it as it really is in the manna moving; a circle or square are the same, whether in idea or existence, in the mind or in the manna; and this, both motion and figure are really in the manna, whether we take notice of them or no: this everybody is ready to agree to. Besides, manna, by the bulk, figure, texture, and motion of its parts, has a power to produce the sensations of sickness, and sometimes of acute pains or gripings, in us. That these ideas of sickness and pain are not in the manna, but effects of its operations on us, and are nowhere when we feel them not: this also every one readily agrees to. And yet men are hardly to be brought to think that sweetness and whiteness are not really in manna, which are but the effects of the operations of manna by the motion, size, and figure of its particles on the eyes and palate: as the pain and sickness caused by manna are confessedly nothing but the effects of its operations on the stomach. Why the pain and sickness, ideas that are the effects of manna, should be thought to be nowhere when they are not felt; and yet the sweetness and whiteness, effects of the same manna on other parts of the body, by ways equally as unknown, should be thought to exist in the manna, when they are not seen nor tasted, would need some reason to explain.

19. Let us consider the red and white colours in porphyry: hinder light but from striking on it, and its colours vanish; it no longer produces any such ideas in us. Upon the return of light, it produces these appearances on us again. Can any one think any real alterations are made in the porphyry by the presence or absence of light, and that those ideas of whiteness and redness are really in porphyry in the light, when it is plain *it has no colour in the dark*? It has indeed such a configuration

---

[1] Berkeley applies the argument of this section to the primary or real qualities as well as to the secondary or imputed qualities. In both cases their *esse* is *percipi*, and they would 'vanish and cease' with the disappearance of sentient life.

of particles, both night and day, as are apt, by the rays of light rebounding from some parts of that hard stone, to produce in us the idea of redness, and from others the idea of whiteness: but whiteness or redness are not in it at any time, but such a texture that hath the power to produce such a sensation in us.

22. I have, in what just goes before, been engaged in physical enquiries a little farther than perhaps I intended. But it being necessary to make the nature of sensation a little understood, and to make the difference between the *qualities* in bodies and the *ideas* produced by them in the mind to be distinctly conceived, without which it were impossible to discourse intelligibly of them, I hope I shall be pardoned this little excursion into natural philosophy, it being necessary in our present enquiry to distinguish the *primary* and *real* qualities of bodies, which are always in them (viz., solidity, extension, figure, number, and motion or rest, and are sometimes perceived by us, viz., when the bodies they are in are big enough singly to be discerned), from those *secondary* and *imputed* qualities, which are but the powers of several combinations of those primary ones, when they operate without being distinctly discerned:[1] whereby we also may come to know what ideas are, and what are not, resemblances of something really existing in the bodies we denominate from them.

23. *Three sorts of qualities in bodies.*—The qualities then that are in bodies, rightly considered, are of three sorts :

First, the bulk, figure, number, situation, and motion or rest of their solid parts. Those are in them, whether we perceive them or no ; and when they are of that size that we can discover them, we have by these an idea of the thing as it is in itself, as is plain in artificial things. These I call *primary qualities*.

Secondly, the power that is in any body, by reason of its insensible primary qualities, to operate after a peculiar manner on any of our senses, and thereby produce in *us* the different ideas of several colours, sounds, smells, tastes, &c. These are usually called *sensible qualities*.

Thirdly, the power that is in any body, by reason of the particular constitution of its primary qualities, to make such a

---

[1] If the constitution of the insensible parts *were* perceptible (if we had 'microscopical eyes'), the secondary qualities, he argues, would disappear for us. (Cf. II. 23. 11–12.)

change in the bulk, figure, texture, and motion of another body, as to make it operate on our senses differently from what it did before. Thus the sun has a power to make wax white, and fire, to make lead fluid. These are usually called *powers*.

The first of these, as has been said, I think may be properly called real, original, or primary qualities, because they are in the things themselves, whether they are perceived or no : and upon their different modifications it is that the secondary qualities depend.

The other two are only powers to act differently upon other things, which powers result from the different modifications of those primary qualities.

24. *The first are resemblances ; the second thought resemblances, but are not ; the third neither are, nor are thought so.*— But though these two latter sorts of qualities are powers barely, and nothing but powers, relating to several other bodies, and resulting from the different modifications of the original qualities, yet they are generally otherwise thought of. V. g., the idea of heat or light which we receive by our eyes or touch from the sun, are commonly thought real qualities existing in the sun, and something more than mere powers in it. But when we consider the sun in reference to wax, which it melts or blanches, we look upon the whiteness and softness produced in the wax, not as qualities in the sun, but effects produced by powers in it : whereas, if rightly considered, these qualities of light and warmth, which are perceptions in me when I am warmed or enlightened by the sun, are no otherwise in the sun than the changes made in the wax, when it is blanched or melted, are in the sun. They are all of them equally powers in the sun, depending on its primary qualities.

25. The reason why the one are ordinarily taken for real qualities, and the other only for bare powers, seems to be because the ideas we have of distinct colours, sounds, &c., containing nothing at all in them of bulk, figure, or motion, we are not apt to think them the effects of these primary qualities which appear not to our senses to operate in their production, and with which they have not any apparent congruity, or conceivable connexion. Hence it is that we are so forward to imagine that those ideas are the resemblances of something really existing in the objects themselves. But, in the other case, in the operations of bodies changing the qualities one of another, we plainly discover that the quality produced hath

commonly no resemblance with anything in the thing producing it; wherefore we look on it as a bare effect of power. [26.] The former, I think, may be called secondary qualities immediately perceivable, the latter secondary qualities mediately perceivable.

## CHAPTER IX [1]

### OF PERCEPTION

1. *It is the first simple idea of reflection.*—Perception, as it is the first faculty of the mind exercised about our ideas, so it is the first and simplest idea we have from reflection, and is by some called thinking in general. Though thinking, in the propriety of the English tongue, signifies that sort of operation of the mind about its ideas wherein the mind is active; where it, with some degree of voluntary attention, considers anything. For in bare, naked perception, the mind is, for the most part, only passive;[2] and what it perceives, it cannot avoid perceiving.

2. *Is only when the mind receives the impression.*—What perception is, every one will know better by reflecting on what he does himself, when he sees, hears, feels, &c., or thinks, than by any discourse of mine. Whoever reflects on what passes in his own mind, cannot miss it: and if he does not reflect, all the words in the world cannot make him have any notion of it. [3.] This is certain, that whatever alterations are made in the body, if they reach not the mind; whatever impressions are made on the outward parts, if they are not taken notice of within, there is no perception. Fire may burn our bodies with no other effect than it does a billet, unless the motion be continued to the brain, and there the sense of heat or idea of pain be produced in the mind, wherein consists actual perception. [4.] How often may a man observe in himself, that whilst his mind is intently employed in the contemplation of some objects, and curiously surveying

---

[1] This and the two following chapters constitute a kind of appendix to the chapter 'Of simple Ideas of Reflection', and describe, under the name of 'faculties', the chief 'sorts' of mental operation distinguishable in the building up of knowledge. They are full of sound psychological observation as well as broad human feeling.

[2] Cf. note 2, p. 52.

some ideas that are there, it takes no notice of impressions of sounding bodies made upon the organ of hearing with the same alteration that uses to be for the producing the idea of sound? Want of sensation in this case is not through any defect in the organ, or that the man's ears are less affected than at other times when he does hear; but that which uses to produce the idea, though conveyed in by the usual organ, not being taken notice of in the understanding, and so imprinting no idea on the mind, there follows no sensation.

5. *Children, though they have ideas in the womb, have none innate.*—Therefore, I doubt not but children, by the exercise of their senses about objects that affect them in the womb, receive some few ideas before they are born, as the unavoidable effects either of the bodies that environ them, or else of those wants or diseases they suffer; amongst which (if one may conjecture concerning things not very capable of examination) I think the ideas of hunger and warmth are two, which probably are some of the first that children have, and which they scarce ever part with again. [6.] Yet these simple ideas are far from those innate principles which some contend for, and we above have rejected, being the effects of sensation, and no otherwise differing in their manner of production from other ideas derived from sense, but only in the precedency of time. [7.] So, after they are born, those ideas are the earliest imprinted which happen to be the sensible qualities which first occur to them: amongst which, light is not the least considerable, nor of the weakest efficacy. And how covetous the mind is to be furnished with all such ideas as have no pain accompanying them, may be a little guessed by what is observable in children new born, who always turn their eyes to that part from whence the light comes, lay them how you please.

8. *Ideas of sensation often changed by the judgement.*—We are farther to consider concerning perception, that the ideas we receive by sensation are often in grown people altered by the judgement [1] without our taking notice of it. When we set before our eyes a round globe of any uniform colour, v. g. gold, alabaster, or jet, it is certain that the idea thereby

---

[1] This opens up the whole question of our 'acquired perceptions', so brilliantly developed in the immediate sequel by Berkeley in his theory of 'divine visual language', and progressively elaborated by psychologists since.

imprinted in our mind is of a flat circle variously shadowed, with several degrees of light and brightness coming to our eyes. But we having by use been accustomed to perceive what kind of appearance convex bodies are wont to make in us, what alterations are made in the reflections of light by the difference of the sensible figures of bodies, the judgement presently, by an habitual custom, alters the appearances into their causes: so that, from that which truly is variety of shadow or colour collecting the figure, it makes it pass for a mark of figure, and frames to itself the perception of a convex figure and an uniform colour; when the idea we receive from thence is only a plane variously coloured, as is evident in painting. [To which purpose I shall here insert a problem of that very ingenious and studious promoter of real knowledge, the learned and worthy Mr. Molineux, which he was pleased to send me in a letter some months since;[1] and it is this: 'Suppose a man born blind, and now adult,

[1] The letter, printed in Locke's correspondence, is dated March 2, 1693, and the second edition of the *Essay*, in which this passage was inserted, appeared, ' some months ' later, in 1694. William Molyneux (1656–98), of Trinity College, Dublin, an enthusiastic admirer of Locke, had sent him in 1692 his *Dioptrica Nova*, which was the beginning of an affectionate correspondence. Berkeley refers to ' Mr. Molyneux's problem ' in his *New Theory of Vision* (section 132), agreeing with Molyneux and Locke in their solution, which he accepts as proof of his own thesis that the objects of sight and of touch are two sets of ideas that have nothing in common. Leibniz, on the contrary, maintained that extension, although not capable of being presented separately as an image, is precisely the element common to the two sets of experiences; and he concluded, therefore, that if the born-blind man knew beforehand by touch only, that the cube and the globe were there, he would be able to distinguish the two by sight, though not perhaps immediately, while still confused by the novelty. This appears to him to be implied in the fact that the blind are capable of learning geometry. We must distinguish carefully, he adds, between ' images ' and ' the exact ideas which consist in definitions ', that is, concepts or notions. Since Cheselden's case (1728), attempts have been made to submit the question to experimental verification. The reports may be taken as confirming the view of Molyneux and Locke that our ordinary perceptions depend on judgements based on experience, but not Berkeley's sweeping denial of any natural correlation between the data of touch and the data of sight. Berkeley says ' there is no idea common to both senses ' (*Theory of Vision*, section 129), but intelligent patients, on the analogy of their tactual experience, soon detected corners or angles in the visual presentation of the cube. The older cases are commented on by Sir W. Hamilton and J. S. Mill and in Carpenter's *Mental Physiology*. Preyer in his *Soul of the Child* gives a list of the chief cases and a careful analysis of results (see English translation, Part II, The Development of the Intellect,

and taught by his touch to distinguish between a cube and a sphere of the same metal, and nighly of the same bigness, so as to tell, when he felt one and the other, which is the cube, which the sphere. Suppose then the cube and sphere placed on a table, and the blind man to be made to see; *quaere*, Whether by his sight, before he touched them, he could now distinguish and tell which is the globe, which the cube?' To which the acute and judicious proposer answers: 'Not. For though he has obtained the experience of how a globe, how a cube, affects his touch; yet he has not yet attained the experience, that what affects his touch so or so, must affect his sight so or so; or that a protuberant angle in the cube, that pressed his hand unequally, shall appear to his eye as it does in the cube.' I agree with this thinking gentleman, whom I am proud to call my friend, in his answer to this his problem; and am of opinion, that the blind man, at first sight, would not be able with certainty to say which was the globe, which the cube, whilst he only saw them; though he could unerringly name them by his touch, and certainly distinguish them by the difference of their figures felt. This I have set down, and leave with my reader, as an occasion for him to consider how much he may be beholden to experience, improvement, and acquired notions, where he thinks he has not the least use of, or help from them; and the rather, because this observing gentleman farther adds, that having upon the occasion of my book proposed this to divers very ingenious men, he hardly ever met with one that at first gave the answer to it which he thinks true, till by hearing his reasons they were convinced.]

9. But this is not, I think, usual in any of our ideas but those received by sight; because sight, the most comprehensive of all our senses, conveying to our minds the ideas of light and colours which are peculiar only to that sense; and also the far different ideas of space, figure, and motion, the several varieties whereof change the appearances of its proper object, viz., light and colours; we bring ourselves by use to judge of the one by the other. This, in many cases, by a settled habit, in things whereof we have frequent experience, is performed so constantly and so quick, that we

Appendix C, pp. 285–317). See also article on 'The Spatial Harmony of Touch and Sight', by G. M. Stratton, *Mind*, N.S., vol. viii, pp. 492 *et seq.*

take that for the perception of our sensation which is an idea formed by our judgement; so that one, viz., that of sensation, serves only to excite the other, and is scarce taken notice of itself; as a man who reads or hears with attention and understanding, takes little notice of the characters or sounds, but of the ideas that are excited in him by them.[1]

10. Nor need we wonder that this is done with so little notice, if we consider how very quick the actions of the mind are performed: for as itself is thought to take up no space, to have no extension, so its actions seem to require no time, but many of them seem to be crowded into an instant. I speak this in comparison to the actions of the body. Any one may easily observe this in his own thoughts who will take the pains to reflect on them. How, as it were in an instant, do our minds with one glance see all the parts of a demonstration, which may very well be called a long one, if we consider the time it will require to put it into words, and step by step show it another? Secondly, we shall not be so much surprised that this is done in us with so little notice, if we consider how the facility which we get of doing things, by a custom of doing, makes them often pass in us without our notice. Habits, especially such as are begun very early, come at last to produce actions in us which often escape our observation. How frequently do we in a day cover our eyes with our eyelids, without perceiving that we are at all in the dark? Men, that by custom have got the use of a byword, do almost in every sentence pronounce sounds which, though taken notice of by others, they themselves neither hear nor observe. And therefore it is not so strange that our mind should often change the idea of its sensation into that of its judgement, and make one serve only to excite the other, without our taking notice of it.

11. *Perception puts the difference between animals and inferior beings.*—This faculty of perception seems to me to be that which puts the distinction betwixt the animal kingdom and the inferior parts of nature. For however vegetables have, many of them, some degrees of motion, and upon the different application of other bodies to them, do very briskly alter

---

[1] Similarly, according to Berkeley, we pass directly from the strictly visual data to the tactual phenomena which they 'signify'.

their figures and motions, and so have obtained the name of sensitive plants from a motion which has some resemblance to that which in animals follows upon sensation; yet I suppose it is all bare mechanism, and no otherwise produced than the turning of a wild oat-beard by the insinuation of the particles of moisture, or the shortening of a rope by the affusion of water. All which is done without any sensation in the subject, or the having or receiving any ideas.

12. Perception, I believe, is in some degree in all sorts of animals; though in some possibly the avenues provided by nature for the reception of sensations are so few, and the perception they are received with so obscure and dull, that it comes extremely short of the quickness and variety of sensations which is in other animals. [13.] We may, I think, from the make of an oyster or cockle, reasonably conclude that it has not so many nor so quick senses as a man, or several other animals; nor if it had, would it, in that state and incapacity of transferring itself from one place to another, be bettered by them. What good would sight and hearing do to a creature that cannot move itself to or from the objects wherein at a distance it perceives good or evil? And would not quickness of sensation be an inconvenience to an animal that must lie still where chance has once placed it, and there receive the afflux of colder or warmer, clean or foul, water, as it happens to come to it? [14.] But yet I cannot but think there is some small dull perception, whereby they are distinguished from perfect insensibility.

15. *Perception the inlet of knowledge.*—Perception then being the first step and degree towards knowledge, and the inlet of all the materials of it, the fewer senses any man as well as any other creature hath; and the fewer and duller the impressions are that are made by them; and the duller the faculties are that are employed about them, the more remote are they from that knowledge which is to be found in some men. But this being in great variety of degrees (as may be perceived amongst men) cannot certainly be discovered in the several species of animals, much less in their particular individuals. It suffices me only to have remarked here, that perception is the first operation of all our intellectual faculties, and the inlet of all knowledge into our minds. And I am apt, too, to imagine that it is perception in the lowest degree

of it which puts the boundaries between animals and the inferior ranks of creatures. But this I mention only as my conjecture by the by, it being indifferent to the matter in hand which way the learned shall determine of it.

## CHAPTER X

### OF RETENTION

1. *Contemplation.*—The next faculty of the mind, whereby it makes a farther progress towards knowledge, is that which I call *retention*, or the keeping of those simple ideas which from sensation or reflection it hath received. This is done two ways. First, by keeping the idea which is brought into it, for some time actually in view, which is called *contemplation*.

2. *Memory.*—The other way of retention is the power to revive again in our minds those ideas which, after imprinting, have disappeared, or have been as it were laid aside out of sight. And thus we do, when we conceive heat or light, yellow or sweet, the object being removed. This is *memory*, which is, as it were, the storehouse of our ideas. For the narrow mind of man not being capable of having many ideas under view and consideration at once, it was necessary to have a repository to lay up those ideas, which at another time it might have use of. [1][But our ideas being nothing but actual perceptions in the mind, which cease to be anything when there is no perception of them, this laying up of our ideas in the repository of the memory, signifies no more but this, that the mind has a power, in many cases, to revive perceptions which it has once had, with this additional perception annexed to them,—that it has had them before. And in this sense it is that our ideas are said to be in our memories, when indeed they are actually nowhere, but only

---

[1] The sentences enclosed in brackets were added by Locke in the second edition, to meet the objection of his earliest critic, John Norris of Bemerton, whose *Cursory Reflections upon a book called an Essay concerning Human Understanding* appeared in 1690, a few months after the publication of the *Essay*. Norris had argued that Locke's language, in the first part of this section, implied the implicit or latent presence in the mind of ideas which are not actual perceptions, and was therefore inconsistent with his argument against innate ideas. Hence Locke's repudiation, in these new sentences, of the customary metaphors he had used, and his insistence that ideas which are said to be laid up in the

there is an ability in the mind, when it will, to revive them again, and, as it were, paint them anew on itself, though some with more, some with less difficulty; some more lively, and others more obscurely.] And thus it is by the assistance of this faculty that we are said to have all those ideas in our understandings, which though we do not actually contemplate, yet we can bring in sight, and make appear again and be the objects of our thoughts, without the help of those sensible qualities which first imprinted them there.

3. *Attention, repetition, pleasure, and pain fix ideas.*—Attention and repetition help much to the fixing any ideas in the memory: but those which naturally at first make the deepest and most lasting impression, are those which are accompanied with pleasure or pain. The great business of the senses being to make us take notice of what hurts or advantages the body, it is wisely ordered by nature (as has been shown) that pain should accompany the reception of several ideas; which, supplying the place of consideration and reasoning in children, and acting quicker than consideration in grown men, makes both the young and old avoid painful objects with that haste which is necessary for their preservation, and in both settles in the memory a caution for the future.

4. *Ideas fade in the memory.*—Concerning the several degrees of lasting wherewith ideas are imprinted on the memory, we may observe, that some of them have been produced in the understanding by an object affecting the senses once only, and no more than once: others, that have more than once offered themselves to the senses, have yet been

memory, are 'actually nowhere'. But merely to reassert in that way the doctrine of Bk. I leaves the characteristic feature of the revived perceptions completely unexplained—their reappearance, namely, 'with this additional perception annexed to them', that the mind has had them before. Leibniz twits Locke with his reliance on 'naked powers and faculties' (*puissances ou facultés nues*). It is obvious that the mind which paints certain ideas anew on itself must have been specifically modified, to enable it to paint just these ideas, which another mind, not having experienced them, would not be in a position to recall. Psychologists are pretty well agreed that the facts of memory cannot be stated without invoking the hypothesis of subconscious dispositions. Stout states the psychological law of retentiveness as being, that 'specific experiences leave behind them specific traces or dispositions which determine the nature and course of subsequent process' (*Manual of Psychology*, Bk. I, ch. 3). Cf. Ward's *Psychological Principles*, pp. 95–101. Professor Ward, following Leibniz, takes these dispositions as 'processes or functions more or less inhibited'.

little taken notice of : the mind, either heedless as in children, or otherwise employed as in men, intent only on one thing, not setting the stamp deep into itself. And in some, where they are set on with care and repeated impressions, either through the temper of the body or some other default, the memory is very weak. In all these cases, ideas in the mind quickly fade, and often vanish quite out of the understanding, leaving no more footsteps or remaining characters of themselves, than shadows do flying over fields of corn; and the mind is as void of them as if they never had been there.

5. Thus many of those ideas which were produced in the minds of children in the beginning of their sensation (some of which perhaps, as of some pleasures and pains, were before they were born, and others in their infancy), if in the future course of their lives they are not repeated again, are quite lost, without the least glimpse remaining of them. This may be observed in those who by some mischance have lost their sight when they were very young, in whom the ideas of colours, having been but slightly taken notice of, and ceasing to be repeated, do quite wear out ; so that some years after there is no more notion nor memory of colours left in their minds, than in those of people born blind. The memory in some men, it is true, is very tenacious, even to a miracle : but yet there seems to be a constant decay of all our ideas, even of those which are struck deepest, and in minds the most retentive ; so that if they be not sometimes renewed by repeated exercise of the senses, or reflection on those kinds of objects which at first occasioned them, the print wears out, and at last there remains nothing to be seen. Thus the ideas, as well as children, of our youth, often die before us : and our minds represent to us those tombs to which we are approaching ; where though the brass and marble remain, yet the inscriptions are effaced by time, and the imagery moulders away. The pictures drawn in our minds are laid in fading colours ; and if not sometimes refreshed, vanish and disappear. How much the constitution of our bodies, and the make of our animal spirits, are concerned in this ; and whether the temper of the brain makes this difference, that in some it retains the characters drawn on it like marble, in others like freestone, and in others little better than sand, I shall not here enquire : though it may seem probable that the constitution of the body does sometimes influence the

memory; since we oftentimes find a disease quite strip the mind of all its ideas, and the flames of a fever in a few days calcine all those images to dust and confusion, which seemed to be as lasting as if graved in marble.

6. *Constantly repeated ideas can scarce be lost.*—But concerning the ideas themselves it is easy to remark, that those that are oftenest refreshed (amongst which are those that are conveyed into the mind by more ways than one) by a frequent return of the objects or actions that produce them, fix themselves best in the memory, and remain clearest and longest there; and therefore those which are of the original qualities of bodies, viz., solidity, extension, figure, motion, and rest; and those that almost constantly affect our bodies, as heat and cold; and those which are the affections of all kinds of beings, as existence, duration, and number, which almost every object that affects our senses, every thought which employs our minds, bring along with them: these, I say, and the like ideas, are seldom quite lost whilst the mind retains any ideas at all.

7. *In remembering, the mind is often active.*—In this secondary perception,[1] as I may so call it, or viewing again the ideas that are lodged in the memory, the mind is oftentimes more than barely passive, the appearance of those dormant pictures depending sometimes on the will.[2] The mind very often sets itself on work in search of some hidden idea, and turns, as it were, the eye of the soul upon it; though sometimes too they start up in our minds of their own accord, and offer themselves to the understanding, and very often are roused and tumbled out of their dark cells into open daylight by some turbulent and tempestuous passion; our affections bringing ideas to our memory which had otherwise lain quiet and unregarded. [This farther is to be observed concerning ideas lodged in the memory, and upon occasion revived by the mind, that they are not only (as the word revive imports) none of them new ones, but also that the mind takes notice of them as of a former impression, and renews its acquaintance

---

[1] So Hobbes calls 'remembrance' a sixth sense. The other five senses take notice of objects without us, but we also notice the ideas or conceptions thus gained, so that when they come again ' we take notice that it is again ' (*Human Nature*, ch. iii. 6).

[2] In active memory or 'recollection (Aristotle's ἀνάμνησις as distinguished from μνήμη) intelligent purpose uses associative law to discover what has been *partly* forgotten. The more numerous the associations, the easier the recollective act' (Fraser).

with them as with ideas it had known before. So that though ideas formerly imprinted are not all constantly in view, yet in remembrance they are constantly known to be such as have been formerly imprinted, i. e., in view, and taken notice of before by the understanding.] [1]

8. *Two defects in the memory, oblivion and slowness.*—Memory, in an intellectual creature, is necessary in the next degree to perception. It is of so great moment, that where it is wanting all the rest of our faculties are in a great measure useless; and we in our thoughts, reasonings, and knowledge, could not proceed beyond present objects, were it not for the assistance of our memories, wherein there may be two defects:—

First, That it loses the idea quite; and so far it produces perfect ignorance. For since we can know nothing farther than we have the idea of it, when that is gone we are in perfect ignorance.

Secondly, That it moves slowly, and retrieves not the ideas that it has, and are laid up in store, quick enough to serve the mind upon occasions. This, if it be to a great degree, is stupidity; and he who through this default in his memory has not the ideas that are really preserved there ready at hand when need and occasion calls for them, were almost as good be without them quite, since they serve him to little purpose. The dull man who loses the opportunity whilst he is seeking in his mind for those ideas that should serve his turn, is not much more happy in his knowledge than one that is perfectly ignorant. It is the business therefore of the memory to furnish to the mind those dormant ideas which it has present occasion for; in the having them ready at hand on all occasions, consists that which we call invention, fancy, and quickness of parts.[2]

---

[1] Added in second edition. Cf. note, p. 79.

[2] 'The marks of a good memory', says Stout, 'are (1) the rapidity with which the power of recalling an experience is acquired; (2) the length of time during which the power of remembering lasts without being refreshed; (3) the rapidity and accuracy of the actual revival. Some persons can learn quickly and easily, but soon forget; others take a long time to learn, but also retain for a long time what they have once learned. Even when memory is retentive, there may yet be slowness and hesitancy in the actual process of reminiscence' (*Manual of Psychology*, Bk. IV, ch. 3). Stout would prefer to restrict the general term memory to the process of revival, but its associations in ordinary usage are rather with what Locke here calls retention, dubbed by Hamilton

9.[1] These are defects we may observe in the memory of one man compared with another. There is another defect which we may conceive to be in the memory of man in general, compared with some superior created intellectual beings, which in this faculty may so far excel man, that they may have constantly in view the whole sense of all their former actions, wherein no one of the thoughts they have ever had may slip out of their sight. The omniscience of God, who knows all things past, present, and to come, and to whom the thoughts of men's hearts always lie open, may satisfy us of the possibility of this. For who can doubt but God may communicate to those glorious spirits, his immediate attendants, any of his perfections in what proportion he pleases, as far as created finite beings can be capable ? It is reported of that prodigy of parts, Monsieur Pascal, that till the decay of his health had impaired his memory, he forgot nothing of what he had done, read, or thought in any part of his rational age. This is a privilege so little known to most men, that it seems almost incredible to those who, after the ordinary way, measure all others by themselves ; but yet, when considered, may help us to enlarge our thoughts towards greater perfections of it in superior ranks of spirits. For this of Monsieur Pascal was still with the narrowness that human minds are confined to here—of having great variety of ideas only by succession, not all at once. Whereas the several degrees of angels may probably have larger views, and some of them be endowed with capacities able to retain together, and constantly set before them, as in one picture, all their past knowledge at once.

10. *Brutes have memory*.—This faculty of laying up and retaining the ideas that are brought into the mind, several other animals seem to have to a great degree, as well as man. For to pass by other instances, birds' learning of tunes, and the endeavours one may observe in them to hit the notes right, put it past doubt with me that they have perception, and retain ideas in their memories, and use them for patterns. For it seems to me impossible that they should endeavour to conform their voices to notes (as it is plain they do) of

the conservative faculty, and distinguished by him from the reproductive or resuscitative faculty, with which the terms remembrance, reminiscence, and recollection are chiefly associated.

[1] Section 9 was added in the second edition.

which they had no ideas. For though I should grant sound may mechanically cause a certain motion of the animal spirits in the brains of those birds whilst the tune is actually playing, and that motion may be continued on to the muscles of the wings, and so the bird mechanically be driven away by certain noises, because this may tend to the bird's preservation; yet that can never be supposed a reason why it should cause mechanically, either whilst the tune was playing, much less after it has ceased, such a motion in the organs of the bird's voice as should conform it to the notes of a foreign sound, which imitation can be of no use to the bird's preservation. But, which is more, it cannot with any appearance of reason be supposed (much less proved) that birds, without sense and memory, can approach their notes, nearer and nearer by degrees, to a tune played yesterday; which if they have no idea of it in their memory, is now nowhere, nor can be a pattern for them to imitate, or which any repeated essays can bring them nearer to.

## CHAPTER XI

### OF DISCERNING, AND OTHER OPERATIONS OF THE MIND

1. *No knowledge without discerning.*—Another faculty we may take notice of in our minds, is that of discerning and distinguishing between the several ideas it has. It is not enough to have a confused perception of something in general: unless the mind had a distinct perception of different objects and their qualities, it would be capable of very little knowledge; though the bodies that affect us were as busy about us as they are now, and the mind were continually employed in thinking. On this faculty of distinguishing one thing from another, depends the evidence and certainty of several even very general propositions, which have passed for innate truths; because men, overlooking the true cause why those propositions find universal assent, impute it wholly to native uniform impressions: whereas it in truth depends upon this clear discerning faculty of the mind, whereby it perceives two ideas to be the same or different. But of this more hereafter.[1]

2. *The difference of wit and judgement.*—How much the imperfection of accurately discriminating ideas one from

[1] Cf. II. 21. 5; IV. 1. 4; 2. 1; 7. 19; 17. 14.

another lies, either in the dullness or faults of the organs of sense, or want of acuteness, exercise, or attention in the understanding, or hastiness and precipitancy natural to some tempers, I will not here examine : it suffices to take notice, that this is one of the operations that the mind may reflect on and observe in itself. If in having our ideas in the memory ready at hand consists quickness of parts ; in this of having them unconfused, and being able nicely to distinguish one thing from another where there is but the least difference, consists in a great measure the exactness of judgement and clearness of reason which is to be observed in one man above another. And hence, perhaps, may be given some reason of that common observation, that men who have a great deal of wit and prompt memories, have not always the clearest judgement or deepest reason. For wit lying most in the assemblage of ideas, and putting those together with quickness and variety wherein can be found any resemblance or congruity, thereby to make up pleasant pictures and agreeable visions in the fancy : judgement, on the contrary, lies quite on the other side, in separating carefully one from another ideas wherein can be found the least difference, thereby to avoid being misled by similitude, and by affinity to take one thing for another. This is a way of proceeding quite contrary to metaphor and allusion, wherein for the most part lies that entertainment and pleasantry of wit which strikes so lively on the fancy, and therefore so acceptable to all people; because its beauty appears at first sight, and there is required no labour of thought to examine what truth or reason there is in it. The mind, without looking any farther, rests satisfied with the agreeableness of the picture and the gaiety of the fancy : and it is a kind of an affront to go about to examine it by the severe rules of truth and good reason ; whereby it appears that it consists in something that is not perfectly conformable to them.

4. *Comparing.*—The *comparing* them one with another, in respect of extent, degrees, time, place, or any other circumstances, is another operation of the mind about its ideas, and is that upon which depends all that large tribe of ideas, comprehended under *relation* ; which of how vast an extent it is, I shall have occasion to consider hereafter.[1]

[1] Chs. 25-8 of this Book.

5. *Brutes compare, but imperfectly.*—How far brutes partake in this faculty is not easy to determine ; I imagine they have it not in any great degree : for though they probably have several ideas distinct enough, yet it seems to me to be the prerogative of human understanding, when it has sufficiently distinguished any ideas so as to perceive them to be perfectly different, and so consequently two, to cast about and consider in what circumstances they are capable to be compared.[1] And therefore, I think, beasts compare not their ideas farther than some sensible circumstances annexed to the objects themselves. The other power of comparing which may be observed in men, belonging to general ideas, and useful only to abstract reasonings, we may probably conjecture beasts have not.

6. *Compounding.*—The next operation we may observe in the mind about its ideas is *composition* ; whereby it puts together several of those simple ones it has received from sensation and reflection, and combines them into complex ones. Under this of composition may be reckoned also that of *enlarging ;*[2] wherein though the composition does not so much appear as in more complex ones, yet it is nevertheless a putting several ideas together, though of the same kind. Thus, by adding several units together we make the idea of a dozen, and putting together the repeated ideas of several perches we frame that of a furlong.

7. *Brutes compound but little.*—In this also, I suppose, brutes come far short of men. For though they take in, and retain together, several combinations of simple ideas, as possibly the shape, smell, and voice of his master make up the complex

---

[1] The sections on ' comparing ' and ' abstracting ' are the heart of this chapter. They concern what Locke rightly calls ' the prerogative of human understanding '—the conceptual reason, as distinguished from the associative processes of the merely animal life. Locke here states, in very simple but very apt words, in what the distinction between these two levels of intelligence consists. The human being is not satisfied with a vague impression of resemblance ; he casts about and considers ' in what circumstances ' the two objects resemble one another, and so arrives at concepts or ' abstract ideas ', clearly defined, on which the possibility of scientific knowledge depends. The frankest acceptance of the evolutionary view of man's animal ancestry ought not to prevent any one from recognizing the ' perfect distinction ' which Locke asserts between the two types of mind in section 10.

[2] This refers, as the examples show, to the variety of complex ideas which Locke calls ' simple modes '. See in particular chs. 13–17.

idea a dog has of him, or rather are so many distinct marks whereby he knows him; yet I do not think they do of themselves ever compound them and make complex ideas. And perhaps even where we think they have complex ideas, it is only one simple one that directs them in the knowledge of several things, which possibly they distinguish less by their sight than we imagine. For I have been credibly informed that a bitch will nurse, play with, and be fond of young foxes, as much as and in place of her puppies, if you can but get them once to suck her so long that her milk may go through them. And those animals which have a numerous brood of young ones at once, appear not to have any knowledge of their number; for though they are mightily concerned for any of their young that are taken from them whilst they are in sight or hearing, yet if one or two of them be stolen from them in their absence or without noise, they appear not to miss them, or to have any sense that their number is lessened.

8. *Naming.*—When children have by repeated sensations got ideas fixed in their memories, they begin by degrees to learn the use of signs. And when they have got the skill to apply the organs of speech to the framing of articulate sounds, they begin to make use of words to signify their ideas to others. These verbal signs they sometimes borrow from others, and sometimes make themselves, as one may observe among the new and unusual names children often give to things in their first use of language.

9. *Abstraction.*—The use of words then being to stand as outward marks of our internal ideas, and those ideas being taken from particular things, if every particular idea that we take in should have a distinct name, names must be endless. To prevent this, the mind makes the particular ideas,[1] received from particular objects, to become general; which is done by considering them as they are in the mind such

[1] Locke asserts emphatically (IV. 17. 8): 'Every man's reasoning and knowledge is only about the ideas existing in his own mind, which are truly every one of them particular existences. . . . So that the perception of the agreement or disagreement of our particular ideas is the whole and utmost of all our knowledge. Universality is but accidental to it.' This account of universality or abstraction should be compared with Bk. III, ch. 3, 'Of General Terms', with the *locus classicus* on 'the general idea of a triangle' (IV. 7. 9), and with Berkeley's criticism of 'abstract ideas', in the Introduction to the *Principles of Human Knowledge* and elsewhere. See the relative Notes, pp. 226, 230, 302, 352.

appearances, separate from all other existences and the circumstances of real existence, as time, place, or any other concomitant ideas. This is called *abstraction*, whereby ideas taken from particular beings become general representatives of all of the same kind; and their names general names, applicable to whatever exists conformable to such abstract ideas. Such precise, naked appearances in the mind, without considering how, whence, or with what others they came there, the understanding lays up (with names commonly annexed to them) as the standards to rank real existences into sorts, as they agree with these patterns, and to denominate them accordingly. Thus, the same colour being observed to-day in chalk or snow, which the mind yesterday received from milk, it considers that appearance alone, makes it a representative of all of that kind; and having given it the name whiteness, it by that sound signifies the same quality wheresoever to be imagined or met with; and thus universals, whether ideas or terms, are made.

10. *Brutes abstract not.*—If it may be doubted whether beasts compound and enlarge their ideas that way to any degree, this, I think, I may be positive in, that the power of abstracting is not at all in them, and that the having of general ideas is that which puts a perfect distinction betwixt man and brutes, and is an excellency which the faculties of brutes do by no means attain to.[1] For it is evident we observe no footsteps in them of making use of general signs for universal ideas; from which we have reason to imagine, that

[1] ' The faculty the brutes have for making *consecutions*', says Leibniz, ' is something inferior to the reason of man. The consecutions of the brutes are like those of simple empirics, who claim that what has sometimes happened will happen again in a case where something strikes them as similar, without being able to judge whether the same reasons hold good.' ' They only guide themselves by examples, for, so far as we can judge of them, they never attain to the formation of necessary propositions; while men are capable of demonstrative sciences ' (*New Essays*, Preface). The emphasis here laid on the fundamental distinction between the conceptual reason of man and the typically animal level of intelligence is not inconsistent with Locke's statement elsewhere that ' in all parts of the creation that fall under human observation there is a gradual connexion of one with another without any great or discernible gaps between, [and therefore] it is a hard matter to say where sensible and rational begin, and where insensible and irrational end. . . . If we compare the understanding and abilities of some men and some brutes, we shall find so little difference that it will be hard to say that that of the man is either clearer or larger ' (IV. 16. 12). Cf. III. 6. 12.

they have not the faculty of abstracting or making general ideas, since they have no use of words or any other general signs.

11. Nor can it be imputed to their want of fit organs to frame articulate sounds, that they have no use or knowledge of general words : since many of them, we find, can fashion such sounds and pronounce words distinctly enough, but never with any such application. And, on the other side, men who, through some defect in the organs, want words, yet fail not to express their universal ideas by signs, which serve them instead of general words, a faculty which we see beasts come short in. And therefore I think we may suppose, that it is in this that the species of brutes are discriminated from man ; and it is that proper difference wherein they are wholly separated, and which at last widens to so vast a distance. For if they have any ideas at all, and are not bare machines (as some[1] would have them), we cannot deny them to have some reason. It seems as evident to me that they do, some of them, in certain instances, reason, as that they have sense ; but it is only in particular ideas, just as they received them from their senses. They are, the best of them, tied up within those narrow bounds, and have not (as I think) the faculty to enlarge them by any kind of abstraction.

14. *Method.*—These, I think, are the first faculties and operations of the mind which it makes use of in understanding ; and though they are exercised about all its ideas in general, yet the instances I have hitherto given have been chiefly in simple ideas ; and I have subjoined the explication of these faculties of the mind to that of simple ideas, before I come to what I have to say concerning complex ones, for these following reasons :—

First, Because, several of these faculties being exercised at first principally about simple ideas, we might, by following nature in its ordinary method, trace and discover them in their rise, progress, and gradual improvements.

Secondly, Because, observing the faculties of the mind, how they operate about simple ideas, which are usually in most men's minds much more clear, precise, and distinct than complex ones, we may the better examine and learn how the mind abstracts, denominates, compares, and exercises its other operations about those which are complex, wherein we are much more liable to mistake.

[1] The Cartesians.

Thirdly, Because these very operations of the mind about ideas received from sensation are themselves, when reflected on, another set of ideas, derived from that other source of our knowledge which I call reflection; and therefore fit to be considered in this place after the simple ideas of sensation. Of compounding, comparing, abstracting, &c., I have but just spoken, having occasion to treat of them more at large in other places.

15. *These are the beginning of human knowledge.*—And thus I have given a short and, I think, true *history of the first beginnings of human knowledge*; whence the mind has its first objects, and by what steps it makes its progress to the laying in and storing up those ideas out of which is to be framed all the knowledge it is capable of; wherein I must appeal to experience and observation whether I am in the right. [16.] This is the only way that I can discover whereby the ideas of things are brought into the understanding. If other men have either innate ideas or infused principles, they have reason to enjoy them; and if they are sure of it, it is impossible for others to deny them the privilege that they have above their neighbours. I can speak but of what I find in myself.

17. *Dark room.*—I pretend not to teach, but to enquire; and therefore cannot but confess here again, that external and internal sensation are the only passages that I can find of knowledge to the understanding. These alone, as far as I can discover, are the windows by which light is let into this *dark room*. For methinks the understanding is not much unlike a closet wholly shut from light, with only some little opening left to let in external visible [1] resemblances or ideas of things without: would the pictures coming into such a dark room but stay there, and lie so orderly as to be found upon occasion, it would very much resemble the understanding of a man, in reference to all objects of sight,[1] and the ideas of them.

These are my guesses concerning the means whereby the understanding comes to have and retain simple ideas, and the modes of them, with some other operations about them. I proceed now to examine some of these simple ideas and their modes a little more particularly.

---

[1] ' Why " visible " or " objects of sight " only ? ' asks Fraser; Locke's simple ideas come in by all the five or more senses.

## CHAPTER XII

### OF COMPLEX IDEAS

**1. *Made by the mind out of simple ones*.**—We have hitherto considered those ideas, in the reception whereof the mind is only passive, which are those simple ones received from sensation and reflection before mentioned, whereof the mind cannot make one to itself, nor have any idea which does not wholly consist of them. [But as the mind is wholly passive in the reception of all its simple ideas, so it exerts several acts of its own, whereby out of its simple ideas, as the materials and foundations of the rest, the other are framed. The acts of the mind wherein it exerts its power over its simple ideas are chiefly these three :[1] (1) Combining several simple ideas into one compound one ; and thus all complex ideas are made.

[1] The insertion of the passage enclosed in brackets, made in the fourth edition, confuses Locke's classification, which was originally, as in ch. 2, into simple and complex ideas, the complex being subdivided into modes, substances, and relations. In the inserted passage, complex ideas appear as one variety of those due to the activity of mind, the other varieties being ideas of relation and general ideas. In the subsequent chapters in this Book, in which he works out his scheme in detail, no special chapter is devoted to general ideas, but they are dealt with under the head of General Terms in Bk. III, ch. 3, and incidentally elsewhere.

Professor Gibson points out very clearly that, in either form, Locke's classification implies the break-down of the conception, with which he apparently starts, of 'a quasi-mechanical composition' of elementary data. Even complex ideas in the narrower sense of compound ideas cannot be adequately explained on such a theory. In the case of 'mixed modes' Locke himself tells us that 'the mind ties the parts into one idea : it is plain it has its unity from an act of the mind combining those several simple ideas together and considering them as one complex one, consisting of those parts' (II. 22. 4) ; and even when experience presents the simple ideas together, as in substances, a similar unifying act is involved, due to the power of the mind ' to consider several of these united together as one idea'. Locke does not think that brutes do of themselves ever compound their simple ideas and make complex ones (II. 11. 7). Ideas of relation, on the other hand, are not the result of compounding at all ; they are due to an overt act of comparison, and, when formed, such an idea ' is for the mind a distinct object of thought over and above the terms from the comparison of which it results'. It is dependent on sensation and reflection only in the sense that the terms to be compared are derived from these sources ; hence, in Locke's phrase, our ideas of relation always ' terminate in ' or are ' ultimately founded on ' such simple ideas (*op. cit.*, pp. 61-7).

(2) The second is bringing two ideas, whether simple or complex, together, and setting them by one another, so as to take a view of them at once, without uniting them into one ; by which it gets all its ideas of relations. (3) The third is separating them from all other ideas that accompany them in their real existence ; this is called abstraction : and thus all its general ideas are made. This shows man's power and its way of operation to be much-what the same in the material and intellectual world. For, the materials in both being such as he has no power over, either to make or destroy, all that man can do is either to unite them together, or to set them by one another, or wholly separate them. I shall here begin with the first of these in the consideration of complex ideas, and come to the other two in their due places.] As simple ideas are observed to exist in several combinations united together, so the mind has a power to consider several of them united together as one idea ; and that not only as they are united in external objects, but as itself has joined them. Ideas thus made up of several simple ones put together I call *complex* ; such as are beauty, gratitude, a man, an army, the universe ; which, though complicated of various simple ideas or complex ideas made up of simple ones, yet are, when the mind pleases, considered each by itself as one entire thing, and signified by one name.

2. *Made voluntarily*.—In this faculty of repeating and joining together its ideas, the mind has great power in varying and multiplying the objects of its thoughts infinitely beyond what sensation or reflection furnished it with : but all this still confined to those simple ideas which it received from those two sources, and which are the ultimate materials of all its compositions. For simple ideas are all from things themselves ; and of these the mind can have no more nor other than what are suggested to it. It can have no other ideas of sensible qualities than what come from without by the senses, nor any ideas of other kind of operations of a thinking substance than what it finds in itself : but when it has once got these simple ideas, it is not confined barely to observation, and what offers itself from without ; it can, by its own power, put together those ideas it has, and make new complex ones which it never received so united.

3. *Are either modes, substances, or relations*.—Complex ideas, however compounded and decompounded, though their

number be infinite, and the variety endless wherewith they fill and entertain the thoughts of men, yet I think they may be all reduced under these three heads: 1. *Modes.* 2. *Substances.* 3. *Relations.*

4. *Modes.*—First, *Modes* I call such complex ideas which, however compounded, contain not in them the supposition of subsisting by themselves, but are considered as dependences on, or affections of substances; such as are the ideas signified by the words triangle, gratitude, murder, &c. And if in this I use the word mode in somewhat a different sense from its ordinary signification, I beg pardon; it being unavoidable in discourses differing from the ordinary received notions, either to make new words, or to use old words in somewhat a new signification: the latter whereof, in our present case, is perhaps the more tolerable of the two.

5. *Simple and mixed modes.*—Of these modes there are two sorts which deserve distinct consideration. First, there are some which are only variations or different combinations of the same simple idea, without the mixture of any other, as a dozen, or score; which are nothing but the ideas of so many distinct units added together: and these I call *simple modes*, as being contained within the bounds of one simple idea. Secondly, there are others compounded of simple ideas of several kinds, put together to make one complex one; v. g., beauty, consisting of a certain composition of colour and figure, causing delight in the beholder; theft, which, being the concealed change of the possession of anything, without the consent of the proprietor, contains, as is visible, a combination of several ideas of several kinds: and these I call *mixed modes*.

6. *Substances, single or collective.*—Secondly, the ideas of *substances* are such combinations of simple ideas as are taken to represent distinct particular things subsisting by themselves, in which the supposed or confused idea of substance, such as it is, is always the first and chief. Thus, if to substance be joined the simple idea of a certain dull whitish colour, with certain degrees of weight, hardness, ductility, and fusibility, we have the idea of lead; and a combination of the ideas of a certain sort of figure, with the powers of motion, thought, and reasoning, joined to substance, make the ordinary idea of a man. Now of substances also there are two sorts of ideas, one of single substances, as they exist separately, as of a man

or a sheep; the other of several of those put together, as an army of men, or flock of sheep; which collective ideas of several substances thus put together, are as much each of them one single idea as that of a man or an unit.

7. *Relation.*—Thirdly, the last sort of complex ideas is that we call *relation*,[1] which consists in the consideration and comparing one idea with another. Of these several kinds we shall treat in their order.

8. *The abstrusest ideas from the two sources.*—If we will trace the progress of our minds, and with attention observe how it repeats, adds together, and unites its simple ideas received from sensation or reflection, it will lead us farther than we at first perhaps we should have imagined. And I believe we shall find, if we warily observe the originals of our notions, that even the most abstruse ideas, how remote soever they may seem from sense, or from any operation of our own minds, are yet only such as the understanding frames to itself, by repeating and joining together ideas that it had either from objects of sense, or from its own operations about them : so that those even large and abstract ideas are *derived from sensation or reflection*, being no other than what the mind, by the ordinary use of its own faculties, employed about ideas received from objects of sense, or from the operations it observes in itself about them, may and does attain unto. This I shall endeavour to show in the ideas we have of space, time, and infinity, and some few other, that seem the most remote from those originals.

## CHAPTER XIII

### OF SIMPLE MODES; AND FIRST, OF THE SIMPLE MODES OF SPACE

1. *Simple modes.*—Those modifications of any one simple idea (which, as has been said, I call simple modes) are as perfectly different and distinct ideas in the mind as those of the greatest distance or contrariety. For the idea of two is as distinct from that of one, as blueness from heat, or either of them from any number; and yet it is made up only of that simple idea of an unit repeated; and repetitions of this kind joined together make those distinct simple modes of a dozen, a gross, a million.

[1] All our ideas, 'when attentively considered', Locke admits, include in them ' some kind of relation ' (II. 21. 3).

2. *Idea of space.*—I shall begin with the simple idea of space. I have showed above (ch. 4), that we get the idea of space both by our sight and touch;[1] which I think is so evident, that it would be as needless to go to prove that men perceive by their sight a distance between bodies of different colours, or between the parts of the same body, as that they see colours themselves: nor is it less obvious that they can do so in the dark by feeling and touch.

3. *Space and extension.*—This space, considered barely in length between any two beings, without considering anything else between them, is called *distance*; if considered in length, breadth, and thickness, I think it may be called *capacity*; [the term *extension* is usually applied to it, in what manner soever considered.][2]

4. *Immensity.*—Each different distance is a different modification of space, and each idea of any different distance or space is a simple mode of this idea. Men, for the use and by the custom of measuring, settle in their minds the ideas of certain stated lengths, such as are an inch, foot, yard, fathom, mile, diameter of the earth, &c., which are so many distinct ideas made up only of space. When any such stated lengths or measures of space are made familiar to men's thoughts, they can in their minds repeat them as often as they will, without mixing or joining to them the idea of body or anything else; and frame to themselves the idea of long, square, or cubic feet, yards, or fathoms, here amongst the bodies of the universe, or else beyond the utmost bounds of all bodies; and, by adding these still one to another, enlarge their idea of space as much as they please. This power of repeating or doubling any idea we have of any distance, and adding it to the former as often as we will, without being ever able to come to any stop or stint, let us enlarge it as much as we will, is that which gives us the idea of *immensity*.

5. *Figure.*—There is another modification of this idea,

---

[1] Locke's vague statement marks only the beginning of the analysis of our spatial perception.

[2] This is the reading of the fourth edition. In the first three editions Locke had been inclined to use 'extension' in a more limited sense 'for an affection of matter, or the distance of the extremities of particular solid bodies; and space in the more general signification, for distance, with or without solid matter possessing it'. In a sentence added to section 27 of this chapter in the fourth edition he makes a similar suggestion.

which is nothing but the relation which the parts of the termination of extension or circumscribed space have amongst themselves. This the touch discovers in sensible bodies, whose extremities come within our reach ; and the eye takes both from bodies and colours, whose boundaries are within its view.

7. *Place.*—Another idea coming under this head and belonging to this tribe, is that we call *place*. As in simple space we consider the relation of distance between any two bodies or points, so in our idea of place we consider the relation of distance betwixt anything and any two or more points which are considered as keeping the same distance one with another, and so considered as at rest ; for when we find any thing at the same distance now which it was yesterday from any two or more points, which have not since changed their distance one with another, and with which we then compared it, we say it hath kept the same place.

8. Thus a company of chess-men standing on the same squares of the chess-board where we left them, we say they are all in the same place, or unmoved,—though perhaps the chess-board hath been in the meantime carried out of one room into another,—because we compared them only to the parts of the chess-board which keep the same distance one with another. The chess-board, we also say, is in the same place it was, if it remain in the same part of the cabin, though perhaps the ship which it is in sails all the while : and the ship is said to be in the same place, supposing it kept the same distance with the parts of the neighbouring land, though perhaps the earth hath turned round, and so both chess-men, and board, and ship have every one changed place, in respect of remoter bodies, which have kept the same distance one with another.

9. But this modification of distance we call place, being made by men for their common use, men consider and determine of this place by reference to those adjacent things which best served to their present purpose, without considering other things which to another purpose would better determine the place of the same thing. So if any one should ask in what place are the verses which report the story of Nisus and Euryalus, it would be very improper to determine this place by saying, they were in such a part of the earth, or in Bodley's library ; but the right designation of the place would be by the parts of Virgil's works, and the proper answer would be,

that these verses were about the middle of the ninth book of his *Aeneid*, and that they have been always constantly in the same place ever since Virgil was printed.

10. That our idea of place is nothing else but such a relative position of anything as I have before mentioned, I think is plain, and will be easily admitted when we consider that we can have no idea of the place of the universe, though we can of all the parts of it; because beyond that we have not the idea of any fixed, distinct, particular beings, in reference to which we can imagine it to have any relation of distance; but all beyond it is one uniform space or expansion, wherein the mind finds no variety, no marks. For to say that the world is somewhere, means no more than that it does exist; this, though a phrase borrowed from place, signifying only its existence, not location; and when one can find out and frame in his mind clearly and distinctly the place of the universe, he will be able to tell us whether it moves or stands still in the undistinguishable inane of infinite space.

11. *Extension and body not the same.*—There are some that would persuade us that body and extension are the same thing;[1] who either change the signification of words, which

---

[1] The remainder of this chapter is occupied with a polemic against Descartes's identification of body with extension. This is, in a sense, a parallel to Locke's argument in the first chapter against the Cartesian doctrine that the soul thinks always. Just as he objected there that the doctrine was arrived at, not as a conclusion from observed facts but from the initial definition of the soul as a thinking substance, so here (and again IV. 7. 12–13) he argues that the doctrine of the impossibility of a vacuum or 'space void of body' is begged in the initial definition of matter as *res extensa*, extension being taken as the 'essence' of matter. The opposition to the Cartesian *plenum* was general among English philosophers of the seventeenth century; it was common ground on which the Cambridge Platonists and Hobbes could meet. Henry More, regarding extension as a characteristic of everything that exists, made it an attribute of God, and Newton refers to space as 'the boundless uniform sensorium' of God. God is substantially present in every portion of space. In a scholium to one of the propositions of the *Principia* (Bk. III, 42) he says: 'He endures for ever and is everywhere present; by existing always and everywhere he constitutes duration and space.' Newton's *Principia* was published in 1687, three years before the *Essay*, and it was no doubt Newton's definition of 'absolute space,' which 'in its own nature, without reference to anything external, remains always similar and immovable', that gave final shape to Locke's view of space, just as the characteristics of Newton's 'absolute, true and mathematical time' reappear in his account of duration. Locke had at one time been inclined to regard

I would not suspect them of, they having so severely condemned the philosophy of others because it hath been too much placed in the uncertain meaning or deceitful obscurity of doubtful or insignificant terms. If therefore they mean by body and extension the same that other people do, viz., by body, something that is solid and extended, whose parts are separable and movable different ways; and by extension, only the space that lies between the extremities of those solid coherent parts, and which is possessed by them, they confound very different ideas one with another. For I appeal to every man's own thoughts, whether the idea of space be not as distinct from that of solidity, as it is from the idea of scarlet colour? It is true, solidity cannot exist without extension, neither can scarlet colour exist without extension; but this hinders not but that they are distinct ideas. Many ideas require others as necessary to their existence or conception, which yet are very distinct ideas. Motion can neither be, nor be conceived, without space; and yet motion is not space, nor space motion; space can exist without it, and they are very distinct ideas; and so, I think, are those of space and solidity. Solidity is so inseparable an idea from body, that upon that depends its filling of space, its contact, impulse, and communication of motion upon impulse. And if it be a reason to prove that spirit is different from body, because thinking includes not the idea of extension in it, the same reason will be as valid, I suppose, to prove that space is not body, because it includes not the idea of solidity [1] in it;

space as 'imaginary'—no more real than number—when separated from matter or body. Subsequently he had tended to treat it as a mere relation—in the case of the extension of bodies 'nothing but the relation of the distance of the extremities', in the case of space without body as 'a bare possibility of body to exist'. On this view 'space, as antecedent to body or some determinate being is in effect nothing'. For his final view, based upon Newton's, space has a positive reality of its own and exists as 'a uniform infinite ocean' prior to the bodies which exist and move within it; and at several points he shows himself inclined to base its existence on the omnipresence of God (e. g. II. 15. 2–3). See Professor Gibson's admirable account of the development of Locke's theory of Space and the influences which shaped it, *Locke's Theory of Knowledge*, pp. 245–54.

[1] Solidity or impenetrability in an absolute sense, it may be argued, cannot be a datum of sense. Hardness, which is all that can properly be claimed under the head of resistance, is treated by Descartes as a secondary quality like colour, and, in that sense, a subjective affection which does not reveal the essence of the object. Cf. note 1, p. 58.

space and soidity being as distinct ideas as thinking and extension, and as wholly separable in the mind one from another. Body, then, and extension, it is evident, are two distinct ideas. For,

12. First, Extension includes no solidity nor resistance to the motion of body, as body does.

13. Secondly, The parts of pure space are inseparable one from the other; so that the continuity cannot be separated, neither really nor mentally. For I demand of any one to remove any part of it from another with which it is continued, even so much as in thought. To divide and separate actually, is, as I think, by removing the parts one from another, to make two superficies, where before there was a continuity: and to divide mentally, is to make in the mind two superficies, where before there was a continuity, and consider them as removed one from the other; which can only be done in things considered by the mind as capable of being separated. It is true, a man may consider so much of such a space as is answerable or commensurate to a foot, without considering the rest; which is indeed a partial consideration, but not so much as mental separation or division.

14. Thirdly, The parts of pure space are immovable, which follows from their inseparability; motion being nothing but change of distance between any two things: but this cannot be between parts that are inseparable; which therefore must needs be at perpetual rest one amongst another.

Thus the determined[1] idea of simple space distinguishes it plainly and sufficiently from body; since its parts are inseparable, immovable, and without resistance to the motion of body.

16.[2] *Division of beings into bodies and spirits, proves not*

[1] For Locke's use of this term see note, p. 204.

[2] This section and the three following discuss what we may call the ontological status of space. Is it to be regarded as a substance, an attribute, a relation, or what? Kant, whose views on space also passed through several phases, refers similarly to the question whether space has a substantial existence of its own or exists only as an attribute of things (or a relation of things to one another). Because he can be satisfied with neither view, he propounds his own theory of space as subjective—a form of human perception. Kant passed, in the course of his own development from a relational or quasi-attributive view, ultimately derived from Leibniz, to an acceptance of Newton's absolute

*space and body the same.*—Those who contend that space and body are the same, bring this dilemma : either this space is something or nothing ; if nothing be between two bodies, they must necessarily touch : if it be allowed to be something, they ask, whether it be body or spirit ? To which I answer by another question, who told them that there was, or could be nothing but solid beings, which could not think, and thinking beings that were not extended ? which is all they mean by the terms body and spirit.

17. *Substance which we know not, no proof against space without body.*—If it be demanded (as usually it is), whether this space, void of body, be *substance* or *accident,* I shall readily answer, I know not ; nor shall be ashamed to own my ignorance, till they that ask show me a clear distinct idea of substance. [18.] Names made at pleasure neither alter the nature of things, nor make us understand them but as they are signs of and stand for determined ideas. And I desire those who lay so much stress on the sound of these two syllables, *substance,* to consider whether, applying it as they do to the infinite incomprehensible God, to finite spirits, and to body, it be in the same sense ; and whether it stands for the same idea, when each of those three so different beings are called substances ? If so, whether it will not thence follow, that God, spirits, and body, agreeing in the same common nature of substance, differ not any otherwise than in a bare different modification of that substance ; as a tree and a pebble, being in the same sense body, and agreeing in the common nature of body, differ only in a bare modification of that common matter ; which will be a very harsh doctrine. If they say that they apply it to God, finite spirits, and matter, in three different significations, and that it stands for one idea when God is said to be a substance, for another when the soul is called substance, and for a third when a body is called so— if the name substance stands for three several distinct ideas, they would do well to make known those distinct ideas, or at least to give three distinct names to them, to prevent, in

space, but eventually became dissatisfied with the conception of space and time as ' two self-subsisting non-entities, which exist for the purpose of containing in themselves everything that is real ' (*Critique of Pure Reason,* Aesthetic, section 8). That the quasi-substantial mode of existence ascribed to Newtonian space involves a real difficulty is shown by the readiness of its supporters to fall back (in the last resort) on the conception of it as a species of divine attribute.

so important a notion, the confusion and errors that will naturally follow from the promiscuous use of so doubtful a term; which is so far from being suspected to have three distinct, that in ordinary use it has scarce one clear distinct signification; and if they can thus make three distinct ideas of substance, what hinders why another may not make a fourth?

19. *Substance and accidents of little use in philosophy.*—They who first ran into the notion of *accidents*, as a sort of real beings that needed something to inhere in, were forced to find out the word *substance* to support them. Had the poor Indian philosopher (who imagined that the earth also wanted something to bear it up) but thought of this word substance, he needed not to have been at the trouble to find an elephant to support it, and a tortoise to support his elephant: the word substance would have done it effectually. And he that enquired, might have taken it for as good an answer from an Indian philosopher, that substance, without knowing what it is, is that which supports the earth, as we take it for a sufficient answer and good doctrine from our European philosophers, that substance, without knowing what it is, is that which supports accidents. So that of substance we have no idea of what it is, but only a confused obscure one of what it does.

20. Whatever a learned man may do here, an intelligent American, who inquired into the nature of things, would scarce take it for a satisfactory account, if, desiring to learn our architecture, he should be told, that a pillar was a thing supported by a basis, and a basis something that supported a pillar. Were the Latin words *inhaerentia* and *substantia* put into the plain English ones that answer them, and were called *sticking on* and *under-propping*, they would better discover to us the very great clearness there is in the doctrine of substance and accidents, and show of what use they are in deciding of questions in philosophy.

21. *A vacuum beyond the utmost bounds of body.*—But to return to our idea of space. If body be not supposed infinite, which I think no one will affirm, I would ask, whether, if God placed a man at the extremity of corporeal beings, he could not stretch his hand beyond his body? If he could, then he would put his arm where there was before space without body; and if there he spread his fingers, there would still be space between them without body.

The truth is, these men must either own that they think body infinite [1] though they are loth to speak it out, or else affirm that space is not body. For I would fain meet with that thinking man, that can in his thoughts set any bounds to space, more than he can to duration; or by thinking, hope to arrive at the end of either: and therefore, if his idea of eternity be infinite, so is his idea of immensity; they are both finite or infinite alike.

22. *The power of annihilation proves a vacuum.*—Farther, those who assert the impossibility of space existing without matter, must not only make body infinite, but must also deny a power in God to annihilate any part of matter. No one, I suppose, will deny that God can put an end to all motion that is in matter, and fix all the bodies of the universe in a perfect quiet and rest, and continue them so as long as he pleases. Whoever then will allow that God can, during such a general rest, *annihilate* either this book or the body of him that reads it, must necessarily admit the possibility of a *vacuum*; for it is evident that the space that was filled by the parts of the annihilated body will still remain, and be a space without body. For the circumambient bodies being in perfect rest, are a wall of adamant, and in that state make it a perfect impossibility for any other body to get into that space. And indeed the necessary motion of one particle of matter into the place from whence another particle of matter is removed, is but a consequence from the supposition of plenitude, which will therefore need some better proof than a supposed matter of fact, which experiment can never make out; our own clear and distinct ideas plainly satisfying us, that there is no necessary connexion between space and solidity, since we can conceive the one without the other. And those who dispute for or against a *vacuum*, do thereby confess they have distinct ideas of *vacuum* and *plenum*.

23. *Motion proves a vacuum.*[2]—But not to go so far as

[1] The Cartesians do say that matter has no limits, but, as Leibniz points out, 'they have changed the term infinite into indefinite, for there is never an infinite whole in the world, although there are always some wholes greater than others to infinity'.

[2] Locke's argument depends on the assumption that matter consists of discrete and absolutely solid corpuscles, whereas the Cartesians held matter to have the same continuity as we commonly attribute to extension. Hence they believed motion to be possible. A particular space, though inseparable from body, is not inseparable from any

beyond the utmost bounds of body in the universe, nor appeal to God's omnipotency to find a *vacuum*, the motion of bodies that are in our view and neighbourhood seems to me plainly to evince it. For I desire any one so to divide a solid body, of any dimension he pleases, as to make it possible for the solid parts to move up and down freely every way within the bounds of that superficies, if there be not left in it a void space as big as the least part into which he has divided the said solid body.

24. *The ideas of space and body distinct.*—But the question being here, whether the idea of space or extension be the same with the idea of body, it is not necessary to prove the real existence of a *vacuum*, but the idea of it ; which it is plain men have when they enquire and dispute whether there be a *vacuum* or no. For if they had not the idea of space without body, they could not make a question about its existence ; and if their idea of body did not include in it something more than the bare idea of space, they could have no doubt about the plenitude of the world ; and it would be as absurd to demand whether there were space without body, as whether there were space without space, or body without body, since these were but different names of the same idea.

25. *Extension being inseparable from body, proves it not the same.*—It is true, the idea of extension joins itself so inseparably with all visible and most tangible qualities, that it suffers us to see no one, or feel very few external objects, without taking in impressions of extension too. This readiness of extension to make itself be taken notice of so constantly with other ideas, has been the occasion, I guess, that some have made the whole essence of body to consist in extension ; which is not much to be wondered at, since some have had their minds, by their eyes and touch (the busiest of all their senses), so filled with the idea of extension, and as it were, wholly possessed with it, that they allowed no existence to anything that had not extension. But I shall desire them to consider, that had they reflected on their ideas of tastes and smells as much as on those of sight and touch ; nay, had they examined their ideas of hunger and thirst, and several other pains, they would have found that they included in them no idea of extension at all ; which is but an affection of body, as well as

particular body. If water is poured from a glass, the space vacated is immediately taken by air.

the rest discoverable by our senses, which are scarce acute enough to look into the pure essences of things.

26. If those ideas which are constantly joined to all others must therefore be concluded to be the essence of those things which have constantly those ideas joined to them, and are inseparable from them, then unity is, without doubt, the essence of everything; for there is not any object of sensation or reflection which does not carry with it the idea of one: but the weakness of this kind of argument we have already shown sufficiently.

27. *Ideas of space and solidity distinct.*—To conclude: Whatever men shall think concerning the existence of a *vacuum*, this is plain to me—that we have as clear an idea of space distinct from solidity, as we have of solidity distinct from motion, or motion from space. We have not any two more distinct ideas; and we can as easily conceive space without solidity, as we can conceive body or space without motion, though it be ever so certain that neither body nor motion can exist without space. But whether any one will take space to be only a relation resulting from the existence of other beings at a distance, or whether they will think the words of the most knowing King Solomon, 'The heaven, and the heaven of heavens, cannot contain thee'; or those more emphatical ones of the inspired philosopher St. Paul, 'In him we live, move, and have our being': are to be understood in a literal sense, I leave every one to consider: only our idea of space is, I think, such as I have mentioned, and distinct from that of body. [But, to avoid confusion in discourses concerning this matter, it were possibly to be wished that the name *extension* were applied only to matter, or the distance of the extremities of particular bodies; and the term *expansion* to space in general, with or without solid matter possessing it, so as to say space is expanded, and body extended. But in this every one has liberty: I propose it only for the more clear and distinct way of speaking.][1]

[1] Added in the fourth edition. Locke does not always adhere to the usage he recommends.

## CHAPTER XIV

### OF DURATION, AND ITS SIMPLE MODES

1. *Duration is fleeting extension.*—There is another sort of distance or length, the idea whereof we get not from the permanent parts of space, but from the fleeting and perpetually perishing parts of succession. This we call *duration*, the simple modes whereof are any different lengths of it whereof we have distinct ideas, as *hours, days, years,* &c., *time,* and *eternity.*

2. *Its idea from reflection on the train of our ideas.*—The answer of a great man [1] to one who asked what time was, *Si non rogas intelligo* (which amounts to this: ' The more I set myself to think of it the less I understand it '), might perhaps persuade one that time, which reveals all other things, is itself not to be discovered. Duration, time, and eternity are, not without reason, thought to have something very abstruse in their nature. But however remote these may seem from our comprehension, yet if we trace them right to their originals, we shall find that the idea of eternity itself is derived from the same common original with the rest of our ideas.

3. To understand *time* and *eternity* aright, we ought with attention to consider what idea it is we have of *duration*, and how we came by it. It is evident to any one who will but observe what passes in his own mind, that there is a train of ideas which constantly succeed one another in his understanding as long as he is awake. Reflection on these appearances of several ideas one after another in our minds, is that which furnishes us with the idea of *succession* ; and the distance between any parts of that succession, or between the appearance of any two ideas in our minds, is that we call *duration.*[2] For whilst we are thinking, or whilst we receive successively several ideas in our minds, we know that we do

[1] St. Augustine.

[2] Recent psychology emphasizes the sense of duration as the more primitive experience. The present as perceived—' the specious present' as it is sometimes called—is not a mathematical point or a line dividing past from future. It is what William James calls a ' duration-block ', within which we have, in the contents, a sense of before and after —a sense of flow in a certain direction. We do not begin, therefore, with discrete units separated by intervals of empty time, but with the sense of a continuous flow or melting of one moment into the next. Hence Bergson's distinction between mathematical or clock time and *la durée réelle.*

exist; and so we call the existence or the continuation of the existence of ourselves, or anything else commensurate to the succession of any ideas in our minds, the duration of ourselves, or any such other thing co-existing with our thinking.

4. That we have our notion of succession and duration from this original, seems plain to me, in that we have no perception of duration but by considering the train of ideas that take their turns in our understandings. When that succession of ideas ceases, our perception of duration ceases with it; which every one clearly experiments in himself whilst he sleeps soundly, whether an hour, or a day, or a month, or a year; of which duration of things whilst he sleeps or thinks not he has no perception at all, but it is quite lost to him; and the moment wherein he leaves off to think till the moment he begins to think again, seems to him to have no distance. And so I doubt not it would be to a waking man, if it were possible for him to keep only one idea in his mind without variation and the succession of others; and we see that one who fixes his thoughts very intently on one thing, so as to take but little notice of the succession of ideas that pass in his mind whilst he is taken up with that earnest contemplation, lets slip out of his account a good part of that duration and thinks that time shorter than it is. But if sleep commonly unites the distant parts of duration, it is because during that time we have no succession of ideas in our minds. For if a man during his sleep dreams, and variety of ideas make themselves perceptible in his mind one after another, he hath then, during such a dreaming, a sense of duration, and of the length of it. By which it is to me very clear that men derive their ideas of duration from their reflection on the train of the ideas they observe to succeed one another in their own understandings.

5. *The idea of duration applicable to things whilst we sleep.*—Indeed a man having, from reflecting on the succession and number of his own thoughts, got the notion or idea of duration, he can apply that notion to things which exist while he does not think; as he that has got the idea of extension from bodies by his sight or touch, can apply it to distances where no body is seen or felt. And therefore, though a man has no perception of the length of duration which passed whilst he slept or thought not; yet having observed the revolution of days and nights, and found the length of their duration

to be in appearance regular and constant, he can imagine and make allowance for the length of duration whilst he slept. But if Adam and Eve (when they were alone in the world) instead of their ordinary night's sleep had passed the whole twenty-four hours in one continued sleep, the duration of that twenty-four hours had been irrecoverably lost to them, and been for ever left out of their account of time.

6. *The idea of succession not from motion.*—Thus, by reflecting on the appearing of various ideas one after another in our understandings, we get the notion of succession; which if any one should think we did rather get from our observation of motion by our senses, he will perhaps be of my mind, when he considers that even motion produces in his mind an idea of succession no otherwise than as it produces there a continued train of distinguishable ideas. For a man, looking upon a body really moving, perceives yet no motion at all, unless that motion produces a constant train of successive ideas; v. g., a man becalmed at sea, out of sight of land, in a fair day may look on the sun, or sea, or ship, a whole hour together, and perceive no motion at all in either; though it be certain that two, and perhaps all of them, have moved during that time a great way; but as soon as he perceives either of them to have changed distance with some other body, as soon as this motion produces any new idea in him, then he perceives that there has been motion. [7.] And this, I think, is the reason why motions very slow, though they are constant, are not perceived by us: because, in their remove from one sensible part towards another, their change of distance is so slow that it causes no new ideas in us but a good while one after another; and so not causing a constant train of new ideas to follow one another immediately in our minds, we have no perception of motion. [8.] On the contrary, things that move so swift as not to affect the senses distinctly with several distinguishable distances of their motion, and so cause not any train of ideas in the mind, are not also perceived to move. For anything that moves round about in a circle in less time than our ideas are wont to succeed one another in our minds, is not perceived to move, but seems to be a perfect, entire circle of that matter or colour, and not a part of a circle in motion.

9. *The train of ideas has a certain degree of quickness.*—Hence I leave it to others to judge, whether it be not probable that

our ideas do, whilst we are awake, succeed one another in our minds at certain distances, not much unlike the images in the inside of a lantern, turned round by the heat of a candle. This appearance of theirs in train, though perhaps it may be sometimes faster and sometimes slower, yet, I guess, varies not very much in a waking man : there seem to be certain bounds to the quickness and slowness of the succession of those ideas one to another in our minds, beyond which they can neither delay nor hasten.[1]

10. The reason I have for this odd conjecture is from observing that, in the impressions made upon any of our senses, we can but to a certain degree perceive any succession ; which if exceeding quick, the sense of succession is lost, even in cases where it is evident that there is a real succession. Let a cannon-bullet pass through a room, and in its way take with it any limb or fleshy parts of a man, it is as clear as any demonstration can be that it must strike successively the two sides of the room ; it is also evident that it must touch one part of the flesh first, and another after, and so in succession : and yet I believe nobody who ever felt the pain of such a shot or heard the blow against the two distant walls, could perceive any succession either in the pain or sound of so swift a stroke. Such a part of duration as this, wherein we perceive no succession, is that which we may call an *instant*, and is that which takes up the time of only one idea in our minds without the succession of another, wherein therefore we perceive no succession at all.

11. This also happens where the motion is so slow as not to supply a constant train of fresh ideas to the senses, as fast as the mind is capable of receiving new ones into it ; and so other ideas of our own thoughts having room to come into our minds between those offered to our senses by the moving body, there the sense of motion is lost ; and the body, though it really moves, yet not changing perceivable distance with some other bodies as fast as the ideas of our own minds do naturally

[1] This passage is quoted by Professor Ward as an instance of Locke's sagacity. Experimental psychology has proved that ' in estimating very short periods of time—of a second or less—there is a certain period for which the mean of a number of estimates is correct, while shorter periods are on the whole over-estimated, and longer periods under-estimated This so-called " indifference-time " we may perhaps take to be evidence of the time occupied in accommodating or fixing attention ' (*Psychological Principles*, p. 217).

follow one another in train, the thing seems to stand still, as is evident in the hands of clocks and shadows of sun-dials, and other constant but slow motions, where, though after certain intervals we perceive by the change of distance that it hath moved, yet the motion itself we perceive not.

12. *This train the measure of other successions.*—So that to me it seems, that the constant and regular succession of ideas in a waking man is, as it were, the measure and standard of all other successions.

13. *The mind cannot fix long on one invariable idea.*—If it be so, that the ideas of our minds, whilst we have any there, do constantly change and shift in a continual succession, it would be impossible, may any one say, for a man to think long of any one thing : by which if it be meant that a man may have one self-same single idea a long time alone in his mind, without any variation at all, I think, in matter of fact, it is not possible : for which (not knowing how the ideas of our minds are framed, of what materials they are made, whence they have their light, and how they come to make their appearances) I can give no other reason but experience : and I would have any one try whether he can keep one unvaried, single idea in his mind, without any other, for any considerable time together.[1]

14. For trial, let him take any figure, any degree of light or whiteness, or what other he pleases ; and he will, I suppose, find it difficult to keep all other ideas out of his mind ; but that some, either of another kind, or various considerations of that idea (each of which considerations is a new idea), will constantly succeed one another in his thoughts, let him be as wary as he can. [15.] All that is in a man's power in this case, I think, is only to mind and observe what the ideas are, that take their turns in his understanding ; or else to direct the sort, and call in such as he hath a desire or use of : but hinder the constant succession of fresh ones I think he cannot, though he may commonly choose whether he will heedfully observe and consider them.

16. *Ideas, however made, include no sense of motion.*—Whether these several ideas in a man's mind be made by certain motions, I will not here dispute : but this I am sure, that they include no idea of motion in their appearance. It is not motion, but the constant train of ideas in our minds, whilst we

[1] ' No one can possibly attend continuously to an object that does not change ' (James, *Principles of Psychology*, i. 421).

# Ch. 14  *Of Duration, and its Simple Modes*

are waking, that furnishes us with the idea of duration, whereof motion no otherwise gives us any perception than as it causes in our minds a constant succession of ideas, as I have before showed : and we have as clear an idea of succession and duration, by the train of other ideas succeeding one another in our minds without the idea of any motion, as by the train of ideas caused by the uninterrupted sensible change of distance between two bodies which we have from motion ; and therefore we should as well have the idea of duration, were there no sense of motion at all.[1]

17. *Time is duration set out by measures.*—Having thus got the idea of duration, the next thing natural for the mind to do, is to get some *measure* of this common duration, whereby it might judge of its different lengths, and consider the distinct order wherein several things exist ; without which a great part of our knowledge would be confused, and a great part of history be rendered very useless. This consideration of duration, as set out by certain periods, and marked by certain measures or epochs, is that, I think, which most properly we call *time*. [18.] What portions of duration are not distinguished or considered as distinguished and measured by such periods come not so properly under the notion of time, as appears by such phrases as these, viz., ' before all time ', and ' when time shall be no more '.

19. *The revolutions of the sun and moon the properest measures of time.*—The diurnal and annual revolutions of the sun, as

---

[1] Kant, however, maintains that external perception is necessary to the idea of change : ' Such a perception is the motion of a point in space, the existence of which in different spaces alone makes the perception of change possible. For in order to make even internal change cogitable, we require to represent time figuratively by a line, and the internal change by the drawing of that line (motion), and consequently are obliged to employ external perception to be able to represent the successive existence of ourselves in different states ' (*Critique of Pure Reason*, Analytic, Bk. II, ch. 2, section 4, *ad fin.*). And Professor Alexander has recently emphasized the interdependence of time and space. If time stood alone, it would ' be for itself and for an observer a mere " now ", and would contain neither earlier nor later '. And, on the other hand, ' space taken by itself in its distinctive character of a whole of coexistence has no distinction of parts '. ' Space so far as merely spatial becomes a blank.' The distinctness of parts which make it a real continuance is supplied by the succession involved in movement. ' Without Space there would be no connexion in Time. Without Time there would be no points to connect. Each of the two is vital to the existence of the other.' Cf. his *Space, Time and Deity*, i. 44–8.

having been from the beginning of nature, constant, regular, and universally observable by all mankind, and supposed equal to one another, have been with reason made use of for the measure of duration. But the distinction of days and years having depended on the motion of the sun, it has brought this mistake with it, that it has been thought that motion and duration were the measure one of another. Whereas any constant periodical appearance or alteration of ideas in seemingly equidistant spaces of duration, if constant and universally observable, would have as well distinguished the intervals of time as those that have been made use of. For supposing the sun, which some have taken to be a fire, had been lighted up at the same distance of time that it now every day comes about to the same meridian, and then gone out again about twelve hours after, and that in the space of an annual revolution it had sensibly increased in brightness and heat, and so decreased again; would not such regular appearances serve to measure out the distances of duration to all that could observe it, as well without as with motion? For if the appearances were constant, universally observable, and in equidistant periods, they would serve mankind for measure of time as well were the motion away. [20.] For the freezing of water or the blowing of a plant, returning at equidistant periods in all parts of the earth, would as well serve men to reckon their years by as the motion of the sun; and in effect we see that some people in America counted their years by the coming of certain birds amongst them at their certain seasons, and leaving them at others.

21. *No two parts of duration can be certainly known to be equal.*—But perhaps it will be said, 'Without a regular motion, such as of the sun or some other, how could it ever be known that such periods were equal?' To which I answer, the equality of any other returning appearances might be known by the same way that that of days was known, or presumed to be so at first: which was only by judging of them by the train of ideas that had passed in men's minds in the intervals. We must therefore carefully distinguish betwixt duration itself and the measures we make use of to judge of its length. Duration in itself is to be considered as going on in one constant, equal, uniform course. But none of the measures of it which we make use of can be known to do so, nor can we be assured that their assigned parts or periods are equal in

# Ch. 14 — Of Duration, and its Simple Modes

duration one to another; for two successive lengths of duration, however measured, can never be demonstrated to be equal. The motion of the sun, which the world used so long and so confidently for an exact measure of duration, has been found in its several parts unequal; and though men have of late made use of a pendulum as a more steady and regular motion than that of the sun or (to speak more truly) of the earth; yet if any one should be asked how he certainly knows that the two successive swings of a pendulum are equal, it would be very hard to satisfy himself that they are infallibly so; since we cannot be sure that the cause of that motion, which is unknown to us, shall always operate equally, and we are sure that the medium in which the pendulum moves is not constantly the same; either of which varying may alter the equality of such periods and thereby destroy the certainty and exactness of the measure by motion. Since then no two portions of succession can be brought together, it is impossible ever certainly to know their equality. All that we can do for a measure of time, is to take such as have continual successive appearances at seemingly equidistant periods; of which seeming equality we have no other measure but such as the train of our own ideas have lodged in our memories, with the concurrence of other probable reasons, to persuade us of their equality.

22. *Time not the measure of motion.*—One thing seems strange to me, that whilst all men manifestly measured time by the motion of the great and visible bodies of the world, time yet should be defined to be the measure of motion; whereas it is obvious to every one who reflects ever so little on it, that to measure motion, space is as necessary to be considered as time. And those who look a little farther will find also the bulk of the thing moved necessary to be taken into the computation by any one who will estimate or measure motion so as to judge right of it. Nor indeed does motion any otherwise conduce to the measuring of duration than as it constantly brings about the return of certain sensible ideas in seeming equidistant periods.

24. *Our measure of time applicable to duration before time.*— The mind having once got such a measure of time as the annual revolution of the sun, can apply that measure to duration wherein that measure itself did not exist. The idea of duration equal to an annual revolution of the sun is as easily

applicable in our thoughts to duration, where no sun nor motion was, as the idea of a foot or yard taken from bodies here can be applied in our thoughts to distances beyond the confines of the world, where are no bodies at all.

27. *Eternity.*—By the same means therefore, and from the same original that we come to have the idea of time, we have also that idea which we call eternity, viz., having got the idea of succession and duration, by reflecting on the train of our own ideas, caused in us either by the natural appearances of those ideas coming constantly of themselves into our waking thoughts, or else caused by external objects successively affecting our senses ; and having from the revolutions of the sun got the ideas of certain lengths of duration, we can [1] in our thoughts add such lengths of duration to one another as often as we please, and apply them, so added, to durations past or to come : and this we can continue to do on, without bounds or limits, and proceed *in infinitum*, and apply thus the length of the annual motion of the sun to duration, supposed before the sun's or any other motion had its being.

31. And thus I think it is plain, that from those two fountains of all knowledge before mentioned, viz. reflection and sensation, we get the ideas of duration, and the measures of it.

For, First, by observing what passes in our minds, how our ideas there in train constantly some vanish, and others begin to appear, we come by the idea of *succession*.

Secondly, by observing a distance in the parts of this succession, we get the idea of *duration*.

Thirdly, by sensation observing certain appearances, at certain regular and seeming equidistant periods, we get the ideas of certain lengths or *measures of duration*, as minutes, hours, days, years, &c.

Fourthly, by being able to repeat those measures of time, or ideas of stated length of duration in our minds, as often as we will, we can come to imagine *duration where nothing does*

[1] ' The notion of eternity, when it means the unbeginning and unending, implies not merely that we *may*, but that we *must*, continue to add to any finite duration, however great ' (Fraser). So Leibniz : ' C'est cette considération des raisons qui achève la notion de l'infini, ou de l'indéfini, dans les progrès possibles. Ainsi les sens seuls ne sauraient suffire à faire former ces notions.' Moreover at bottom, he adds, the idea of the absolute is prior in the nature of things to that of the limits which we add to it.

## Ch. 14 *Of Duration, and its Simple Modes*

*really endure or exist*; and thus we imagine to-morrow, next year, or seven years hence.

Fifthly, by being able to repeat any such idea of any length of time, as of a minute, a year, or an age, as often as we will in our own thoughts, and add them one to another, without ever coming to the end of such addition, any nearer than we can to the end of number, to which we can always add, we come by the idea of *eternity*, as the future eternal duration of our souls, as well as the eternity of that infinite Being which must necessarily have always existed.

Sixthly, by considering any part of infinite duration, as set out by periodical measures, we come by the idea of what we call *time* in general.

## CHAPTER XV

### OF DURATION AND EXPANSION CONSIDERED TOGETHER

1. *Both capable of greater and less.*—Though we have in the precedent chapters dwelt pretty long on the considerations of space and duration, yet they being ideas of general concernment, that have something very abstruse and peculiar in their nature, the comparing them one with another may perhaps be of use for their illustration; and we may have the more clear and distinct conception of them by taking a view of them together. Distance or space, in its simple abstract conception, to avoid confusion, I call *expansion*, to distinguish it from extension, which by some is used to express this distance only as it is in the solid parts of matter, and so includes, or at least intimates, the idea of body: whereas, the idea of pure distance includes no such thing. I prefer also the word expansion to space, because space is often applied to distance of fleeting successive parts, which never exist together,[1] as well as to those which are permanent. In both these (viz. expansion and duration) the mind has this common idea of continued lengths, capable of greater or less quantities; for a man has as clear an idea of the difference of the length of an hour and a day as of an inch and a foot.

2. *Expansion not bounded by matter.*—The mind having got the idea of the length of any part of expansion, let it be a span,

[1] e.g. 'There was silence in heaven about the space of half an hour' (*Rev.* 8. 1).

or a pace, or what length you will, *can*, as has been said, repeat that idea ; and so adding it to the former, enlarge its idea of length, till it amounts to the distance of the sun or remotest star. By such a progression as this, setting out from the place where it is, or any other place, it can proceed and pass beyond all those lengths, and find nothing to stop its going on, either in or without body. It is true we can easily in our thoughts come to the end of solid extension ; the extremity and bounds of all body we have no difficulty to arrive at : but when the mind is there, it finds nothing to hinder its progress into this endless expansion ; of that it can neither find nor conceive any end. Nor let any one say, that beyond the bounds of body there is nothing at all, unless he will confine God within the limits of matter. Solomon, whose understanding was filled and enlarged with wisdom, seems to have other thoughts, when he says, ' Heaven and the heaven of heavens cannot contain thee '. And he, I think, very much magnifies to himself the capacity of his own understanding who persuades himself that he can extend his thoughts farther than God exists, or imagine any expansion where he is not.

3. *Nor duration by motion.*—Just so is it in duration. The mind, having got the idea of any length of duration, can double, multiply, and enlarge it, not only beyond its own, but beyond the existence of all corporeal beings and all the measures of time, taken from the great bodies of the world and their motions. But yet every one easily admits, that though we make duration boundless, as certainly it is, we cannot yet extend it beyond all being. God, every one easily allows, fills eternity ; and it is hard to find a reason why any one should doubt that he likewise fills immensity. His infinite being is certainly as boundless one way as another ; and methinks it ascribes a little too much to matter to say, where there is no body, there is nothing.[1]

4. *Why men more easily admit infinite duration, than infinite expansion.*—Hence I think we may learn the reason why every one familiarly, and without the least hesitation, speaks of and supposes eternity, and sticks not to ascribe infinity to duration; but it is with more doubting and reserve that many admit or suppose the infinity of space. The reason whereof seems to me to be this, that duration and extension being used as names of affections belonging to other beings, we easily conceive in God

[1] Cf. note, p. 98, *supra.*

infinite duration, and we cannot avoid doing so : but not attributing to him extension, but only to matter, which is finite, we are apter to doubt of the existence of expansion without matter; of which alone we commonly suppose it an attribute. And therefore, when men pursue their thoughts of space, they are apt to stop at the confines of body : as if space were there at an end too, and reached no farther. Or if their ideas, upon consideration, carry them farther, yet they term what is beyond the limits of the universe, imaginary space; as if it were nothing, because there is no body existing in it.[1] Whereas duration, antecedent to all body, and to the motions which it is measured by, they never term imaginary ; because it is never supposed void of some other real existence. And if the names of things may at all direct our thoughts towards the originals of men's ideas (as I am apt to think they may very much), one may have occasion to think by the name *duration* that the continuation of existence, with a kind of resistance to any destructive force, and the continuation of solidity (which is apt to be confounded with, and if we will look into the minute atomical parts of matter, is little different from, hardness), were thought to have some analogy, and gave occasion to words so near of kin as *durare* and *durum esse*.

5. *Time to duration is as place to expansion.*—Time in general is to duration as place to expansion. They are so much of those boundless oceans of eternity and immensity, as is set out and distinguished from the rest as it were by landmarks ; and so are made use of to denote the position of finite real beings, in respect one to another, in those uniform infinite oceans of duration and space. [6.] Time and place taken thus have each of them a twofold acceptation. *First*, time in general is commonly taken for so much of infinite duration, as is measured out by and coexistent with the existence and motions of the great bodies of the universe, as far as we know anything of them ; and in this sense, time begins and ends with the frame of this sensible world, as in these phrases before mentioned, ' before all time ', or ' when time

[1] Locke himself, as we have seen, at one time held this view of space. ' We are apt to think that it as really exists beyond the utmost extent of all bodies or finite beings, though there are no beings there to sustain it, as it does here amongst bodies ; yet it is no more true that there is any real distance in that which we call imaginary space, than that there is any real figure there ' (*Miscellaneous Papers* of 1677–8, in Lord King's *Life*, ii. 175–85). Cf. note, p. 98, *supra*.

shall be no more'. Place likewise is taken sometimes for that portion of infinite space which is possessed by and comprehended within the material world, and is thereby distinguished from the rest of expansion; though this may more properly be called extension than place. [7.] *Secondly*, sometimes the word time is used in a larger sense, and is applied to parts of that infinite uniform duration which we upon any occasion do suppose equal to certain lengths of measured time; and so consider them as bounded and determined. And likewise we sometimes speak of place, distance, or bulk in the great inane beyond the confines of the world, when we consider so much of that space as is equal to or capable to receive a body of any assigned dimensions.

8. *They belong to all beings.*—*Where* and *When* are questions belonging to all finite existences, and are by us always reckoned from some known parts of this sensible world, and from some certain epochs marked out to us by the motions observable in it. Without some such fixed parts or periods, the order of things would be lost to our finite understandings in the boundless, invariable oceans of duration and expansion; which comprehend in them all finite beings, and in their full extent belong only to the Deity. And therefore we are not to wonder that we comprehend them not, and do so often find our thoughts at a loss, when we would consider them either abstractly in themselves, or as any way attributed to the first incomprehensible Being.

9. *All the parts of extension are extension, and all the parts of duration are duration.*—There is one thing more wherein space and duration have a great conformity, and that is, though they are justly reckoned amongst our *simple ideas*, yet none of the distinct ideas we have of either is without all manner of composition;[1] it is the very nature of both of them

---

[1] M. Coste in the French version of the *Essay* quotes a criticism of Locke's position here which he received from a Dutch professor together with a reply dictated by Locke. (The critic objected that, as involving 'composition', our ideas of space and time cannot be classed among 'simple ideas', and complained at the same time that in the second chapter where he introduces his classification of ideas Locke has not given an exact enough definition of what he means by simplicity. Locke replied that what he had strictly meant to exclude in his definition was ' a composition of *different* ideas in the mind and not a composition of ideas of the same kind, where we never come to an ultimate idea completely devoid of this composition '. Hence if the idea of extension

to consist of parts : but their parts, being all of the same kind, and without the mixture of any other idea, hinder them not from having a place amongst simple ideas. Could the mind, as in number, come to so small a part of extension or duration as excluded divisibility, that would be, as it were, the indivisible unit or idea ; by repetition of which, it would make its more enlarged ideas of extension and duration. But since the mind is not able to frame an idea of any space without parts, instead thereof it makes use of the common measures, which by familiar use in each country have imprinted themselves on the memory : and these are the component parts of larger ideas, which the mind, upon occasion, makes by the addition of such known lengths which it is acquainted with. On the other side, the ordinary smallest measure we have of either is looked on as an unit in number, when the mind by division would reduce them into less fractions. Though on both sides, both in addition and division, either of space or duration, when the idea under consideration becomes very big or very small, its precise bulk becomes very obscure and confused ; and it is the number of its repeated additions or divisions, that alone remains clear and distinct ; as will easily appear to any one who will let his thoughts loose in the vast expansion of space, or divisibility of matter. Every part of duration is duration too ; and every part of extension is extension ; both of them capable of addition or division *in infinitum*.[1] But the least portions of either of them, whereof we have clear and distinct ideas, may

consists in having *partes extra partes*, in the language of the Schools, it still remains a simple idea, because the idea of having *partes extra partes* cannot be resolved into two other ideas. He goes on to refer to his own suggestion in this section that the least portions of space and time which we can clearly and distinctly perceive may be regarded as the simple ideas of that kind out of which the complex ideas of extension and duration in their various modes are composed. If this is not sufficient to clear up the difficulty, Locke has nothing more to add (writes M. Coste) than that, ' if the idea of extension is so peculiar that it cannot be brought into exact agreement with the definition he has given, in that it differs in some way from all the others of that kind, he believes it is better to leave it exposed to that difficulty than to try to accommodate it by making a new division '.

[1] Locke here emphasizes the *continuity* of space and time which implies, on the one hand, their infinity, on the other their infinite divisibility. So Kant : ' Space consists only of spaces, and time of times ; we cannot conceive either space or time as composed of constituent parts which are given before space and time ' (*Critique of Pure Reason*, Analytic, Bk. II, ch. 2, section 3 (2)).

perhaps be fittest to be considered by us as the *simple ideas* of that kind, out of which our complex modes of space, extension, and duration are made up, and into which they can again be distinctly resolved.[1] Such a small part in duration may be called a *moment*, and is the time of one idea in our minds, in the train of their ordinary succession there. The other, wanting a proper name, I know not whether I may be allowed to call a *sensible point*, meaning thereby the least particle of matter or space we can discern, which is ordinarily about a minute, and to the sharpest eyes seldom less than thirty seconds, of a circle whereof the eye is the centre.

10. *Their parts inseparable.*—Expansion and duration have this farther agreement, that though they are both considered by us as having parts, yet their parts are not separable one from another, no not even in thought. [11.] But yet there is this manifest difference between them, that the ideas of length which we have of expansion are turned every way, and so make figure, and breadth, and thickness ; but duration is but as it were the length of one straight line extended *in infinitum*, not capable of multiplicity, variation, or figure, but is one common measure of all existence whatsoever, wherein all things, whilst they exist, equally partake. For this present moment is common to all things that are now in being, and equally comprehends that part of their existence as much as if they were all but one single being ; and we may truly say, they all exist in the same moment of time.

12. *Duration has never two parts together, expansion all together.*—Duration, and time which is a part of it, is the idea we have of *perishing* distance, of which no two parts exist together, but follow each other in succession ; as *expansion* is the idea of *lasting* distance, all whose parts exist together, and are not capable of succession. And therefore, though we cannot conceive any duration without succession, nor can put it together in our thoughts that any being does now exist to-morrow, or possess at once more than the present moment of

[1] This was the line taken by Berkeley and Hume, who limited the term idea to that which can be sensed or imaged. Berkeley's Commonplace Book and his early works are full of the *minimum visibile* and the *minimum tangibile*. The magnitude of objects is determined, he says, 'according as they contain in them more or fewer points, they being made up of points or minimums. For whatever may be said of extension in abstract, it is certain sensible extension is not infinitely divisible' (*New Theory of Vision*, section 54).

duration; yet we can conceive the eternal duration of the Almighty far different from that of man, or any other finite being. Because man comprehends not in his knowledge or power all past and future things: his thoughts are but of yesterday, and he knows not what to-morrow will bring forth. What is once past he can never recall; and what is yet to come, he cannot make present. What I say of man, I say of all finite beings, who, though they may far exceed man in knowledge and power, yet are no more than the meanest creature in comparison with God himself. Finite of any magnitude holds not any proportion to infinite. God's infinite duration being accompanied with infinite knowledge and infinite power, he sees all things past and to come; and they are no more distant from his knowledge, no farther removed from his sight, than the present: they all lie under the same view: and there is nothing which he cannot make exist each moment he pleases. For the existence of all things depending upon his good pleasure, all things exist every moment that he thinks fit to have them exist. To conclude: expansion and duration do mutually embrace and comprehend each other; every part of space being in every part of duration, and every part of duration in every part of expansion. Such a combination of two distinct ideas is, I suppose, scarce to be found in all that great variety we do or can conceive, and may afford matter to farther speculation.[1]

## CHAPTER XVI

### OF NUMBER

1. *Number the simplest and most universal idea.*—Amongst all the ideas we have, as there is none suggested to the mind by more ways, so there is none more simple, than that of *unity*, or one. It has no shadow of variety of composition in it: every object our senses are employed about, every idea in our understandings, every thought of our minds, brings this idea along with it. And therefore it is the most intimate to our thoughts, as well as it is, in its agreement to all other things, the most

[1] Following out this line of speculation, Professor Alexander arrives at the result that ' there is no mere Space or mere Time but only Space-Time or Time-Space. Space and Time by themselves are abstractions from Space-Time' (*Space, Time and Deity*, p. 48). Cf. note, p. 111, *supra.*

universal idea we have. For number applies itself to men, angels, actions, thoughts,—everything that either doth exist or can be imagined.

2. *Its modes made by addition.*—By repeating this idea in our minds, and adding the repetitions together, we come by the *complex* ideas of the *modes* of it. Thus by adding one to one we have the complex idea of a couple : by putting twelve units together we have the complex idea of a dozen ; and so of a score, or a million, or any other number.

3. *Each mode distinct.*—The simple modes of number are of all other the most distinct ; every the least variation which is an unit, making each combination as clearly different from that which approacheth nearest to it, as the most remote : two being as distinct from one, as two hundred ; and the idea of two as distinct from the idea of three, as the magnitude of the whole earth is from that of a mite. This is not so in other simple modes, in which it is not so easy, nor perhaps possible, for us to distinguish betwixt two approaching ideas, which yet are really different. For who will undertake to find a difference between the white of this paper and that of the next degree to it : or can form distinct ideas of every the least excess in extension ?

4. *Therefore demonstrations in numbers the most precise.*—The clearness and distinctness of each mode of number from all others, even those that approach nearest, makes me apt to think that demonstrations in numbers, if they are not more evident and exact than in extension, yet they are more general in their use, and more determinate in their application. Because our thoughts cannot in space arrive at any determined smallness beyond which it cannot go, as an unit ; and therefore the quantity or proportion of any the least excess cannot be discovered.

5. *Names necessary to numbers.*—By the repeating, as has been said, of the idea of an unit, and joining it to another unit, we make thereof one collective idea, marked by the name two. And whosoever can do this and proceed on, still adding one more to the last collective idea which he had of any number, and give a name to it, may count, or have ideas for several collections of units, distinguished one from another, as far as he hath a series of names for following numbers, and a memory to retain that series with their several names : all numeration being but still the adding of one unit more, and

giving to the whole together, as comprehended in one idea, a new or distinct name or sign, whereby to know it from those before and after, and distinguish it from every smaller or greater multitude of units. For, the several simple modes of numbers being in our minds but so many combinations of units, which have no variety, nor are capable of any other difference but more or less, names or marks for each distinct combination seem more necessary than in any other sort of ideas. For without such names or marks we can hardly well make use of numbers in reckoning, especially where the combination is made up of any great multitude of units; which, put together without a name or mark to distinguish that precise collection, will hardly be kept from being a heap in confusion.

6. This I think to be the reason why some Americans I have spoken with (who were otherwise of quick and rational parts enough) could not, as we do, by any means count to one thousand, nor had any distinct idea of that number, though they could reckon very well to twenty. Because their language being scanty, and accommodated only to the few necessaries of a needy, simple life, unacquainted either with trade or mathematics, had no words in it to stand for one thousand; so that when they were discoursed with of those greater numbers, they would show the hairs of their head, to express a great multitude which they could not number; which inability, I suppose, proceeded from their want of names. The Tououpinambos had no names for numbers above five; any number beyond that they made out by showing their fingers, and the fingers of others who were present.

7. *Why children number not earlier.*—Thus children, either for want of names to mark the several progressions of numbers, or not having yet the faculty to collect scattered ideas into complex ones, and range them in a regular order, and so retain them in their memories as is necessary to reckoning, do not begin to number very early, nor proceed in it very far or steadily, till a good while after they are well furnished with good store of other ideas; and one may often observe them discourse and reason pretty well, and have very clear conceptions of several other things, before they can tell twenty. For he that will count twenty, or have any idea of that number, must know that nineteen went before, with the distinct name or sign of every one of them, as they stand

marked in their order; for wherever this fails, a gap is made, the chain breaks, and the progress in numbering can go no farther. So that to reckon right it is required, (1) That the mind distinguish carefully two ideas which are different one from another only by the addition or subtraction of one unit. (2) That it retain in memory the names or marks of the several combinations from an unit to that number; and that not confusedly, and at random; but in that exact order that the numbers follow one another.

8. *Number measures all measurables.*—This farther is observable in number, that it is that which the mind makes use of in measuring all things that by us are measurable, which principally are expansion and duration; and our idea of infinity even when applied to those seems to be nothing but the infinity of number. For what else are our ideas of eternity and immensity, but the repeated additions of certain ideas of imagined parts of duration and expansion, with the infinity of number, in which we can come to no end of addition? For let a man collect into one sum as great a number as he pleases, this multitude, how great soever, lessens not one jot the power of adding to it, or brings him any nearer the end of the inexhaustible stock of number, where still there remains as much to be added as if none were taken out. And this endless addition or *addibility* (if any one like the word better) of numbers, so apparent to the mind, is that, I think, which gives us the clearest and most distinct idea of infinity; of which more in the following chapter.

## CHAPTER XVII

### OF INFINITY

1. *Infinity, in its original intention, attributed to space, duration, and number.*—He that would know what kind of idea it is to which we give the name of infinity, cannot do it better than by considering to what infinity is by the mind more immediately attributed, and then how the mind comes to frame it.

Finite and infinite seem to me to be looked upon by the mind as the modes of quantity, and to be attributed primarily in their first designation only to those things which have parts, and are capable of increase or diminution by the addition or subtraction of any the least part ; and such are the ideas of space, duration, and number, which we have considered in the foregoing chapters. It is true that we cannot but be assured that the great God, of whom and from whom are all things, is incomprehensibly infinite : but yet when we apply to that first and supreme Being our idea of infinite, in our weak and narrow thoughts, we do it primarily in respect of his duration and ubiquity; and, I think, more figuratively to his power, wisdom, and goodness, and other attributes, which are properly inexhaustible and incomprehensible, &c. For when we call them infinite, we have no other idea of this infinity but what carries with it some reflection on and intimation of that number or extent of the acts or objects of God's power, wisdom, and goodness, which can never be supposed so great or so many, which these attributes will not always surmount and exceed, let us multiply them in our thoughts as far as we can, with all the infinity of endless number. I do not pretend to say how these attributes are in God, who is infinitely beyond the reach of our narrow capacities ; they do without doubt contain in them all possible perfection ; but this, I say, is our way of conceiving them, and these our ideas of their infinity.

2. *How we come by the idea of infinity.*—Finite then and infinite being by the mind looked on as modifications [1] of expansion and duration, the next thing to be considered is how the mind comes by them. As for the idea of finite, there is no great difficulty. The obvious portions of extension that affect our senses carry with them into the mind the idea of finite ; and the ordinary periods of succession whereby we measure time and duration, as hours, days, and years, are bounded lengths. The difficulty is, how we come by those boundless ideas of eternity and immensity, since the objects which we converse with come so much short of any approach or proportion to that largeness. [3.] Every one that has any idea of any stated lengths of space, as a foot, finds that he can repeat that idea ; and joining it to the former, make the idea of two feet ; and by the addition of a third, three feet, and so on, without ever coming to an end of his additions, and how often soever he doubles or any otherwise multiplies it, he finds that, after he has continued this doubling in his thoughts and

[1] The true infinite, says Leibniz, is not a modification. ' In strictness it is to be found only in the absolute, which is prior to all composition and is not formed by the addition of parts.'

enlarged his idea as much as he pleases, he has no more reason to stop, nor is one jot nearer the end of such addition than he was at first setting out.

4. *Our idea of space boundless.*—This, I think, is the way whereby the mind gets the idea of infinite space.[1] It is a quite different consideration to examine whether the mind has the idea of such a boundless space actually existing, since our ideas are not always proofs of the existence of things; but yet, since this comes here in our way, I suppose I may say that we are apt to think that space in itself is actually boundless, to which imagination the idea of space or expansion of itself naturally leads us. For it being considered by us either as the extension of body, or as existing by itself, without any solid matter taking it up, it is impossible the mind should be stopped anywhere in its progress in this space, how far soever it extends its thoughts. Any bounds made with body, even adamantine walls, are so far from putting a stop to the mind in its farther progress in space and extension, that it rather facilitates and enlarges it : for so far as that body reaches, so far no one can doubt of extension ; and when we are come to the utmost extremity of body, what is there that can there put a stop, and satisfy the mind that it is at the end of space, when it perceives it is not ; nay, when it is satisfied that body itself can move into it ?

5. *And so of duration.*—As, by the power we find in ourselves of repeating as often as we will any idea of space, we get the idea of immensity; so, by being able to repeat the idea of any length of duration we have in our minds, with all the endless addition of number, we come by the idea of eternity. For we find in ourselves, we can no more come to an end of such repeated ideas than we can come to the end of number; which every one perceives he cannot. But here again it is another question, quite different from our having an idea of eternity, to know whether there were any real being whose duration has been eternal. And as to this, I say, he that considers something now existing must necessarily come to

[1] ' A merely empirical "repetition" of phenomena does not explain the *intellectual need* for *continuing without end* the process of repetition which, Locke himself seems to allow, is implied in the idea of space ' (Fraser). In the next section, it may perhaps be noted, we are said to find ' in ourselves ' this ' power ' or obligation, which forbids us to rest in any limited duration.

Something eternal. But having spoke of this in another place,[1] I shall say here no more of it, but proceed on to some other considerations of our idea of infinity.

6. *Why other ideas are not capable of infinity.*—If it be so, that our idea of infinity be got from the power we observe in ourselves of repeating without end our own ideas, it may be demanded, why we do not attribute infinity to other ideas, as well as those of space and duration; since they may be as easily and as often repeated in our minds as the other; and yet nobody ever thinks of infinite sweetness or infinite whiteness, though he can repeat the idea of sweet or white as frequently as those of a yard or a day? To which I answer, All the ideas that are considered as having parts, and are capable of increase by the addition of any equal or less parts, afford us, by their repetition, the idea of infinity; because with this endless repetition there is continued an enlargement, of which there can be no end. But in other ideas it is not so. To the perfectest idea I have of the whitest whiteness, if I add another of a less or equal whiteness (and of a whiter than I have, I cannot add the idea), it makes no increase, and enlarges not my idea at all; and therefore the different ideas of whiteness, &c., are called degrees. If you take the idea of white which one parcel of snow yielded yesterday to your sight, and another idea of white from another parcel of snow you see to-day, and put them together in your mind, they embody, as it were, and run into one, and the idea of whiteness is not at all increased; and if we add a less degree of whiteness to a greater, we are so far from increasing that we diminish it.

7. *Difference between infinity of space and space infinite.*—Though our idea of infinity arise from the contemplation of quantity, and the endless increase the mind is able to make in quantity; yet I guess we cause great confusion in our thoughts when we discourse or reason about an infinite quantity, as an infinite space or an infinite duration. For our idea of infinity being, as I think, *an endless growing idea,* but the idea of any quantity the mind has, being at that time terminated in that idea (for be it as great as it will, it can be no greater than it is), to join infinity to it, is to adjust a standing measure to a growing bulk; and therefore I think it is not an insignificant subtilty if I say that we are carefully to distinguish between the

---

[1] Bk. IV, ch. 10, 'Of our Knowledge of the Existence of a God'.

idea of the infinity of space and the idea of a space infinite : [1] the first is nothing but a supposed endless progression of the mind over what repeated ideas of space it pleases ; but to have actually in the mind the idea of a space infinite, is to suppose the mind already passed over, and actually to have a view of all those repeated ideas of space which an endless repetition can never totally represent to it ; which carries in it a plain contradiction.

8. *We have no idea of infinite space.*—This, perhaps, will be a little plainer if we consider it in numbers. The infinity of numbers, to the end of whose addition every one perceives there is no approach, easily appears to any one that reflects on it : but how clear soever this idea of the infinity of number be, there is nothing yet more evident than the absurdity of the actual idea of an infinite number. Whatsoever positive ideas we have in our minds of any space, duration, or number, let them be never so great, they are still finite ; but when we suppose an inexhaustible remainder from which we remove all bounds, and wherein we allow the mind an endless progression of thought, without ever completing the idea, there we have our idea of infinity ; which though it seems to be pretty clear when we consider nothing else in it but the negation of an end, yet when we would frame in our minds the idea of an infinite space or duration, that idea is very obscure and confused, because it is made up of two parts very different, if not inconsistent. For let a man frame in his mind an idea of any space or number, as great as he will, it is plain the mind rests and terminates in that idea ; which is contrary to the idea of infinity, which consists in a supposed endless progression. And therefore I think it is that we are so easily confounded when we come to argue and reason about infinite space or duration, &c.

10. *Our different conception of the infinity of number, duration, and expansion.*—It will, perhaps, give us a little farther light into the idea we have of infinity, and discover to us that it is *nothing but the infinity of number applied to determinate parts*, of which we have in our minds the distinct ideas, if we consider that number is not generally thought by us infinite, whereas duration and extension are apt to be so ; which arises from hence, that in number we are at one end as it were : for there

[1] The same distinction is drawn by Kant and constitutes his key to the solution of the Antinomies arising from the nature of space and time.

being in number nothing less than an unit, we there stop, and are at an end; it is like a line, whereof one end terminating with us, the other is extended still forwards beyond all that we can conceive; but in space and duration it is otherwise. For in duration we consider it as if this line of number were extended both ways to an unconceivable, undeterminate, and infinite length; which is evident to any one that will but reflect on what consideration he hath of eternity; which, I suppose, he will find to be nothing else but the turning this infinity of number both ways, *à parte ante* and *à parte post*, as they speak. [11.] The same happens also in space, wherein conceiving our selves to be as it were in the centre, we do on all sides pursue those indeterminable lines of number.

12. *Infinite divisibility.*—And since in any bulk of matter our thoughts can never arrive at the utmost divisibility, therefore there is an apparent infinity to us also in that; but with this difference, that in the former considerations of the infinity of space and duration, we only use addition of numbers; whereas this is like the division of an unit into its fractions, wherein the mind also can proceed *in infinitum*, as well as in the former additions: though in the addition of the one we can have no more the positive idea of a space infinitely great, than in the division of the other we can have the idea of a body infinitely little; our idea of infinity being, as I may so say, a growing and fugitive idea, still in a boundless progression that can stop nowhere.

13. *No positive idea of infinite.*—Though it be hard, I think, to find any one so absurd as to say he has the positive idea of an actual infinite number, yet there be those who imagine they have *positive* ideas of infinite duration and space. It would, I think, be enough to destroy any such positive idea of infinite to ask him that has it, whether he could add to it or no; which would easily show the mistake of such a positive idea. For I think it is evident that the addition of finite things together (as are all lengths whereof we have the positive ideas) can never otherwise produce the idea of infinite than as number does; which, consisting of additions of finite units one to another, suggests the idea of infinite only by a power we find we have of still increasing the sum, and adding more of the same kind, without coming one jot nearer the end of such progression.

15. *What is positive, what negative, in our idea of infinite.*—The idea of infinite has, I confess, something of positive in all those things we apply it to. When we would think of infinite space or duration, we at first step usually make some very large idea, as, perhaps, of millions of ages or miles, which possibly we double and multiply several times. All that we thus amass together in our thoughts is positive. But what still remains beyond this, we have no more a positive, distinct notion of, than a mariner has of the depth of the sea, where having let down a large portion of his sounding-line, he reaches no bottom: whereby he knows the depth to be so many fathoms, and more; but how much that more is, he hath no distinct notion at all. Let this line be ten or ten thousand fathoms long, it equally discovers what is beyond it; and gives only this confused and comparative idea, that this is not all, but one may yet go farther.

16. *We have no positive idea of an infinite duration.*—I ask those who say they have a positive idea of eternity, whether their idea of duration includes in it succession or not? If it does not, they ought to show the difference of their notion of duration, when applied to an eternal being, and to a finite; since perhaps there may be others, as well as I, who will own to them their weakness of understanding in this point, and acknowledge that the notion they have of duration forces them to conceive, that whatever has duration is of a longer continuance to-day than it was yesterday. If to avoid succession in eternal existence, they recur to the *punctum stans* of the schools, I suppose they will thereby very little mend the matter or help us to a more clear and positive idea of infinite duration, there being nothing more inconceivable to me than duration without succession. Besides that *punctum stans*, if it signify anything, being not *quantum*, finite or infinite cannot belong to it. But if our weak apprehensions cannot separate succession from any duration whatsoever, our idea of eternity can be nothing but of infinite succession of moments of duration wherein anything does exist; and whether any one has or can have a positive idea of an actual infinite number, I leave him to consider, till his infinite number be so great that he himself can add no more to it: and as long as he can increase it, I doubt, he himself will think the idea he hath of it a little too scanty for positive infinity.

17. I think it unavoidable for every considering rational

creature, that will but examine his own or any other existence, to have the notion of an eternal wise Being, who had no beginning: and such an idea of infinite duration I am sure I have. But this negation of a beginning, being but the negation of a positive thing, scarce gives me a positive idea of infinity.

20. *Some think they have a positive idea of eternity, and not of infinite space.*—There are some I have met with that put so much difference between infinite duration and infinite space, that they persuade themselves that they have a positive idea of eternity, but that they have not nor can have any idea of infinite space. The reason of which mistake I suppose to be this, that finding by a due contemplation of causes and effects that it is necessary to admit some eternal Being, and so to consider the real existence of that Being as taken up and commensurate to their idea of eternity: but, on the other side, not finding it necessary, but on the contrary apparently absurd, that body should be infinite, they forwardly conclude they can have no idea of infinite space, because they can have no idea of infinite matter. Which consequence, I conceive, is very ill collected; because the existence of matter is no ways necessary to the existence of space, no more than the existence of motion, or the sun, is necessary to duration, though duration uses to be measured by it. And why should we think our idea of infinite space requires the real existence of matter to support it, when we find that we have as clear an idea of infinite duration to come, as we have of infinite duration past. Though I suppose, nobody thinks it conceivable that anything does or has existed in that future duration. But if these men are of the mind, that they have clearer ideas of infinite duration than of infinite space, because it is past doubt that God has existed from all eternity, but there is no real matter co-extended with infinite space; yet those philosophers who are of opinion that infinite space is possessed by God's infinite omnipresence, as well as infinite duration by his eternal existence,[1] must be allowed to have as clear an idea of infinite space as of infinite duration; though neither of them, I think, has any positive idea of infinity in either case.

21. I have been hitherto apt to think that the great and inextricable difficulties which perpetually involve all discourses

[1] This, as we have seen, was Locke's own view, which he shared with Newton and others. Cf. ch. 15. 2-3 and note to p. 98.

concerning infinity, whether of space, duration, or divisibility, have been the certain marks of a defect in our ideas of infinity, and the disproportion the nature thereof has to the comprehension of our narrow capacities. For whilst men talk and dispute of infinite space or duration, as if they had as complete and positive ideas of them as they have of the names they use for them, or as they have of a yard, or an hour, or any other determinate quantity, it is no wonder if the incomprehensible nature of the thing they discourse of, or reason about, leads them into perplexities and contradictions, and their minds be overlaid by an object too large and mighty to be surveyed and managed by them.

22. *All these ideas from sensation and reflection.*—If I have dwelt pretty long on the considerations of duration, space, and number, and what arises from the contemplation of them, infinity, it is possibly no more than the matter requires, there being few simple ideas whose modes give more exercise to the thoughts of men than these do. I pretend not to treat of them in their full latitude ; it suffices to my design to show how the mind receives them, such as they are, from sensation and reflection : and how even the idea we have of infinity, how remote soever it may seem to be from any object of sense or operation of our mind, has nevertheless, as all our other ideas, its original there.[1] Some mathematicians, perhaps, of advanced speculations, may have other ways to introduce into their minds ideas of infinity ; but this hinders not but that they themselves, as well as all other men, got the first ideas which they had of infinity from sensation and reflection, in the method we have here set down.

Chapter 18, 'Of other Simple Modes', is inserted, as Locke says, only 'for method's sake', and the same is true in the main of chapter 19, 'Of the Modes of Thinking', and chapter 20, 'Of Modes of Pleasure and Pain'. Chapters 18 and 20 are here omitted, but chapter 19 is retained for the explanation it gives of the terms Locke uses about mental operations.

[1] See Introduction, pp. xxvi–vii.

## CHAPTER XIX

#### OF THE MODES OF THINKING

1. *Sensation, remembrance, contemplation, &c.*—When the mind turns its view inwards upon itself, and contemplates its own actions, thinking is the first that occurs. In it the mind observes a great variety of modifications, and from thence receives distinct ideas. Thus the perception which actually accompanies and is annexed to any impression on the body made by an external object, being distinct from all other modifications of thinking, furnishes the mind with a distinct idea which we call *sensation*; which is, as it were, the actual entrance of any idea into the understanding by the senses. The same idea, when it again recurs without the operation of the like object on the external sensory, is *remembrance*: if it be sought after by the mind, and with pain and endeavour found, and brought again in view, it is *recollection*: if it be held there long under attentive consideration, it is *contemplation*: when ideas float in our mind without any reflection or regard of the understanding, it is that which the French call *rêverie*; our language has scarce a name for it: when the ideas that offer themselves (for, as I have observed in another place, whilst we are awake there will always be a train of ideas succeeding one another in our minds) are taken notice of, and, as it were, registered in the memory, it is *attention*: when the mind with great earnestness, and of choice, fixes its view on any idea, considers it on all sides, and will not be called off by the ordinary solicitation of other ideas, it is that we call *intention*, or *study*; sleep, without dreaming, is rest from all these: and *dreaming* itself is the having of ideas (whilst the outward senses are stopped, so that they receive not outward objects with their usual quickness) in the mind, not suggested by any external objects or known occasion, nor under any choice or conduct of the understanding at all; and whether that which we call *ecstasy* be not dreaming with the eyes open, I leave to be examined.

2. These are some few instances of those various modes of thinking which the mind may observe in itself, and so have as distinct ideas of as it hath of white and red, a square or a circle. I do not pretend to enumerate them all, nor to treat at large

of this set of ideas which are got from reflection ; that would be to make a volume. It suffices to my present purpose to have shown here, by some few examples, of what sort these ideas are, and how the mind comes by them ; especially since I shall have occasion hereafter to treat more at large of *reasoning, judging, volition*, and *knowledge*, which are some of the most considerable operations of the mind, and modes of thinking.[1]

3. *The various attention of the mind in thinking.*—But perhaps it may not be an unpardonable digression, nor wholly impertinent to our present design, if we reflect here upon the different state of the mind in thinking which those instances of attention, *rêverie*, and dreaming, &c., before mentioned, naturally enough suggest. That there are ideas, some or other, always present in the mind of a waking man, every one's experience convinces him ; though the mind employs itself about them with several degrees of attention. Sometimes the mind fixes itself with so much earnestness on the contemplation of some objects, that it turns their ideas on all sides ; remarks their relations and circumstances, and views every part so nicely, and with such intention, that it shuts out all other thoughts, and takes no notice of the ordinary impressions made then on the senses, which at another season would produce very sensible perceptions : at other times, it barely observes the train of ideas that succeed in the understanding, without directing and pursuing any of them ; and at other times it lets them pass almost quite unregarded, as faint shadows that make no impression.

4. *Hence it is probable that thinking is the action, not essence, of the soul.*—This difference of intention and remission of the mind, with a great variety of degrees between earnest study and very near minding nothing at all, every one, I think, has experimented in himself. Trace it a little farther, and you find the mind in sleep, retired as it were from the senses, and out of the reach of those motions made on the organs of sense, which at other times produce very vivid and sensible ideas. But in this retirement of the mind from the senses, it often retains a yet more loose and incoherent manner of thinking, which we call dreaming ; and last of all, sound sleep closes the scene quite, and puts an end to all appearances. That

[1] Chiefly in Bk. IV. Volition is considered as a mode of ' power ' in ch. 21 of this Book.

which I would conclude from hence is, whether it be not probable, that thinking is the action and not the essence of the soul? Since the operations of agents will easily admit of intention and remission; but the essences of things are not conceived capable of any such variation. But this by the by.[1]


## CHAPTER XXI [2]

### OF POWER

**1.** *This idea how got.*—The mind being every day informed, by the senses, of the alteration of those simple ideas it observes in things without; and taking notice how one comes to an end and ceases to be, and another begins to exist which was not before; reflecting also, on what passes within itself, and observing a constant change of its ideas, sometimes by the impression of outward objects on the senses, and sometimes by the determination of its own choice; and concluding from what it has so constantly observed to have been, that the like changes will for the future be made in the same things by like agents, and by the like ways; considers [3] in one thing the possibility of having any of its simple ideas changed, and in another the possibility of making that change; and so comes by that idea which we call *power*. Thus we say, fire has a power to melt gold, i. e., to destroy the consistency of its insensible parts, and consequently its hardness, and make it fluid; and gold has a power to be melted: that the sun

---

[1] Locke's 'digression' in these two sections connects itself with the controversy with the Cartesians in the first chapter of this Book.

[2] This chapter is much the longest in the *Essay*, but, with the exception of the first four sections and the concluding sections, it has little connexion with the problem of the *Essay* or the characteristic doctrines which Locke expounds in the course of it. The rest of the chapter is devoted to a lengthy discussion of the question of the freedom of the will, which is more tedious than instructive to a modern reader. The length is partly due to the fact that between the first and the second edition Locke changed his view as to what finally determines us to action. In these circumstances, only enough has been retained here to indicate the general drift of the argument, or to preserve some incidental statement for the sake of its happy expression.

[3] Cf. Introduction, pp. xxiii–iv. The first four sections of this chapter should be read in connexion with the opening sections of ch. 23, on the idea of Substance, as bearing upon the question of the necessary implication of both ideas in our experience.

has a power to blanch wax; and wax a power to be blanched by the sun, whereby the yellowness is destroyed, and whiteness made to exist in its room. In which and the like cases, the power we consider is in reference to the change of perceivable ideas. For we cannot observe any alteration to be made in, or operation upon, anything, but by the observable change of its sensible ideas: nor conceive any alteration to be made, but by conceiving a change of some of its ideas.

2. *Power active and passive.*—Power thus considered is twofold, viz., as able to make, or able to receive, any change: the one may be called *active*, and the other *passive*, power.[1] Whether matter be not wholly destitute of active power, as its author, God, is truly above all passive power; and whether the intermediate state of created spirits be not that alone which is capable of both active and passive power, may be worth consideration. I shall not now enter into that enquiry: my present business being not to search into the original of power, but how we come by the idea of it. But since active powers make so great a part of our complex ideas of natural substances (as we shall see hereafter),[2] yet they being not, perhaps, so truly active powers as our hasty thoughts are apt to represent them, I judge it not amiss, by this intimation, to direct our minds to the consideration of God and spirits, for the clearest idea of active power.[3]

3. *Power includes relation.*—I confess power includes in it some kind of *relation*[4] (a relation to action or change), as, indeed, which of our ideas, of what kind soever, when atten-

---

[1] The distinction between active and passive power was familiar in mediaeval philosophy, going back to Aristotle's *Metaphysics*, Bk. V. 12 and Bk. IX. 1. Passive powers are frequently spoken of as 'capacities'. So Locke (II. 23. 7) speaks of 'active powers and passive capacities'.

[2] Ch. 23. 7–13.

[3] This section and section 4 (cf. also ch. 23, section 28) are historically important because the contrast between the 'passiveness and inertness' of the 'things which we perceive', and the activity of spirit as the only real 'agent' or efficient cause, formed the starting-point of Berkeley's philosophy. Spirit is defined by him as 'that which acts'—causes and effects in the material world coming to mean for him no more than an orderly system of signs and significates, which forms for finite spirits a medium of intercourse with one another and with the supreme Spirit. (Cf. *Principles of Human Knowledge*, sections 25, 27, &c.)

[4] By acknowledging that 'some kind of relation' is implied in all our ideas, Locke again (as in the case of extension) admits the breakdown of his division of ideas into simple and complex (or compounded) ideas. He never really defines what he means by a simple idea.

tively considered, does not? For our ideas of extension, duration, and number, do they not all contain in them a secret relation of the parts? Figure and motion have something relative in them much more visibly: and sensible qualities, as colours and smells, &c., what are they but the powers of different bodies in relation to our perception? And if considered in the things themselves, do they not depend on the bulk, figure, texture, and motion of the parts? All which include some kind of relation in them. Our idea therefore of power, I think, may well have a place amongst other simple ideas, and be considered as one of them, being one of those that make a principal ingredient in our complex ideas of substances, as we shall hereafter have occasion to observe.[1]

4. *The clearest idea of active power had from spirit.*—We are abundantly furnished with the idea of passive power, by almost all sorts of sensible things. In most of them we cannot avoid observing their sensible qualities, nay, their very substances, to be in a continual flux: and therefore with reason we look on them as liable still to the same change. Nor have we of active power (which is the more proper signification of the word power) fewer instances. Since whatever change is observed, the mind must collect a power somewhere, able to make that change, as well as a possibility in the thing itself to receive it.[2] But yet, if we will consider it attentively, bodies by our senses do not afford us so clear and distinct an idea of active power as we have from reflection on the operations of our minds. For all power relating to action, and there being but two sorts of action whereof we have any idea, viz., thinking and motion, let us consider whence we have the clearest ideas of the powers which produce these actions. (1) Of thinking, body affords us no idea at all: it is only from

[1] In the present chapter power, in the sense of active power ('which is the more proper signification of the word') is connected with our own experience of volitional activity in the initiation of movement. In ch. 23 the idea comes up again (as he here indicates) in connexion with the qualities of substances which he had already told us (in ch. 8) are ' powers to produce ideas in us ' or to produce changes in other material things. There he again tells us that ' these powers considered in themselves are truly complex ideas ' (ch. 23. 7). Under the title 'Cause and Effect' the same idea, now specifically classed as an 'idea of relation', reappears at a later stage for special treatment (ch. 26).

[2] As pointed out in the Introduction, this is as frank an acknowledgement as could be desired of the necessity of the idea of causality to interpret the phenomenon of change. Cf. note 1, p. 180.

reflection that we have that. (2) Neither have we from body any idea of the beginning of motion. A body at rest affords us no idea of any active power to move ; and when it is set in motion itself, that motion is rather a passion than an action in it. For when the ball obeys the stroke of a billiard-stick, it is not any action of the ball, but bare passion : also when by impulse it sets another ball in motion that lay in its way, it only communicates the motion it had received from another, and loses in itself so much as the other received ; which gives us but a very obscure idea of an active power of moving in body, whilst we observe it only to transfer but not produce any motion. The idea of the beginning of motion we have only from reflection on what passes in ourselves, where we find by experience, that, barely by willing it, barely by a thought of the mind, we can move the parts of our bodies which were before at rest. So that it seems to me, we have, from the observation of the operation of bodies by our senses, but a very imperfect, obscure idea of active power, since they afford us not any idea in themselves of the power to begin any action, either motion or thought. But if, from the impulse bodies are observed to make one upon another, any one thinks he has a clear idea of power, it serves as well to my purpose, sensation being one of those ways whereby the mind comes by its ideas : only I thought it worth while to consider here by the way, whether the mind doth not receive its idea of active power clearer from reflection on its own operations, than it doth from any external sensation.

5. *Will and Understanding, two powers.*—This at least I think evident, that we find in ourselves a power to begin or forbear, continue or end, several actions of our minds and motions of our bodies, barely by a thought or preference of the mind ordering, or as it were commanding, the doing or not doing such or such a particular action. This power is that which we call the *Will*. The actual exercise of that power, by directing any particular action or its forbearance, is that which we call *volition* or *willing*. The forbearance of that action consequent to such order or command of the mind, is called *voluntary* ; and whatsoever action is performed without such a thought of the mind, is called *involuntary*. The power of perception is that which we call the *Understanding*. Perception, which we make the act of the understanding, is of three sorts : (1) The perception of ideas in our minds. (2) The per-

ception of the signification of signs. (3) The perception of the connexion or repugnancy, agreement or disagreement, that there is between any of our ideas. All these are attributed to the understanding, or perceptive power, though it be the two latter only that use allows us to say we understand.

6. *Faculties.*—These powers of the mind, viz., of perceiving and of preferring, are usually called by another name : and the ordinary way of speaking, is that the understanding and will are two *faculties* of the mind ; a word proper enough, if it be used, as all words should be, so as not to breed any confusion in men's thoughts by being supposed (as I suspect it has been) to stand for some real beings in the soul, that performed those actions of understanding and volition. For when we say, the will is the commanding and superior faculty of the soul ; that it is or is not free ; that it determines the inferior faculties ; that it follows the dictates of the understanding, &c. ; though these and the like expressions, by those that carefully attend to their own ideas, and conduct their thoughts more by the evidence of things than the sound of words, may be understood in a clear and distinct sense : yet I suspect, I say, that this way of speaking of *faculties* has misled many into a confused notion of so many distinct agents in us, which had their several provinces and authorities, and did command, obey, and perform several actions, as so many distinct beings ; which has been no small occasion of wrangling, obscurity, and uncertainty in questions relating to them.

7. *Whence the ideas of liberty and necessity.*—Every one, I think, finds in himself a power to begin or forbear, continue or put an end to, several actions in himself. From the consideration of the extent of this power of the mind over the actions of the man, which every one finds in himself, arise the ideas of *liberty* and *necessity*. [8.] The idea of liberty is the idea of a power in any agent to do or forbear any particular action, according to the determination or thought of the mind, whereby either of them is preferred to the other ; where either of them is not in the power of the agent, to be produced by him according to his volition, there he is not at liberty. So a man striking himself, or his friend, by a convulsive motion of his arm, which it is not in his power, by volition or the direction of his mind, to stop or forbear, nobody thinks he has in that liberty. [12.] As it is in the motions of the body, so it is in the thoughts of our minds. A waking man, being under

the necessity of having some ideas constantly in his mind, is not at liberty to think or not to think; but whether he will remove his contemplation from one idea to another is many times in his choice. But yet some ideas to the mind, like some motions to the body, are such as in certain circumstances it cannot avoid, nor obtain their absence by the utmost effort it can use. A man on the rack is not at liberty to lay by the idea of pain and divert himself with other contemplations; and sometimes a boisterous passion hurries our thoughts as a hurricane does our bodies, without leaving us the liberty of thinking on other things, which we would rather choose.

14. *Liberty belongs not to the will.*—If this be so (as I imagine it is), I leave it to be considered, whether it may not help to put an end to that long agitated, and I think unreasonable, because unintelligible, question, viz., *Whether man's will be free or no?* For, if I mistake not, it follows, from what I have said, that the question itself is altogether improper; and it is as insignificant to ask whether man's will be free, as to ask whether his sleep be swift, or his virtue square. Liberty, which is but a power, belongs only to agents, and cannot be an attribute or modification of the will, which is also but a power. [20.] Not that I deny there are faculties, both in the body and mind. Nor do I deny that those words, and the like, are to have their place in the common use of languages that have made them current. It looks like too much affectation wholly to lay them by: and philosophy itself, though it likes not a gaudy dress, yet when it appears in public, must have so much complacency as to be clothed in the ordinary fashion and language of the country, so far as it can consist with truth and perspicuity. But the fault has been that faculties have been spoken of and represented as so many distinct agents. For it being asked, what it was that digested the meat in our stomachs, it was a ready and very satisfactory answer, to say, that it was the *digestive faculty*, and so in the mind, the *intellectual faculty*, or the understanding, understood; and the *elective faculty*, or the will, willed or commanded; which is, in short, to say that the ability to digest, digested; and the ability to move, moved; and the ability to understand, understood.

21. *But to the agent or man.*—To return then to the inquiry about liberty, I think *the question is not proper, whether the will be free, but whether a man be free.* Thus, I think,

(1) That so far as any one can, by the direction of choice of

his mind preferring the existence of any action to the non-existence of that action, and vice versa, make it to exist or not exist, so far he is free. For how can we think any one freer than to have the power to do what he will ?. [22.] But the inquisitive mind of man, willing to shift off from himself, as far as he can, all thoughts of guilt, is not content with this : and it passes for a good plea, that a man is not free at all, if he be not as free to will as he is to act what he wills. Concerning a man's liberty, there yet therefore is raised this farther question, *whether a man be free to will*; which, I think, is what is meant, when it is disputed whether the will be free. And as to that I imagine,

23. (2) That willing or volition being an action, and freedom consisting in a power of acting or not acting, a man, in respect of willing or the act of volition, when any action in his power is once proposed to his thoughts, as presently to be done, cannot be free. For it is unavoidably necessary to prefer the doing or forbearance of an action in a man's power, which is once so proposed to his thoughts ; a man must necessarily will the one or the other of them : upon which preference or volition, the action or its forbearance certainly follows, and is truly voluntary. But the act of volition, or preferring one of the two, being that which he cannot avoid, a man, in respect of that act of willing, is under a necessity, and so cannot be free.

25. Since then it is plain that in most cases a man is not at liberty whether he will or no ; the next thing demanded is, *whether a man be at liberty to will which of the two he pleases, motion or rest*. This question carries the absurdity of it so manifestly in itself, that one might thereby sufficiently be convinced that liberty concerns not the will. For to ask, whether a man be at liberty to will either motion or rest, speaking or silence, which he pleases, is to ask, whether a man can will what he wills, or be pleased with what he is pleased with. A question which, I think, needs no answer : and they who can make a question of it, must suppose one will to determine the acts of another, and another to determine that ; and so on *in infinitum*.

26. To avoid these and the like absurdities, nothing can be of greater use than to establish in our minds determined ideas of the things under consideration. [27.] First, then, it is carefully to be remembered, that freedom consists in our being able

to act, or not to act, according as we shall choose or will. [28.] Secondly, we must remember that volition, or willing, is an act of the mind directing its thought to the production of any action, and thereby exerting its power to produce it. To avoid multiplying of words, I would crave leave here, under the word action, to comprehend the forbearance too, of any action proposed. [29.] Thirdly, the will being nothing but a power in the mind to direct the operative faculties of a man to motion or rest, as far as they depend on such direction : to the question, What is it determines the will ? the true and proper answer is, The mind. For that which determines the general power of directing to this or that particular direction, is nothing but the agent itself exercising the power it has, that particular way. If this answer satisfies not, it is plain the meaning of the question, what determines the will, is this, What moves the mind in every particular instance, to determine its general power of directing to this or that particular motion or rest ? And to this I answer, the motive for continuing in the same state or action, is only the present satisfaction in it ; the motive to change, is always some uneasiness ; nothing setting us upon the change of state, or upon any new action, but some uneasiness. This is the great motive that works on the mind to put it upon action, which for shortness' sake we will call determining of the will : which I shall more at large explain.

30. *Will and desire must not be confounded.*—But in the way to it, it will be necessary to premise, that though I have above endeavoured to express the act of volition by choosing, preferring, and the like terms, that signify desire as well as volition, for want of other words to mark that act of the mind, whose proper name is *willing* or *volition* ; yet, it being a very simple act, whosoever desires to understand what it is, will better find it by reflecting on his own mind, and observing what it does when it wills, than by any variety of articulate sounds whatsoever. This caution I think the more necessary, because I find the will often confounded with several of the affections, especially *desire*, and one put for the other ; and that by men, who would not willingly be thought not to have had very distinct notions of things, and not to have writ very clearly about them. This, I imagine, has been no small occasion of obscurity and mistake in this matter ; and therefore is, as much as may be, to be avoided. For he that shall turn his thoughts inwards upon what passes in his mind when he wills, shall see that the will or power of volition is conversant about

nothing, but our own actions; terminates there, and reaches no further; and that volition is nothing but that particular determination of the mind, whereby barely by a thought the mind endeavours to give rise, continuation, or stop, to any action which it takes to be in its power. This, well considered, plainly shows that the will is perfectly distinguished from desire; which in the very same action may have a quite contrary tendency from that which our will sets us upon. A man whom I cannot deny, may oblige me to use persuasions to another, which, at the same time I am speaking, I may wish may not prevail on him. In this case, it is plain the will and desire run counter.

31. *Uneasiness determines the will.*—To return then to the enquiry, ' What is it that determines the will in regard to our actions? ' That, upon second thoughts,[1] I am apt to imagine is not, as is generally supposed, the greater good in view, but some (and, for the most part, the most pressing) uneasiness a man is at present under. This is that which successively determines the will, and sets us upon those actions we perform. This uneasiness we may call, as it is, *desire*, which is an uneasiness of the mind for want of some absent good. As much as we desire any absent good, so much are we in pain for it.

35. *The greatest positive good determines not the will, but uneasiness.*—It seems so established and settled a maxim, by the general consent of all mankind, that good, the greater good, determines the will, that I do not at all wonder that, when I first published my thoughts on this subject, I took it for granted; and I imagine, that by a great many I shall be thought more excusable for having then done so, than that now I have ventured to recede from so received an opinion. But yet upon a stricter inquiry, I am forced to conclude that *good*, the *greater good*, though apprehended and acknowledged to be so, does not determine the will until our desire, raised proportionably to it, makes us uneasy in the want of it. Convince a man never so much that plenty has its advantages over poverty; make him see and own that the handsome conveniences of life are better than nasty penury; yet as long as he is content with the latter, and finds no uneasiness in it, he moves not; his will never is determined to any action that shall bring him out of it. Let a man be never so well persuaded of the advantages of virtue, that it is as necessary to a man

[1] From section 28 to the end of section 60, this chapter was rewritten in the second edition.

who has any great aims in this world or hopes in the next, as food to life : yet till he ' hungers and thirsts after righteousness', till he feels an uneasiness in the want of it, his will will not be determined to any action in pursuit of this confessed greater good ; but any other uneasiness he feels in himself shall take place and carry his will to other actions. On the other side, let a drunkard see that his health decays, his estate wastes ; discredit and diseases, and the want of all things, even of his beloved drink, attends him in the course he follows : yet the returns of uneasiness to miss his companions, the habitual thirst after his cups, at the usual time, drives him to the tavern, though he has in his view the loss of health and plenty, and perhaps the joys of another life : the least of which is no inconsiderable good, but such as he confesses is far greater than the tickling of his palate with a glass of wine, or the idle chat of a soaking club. It is not for want of viewing the greater good ; for he sees and acknowledges it, and in the intervals of his drinking hours will take resolutions to pursue the greater good ; but when the uneasiness to miss his accustomed delight returns, the greater acknowledged good loses its hold, and the present uneasiness determines the will to the accustomed action ; which thereby gets stronger footing to prevail against the next occasion, though he at the same time makes secret promises to himself that he will do so no more ; this is the last time he will act against the attainment of those greater goods. And thus he is, from time to time, in the state of that unhappy complainer,[1] *Video meliora proboque, deteriora sequor* : which sentence, allowed for true, and made good by constant experience, may this, and possibly no other, way be easily made intelligible.

36. *Because the removal of uneasiness is the first step to happiness.*—If we enquire into the reason of what experience makes so evident in fact, and examine why it is uneasiness alone operates on the will, and determines it in its choice, we shall find that, forasmuch as whilst we are under any uneasiness, we cannot apprehend ourselves happy, or in the way to it, therefore that which of course determines the choice of our will to the next action, will always be the removing of pain, as long as we have any left, as the first and necessary step towards happiness. [37.] Another reason may be this : because that alone is present, and it is against the nature of things that

[1] Ovid, *Metamorph.* lib. vii, vv. 20–1.

what is absent should operate where it is not. It may be said, that absent good may, by contemplation, be brought home to the mind, and made present. The idea of it indeed may be in the mind, and viewed as present there; but nothing will be in the mind as a present good, able to counterbalance the removal of any uneasiness which we are under, till it raises our desire, and the uneasiness of that has the prevalency in determining the will. Till then, the idea in the mind of whatever good, is there only like other ideas, the object of bare unactive speculation, but operates not on the will, nor sets us on work. [38.] Were the will determined by the views of good, as it appears in contemplation greater or less to the understanding, I do not see how it could ever get loose from the infinite eternal joys of heaven, once proposed and considered as possible. But that it is not so, is visible in experience, the infinitely greatest confessed good being often neglected to satisfy the successive uneasiness of our desires pursuing trifles.

40. *The most pressing uneasiness naturally determines the will.* But we being in this world beset with sundry uneasinesses, distracted with different desires, the next enquiry naturally will be, which of them has the precedency in determining the will to the next action? And to that the answer is, That ordinarily, which is the most pressing of those that are judged capable of being then removed. Very great uneasinesses move not the will when they are judged not capable of a cure: they, in that case, put us not upon endeavours. But these set apart, the most important and urgent uneasiness we at that time feel, is that which ordinarily determines the will successively in that train of voluntary actions which make up our lives.

41. *All desire happiness.*—If it be farther asked, what it is moves desire, I answer, Happiness, and that alone. Happiness and misery are the names of two extremes, the utmost bounds whereof we know not. But of some degrees of both we have very lively impressions, which, for shortness' sake, I shall comprehend under the names of pleasure and pain, there being pleasure and pain of the mind as well as the body. Or, to speak truly, they are all of the mind; though some have their rise in the mind from thought, others in the body from certain modifications of motion. [42.] What has an aptness to produce pleasure in us is that we call good, and what is apt to produce pain in us we call evil; for no other reason but for its aptness to produce pleasure and

pain in us, wherein consists our happiness and misery. Farther, though what is apt to produce any degree of pleasure be in itself good, and what is apt to produce any degree of pain be evil, yet it often happens that we do not call it so when it comes in competition with a greater of its sort. So that if we will rightly estimate what we call good and evil, we shall find it lies much in comparison : for the cause of every less degree of pain, as well as every greater degree of pleasure, has the nature of good and vice versa.

43. *What good is desired, what not.*—Though this be that which is called good and evil, and all good be the proper object of desire in general, yet all good, even seen and confessed to be so, does not necessarily move every particular man's desire ; but only that part, or so much of it, as is considered and taken to make a necessary part of his happiness. Let one man place his satisfaction in sensual pleasures, another in the delight of knowledge : though each of them cannot but confess there is great pleasure in what the other pursues, yet neither of them making the other's delight a part of his happiness, their desires are not moved, but each is satisfied without what the other enjoys, and so his will is not determined to the pursuit of it.

47. *The power to suspend the prosecution of any desire, makes way for consideration.*—There being in us a great many uneasinesses always soliciting, and ready to determine the will, it is natural, as I have said, that the greatest and most pressing should determine the will to the next action ; and so it does for the most part, but not always. For the mind having in most cases, as is evident in experience, a power to *suspend* the execution and satisfaction of any of its desires, and so all, one after another, is at liberty to consider the objects of them, examine them on all sides, and weigh them with others. In this lies the liberty man has ; and from the not using of it right, comes all that variety of mistakes, errors, and faults which we run into in the conduct of our lives, and our endeavours after happiness ; whilst we precipitate the determination of our wills, and engage too soon before due examination. This seems to me the source of all liberty; in this seems to consist that which is (as I think improperly) called *free-will*. For during this suspension of any desire, before the will be determined to action, and the action (which follows that determination) done, we have opportunity to examine, view,

and judge of the good or evil of what we are going to do ; and when upon due examination we have judged, we have done our duty, all that we can or ought to do in pursuit of our happiness ; and it is not a fault, but a perfection of our nature, to desire, will, and act, according to the last result of a fair examination.

48. *To be determined by our own judgement, is no restraint to liberty.*—This is so far from being a restraint or diminution of freedom, that it is the very improvement and benefit of it ; it is not an abridgement, it is the end and use, of our liberty ; and the farther we are removed from such a determination, the nearer we are to misery and slavery. Were we determined by anything but the last result of our own minds, judging of the good or evil of any action, we were not free. [49.] If we look upon those superior beings above us who enjoy perfect happiness, we shall have reason to judge, that they are more steadily determined in their choice of good than we ; and yet we have no reason to think they are less happy or less free than we are. And if it were fit for such poor finite creatures as we are to pronounce what infinite wisdom and goodness could do, I think we might say that God himself cannot choose what is not good ; the freedom of the Almighty hinders not his being determined by what is best. [50.] If to break loose from the conduct of reason, and to want that restraint of examination and judgement which keeps us from choosing or doing the worse, be liberty, true liberty, madmen and fools are the only freemen.

52. This is the hinge on which turns the *liberty* of intellectual beings, in their constant endeavours after, and steady prosecution of true felicity, that they can *suspend* this prosecution in particular cases, till they have looked before them, and informed themselves whether that particular thing which is then proposed or desired lie in the way to their main end, and make a real part of that which is their greatest good. This, as seems to me, is the great privilege of finite intellectual beings. [53.] Nor let any one say, he cannot govern his passions, nor hinder them from breaking out, and carrying him into action ; for what he can do before a prince or a great man, he can do alone, or in the presence of God, if he will.

72. [Before I close this chapter, it may perhaps be to our purpose, and help to give us clearer conceptions about *power*,

if we make our thoughts take a little more exact survey of *action*. I have said above, that we have ideas but of two sorts of action, viz., motion and thinking. These, in truth, though called and counted actions, yet, if nearly considered, will not be found to be always perfectly so. For, if I mistake not, there are instances of both kinds, which, upon due consideration, will be found rather *passions* than actions, and consequently so far the effects barely of passive powers in those subjects which yet on their account are thought agents. For in these instances the substance that hath motion or thought receives the impression, whereby it is put into that action, purely from without, and so acts merely by the capacity it has to receive such an impression from some external agent; and such a power is not properly an active power, but a mere passive capacity in the subject. Sometimes the substance or agent puts itself into action by its own power; and this is properly *active power*. Whatsoever modification a substance has, whereby it produces any effect, that is called action : v. g., a solid substance by motion operates on or alters the sensible ideas of another substance, and therefore this modification of motion we call action. But yet this motion in that solid substance is, when rightly considered, but a passion, if it received it only from some external agent. So that the active power of motion is in no substance which cannot begin motion in itself, or in another substance, when at rest. So likewise in thinking, a power to receive ideas or thoughts from the operation of any external substance, is called a power of thinking : but this is but a passive power or capacity. But to be able to bring into view ideas out of sight at one's own choice, and to compare which of them one thinks fit, this is an active power. This reflection may be of some use to preserve us from mistakes about powers and actions, which grammar and the common frame of languages may be apt to lead us into : since what is signified by verbs that grammarians call active, does not always signify action; v. g., this proposition, 'I see the moon or a star', or, 'I feel the heat of the sun', though expressed by a verb active, does not signify any action in me whereby I operate on those substances, but the reception of the ideas of light, roundness, and heat; wherein I am not active, but barely passive, and cannot, in that position of my eyes or body, avoid receiving them. But when I turn my eyes another way, or remove my body out of the sunbeams, I am properly active;

because of my own choice, by a power within myself, I put myself into that motion. Such an action is the product of active power.][1]

73. And thus I have, in a short draft, given a view of our *original ideas*, from whence all the rest are derived, and of which they are made up;[2] which if I would consider as a philosopher,[3] and examine on what causes they depend, and of what they are made, I believe they all might be reduced to these very few primary and original ones, viz., *extension, solidity, mobility*, or the power of being moved ; which by our senses we receive from body : *perceptivity*, or the power of perception, or thinking; *motivity*, or the power of moving; which by reflection we receive from our minds. I crave leave to make use of these two new words, to avoid the danger of being mistaken in the use of those which are equivocal. To which if we add *existence, duration, number*, which belong both to the one and the other, we have perhaps all the original ideas on which the rest depend. For by these, I imagine, might be explained the nature of colours, sounds, tastes, smells, and all other ideas we have, if we had but faculties

[1] This paragraph was added in the fourth edition. It returns to the distinction between active and passive power suggested in sections 2 and 4. Locke recurs to the subject again at the end of the following chapter (II. 22. 11).

[2] Locke has now completed his account of the 'simple modes'. Although these are themselves 'complex ideas', they are in Locke's scheme (at any rate in the case of space, time, and number) only repetitions of simple ideas. Hence Locke interposes this section to mark the stage he has arrived at. The idea of power is not covered by his definition of simple modes as 'only variations or combinations of the same simple idea' ; neither are the modes of thinking or the modes of pleasure and pain.

[3] i. e. a natural philosopher, or physicist. The list here, it should be noted, is not really of our 'original ideas', for these, as expounded in chapters 3-7, consist largely of secondary qualities. The primary qualities, summarized as extension, solidity, and mobility, are here regarded, from the point of view of physical and physiological science, as the real causes whereby bodies produce in us 'the rest' of our original ideas, exemplified by 'colours, sounds, tastes, smells', to which, apparently, the term 'sensible qualities' is here more specially applied. Formerly, as Professor Sorley points out, 'Locke was trying to get back to the primary data of our individual experience'; in this list he is thinking of 'the objective reality on which our experience depends and which, he assumes, it reveals'. Unfortunately he is always in danger of confusing the two points of view. (Cf. Sorley's *English Philosophy*, pp. 114-16.)

acute enough to perceive the severally modified extensions and motions of these minute bodies which produce those several sensations in us. But my present purpose being only to enquire into the knowledge the mind has of things by those ideas and appearances which God has fitted it to receive from them, and how the mind comes by that knowledge, rather than into their causes or manner of production, I shall not, contrary to the design of this *Essay*, set myself to enquire philosophically into the peculiar constitution of bodies and the configuration of parts, whereby they have the power to produce in us the ideas of their sensible qualities. I shall not enter any further into that disquisition,[1] it sufficing to my purpose to observe, that gold or saffron has a power to produce in us the idea of yellow ; and snow or milk, the idea of white ; which we can only have by our sight, without examining the texture of the parts of those bodies, or the particular figures or motion of the particles which rebound from them, to cause in us that particular sensation : though when we go beyond the bare ideas in our minds, and would enquire into their causes, we cannot conceive anything else to be in any sensible object whereby it produces different ideas in us, but the different bulk, figure, number, texture, and motion of its insensible parts.

## CHAPTER XXII

### OF MIXED MODES

1. *Mixed modes, what.*—Having treated of *simple modes* in the foregoing chapters, and given several instances of some of the most considerable of them, to show what they are, and how we come by them ; we are now, in the next place, to consider those we call *mixed modes* : such are the complex ideas we mark by the names obligation, drunkenness, a lie, &c., which, consisting of several combinations of simple ideas of different kinds, I have called mixed modes, to distinguish them from the more simple modes, which consist only of simple ideas of the same kind. These mixed modes, being also such combinations of simple ideas as are not looked upon to be characteristical marks of any real beings that have a steady

[1] Locke touches upon this topic repeatedly in the sequel, e. g. ch. 23. 11-13, IV. 3, &c.

existence, but scattered and independent ideas put together by the mind, are thereby distinguished from the complex ideas of substances.

2. *Made by the mind.*—That the mind, in respect of its simple ideas, is wholly passive, and receives them all from the existence and operations of things, such as sensation or reflection offers them, without being able to make any one idea, experience shows us. But if we attentively consider these ideas I call mixed modes, we are now speaking of, we shall find their original quite different. The mind often exercises an active power in making these several combinations: for, it being once furnished with simple ideas, it can put them together in several compositions, and so make variety of complex ideas, without examining whether they exist so together in nature. And hence, I think, it is that these ideas are called *notions*;[1] as if they had their original and constant existence more in the thoughts of men, than in the reality of things; and to form such ideas it sufficed that the mind put the parts of them together, and that they were consistent in the understanding, without considering whether they had any real being: though I do not deny but several of them might be taken from observation.

4. *The name ties the parts of mixed modes into one idea.*—Every mixed mode consisting of many distinct simple ideas, it seems reasonable to enquire, whence it has its unity, and how such a precise multitude comes to make but one idea, since that combination does not always exist together in nature. To which I answer, It is plain it has its unity from an act of the mind combining those several simple ideas together, and considering them as one complex one, consisting of those parts; and the mark of this union, or that which is looked on generally to complete it, is one name given to that combination. For it is by their names that men commonly regulate their account of their distinct species of mixed modes, seldom allowing or considering any number of simple ideas to make one complex one,

---

[1] Notions, as actively formed and tied together by the mind, are all, in Locke's sense of the word, abstract ideas, and therefore this suggestion (repeated III. 5. 12) may have led Berkeley to his distinction between 'ideas' (perceived by the senses or represented in imagination) and the 'notions' of spirits and relations, which are essentially unpicturable but the meaning of which we nevertheless understand. Abstract idea, notion, concept mean the same thing. (Cf. II. 11. 9–11; IV. 9. 1.)

but such collections as there be names for. Thus, though the killing of an old man be as fit in nature to be united into one complex idea as the killing a man's father; yet, there being no name standing precisely for the one, as there is the name of parricide to mark the other, it is not taken for a particular complex idea, nor a distinct species of actions from that of killing a young man, or any other man.

5. *The cause of making mixed modes.*—If we should enquire a little farther, to see what it is that occasions men to make several combinations of simple ideas into distinct and, as it were, settled modes, and neglect others which, in the nature of things themselves, have as much an aptness to be combined and make distinct ideas, we shall find the reason of it to be the end of language; which being to mark or communicate men's thoughts to one another with all the dispatch that may be, they usually make such collections of ideas into complex modes, and affix names to them, as they have frequent use of in their way of living and conversation. [6.] This shows us how it comes to pass, that there are in every language many particular words which cannot be rendered by any one single word of another. For the several fashions, customs, and manners of one nation, making several combinations of ideas familiar and necessary in one, which another people have had never any occasion to make, or perhaps so much as take notice of, names come of course to be annexed to them, to avoid long periphrases in things of daily conversation. Thus ὀστρακισμός amongst the Greeks, and *proscriptio* amongst the Romans, were words which other languages had no names that exactly answered. [7.] Hence also we may see the reason why languages constantly change, take up new and lay by old terms. What a number of different ideas are by this means wrapped up in one short sound, and how much of our time and breath is thereby saved, any one will see who will but take the pains to enumerate all the ideas that either *reprieve* or *appeal* stand for; and instead of either of those names use a periphrasis to make any one understand their meaning.

10. *Motion, thinking, and power have been most modified.*— It is worth our observing which of all our simple ideas have been most modified, and had most mixed modes made out of them, with names given to them : and those have been these three : thinking, and motion (which are the two ideas which comprehend in them all action), and power, from whence these

actions are conceived to flow. For action being the great business of mankind, and the whole matter about which all laws are conversant, it is no wonder that the several modes of thinking and motion should be taken notice of, the ideas of them observed and laid up in the memory, and have names assigned to them; without which, laws could be but ill made, or vice and disorder repressed.

11. *Several words seeming to signify action, signify but the effect.*—*Power* being the source from whence all action proceeds, the substances wherein these powers are, when they exert this power into act, are called *causes*; and the substances which thereupon are produced, or the simple ideas which are introduced into any subject by the exerting of that power, are called *effects*. The *efficacy* whereby the new substance or idea is produced, is called, in the subject exerting that power, *action*; but in the subject, wherein any simple idea is changed or produced, it is called *passion*: which efficacy however various, and the effects almost infinite, yet we can, I think, conceive it, in intellectual agents, to be nothing else but modes of thinking and willing; in corporeal agents, nothing else but modifications of motion. And therefore many words which seem to express some action, signify nothing of the action, or *modus operandi*, at all, but barely the effect, with some circumstances of the subject wrought on, or cause operating; v. g., creation, annihilation, contain in them no idea of the action or manner whereby they are produced, but barely of the cause, and the thing done. And when a countryman says the cold freezes water, though the word freezing seems to import some action, yet truly it signifies nothing but the effect; viz., that water, that was before fluid, is become hard and consistent; without containing any idea of the action whereby it is done.[1]

---

[1] We may trace the development of Locke's thought here in Berkeley's denial of real causation in the physical world—in his interpretation, that is to say, of the causal relation in the physical world as no more than orderly sequence or the relation of sign and thing signified—and in Hume's polemic against the notion of any ' tie or connexion between the cause and effect which binds them together '.

## CHAPTER XXIII[1]

### OF OUR COMPLEX IDEAS OF SUBSTANCES

1. *Ideas of substances, how made.*—The mind being, as I have declared, furnished with a great number of the simple ideas conveyed in by the senses, as they are found in exterior things, or by reflection on its own operations, takes notice also, that a certain number of these simple ideas go constantly together; which being presumed to belong to one thing, and words being suited to common apprehensions, and made use of for quick dispatch, are called, so united in one subject, by one name;

---

[1] This is one of the most important chapters in the *Essay*. Its nominal subject is our complex ideas of particular sorts of substances, but it is chiefly concerned with the idea of 'pure substance in general', the substratum or support which, in each case, we 'suppose' to be present in addition to the group of simple ideas which we observe to go constantly together. Other passages in which Locke deals with this idea are I. 4. 18; II. 12. 6; 13. 17–20; our knowledge of substances is further discussed in Bk. III. 6 ('Names of Substances'), Bk. IV. 3. 6–16; 4. 11–17, &c. For Locke's position in regard to the idea of 'substance in general', which 'we neither have nor can have by sensation and reflection', but which he pronounces nevertheless to be a necessary idea which 'all simple ideas carry with them', cf. Introduction, pp. xxiv–vi. His further difficulties in regard to the obscurity of the idea, our inability to give it any determinate content, and our consequent ignorance, as he holds, of the real essence of any substance, whether material or immaterial, arise from the inconsistent demand to know the substance as 'something besides' the qualities that characterize it, i.e., in effect, to know it as an additional quality. Otherwise expressed, they are due to the desire to know as a simple idea of sensation or reflection what he has acknowledged cannot come to us by either of these channels. Or again, it might be said, he insists on treating as an absolute or independent fact a conception which he has expressly described as 'a relative idea'. Hence he tells us (section 16 of this chapter) that 'by the complex idea of extended, figured, coloured and *all other sensible qualities*, which is all that we know of it, we are as far from the idea of the substance of body, *as if we knew nothing at all*'. But our supposed ignorance arises, as Leibniz rightly pointed out (*New Essays*, Bk. II. 23), because we demand a knowledge of which the subject does not admit. Locke's agnosticism in this respect was the object of Berkeley's delicate raillery; but, reinforced by Kant's analogous doctrine of the thing-in-itself, it continued to haunt English philosophy in Hamilton, Mansel, and Spencer. Spencer's Unknown and Unknowable is the lineal descendant of Locke's 'unknown common subject which inheres not in anything else' (section 6). Cf. the Editor's *Scottish Philosophy*, Lecture V, The Relativity of Knowledge, or *The Idea of God*, Lecture VIII, Positivism and Agnosticism.

Ch. 23      *Of our Complex Ideas of Substances*      155

which, by inadvertency,[1] we are apt afterward to talk of and consider as one simple idea, which indeed is a complication of many ideas together : because, as I have said, not imagining how these simple ideas can subsist by themselves, we accustom ourselves to suppose [2] some *substratum* wherein they do subsist, and from which they do result, which therefore we call *substance*.

2. <u>*Our idea of substance in general*</u>.—So that if any one will examine himself concerning his notion of pure substance in general, he will find he has no other idea of it at all, but only a supposition of he knows not what support of such qualities which are capable of producing simple ideas in us ; which qualities are commonly called accidents. If any one should be asked, what is the subject wherein colour or weight inheres, he would have nothing to say, but the solid extended parts : and if he were demanded, what is it that that solidity and extension inhere in, he would not be in a much better case than the Indian before mentioned,[3] who saying that the world was supported by a great elephant, was asked, what the elephant rested on ; to which his answer was, a great tortoise: but being again pressed to know what gave support to the broad-backed tortoise, replied, something, he knew not what. And thus here, as in all other cases where we use words without having clear and distinct ideas, we talk like children ; who being questioned what such a thing is which they know not, readily give this satisfactory answer, that it is *something*; which in truth signifies no more, when so used, either by children or men, but that they know not what ; and that the thing they pretend to know, and

---

[1] Leibniz justly takes exception to this phrase. The unity, he points out, is the unity of the subject, the concrete individual of which we predicate the qualities, and in no way suggests the simplicity of a simple idea. We do not begin in knowledge with the qualities as abstractions which we afterwards tie together and refer to a subject. ' It is rather the *concretum*, as wise, warm, or shining, which arises in our mind, than abstractions like knowledge, heat, light, &c.'

[2] Locke makes it quite clear in the controversy with Stillingfleet that, in his somewhat ambiguous phraseology here, he has no intention of throwing doubt on the necessity and objective validity of the idea. Perhaps the strongest statement is that quoted by Professor Gibson (*op. cit.*, 191) from the *First Letter* : ' Having everywhere affirmed and built upon it that man is a substance, I cannot be supposed to question or doubt the being of substance, till I can question or doubt of my own being.'

[3] Ch. 13, section 20.

talk of, is what they have no distinct idea of at all, and so are perfectly ignorant of it, and in the dark. The idea, then, we have, to which we give the general name substance, being nothing but the supposed, but unknown, support of those qualities we find existing, which we imagine cannot subsist *sine re substante*, without something to support them, we call that support *substantia*; which, according to the true import of the word, is, in plain English, standing under, or upholding.

3. *Of the sorts of substances.*—An obscure and relative idea of substance in general being thus made, we come to have the ideas of *particular sorts of substances*, by collecting such combinations of simple ideas as are, by experience and observation of men's senses, taken notice of to exist together, and are therefore supposed to flow from the particular internal constitution or unknown essence of that substance. Thus we come to have the ideas of a man, horse, gold, water, &c., of which substances, whether any one has any other clear idea, farther than of certain simple ideas coexisting together, I appeal to every one's own experience. It is the ordinary qualities observable in iron or a diamond, put together, that make the true complex idea of those substances, which a smith or a jeweller commonly knows better than a philosopher; who, whatever substantial forms[1] he may talk of, has no other idea of those substances than what is framed by a collection of those simple ideas which are to be found in them. Only we must take notice, that our complex ideas of substances, besides all these simple ideas they are made up of, have always the confused idea of something to which they belong and in which they subsist. And therefore, when we speak of any sort of substance, we say it is a thing having such or such qualities; as body is a thing that is extended, figured, and capable of motion; a spirit, a thing capable of thinking; and so hardness, friability, and power to draw iron, we say, are qualities to be found in a loadstone. These and the like fashions of speaking intimate that the substance is supposed always something besides the extension, figure, solidity, motion, thinking, or other observable ideas, though we know not what it is.

---

[1] This scholastic doctrine is criticized at some length in Bk. III, chs. 3 and 6, in connexion with the problem of classification. Locke attacks the doctrine there for its assumption of a fixed number of species or kinds in nature. 'Form' is the Aristotelian εἶδος, considered as the essence of the species. Cf. II. 31. 6–7; III. 3. 17; 6. 14–17

4. *No clear idea of substance in general.*—Hence, when we talk or think of any particular sort of corporeal substances, as horse, stone, &c., though the idea we have of either of them be but the complication or collection of those several simple ideas of sensible qualities which we use to find united in the thing called horse or stone ; yet because we cannot conceive how they should subsist alone, nor one in another, we suppose them existing in, and supported by, some common subject ; which support we denote by the name substance, though it be certain we have no clear or distinct idea of that thing we suppose a support.

5. *As clear an idea of spirit as body.*—The same happens concerning the operations of the mind, viz., thinking, reasoning, fearing, &c., which we concluding not to subsist of themselves, nor apprehending how they can belong to body, or be produced by it, we are apt to think these the actions of some other substance, which we call spirit ; whereby yet it is evident, that having no other idea or notion of matter, but something wherein those many sensible qualities which affect our senses do subsist ; by supposing a substance wherein thinking, knowing, doubting, and a power of moving, &c. do subsist ; we have as clear a notion of the substance of spirit as we have of body ; the one being supposed to be (without knowing what it is) the *substratum* to those simple ideas we have from without ; and the other supposed (with a like ignorance of what it is) to be the *substratum* to those operations which we experiment in ourselves within. It is plain, then, that the idea of corporeal substance in matter is as remote from our conceptions and apprehensions as that of spiritual substance or spirit ; and therefore, from our not having any notion of the substance of spirit, we can no more conclude its non-existence than we can, for the same reason, deny the existence of body : it being as rational to affirm there is no body, because we have no clear and distinct idea of the substance of matter, as to say there is no spirit, because we have no clear and distinct idea of the substance of a spirit.

6. *Of the sorts of substances.*—Whatever therefore be the secret and abstract nature of substance in general, all the ideas we have of particular distinct sorts of substances are nothing but several combinations of simple ideas coexisting in such, though unknown, cause of their union, as makes the whole subsist of itself. It is by such combinations of simple ideas,

and nothing else, that we represent particular sorts of substances to ourselves. Such are the ideas we have of their several species in our minds; and such only do we, by their specific names, signify to others, v. g., man, horse, sun, water, iron; upon hearing which words, every one who understands the language frames in his mind a combination of those several simple ideas which he has usually observed or fancied to exist together under that denomination; all which he supposes to rest in, and be, as it were, adherent to, that unknown common subject, which inheres not in anything else. Though in the meantime it be manifest, and every one upon enquiry into his own thoughts will find, that he has no other idea of any substance but what he has barely of those sensible qualities, which he supposes to inhere, with a supposition of such a substratum, as gives, as it were, a support to those qualities or simple ideas, which he has observed to exist united together. Thus the idea of the sun, what is it but an aggregate of those several simple ideas, bright, hot, roundish, having a constant regular motion, at a certain distance from us, and perhaps some other? As he who thinks and discourses of the sun, has been more or less accurate in observing those sensible qualities, ideas, or properties, which are in that thing which he calls the sun.

7. *Powers a great part of our complex ideas of substances.*—For he has the perfectest idea of any of the particular sorts of substances who has gathered and put together most of those simple ideas which do exist in it, among which are to be reckoned its active powers and passive capacities; which, though not simple ideas, yet in this respect, for brevity's sake, may conveniently enough be reckoned amongst them;[1] v. g., we immediately by our senses perceive in fire its heat and colour; which are, if rightly considered, nothing but powers in it to produce those ideas in us: we also by our senses perceive the colour and brittleness of charcoal, whereby we come by the knowledge of another power in fire, which it has to change the colour and consistency of wood. By the former, fire immediately, by the latter it mediately, discovers to us these several powers, which therefore we look upon to be a part of the qualities of fire, and so make them a part of the complex idea of it. For all those powers that we take cognizance of, terminating only in the alteration of some sensible qualities in

[1] Cf. ch. 21. 3.

those subjects on which they operate, and so making them exhibit to us new sensible ideas ; therefore it is that I have reckoned these powers amongst the simple ideas which make the complex ones of the sorts of substances ; though these powers, considered in themselves, are truly complex ideas.

8. *And why.*—Nor are we to wonder that powers make a great part of our complex ideas of substances, since their secondary qualities are those which, in most of them, serve principally to distinguish substances one from another, and commonly make a considerable part of the complex idea of the several sorts of them. For our senses failing us in the discovery of the bulk, texture, and figure of the minute parts of bodies, on which their real constitutions and differences depend, we are fain to make use of their secondary qualities as the characteristical notes and marks whereby to frame ideas of them in our minds, and distinguish them one from another. All which secondary qualities, as has been shown, are nothing but bare powers. For the colour and taste of opium are, as well as its soporific or anodyne virtues, mere powers depending on its primary qualities, whereby it is fitted to produce different operations on different parts of our bodies.

9. *Three sorts of ideas make our complex ones of substances.*— The ideas that make our complex ones of corporeal substances are of these three sorts. First, the ideas of the primary qualities of things which are discovered by our senses, and are in them even when we perceive them not : such are the bulk, figure, number, situation, and motion of the parts of bodies, which are really in them, whether we take notice of them or no. Secondly, the sensible secondary qualities which, depending on these, are nothing but the powers those substances have to produce several ideas in us by our senses ; which ideas are not in the things themselves otherwise than as anything is in its cause. Thirdly, the aptness we consider in any substance to give or receive such alterations of primary qualities as that the substance so altered should produce in us different ideas from what it did before ; these are called active and passive powers : all which powers, as far as we have any notice or notion of them, terminate only in sensible simple ideas. For whatever alteration a loadstone has the power to make in the minute particles of iron, we should have no notion of any power it had at all to operate on iron, did not its sensible motion discover it ; and I doubt not but there are a thousand changes

that bodies we daily handle have a power to cause in one another, which we never suspect, because they never appear in sensible effects.[1]

10. *Powers make a great part of our complex ideas of substances.*—Powers therefore justly make a great part of our complex ideas of substances. He that will examine his complex idea of gold, will find several of its ideas that make it up to be only powers: as the power of being melted, but of not spending itself in the fire, of being dissolved in *aqua regia*, are ideas as necessary to make up our complex idea of gold, as its colour and weight: which, if duly considered, are also nothing but different powers. For to speak truly, yellowness is not actually in gold, but is a power in gold to produce that idea in us by our eyes when placed in a due light: and the heat which we cannot leave out of our idea of the sun, is no more really in the sun than the white colour it introduces into wax.[2]

11. *The now secondary qualities of bodies would disappear, if we could discover the primary ones of their minute parts.*—Had

---

[1] This thought is elaborated in a fine passage, Bk. IV. 6. 11.

[2] In sections 7–10 Locke returns upon the distinctions he had drawn in ch. 8 between primary qualities, secondary qualities, and powers. Secondary qualities, he had there said, 'are usually called *sensible* qualities' as distinguished from the primary, which are in bodies 'whether we perceive them or no', and by which we have 'an idea of the thing as it is in itself' (II. 8. 23). This usage he follows here, although it is not quite easy to maintain, seeing he is bound to acknowledge that the primary qualities also are 'discovered by our senses' (section 9). The point, however, is the generalized use of the term 'powers' to include both the secondary qualities and what are popularly known as powers, and to distinguish both from what he calls 'positive qualities' (section 36). Both are regarded as depending on the 'bulk, texture, and figure of the minute parts of bodies' which 'our senses fail to discover' (section 8). This is repeatedly spoken of as 'the real constitution' of bodies (the 'internal constitution', the 'secret composition and radical texture' in section 12) and it is subsequently (in Bks. III and IV) identified with the 'real essence' of bodies, although the term essence appears to be used in the present chapter as equivalent to 'substance', e. g. in sections 3 and 35. The internal constitution of bodies would disclose itself to 'microscopical eyes', but substance, as Locke understands it, is inherently unknowable. It is for ever hidden behind its own manifestations.

Berkeley's contention was that the primary qualities are on the same level as the so-called *sensible* qualities, being equally effects 'in us' of a power which he identifies with the Divine Agent. He therefore eliminates substance in the case of material bodies, a body being for him only the group or cluster of sense-ideas which 'go constantly together'.

## Ch. 23    *Of our Complex Ideas of Substances*

we senses acute enough to discern the minute particles of bodies, and the real constitution on which their sensible qualities depend, I doubt not but they would produce quite different ideas in us, and that which is now the yellow colour of gold would then disappear, and instead of it we should see an admirable texture of parts of a certain size and figure. This microscopes plainly discover to us; for what to our naked eyes produces a certain colour is, by thus augmenting the acuteness of our senses, discovered to be quite a different thing; and the thus altering, as it were, the proportion of the bulk of the minute parts of a coloured object to our usual sight, produces different ideas from what it did before. Thus sand, or pounded glass, which is opaque and white to the naked eye, is pellucid in a microscope: Blood to the naked eye appears all red; but by a good microscope, wherein its lesser parts appear, shows only some few globules of red, swimming in a pellucid liquor; and how these red globules would appear, if glasses could be found that yet could magnify them one thousand or ten thousand times more, is uncertain.

12. *Our faculties of discovery suited to our state.*—The infinite wise Contriver of us and all things about us hath fitted our senses, faculties, and organs to the conveniences of life, and the business we have to do here. We are able by our senses to know and distinguish things, and to examine them so far as to apply them to our uses, and several ways to accommodate the exigencies of this life. We have insight enough into their admirable contrivances and wonderful effects to admire and magnify the wisdom, power, and goodness of their Author. Such a knowledge as this, which is suited to our present condition, we want not faculties to attain. But it appears not that God intended we should have a perfect, clear, and adequate knowledge of them: that perhaps is not in the comprehension of any finite being. We are furnished with faculties (dull and weak as they are) to discover enough in the creatures to lead us to the knowledge of the Creator, and the knowledge of our duty; and we are fitted well enough with abilities to provide for the conveniences of living: these are our business in this world. But were our senses altered, and made much quicker and acuter, the appearance and outward scheme of things would have quite another face to us; and I am apt to think, would be inconsistent with our being, or at least well-being, in this part of the universe which we inhabit. He that considers how

little our constitution is able to bear a remove into parts of this air not much higher than that we commonly breathe in, will have reason to be satisfied that, in this globe of earth allotted for our mansion, the all-wise Architect has suited our organs and the bodies that are to affect them one to another. If our sense of hearing were but a thousand times quicker than it is, how would a perpetual noise distract us. And we should, in the quietest retirement, be less able to sleep or meditate than in the middle of a sea-fight. Nay, if that most instructive of our senses, seeing, were in any man a thousand or a hundred thousand times more acute than it is now by the best microscope, things several millions of times less than the smallest object of his sight now would then be visible to his naked eyes, and so he would come nearer the discovery of the texture and motion of the minute parts of corporeal things, and in many of them probably get ideas of their internal constitutions: but then he would be in a quite different world from other people: nothing would appear the same to him and others: the visible ideas of everything would be different. So that I doubt whether he and the rest of men could discourse concerning the objects of sight, or have any communication about colours, their appearances being so wholly different. And perhaps such a quickness and tenderness of sight could not endure bright sunshine, or so much as open daylight; nor take in but a very small part of any object at once, and that too only at a very near distance. And if by the help of such microscopical eyes [1] (if I may so call them) a man could penetrate farther than ordinary into the secret composition and radical texture of bodies, he would not make any great advantage by the change, if such an acute sight would not serve to conduct him to the market and exchange; if he could not see things he was to avoid at a convenient distance, nor distinguish things he had to do with by those sensible qualities others do. He that was sharp-sighted enough to see the configuration of the minute particles of the spring of a clock, and observe upon what peculiar structure and impulse its elastic motion depends, would no doubt discover something very admirable. But if eyes so framed could not view at once the hand, and the characters of the hour-plate, and thereby at a distance see what o'clock it was, their owner could not be much benefited

[1] Cf. Pope in the *Essay on Man*:
    Why has not man a microscopic eye?
    For this plain reason,—man is not a fly.

by that acuteness ; which, whilst it discovered the secret contrivance of the parts of the machine, made him lose its use.

13. *Conjecture about spirits.*—And here give me leave to propose an extravagant conjecture of mine, viz., that since we have some reason (if there be any credit to be given to the report of things, that our philosophy cannot account for) to imagine, that spirits can assume to themselves bodies of different bulk, figure, and conformation of parts—whether one great advantage some of them have over us, may not lie in this, that they can so frame and shape to themselves organs of sensation or perception, as to suit them to their present design, and the circumstances of the object they would consider. For how much would that man exceed all others in knowledge, who had but the faculty so to alter the structure of his eyes, that one sense, as to make it capable of all the several degrees of vision which the assistance of glasses (casually at first light on) has taught us to conceive ? What wonders would he discover, who could so fit his eye to all sorts of objects, as to see, when he pleased, the figure and motion of the minute particles in the blood, and other juices of animals, as distinctly as he does, at other times, the shape and motion of the animals themselves ? But to us, in our present state, alterable organs so contrived, as to discover the figure and motion of the minute parts of bodies, whereon depend those sensible qualities we now observe in them, would perhaps be of no advantage. God has no doubt made us so, as is best for us in our present condition. He hath fitted us for the neighbourhood of the bodies that surround us, and we have to do with : and though we cannot, by the faculties we have, attain to a perfect knowledge of things, yet they will serve us well enough for those ends above mentioned, which are our great concernment. I beg my reader's pardon for laying before him so wild a fancy, concerning the ways of perception in beings above us ; but how extravagant soever it be, I doubt whether we can imagine anything about the knowledge of angels, but after this manner, some way or other, in proportion to what we find and observe in ourselves. And though we cannot but allow that the infinite power and wisdom of God may frame creatures with a thousand other faculties and ways of perceiving things without them, than what we have, yet our thoughts can go no farther than our own : so impossible it is for us to enlarge our very guesses beyond the ideas received from our own sensation and

reflection. The supposition at least, that angels do sometimes assume bodies, needs not startle us ; since some of the most ancient and most learned Fathers of the church seemed to believe that they had bodies : and this is certain, that their state and way of existence is unknown to us.

14. *Complex ideas of substances.*—But to return to the matter in hand, the ideas we have of substances, and the ways we come by them : I say, Our *specific* ideas of substances are nothing else but a *collection of a certain number of simple ideas, considered as united in one thing.* These ideas of substances, though they are commonly called simple apprehensions, and the names of them simple terms; yet, in effect, are complex and compounded. Thus the idea which an Englishman signifies by the name swan is white colour, long neck, red beak, black legs, and whole feet, and all these of a certain size, with a power of swimming in the water, and making a certain kind of noise ; and perhaps to a man who has long observed those kind of birds, some other properties, which all terminate in sensible simple ideas, all united in one common subject.

15. *Idea of spiritual substances as clear as of bodily substances.* —Besides the complex ideas we have of material sensible substances, of which I have last spoken,—by the simple ideas we have taken from those operations of our own minds, which we experiment daily in ourselves, we are able to frame the *complex idea of an immaterial spirit.*[1] For putting together the

[1] The rest of this chapter is mainly occupied with the argument that the idea of an immaterial substance is as clear as that of a material substance and presents no more difficulty, (1) for the paradoxical reason that we are equally—indeed totally—ignorant of the substance of both, (2) because it is as difficult to understand how the solid parts of matter cohere as it is to understand how the soul thinks, (3) because it is no more difficult to conceive ' how a substance we know not should, by thought, set body into motion than how a substance we know not should, by impulse, set body into motion '. Following the Scholastic and Cartesian tradition, Locke assumes in this chapter that the thinking substance is immaterial, although he argues elsewhere that it is as easy to conceive that God ' should superadd to matter a faculty of thinking [as] that he should superadd to it another substance with a faculty of thinking ', and that ' it becomes the modesty of philosophy, not to pronounce magisterially, where we want that evidence that can produce knowledge' (IV. 3. 6). Certainly if we are completely ignorant of the substance in both cases, and if, as he says in his *First Letter* to Stillingfleet, ' the general idea of substance is everywhere the same ', it is hard to see what grounds we can have for supposing two different sorts of

ideas of thinking and willing, or the power of moving or quieting corporeal motion, joined to substance, of which we have no distinct idea, we have the idea of an immaterial spirit; and by putting together the ideas of coherent solid parts, and a power of being moved, joined with substance, of which likewise we have no positive idea, we have the idea of matter. The one is as clear and distinct an idea as the other: the idea of thinking and moving a body being as clear and distinct ideas as the ideas of extension, solidity, and being moved. For our idea of substance is equally obscure, or none at all, in both; it is but a supposed I know not what, to support those ideas we call accidents. [It is for want of reflection that we are apt to think that our senses show us nothing but material things. Every act of sensation, when duly considered, gives us an equal view of both parts of nature, the corporeal and spiritual. For whilst I know, by seeing or hearing, &c., that there is some corporeal being without me, the object of that sensation, I do more certainly know that there is some spiritual being within me that sees and hears. This I must be convinced cannot be the action of bare insensible matter, nor ever could be without an immaterial thinking being.][1]

16. *No idea of abstract substance.*—By the complex idea of extended, figured, coloured, and all other sensible qualities which is all that we know of it, we are as far from the idea of

substances. If substance is the purely indeterminate support of accidents that Locke represents it as being, the qualities of a substance are in no wise grounded in its nature (for it has no nature) and it will support any quality with equal indifferency. Leibniz, who discusses this question in the Preface to his *New Essays*, protests against this conception of substances 'in their naked essence without activity', i.e. without a determinate nature and mode of self-expression.

[1] Added in the fourth edition. The idea of the self is given not only in reflection, but is implied in every act of sense-perception. Locke says he is 'more certain' of the spiritual being within than of the corporeal being without, because, although he cannot doubt his act of perception, he can doubt the reality of the object perceived. As he explains in Book IV, he knows his own existence intuitively, that of material things by sensation, which is not strictly knowledge at all but only 'an assurance that deserves the name of knowledge' (IV. 2. 14; 9. 3; 11. 1–3). The words 'nor ever could be without an immaterial being' are probably not intended to exclude the possibility of a material soul endowed by God with the power of thinking, but only to negate the possibility of matter developing such a faculty by its own unaided powers (as he argues in Bk. IV. 10. 9–17).

the substance of body as if we knew nothing at all : nor, after all the acquaintance and familiarity which we imagine we have with matter, and the many qualities men assure themselves they perceive and know in bodies, will it, perhaps, upon examination be found, that they have any more or clearer primary ideas belonging to body than they have belonging to immaterial spirit.

17. *The cohesion of solid parts and impulse, the primary ideas of body.*—The primary ideas we have *peculiar to body*, as contra-distinguished to spirit, are *the cohesion of solid*, and consequently separable *parts, and a power of communicating motion by impulse.* These, I think, are the original ideas proper and peculiar to body ; for figure is but the consequence of finite extension.

18. *Thinking and motivity, the primary ideas of spirit.*—The ideas we have belonging and *peculiar to spirit* are *thinking*, and *will*, or a power of putting body into motion by thought, and, which is consequent to it, liberty. For as body cannot but communicate its motion by impulse to another body, which it meets with at rest ; so the mind can put bodies into motion, or forbear to do so, as it pleases. The ideas of existence, duration, and mobility,[1] are common to them both.

19. *Spirits capable of motion.*—There is no reason why it should be thought strange that I make mobility belong to spirit : for having no other idea of motion but change of distance with other beings that are considered as at rest, and finding that spirits as well as bodies cannot operate but where they are, and that spirits do operate at several times in several places, I cannot but attribute change of place to all finite spirits ; (for of the infinite Spirit I speak not here). For my soul, being a real being, as well as my body, is certainly as capable of changing distance with any other body or being as body itself, and so is capable of motion. And if a mathematician can consider a certain distance or a change of that distance between two points, one may certainly conceive a distance and a change of distance between two spirits ; and so conceive their motion, their approach or removal, one from another.

20. Every one finds in himself, that his soul can think, will,

---

[1] ' Existence, duration, number ' was Locke's previous enumeration (II. 21. 75) of the ideas common to both ; mobility is asserted here of spirits for the first time.

and operate on his body, in the place where that is; but cannot operate on a body, or in a place, an hundred miles distant from it. Nobody can imagine, that his soul can think or move a body at Oxford, whilst he is at London; and cannot but know that, being united to his body, it constantly changes place all the whole journey between Oxford and London, as the coach or horse does that carries him; and I think may be said to be truly all that while in motion: or if that will not be allowed to afford us a clear idea enough of its motion, its being separated from the body in death, I think, will: for to consider it as going out of the body, or leaving it, and yet to have no idea of its motion, seems to me impossible.

21. If it be said by any one, that it cannot change place, because it hath none, for spirits are not *in loco*, but *ubi*,[1] I suppose that way of talking will not now be of much weight to many, in an age that is not much disposed to admire, or suffer themselves to be deceived by such unintelligible ways of speaking. But if any one thinks there is any sense in that distinction, and that it is applicable to our present purpose, I desire him to put it into intelligible English; and then from thence draw a reason to show, that immaterial spirits are not capable of motion. Indeed motion cannot be attributed to God; not because he is an immaterial, but because he is an infinite Spirit.

22. *Idea of soul and body compared.*—Let us compare, then, our complex idea of an immaterial spirit with our complex idea of body, and see whether there be any more obscurity in one than in the other, and in which most. Our idea of body, as I think, is an extended solid substance, capable of communicating motion by impulse, and our idea of soul, as an immaterial spirit, is of a substance that thinks, and has a power

[1] The Scholastics taught that the presence of a spirit in a place is defined by its operation on the body occupying the place, and the succession of its operations—by virtue of which it is said to be in different places—is said to be its movement. But neither place nor movement is predicated univocally of spirits and bodies. Place in the former case does not mean that a spirit is quantitatively determined as commensurate with a certain space or that it traverses space by a movement of transition as a body does. ' Ubication ' is the title under which they discuss the subject. But just as Locke tends to speak of the omnipresence of God as equivalent to an actual *occupation* of infinite space, so here he treats spirits as if they were space-occupying bodies moving from place to place.

of exciting motion in body by will or thought. I know that people, whose thoughts are immersed in matter, and have so subjected their minds to their senses that they seldom reflect on anything beyond them, are apt to say, they cannot comprehend a thinking thing, which perhaps is true : but I affirm, when they consider it well, they can no more comprehend an extended thing.

23. *Cohesion of solid parts in body, as hard to be conceived as thinking in a soul.*—If any one says, he knows not what it is thinks in him ; he means, he knows not what the substance is of that thinking thing : no more, say I, knows he what the substance is of that solid thing. Farther, if he says, he knows not how he thinks :[1] I answer, Neither knows he how he is extended ; how the solid parts of body are united or cohere together to make extension.[2] For though the pressure of the particles of air may account for the cohesion of several parts of matter that are grosser than the particles of air, and have pores less than the corpuscles of air ; yet the weight or pressure of the air will not explain, nor can be a cause of, the coherence of the particles of air themselves. And if the pressure of the ether,[3] or any subtiler matter than the air, may unite and hold fast together the parts of a particle of air, as well as other bodies ; yet it cannot make bonds for itself, and hold together the parts that make up every the least corpuscle of that *materia subtilis*. [24.] So that perhaps, how clear an idea soever we think we have of the extension of body, which is nothing but the cohesion of solid parts, he that shall well consider it in his mind, may have reason to conclude, that it is as easy

[1] So Locke says again (IV. 3. 6), ' Since we know not wherein thinking consists ', and Hume (*Dialogues concerning Natural Religion*, Part VII) says, ' Reason, in its internal fabric and structure, is really as little known to us as instinct or vegetation. The effects of these principles are all known to us from experience ; but the principles themselves and their manner of operation are totally unknown.' What is it we desire, in such a case, to know ?

[2] For the Cartesians matter, its essence being extension, is naturally continuous ; but an atomistic theory finds a difficulty in explaining how the ultimate discrete atoms unite and cohere so as to form ' the grosser sensible bodies ' we perceive. Professor Gibson shows that Henry More and Glanville, as well as Boyle, the chemist, all occupied themselves with this problem and, like Locke, pronounced it insoluble (*op. cit.*, 255–7).

[3] The reference is to a theory put forward by Malebranche, *Recherche de la Vérité*, Bk. VI, part 2, ch. 9, and expounded in James Bernoulli's *De Gravitate Aetheris* (1680).

for him to have a clear idea how the soul thinks, as how body is extended.

25. I allow it is usual for most people to wonder how any one should find a difficulty in what they think they every day observe. Do we not see, will they be ready to say, the parts of bodies stick firmly together? Is there anything more common? And what doubt can there be made of it? And the like I say concerning thinking and voluntary motion: Do we not every moment experiment it in ourselves; and therefore can it be doubted? The matter of fact is clear, I confess; but when we would a little nearer look into it, and consider how it is done, there, I think, we are at a loss, both in the one and the other, and can as little understand how the parts of body cohere, as how we ourselves perceive or move. [27.] For to extend our thoughts a little farther, that pressure, which is brought to explain the cohesion of bodies, is as unintelligible as the cohesion itself. For if matter be considered, as no doubt it is, finite, let any one send his contemplation to the extremities of the universe, and there see what conceivable hoops, what bond, he can imagine to hold this mass of matter in so close a pressure together; from whence steel has its firmness, and the parts of a diamond their hardness and indissolubility. If matter be finite, it must have its extremes; and there must be something to hinder it from scattering asunder. If, to avoid this difficulty, any one will throw himself into the supposition and abyss of infinite matter, let him consider what light he thereby brings to the cohesion of body; and whether he be ever the nearer making it intelligible, by resolving it into a supposition the most absurd and most incomprehensible of all other: so far is our extension of body (which is nothing but the cohesion of solid parts) from being clearer, or more distinct, when we would enquire into the nature, cause, or manner of it, than the idea of thinking.

28. *Communication of motion by impulse, or by thought, equally intelligible.*—Another idea we have of body, is the power of *communication of motion by impulse*; and of our souls, the power of *exciting motion by thought*. These ideas, the one of body, the other of our minds, every day's experience clearly furnishes us with: but if here again we enquire how this is done, we are equally in the dark. For in the communication of motion by impulse, wherein as much motion is lost to

one body as is got to the other, which is the ordinariest case, we can have no other conception but of the passing of motion out of one body into another; which, I think, is as obscure and inconceivable, as how our minds move or stop our bodies by thought; which we every moment find they do. The increase of motion by impulse, which is observed or believed sometimes to happen, is yet harder to be understood. We have by daily experience clear evidence of motion produced both by impulse and by thought; but the manner how, hardly comes within our comprehension; we are equally at a loss in both. So that, however we consider motion, and its communication either from body or spirit, the idea which belongs to spirit is at least as clear as that which belongs to body. And if we consider the active power of moving, or, as I may call it, motivity, it is much clearer in spirit than body, since two bodies, placed by one another at rest, will never afford us the idea of a power in the one to move the other, but by a borrowed motion: whereas the mind every day affords us ideas of an active power of moving of bodies; and therefore it is worth our consideration, whether active power be not the proper attribute of spirits, and passive power of matter.[1] Hence may be conjectured, that created spirits are not totally separate from matter; because they are both active and passive. Pure spirit, viz., God, is only active; pure matter is only passive; those beings that are both active and passive, we may judge to partake of both. But be that as it will, I think we have as many and as clear ideas belonging to spirit as we have belonging to body, the substance of each being equally unknown to us; and the idea of thinking in spirit as clear as of extension in body; and the communication of motion by thought, which we attribute to spirit, is as evident as that by impulse which we ascribe to body. Constant experience makes us sensible of both of these, though our narrow understandings can comprehend neither.[2]

29. To conclude: Sensation convinces us, that there are

[1] Cf. II. 21. 1-4 and relative notes.

[2] In this section the action of mind on body which, by its inexplicability, drove the Cartesians to develop the theory of Occasionalism, is accepted by Locke as no more and no less mysterious than the communication of motion by impulse. It is to be noted that the most consistent occasionalists extended their theory to the action of one body upon another, thus anticipating Hume's resolution of causation into observed sequence. Cf. IV. 3. 28 and note.

solid, extended substances; and reflection, that there are thinking ones : experience assures us of the existence of such beings; and that the one hath a power to move body by impulse, the other by thought; this we cannot doubt of. Experience, I say, every moment furnishes us with the clear ideas both of the one and the other. But beyond these ideas, as received from their proper sources, our faculties will not reach. If we would enquire farther into their nature, causes, and manner, we perceive not the nature of extension clearer than we do of thinking. If we would explain them any farther, one is as easy as the other; and there is no more difficulty to conceive how a substance we know not should by thought set body into motion, than how a substance we know not should by impulse set body into motion. So that we are no more able to discover wherein the ideas belonging to body consist, than those belonging to spirit. From whence it seems probable to me, that the simple ideas we receive from sensation and reflection are the boundaries of our thoughts; beyond which, the mind, whatever efforts it would make, is not able to advance one jot; nor can it make any discoveries, when it would pry into the nature and hidden causes of those ideas.

30. *Ideas of body and spirit compared.*—So that, in short, the idea we have of spirit, compared with the idea we have of body, stands thus : The substance of spirit is unknown to us ; and so is the substance of body equally unknown to us. Two primary qualities or properties of body, viz., solid coherent parts and impulse, we have distinct clear ideas of : so likewise we know and have distinct clear ideas of two primary qualities or properties of spirit, viz., thinking, and a power of action ; i.e., a power of beginning or stopping several thoughts or motions. We have also the ideas of several qualities inherent in bodies, and have the clear distinct ideas of them : which qualities are but the various modifications of the extension of cohering solid parts and their motion. We have likewise the ideas of the several modes of thinking, viz., believing, doubting, intending, fearing, hoping; all which are but the several modes of thinking. We have also the ideas of willing, and moving the body consequent to it, and with the body itself too; for, as has been showed, spirit is capable of motion.

31. *The notion of spirit involves no more difficulty in it than that of body.*—Lastly, if this notion of immaterial spirit may have, perhaps, some difficulties in it not easy to be explained,

we have therefore no more reason to deny or doubt the existence of such spirits, than we have to deny or doubt the existence of body because the notion of body is cumbered with some difficulties, very hard and perhaps impossible to be explained or understood by us. For I would fain have instanced anything in our notion of spirit more perplexed, or nearer a contradiction, than the very notion of body includes in it; the divisibility *in infinitum* of any finite extension involving us, whether we grant or deny it, in consequences impossible to be explicated, or made in our apprehensions consistent; consequences that carry greater difficulty and more apparent absurdity, than anything can follow from the notion of an immaterial knowing substance. [32.] For it being no more a contradiction that thinking should exist separate and independent from solidity, than it is a contradiction that solidity should exist separate and independent from thinking, they being both but simple ideas, independent one from another; and having as clear and distinct ideas in us of thinking as of solidity, I know not why we may not as well allow a thinking thing without solidity, i.e., immaterial, to exist, as a solid thing without thinking, i.e., matter, to exist; especially since it is no harder to conceive how thinking should exist without matter, than how matter should think. But whichever of these complex ideas be clearest, that of body or immaterial spirit, this is evident, that the simple ideas that make them up are no other than what we have received from sensation or reflection; and so is it of all our other ideas of substances, even of God himself.

33. *Idea of God.*—For if we examine the idea we have of the incomprehensible Supreme Being, we shall find, that we come by it the same way; and that the complex ideas we have both of God and separate spirits are made up of the simple ideas we receive from reflection: v.g., having, from what we experiment in ourselves, got the ideas of existence and duration, of knowledge and power, of pleasure and happiness, and of several other qualities and powers which it is better to have than to be without; when we would frame an idea the most suitable we can to the Supreme Being, we enlarge every one of these with our idea of infinity; and so, putting them together, make our complex idea of God. For that the mind has such a power of enlarging some of its ideas, received from sensation and reflection, has been already showed.

35. It is infinity which, joined to our ideas of existence, power, knowledge, &c., makes that complex idea whereby we represent to ourselves, the best we can, the Supreme Being. For though in his own essence (which certainly we do not know, not knowing the real essence [1] of a pebble, or a fly, or of our own selves) God be simple and uncompounded; yet, I think, I may say we have no other idea of him but a complex one of existence, knowledge, power, happiness, &c., infinite and eternal : which are all distinct ideas, and some of them being relative are again compounded of others ; all which being, as has been shown, originally got from sensation and reflection, go to make up the idea or notion we have of God.

36. *No ideas in our complex one of spirits, but those got from sensation or reflection.*—This farther is to be observed, that there is no idea we attribute to God, bating infinity, which is not also a part of our complex idea of other spirits. Because, being capable of no other simple ideas belonging to any thing but body, but those which by reflection we receive from the operation of our own minds, we can attribute to spirits no other but what we receive from thence : and all the difference we can put between them in our contemplation of spirits, is only in the several extents and degrees of their knowledge, power, duration, happiness, &c. For that in our ideas, as well of spirits, as of other things, we are *restrained to those we receive from sensation and reflection,* is evident from hence, that in our ideas of spirits,[2] how much soever advanced in perfection beyond those of bodies, even to that of infinite, we cannot yet have any idea of the manner wherein they discover their thoughts one to another ; though we must necessarily conclude, that separate spirits, which are beings that have perfecter knowledge and greater happiness than we, must needs have also a perfecter way of communicating their thoughts than we have, who are fain to make use of corporeal

[1] Cf. Berkeley, *Principles*, section 101, where Berkeley rallies the sceptics on ' the stock of arguments they produce to depreciate our faculties.' ' We are miserably bantered, say they, by our senses, and amused only with the outside and show of things. The real essence—the internal qualities and constitution—of every the meanest object is hid from our view ; something there is in every drop of water, every grain of sand, which it is beyond the power of human understanding to fashion or comprehend.'

[2] That is, separate or unembodied spirits.

signs and particular sounds; which are therefore of most general use, as being the best and quickest we are capable of. But of immediate [1] communication, having no experiment in ourselves, and consequently no notion of it at all, we have no idea how spirits, which use not words, can with quickness, or much less how spirits, that have no bodies, can be masters of their own thoughts, and communicate or conceal them at pleasure, though we cannot but necessarily suppose they have such a power.

37. *Recapitulation.*—And thus we have seen *what kind of ideas we have of substances of all kinds*, wherein they consist, and how we come by them. From whence, I think, it is very evident,

First, That all our ideas of the several sorts of substances are nothing but collections of simple ideas, with a supposition of something to which they belong, and in which they subsist; though of this supposed something we have no clear distinct idea at all.

Secondly, That all the simple ideas that, thus united in one common substratum, make up our complex ideas of several sorts of substances, are no other but such as we have received from sensation or reflection.

Thirdly, That most of the simple ideas that make up our complex ideas of substances, when truly considered, are only powers, however we are apt to take them for positive qualities: v.g., the greatest part of the ideas that make our complex idea of gold are yellowness, great weight, ductility, fusibility, and solubility in *aqua regia*, &c., all united together in an unknown substratum; all which ideas are nothing else but so many relations to other substances, and are not really in the gold considered barely in itself, though they depend on those real and primary qualities of its internal constitution, whereby it has a fitness differently to operate and be operated on by several other substances.

---

[1] Immediate, i.e. independently of sense-organs

## CHAPTER XXIV

#### OF COLLECTIVE IDEAS OF SUBSTANCES

1. *One idea.*—Besides these complex ideas of several single substances, as of man, horse, gold, violet, apple, &c., the mind hath also complex collective ideas of substances; which I so call, because such ideas are made up of many particular substances considered together, as united into one idea, and which so joined are looked on as one; v.g., the idea of such a collection of men as make an army, though consisting of a great number of distinct substances, is as much one idea as the idea of a man: and the great collective idea of all bodies whatsoever, signified by the name world, is as much one idea as the idea of any the least particle of matter in it; it sufficing to the unity of any idea, that it be considered as one representation or picture, though made up of ever so many particulars. [3.] And in truth, if we consider all these collective ideas aright, as army, constellation, universe, they are but the artificial draughts of the mind, bringing things very remote, and independent on one another, into one view, the better to contemplate and discourse of them, united into one conception, and signified by one name. For there are no things so remote, nor so contrary, which the mind cannot, by this art of composition, bring into one idea, as is visible in that signified by the name universe.

## CHAPTER XXV

#### OF RELATION

1. *Relation, what.*—Besides the ideas, whether simple or complex, that the mind has of things, as they are in themselves, there are others it gets from their comparison one with another.[1] The understanding, in the consideration of anything,

---

[1] Relations are regarded throughout this chapter as due to the relating or 'comparing' or 'considering' act of the mind and 'extrinsical' to 'things as they are in themselves'. Relative names are distinguished from positive or absolute names which signify only 'what does or is supposed really to exist in the thing they denominate'. The strongest expression of the view taken is in section 8: relation is

is not confined to that precise object : it can carry any idea, as it were, beyond itself, or, at least, look beyond it to see how it stands in conformity to any other. When the mind so considers one thing, that it does, as it were, bring it to and set it by another, and carry its view from one to the other : this is, as the words import, *relation* and *respect*; and the denominations given to positive things, intimating that respect, and serving as marks to lead the thoughts beyond the subject itself denominated to something distinct from it, are what we call *relatives*; and the things so brought together, *related*. Thus when the mind considers Caius as such a positive being, it takes nothing into that idea, but what really exists in Caius ; v. g., when I consider him as man, I have nothing in my mind but the complex idea of the species man. So likewise, when I say, ' Caius is a white man ', I have nothing but the bare consideration of man who hath that white colour. But when I give Caius the name *husband*, I intimate some other

' not contained in the real existence of things, but something extraneous and superinduced '. The position, as Professor Kemp Smith has pointed out, is the direct consequence of Locke's unquestioning acceptance of the Scholastic doctrine of substance as ' the unchanging ground of the unchanging nature of the thing ' (*Studies in the Cartesian Philosophy*, p. 204). In this sense Locke speaks (Bk. III. 6. 6) of the ' real essence ' as ' the real constitution of anything, which is the foundation of all those properties that are combined in and are constantly found to coexist with the nominal essence, *that particular constitution which everything has within itself, without relation to anything without it'*. For this theory the world would consist of a collection of such self-contained and unrelated ' reals '. But, as so often happens, Locke himself, in another part of his work, when he is following out another line of thought, supplies us with the best corrective of his own statements here. Cf. the fine passage (IV. 6. 11), in the course of which he tells us this, ' we are quite out of the way when we think that things contain within themselves the qualities that appear to us in them . . . for which perhaps, to understand them aright, we ought to look not only beyond this our earth and atmosphere, but even beyond the sun or remotest star our eyes have yet discovered. . . . This is certain, things, however absolute and entire they seem in themselves, are but retainers to other parts of nature for that which they are most taken notice of by us. . . . There is not so complete and perfect a part that we know of nature which does not owe the being it has, and the excellence of it, to its neighbours.' Unfortunately the later statement cannot be taken to mean the explicit abandonment of the earlier view ; for in the next section Locke is found still clinging to the notion of independent substances with real essences from which these properties might be deduced, only insisting that what has been said ' is enough to put an end to all our hopes of ever having the ideas of their real essences '.

person; and when I give him the name *whiter*, I intimate some other thing: in both cases my thought is led to something beyond Caius, and there are two things brought into consideration. And since any idea, whether simple or complex, may be the occasion why the mind thus brings two things together, and as it were, takes a view of them at once, though still considered as distinct: therefore any of our ideas may be the foundation of relation.

2. *Relations without correlative terms, not easily perceived.*— These, and the like relations, expressed by relative terms, that have others answering them with a reciprocal intimation, as father and son, bigger and less, cause and effect, are very obvious to every one. But where languages have failed to give correlative names, the relation is not always so easily taken notice of. Hence it is that many of those names which, duly considered, do include evident relations, have been called external denominations. But all names, that are more than empty sounds, must signify some idea which is either in the thing to which the name is applied; and then it is positive, and is looked on as united to and existing in the thing to which the denomination is given: or else it arises from the respect the mind finds in it to something distinct from it, with which it considers it; and then it includes a relation.

3. *Some seemingly absolute terms contain relations.*—Another sort of relative terms there is, which are not looked on to be either relative or so much as external denominations; which yet, under the form and appearance of signifying something absolute in the subject, do conceal a tacit, though less observable relation. Such are the seemingly positive terms of old, great, imperfect, &c., whereof I shall have occasion to speak more at large in the following chapters.[1]

4. *Relation different from the things related.*—This farther may be observed, that the ideas of relation may be the same in men who have far different ideas of the things that are related, or that are thus compared: v. g., those who have far different ideas of a man, may yet agree in the notion of a father: which is a notion superinduced to the substance, or man, and refers only to an act of that thing called man, whereby he contributed to the generation of one of his own kind, let man be what it will.

[1] e.g. ch. 26. 4–6.

7. *All things capable of relation.*—Concerning relation in general, these things may be considered:

First, That there is no one thing, whether simple idea, substance, mode, or relation, or name of either of them, which is not capable of almost an infinite number of considerations in reference to other things; and therefore this makes no small part of men's thoughts and words: v. g., one single man may at once be concerned in and sustain all these following relations, and many more, viz., father, brother, son, grandfather, grandson, father-in-law, son-in-law, husband, friend, enemy, subject, general, judge, patron, client, professor, European, Englishman, islander, servant, master, possessor, captain, superior, inferior, bigger, less, older, younger, contemporary, like, unlike, &c., to an almost infinite number: he being capable of as many relations as there can be occasions of comparing him to other things, in any manner of agreement, disagreement, or respect whatsoever.

8. *The ideas of relations clearer often than of the subjects related.*—Secondly, This farther may be considered concerning relation, that though it be not contained in the real existence of things, but something extraneous and superinduced,[1] yet the ideas which relative words stand for are often clearer and more distinct than of those substances to which they do belong. The notion we have of a father or brother is a great deal clearer and more distinct than that we have of a man : or, if you will, paternity is a thing whereof it is easier to have a clear idea than of humanity. Because the knowledge of one action, or one simple idea, is oftentimes sufficient to give me the notion of a relation; but to the knowing of any substantial being, an accurate collection of sundry ideas is necessary. A man, if he compares two things together, can hardly be supposed not to know what it is wherein he compares them : so that when he compares any things together, he cannot but have a very clear idea of that relation. The ideas then of relations are capable at least of being more perfect and distinct in our minds than those of substances. Because it is commonly hard

Cf. note, p. 175. Green argued from this statement and others like it that, if all relations are superinduced by the mind, then the really existent, as distinguished from ' the workmanship of the mind ', must be the momentary sensation, which we cannot even qualify as ' this ' or ' that ', without infecting it with relation and so making it fictitious. Hence, ' as Plato long ago taught, a consistent sensationalism must be speechless ' (Introduction to Hume, section 45, *Works*, vol. i, p. 36).

to know all the simple ideas which are really in any substance, but for the most part easy enough to know the simple ideas that make up any relation I think on, or have a name for.

9. *Relations all terminate in simple ideas.*—Thirdly, Though there be a great number of considerations wherein things may be compared one with another, and so a multitude of relations, yet they all terminate in, and are concerned about, those simple ideas either of sensation or reflection, which I think to be the whole materials of all our knowledge.

10. *Terms leading the mind beyond the subject denominated are relative.*—Fourthly, That relation being the considering of one thing with another which is extrinsical to it, it is evident that all words that necessarily lead the mind to any other ideas than are supposed really to exist in that thing to which the word is applied, are relative words : v. g., a man, black, merry, thoughtful, thirsty, angry, extended; these and the like are all absolute, because they neither signify nor intimate anything but what does or is supposed really to exist in the man thus denominated : but father, brother, king, husband, blacker, merrier, &c., are words which, together with the thing they denominate, imply also something else separate, and exterior to the existence of that thing.

11. *Conclusion.*—Having laid down these premisses concerning relation in general, I shall now proceed to show in some instances, how all the ideas we have of relation are made up, as the others are, only of simple ideas ; and that they all, how refined or remote from sense soever they seem, terminate at last in simple ideas. I shall begin with the most comprehensive relation, wherein all things that do or can exist are concerned ; and that is the relation of *cause* and *effect*. The idea whereof, how derived from the two fountains of all our knowledge, sensation and reflection,[1] I shall in the next place consider.

---

[1] Note the variety of the phraseology in the last three sections : 'derived from', 'terminate in', 'concerned about'. Cf. note, p. 92.

## CHAPTER XXVI

### OF CAUSE AND EFFECT, AND OTHER RELATIONS

1. *Whence their ideas got.*—In the notice that our senses take of the constant vicissitude of things, we cannot but observe that several particular both qualities and substances begin to exist; and that they receive this their existence from the due application and operation of some other being. From this observation we get our ideas of *cause* and *effect*. That which produces any simple or complex idea, we denote by the general name *cause*; and that which is produced, *effect*.[1] Thus finding that in that substance which we call wax fluidity, which is a simple idea that was not in it before, is constantly produced by the application of a certain degree of heat, we call the simple idea of heat, in relation to fluidity in wax, *the cause* of it, and fluidity *the effect*.

2. *Creation, generation, making, alteration.*—Having thus, from what our senses are able to discover in the operations of bodies on one another,[2] got the notion of cause and effect, the mind finds no great difficulty to distinguish the several originals of things into two sorts:

First, When the thing is wholly made new, so that no part thereof did ever exist before; as when a new particle of matter doth begin to exist, *in rerum naturâ*, which had before no being: and this we call *creation*.

---

[1] ' Should any one pretend to define a cause, by saying it is something productive of another, 'tis evident he would say nothing. For what does he mean by *production* ? Can he give any definition of it, that will not be the same with that of causation ?' (Hume, *Treatise*, Bk. I, part 3, section 2). Ultimate conceptions of reason cannot, however, in strictness be defined, any more than simple ideas of sense. Hume's attempt to resolve the idea of necessary connexion or *consequence* into that of repeated *sequence* is, in effect, to deny that we can frame the idea of consequence at all. Although Locke here loosely traces the origin of the idea to the 'observation' of the senses, he says, in his *First Letter* to Stillingfleet, that 'everything that has a beginning must have a cause is a true principle of reason, which we come to know by perceiving that *the idea of beginning to be* is *necessarily connected* with *the idea of some operation*; and the idea of *operation* with *something operating, which we call a cause*' (*Works*, i. 495).

[2] This should be compared with the more careful statement in ch. 21, sections 1 and 4. What 'our senses are able to discover' is only 'the constant vicissitude of things'.

Secondly, When a thing is made up of particles which did all of them before exist, but that very thing, so constituted of pre-existing particles, had not any existence before, as this man, this egg, rose, or cherry, &c. And this, when referred to a substance produced in the ordinary course of nature by an internal principle, but set on work by, and received from, some external agent or cause, and working by insensible ways which we perceive not, we call *generation*. When the cause is extrinsical, and the effect produced by a sensible separation or juxtaposition of discernible parts, we call it *making*; and such are all artificial things. When any simple idea is produced which was not in that subject before, we call it *alteration*. Thus a man is generated, a picture made, and either of them altered, when any new sensible quality or simple idea is produced in either of them, which was not there before. In which, and all other cases, we may observe, that the notion of cause and effect has its rise from ideas received by sensation or reflection; and that this relation, how comprehensive soever, terminates at last in them.

3. *Relations of time.*—Time and place are also the foundations of very large relations, and all finite beings at least are concerned in them. But having already shown in another place [1] how we get these ideas, it may suffice here to intimate, that most of the denominations of things received from time are only relations: thus, when any one says that Queen Elizabeth lived sixty-nine years, these words import only the relation of that duration to some other, and mean no more but this, that the duration of her existence was equal to sixty-nine annual revolutions of the sun. [4.] There are yet, besides those, other words of time that ordinarily are thought to stand for positive ideas, which yet will, when considered, be found to be relative, such as are young, old, &c. Thus having settled in our thoughts the idea of the ordinary duration of a man to be seventy years, when we say a man is *young*, we mean that his age is yet but a small part of that which usually men attain to; and when we denominate him *old*, we mean that his duration is run out almost to the end of that which men do not usually exceed. But yet a horse we call old at twenty, and a dog at seven years; because in each of these we compare their age to different

---

[1] II. 5. 1; 7. 9; 13 and 14

ideas of duration which are settled in our minds as belonging to these several sorts of animals, in the ordinary course of nature. But the sun and stars, though they have outlasted several generations of men, we call not old, because we do not know what period God hath set to that sort of beings. This term belonging properly to those things which we can observe, in the ordinary course of things, by a natural decay, to come to an end in a certain period of time; and so have in our minds, as it were, a standard, to which we can compare the several parts of their duration.

5. *Relations of place and extension.*—The relation also that things have to one another in their *places* and distances, is very obvious to observe. Here also, having by observation settled in our minds the ideas of the bigness of several species of things from those we have been most accustomed to, we make them, as it were, the standards whereby to denominate the bulk of others. Thus we call a great apple, such an one as is bigger than the ordinary sort of those we have been used to; and a little horse, such an one as comes not up to the size of that idea which we have in our minds to belong ordinarily to horses, and that will be a great horse to a Welshman which is but a little one to a Fleming. [6.] And so abundance of words, in ordinary speech, stand only for relations, which at first sight seem to have no such signification: v. g., 'The ship has necessary stores'. *Necessary* and *stores* are both relative words; one having a relation to the accomplishing the voyage intended, and the other to future use. All which relations, how they are confined to, and terminate in ideas derived from sensation or reflection, is too obvious to need any explication.

## CHAPTER XXVII

### OF IDENTITY AND DIVERSITY [1]

1. *Wherein identity consists.*—Another occasion the mind often takes of comparing, is the very being of things, when, considering anything as existing at any determined time and place, we compare it with itself existing at another time, and thereon form the ideas of *identity* and *diversity*. When we see

[1] This chapter was added in the second edition, on the suggestion of Molyneux, who urged Locke to 'insist more particularly and at large on the *principium individuationis*'.

anything to be in any place in any instant of time, we are sure (be it what it will) that it is that very thing, and not another, which at that same time exists in another place, how like and undistinguishable soever it may be in all other respects: and in this consists *identity*, when the ideas it is attributed to vary not at all from what they were that moment wherein we consider their former existence, and to which we compare the present. For we never finding, nor conceiving it possible, that two things of the same kind should exist in the same place at the same time, we rightly conclude that whatever exists anywhere at any time, excludes all of the same kind, and is there itself alone. When therefore we demand whether anything be the same or no, it refers always to something that existed such a time in such a place, which it was certain at that instant was the same with itself and no other: from whence it follows, that one thing cannot have two beginnings of existence, nor two things one beginning, it being impossible for two things of the same kind to be or exist in the same instant, in the very same place, or one and the same thing in different places. That therefore that had one beginning, is the same thing; and that which had a different beginning in time and place from that, is not the same, but diverse. That which has made the difficulty about this relation, has been the little care and attention used in having precise notions of the things to which it is attributed.

2. *Identity of substances.*—We have the ideas but of three sorts of substances: 1. *God.* 2. *Finite intelligences.* 3. *Bodies.* First, God is without beginning, eternal, unalterable, and everywhere; and therefore concerning his identity, there can be no doubt. Secondly, Finite spirits having had each its determinate time and place of beginning to exist, the relation to that time and place will always determine to each of them its identity, as long as it exists. Thirdly, The same will hold of every particle of matter, to which no addition or subtraction of matter being made, it is the same. For though these three sorts of substances, as we term them, do not exclude one another out of the same place,[1] yet we cannot conceive but that they must necessarily each of them exclude any of the same kind out of the same place: or else the notions and names of identity and diversity would be in vain, and

[1] A spirit and a body, that is to say, may occupy the same place, and God is omnipresent.

there could be no such distinction of substances, or anything else, one from another.

*Identity of modes.* All other things being but modes or relations ultimately terminated in substances, the identity and diversity of each particular existence of them too will be by the same way determined : only as to things whose existence is in succession, such as are the actions of finite beings, v. g., *motion* and *thought*, both which consist in a continued train of succession, concerning their diversity there can be no question : because, each perishing the moment it begins, they cannot exist in different times, or in different places, as permanent beings can at different times exist in distant places ; and therefore no motion or thought, considered as at different times, can be the same, each part thereof having a different beginning of existence.

3. *Principium individuationis.*—From what has been said, it is easy to discover, what is so much enquired after, the *principium individuationis* ; and that, it is plain, is existence itself, which determines a being of any sort to a particular time and place incommunicable to two beings of the same kind.[1] This, though it seems easier to conceive in simple substances or modes, yet when reflected on, is not more difficult in compounded ones, if care be taken to what it is applied ; v. g., let us suppose an atom, i. e., a continued body under one immutable superficies, existing in a determined time and place ; it is evident, that, considered in any instant of its existence, it is, in that instant, the same with itself. For being at that instant what it is and nothing else, it is the same, and so must continue as long as its existence is continued. In like manner, if two or more atoms be joined together into the same mass, every one of those atoms will be the same, by the foregoing

[1] Leibniz contends that ' besides the difference of time and place there must be an internal principle of distinction, and though there are many things of the same kind still none of them are ever perfectly alike '. This is in accordance with the principle of ' the identity of indiscernibles ', which is fundamental in his philosophy. As he states it in this connexion, ' if two individuals were perfectly alike and equal and (in a word) *indistinguishable* in themselves, there would be no principle of individuation.' The external relations of space and time serve us practically, he says, to distinguish things which we do not easily distinguish by themselves; but the things do not on that account cease to be distinguishable in themselves. Moreover space and time are themselves perfectly alike in all their parts, and it is rather by the things that we distinguish one time or place from another than vice versa.

rule: and whilst they exist united together, the mass, consisting of the same atoms, must be the same mass, or the same body, let the parts be never so differently jumbled: but if one of these atoms be taken away, or one new one added, it is no longer the same mass, or the same body. In the state of living creatures, their identity depends not on a mass of the same particles, but on something else. For in them the variation of great parcels of matter alters not the identity; an oak, growing from a plant to a great tree, and then lopped, is still the same oak: and a colt, grown up to a horse, sometimes fat, sometimes lean, is all the while the same horse. The reason whereof is that in these two cases—a mass of matter and a living body—identity is not applied to the same thing.

4. *Identity of vegetables.*—We must therefore consider wherein an oak differs from a mass of matter; and that seems to me to be in this, that the one is only the cohesion of particles of matter anyhow united, the other such a disposition of them as constitutes the parts of an oak, and such an organization of those parts as is fit to receive and distribute nourishment, so as to continue and frame the wood, bark, and leaves, &c., of an oak, in which consists the vegetable life. That being then one plant which has such an organization of parts in one coherent body, partaking of one common life, it continues to be the same plant as long as it partakes of the same life, though that life be communicated to new particles of matter vitally united to the living plant in a like continued organization, conformable to that sort of plants. For this organization being at any one instant in any one collection of matter, is in that particular concrete distinguished from all other, and is that individual life which existing constantly from that moment both forwards and backwards, in the same continuity of insensibly succeeding parts united to the living body of the plant, it has that identity which makes the same plant, and all the parts of it parts of the same plant, during all the time that they exist united in that continued organization, which is fit to convey that common life to all the parts so united.[1]

---

[1] Bishop Butler treats this account of the identity of plants as being only true 'in a loose and popular sense'. 'If they have not one common particle of matter they cannot be the same tree in the proper philosophical sense of the word *same*; it being evidently a contradiction in terms to say they are, when no part of their substance and no one of their properties is the same; no part of their substance by the

5. *Identity of animals.*—The case is not so much different in *brutes*, but that any one may hence see what makes an animal, and continues it the same. Something we have like this in machines, and may serve to illustrate it. For example, what is a watch ? It is plain it is nothing but a fit organization or construction of parts to a certain end, which, when a sufficient force is added to it, it is capable to attain. If we would suppose this machine one continued body, all whose organized parts were repaired, increased, or diminished, by a constant addition or separation of insensible parts, with one common life, we should have something very much like the body of an animal, with this difference, that in an animal the fitness of the organization, and the motion wherein life consists, begin together, the motion coming from within ; but in machines, the force coming sensibly from without, is often away when the organ is in order, and well fitted to receive it.

6. *Identity of man.*—This also shows wherein the identity of the same *man* consists ; viz., in nothing but a participation of the same continued life by constantly fleeting particles of matter, in succession vitally united to the same organized body. He that shall place the identity of man in anything else will find it hard to make an embryo, one of years, mad, and sober, the same man, by any supposition that will not make it possible for Socrates, Pilate, St. Austin, and Caesar Borgia, to be the same man. For if the identity of soul alone makes the same man, and there be nothing in the nature of matter why the same individual spirit may not be united to different bodies, it will be possible that those men living in distant ages, and of different tempers, may have been the same man : which way of speaking must be, from a very strange use of the word man, applied to an idea out of which body and shape are excluded. And that way of speaking would agree yet worse with the notions of those philosophers who allow of transmigration, and are of opinion that the souls of men may, for their miscarriages, be detruded into the bodies of beasts, as fit habitations, with organs suited to the satisfaction of their brutal inclina-

supposition ; no one of their properties, because it is allowed that the same property cannot be transferred from one substance to another ' (Dissertation on Personal Identity, appended to the *Analogy*). But this is to burke the whole question by reiterating a technical terminology. Locke's usage would nowadays be recognized as much more ' philosophical ' than that of the bishop.

tions. But yet I think nobody, could he be sure that the soul of Heliogabalus were in one of his hogs, would yet say that hog were a man or Heliogabalus.

7. *Identity suited to the idea.*—It is not therefore unity of substance that comprehends all sorts of identity, or will determine it in every case : but to conceive and judge of it aright, we must consider what idea the word it is applied to stands for : it being one thing to be the same *substance,* another the same *man,* and a third the same *person,* if *person, man,* and *substance* are three names standing for three different ideas ; [1] for such as is the idea belonging to that name, such must be the identity : which if it had been a little more carefully attended to, would possibly have prevented a great deal of that confusion which often occurs about this matter, with no small seeming difficulties, especially concerning personal identity, which therefore we shall in the next place a little consider.

8. *Same man.*—An animal is a living organized body ; and consequently the same animal, as we have observed, is the same continued life communicated to different particles of matter, as they happen successively to be united to that organized living body. And, whatever is talked of other definitions, ingenious observation puts it past doubt, that the idea in our minds of which the sound man in our mouths is the sign, is nothing else but of an animal of such a certain form : since I think I may be confident, that whoever should see a creature of his own shape and make, though it had no more reason all its life than a cat or a parrot, would call him still a *man* ; or whoever should hear a cat or a parrot discourse, reason, and philosophize, would call or think it nothing but a *cat* or a *parrot* ; and say, the one was a dull irrational man and the other a very intelligent rational parrot. For I presume it is not the idea of a thinking or rational being alone that makes the idea of a man in most people's sense, but of a body, so and so shaped, joined to it ; and if that be the idea of a man, the same successive body not shifted all at once must, as well as the same immaterial spirit, go to the making of the same man.

9. *Personal identity.*—This being premised, to find wherein

[1] The argument throughout the rest of the chapter turns on the difference between these three ideas—between identity of soul-substance, the identity of a ' man ' as a *compositum* of soul and body, and the personal identity which depends upon ' consciousness ' or memory.

personal identity consists, we must consider what *person* stands for; which, I think, is a thinking intelligent being,[1] that has reason and reflection, and can consider itself as itself, the same thinking thing, in different times and places; which it does only by that consciousness [2] which is inseparable from thinking, and as it seems to me essential to it; it being impossible for any one to perceive without perceiving that he does perceive. When we see, hear, smell, taste, feel, meditate, or will anything, we know that we do so. Thus it is always as to our present sensations and perceptions : and by this every one is to himself that which he calls *self*; it not being considered, in this case, whether the same self be continued in the same or diverse substances. For since consciousness always accompanies thinking and it is that that makes every one to be what he calls self, and thereby distinguishes himself from all other thinking things; in this alone consists personal identity, i. e., the sameness of a rational being : and as far as this consciousness can be extended backwards to any past action or thought, so far reaches the identity of that person; it is the same self now it was then; and it is by the same self with this present one that now reflects on it, that that action was done.

10. *Consciousness makes personal identity.*—But it is farther enquired, whether it be the same identical substance. This few would think they had reason to doubt of, if these perceptions, with their consciousness, always remained present in the mind, whereby the same thinking thing would be always consciously present, and, as would be thought, evidently the same to itself. But that which seems to make the difficulty is this, that this consciousness being interrupted always by forgetfulness, there being no moment of our lives wherein we have the whole train of all our past actions before our eyes in one view; but even the best memories losing the sight of one part whilst they are viewing another; and we sometimes, and that the greatest part of our lives, not reflecting on our past selves,

[1] This definition of personality is treated by Butler as giving Locke's case away, ' because being and substance, in this place, stand for the same idea ' (Dissertation on Personal Identity).

[2] Consciousness is used by Locke throughout this chapter for the reflective consciousness of our actions and states as ours, for which the term self-consciousness is now often used. He calls it in section 13 ' a reflex act of perception accompanying ' any action we perform. The word is not much used elsewhere in the *Essay*, except in the discussion of the question whether the soul always thinks (II. 1. 10–19).

being intent on our present thoughts, and in sound sleep having no thoughts at all, or, at least, none with that consciousness which remarks our waking thoughts : I say, in all these cases, our consciousness being interrupted, and we losing the sight of our past selves, doubts are raised whether we are the same thinking thing, i. e., the same substance, or no. Which, however reasonable or unreasonable, concerns not *personal identity* at all : the question being what makes the same person, and not, whether it be the same identical substance which always thinks in the same person, which in this case matters not at all ; different substances, by the same consciousness (where they do partake in it), being united into one person, as well as different bodies by the same life are united into one animal, whose identity is preserved, in that change of substances, by the unity of one continued life. For it being the same consciousness that makes a man be himself to himself, personal identity depends on that only, whether it be annexed only to one individual substance, or can be continued in a succession of several substances.[1] For as far as any intelligent being can repeat the idea of any past action with the same consciousness it had of it at first, and with the same consciousness it has of any present action ; so far it is the same personal self. For it is by the consciousness it has of its present thoughts and actions that it is *self to itself* now, and so will be the same self, as far as the same consciousness can extend to actions past or to come ; and would be by distance of time, or change of substance, no more two persons, than a man be two men by wearing other clothes to-day than he did yesterday, with a long or short sleep between : the same consciousness uniting those distant actions into the same person, whatever substances contributed to their production.

11. *Personal identity in change of substances.*—That this is so, we have some kind of evidence in our very bodies, all whose particles, whilst vitally united to this same thinking conscious self, so that we feel when they are touched, and are affected by and conscious of good or harm that happens to them, are a part of ourselves, i. e., of our thinking conscious self. Thus the limbs of his body are to every one a part of himself : he sympathizes and is concerned for them. Cut off a hand and thereby separate it from that consciousness we had of its heat, cold,

[1] Section 13 and note, p. 191.

and other affections, and it is then no longer a part of that which is himself, any more than the remotest part of matter. Thus we see the substance, whereof personal self consisted at one time, may be varied at another, without the change of personal identity; there being no question about the same person, though the limbs which but now were a part of it, be cut off.[1]

12. *Whether in the change of thinking substances.*—But the question is, whether, if the same substance which thinks be changed, it can be the same person, or remaining the same, it can be different persons. [13.] As to the first part of the question, whether, if the same thinking substance (supposing immaterial substances only to think) be changed, it can be the same person, I answer, That cannot be resolved but by those who know what kind of substances they are that do think; and whether the consciousness of past actions can be transferred from one thinking substance to another. I grant, were the same consciousness the same individual action, it could not; but it being but a present representation of a past action, why it may not be possible that that may be represented to the mind to have been, which really never was, will remain to be shown. And therefore, how far the consciousness of past actions is annexed to any individual agent, so that another cannot possibly have it, will be hard for us to determine, till we know what kind of action it is, that cannot be done without a reflex act of perception accompanying it, and how performed by thinking substances, who cannot think without being conscious of it. But that which we call the same consciousness, not being the same individual act, why one intellectual substance may not have represented to it as done by itself what it never did, and was perhaps done by some other agent; why, I say, such a representation may not possibly be without reality of matter of fact, as well as several

[1] It is a somewhat loose use of his own terminology to speak of the limbs as part of the ' person '. The particles of the body are ' vitally united ', he says, to the conscious thinking self; and from that he passes to think of the body as represented in that self by the feelings it occasions, and therefore as ' a part of ourselves '. In IV. 10. 18 he says distinctly, ' that frame of particles is not you, it makes not the thinking thing you are '. This argument from the change of the material substances with which the ' same thinking conscious self ' is associated is aside from the main argument which he goes on to develop about ' change of thinking substances '. He repeats it, however, in the same terms in section 25.

## Ch. 27 — Of Identity and Diversity

representations in dreams are, which yet whilst dreaming we take for true, will be difficult to conclude from the nature of things. And that it never is so, will by us, till we have clearer views of the nature of thinking substances, be best resolved into the goodness of God, who, as far as the happiness or misery of any of his sensible creatures is concerned in it, will not by a fatal error of theirs transfer from one to another that consciousness which draws reward or punishment with it. How far this may be an argument against those who would place thinking in a system of fleeting animal spirits, I leave to be considered. But yet, to return to the question before us, it must be allowed that if the same consciousness (which, as has been shown, is quite a different thing from the same numerical figure or motion in body) can be transferred from one thinking substance to another, it will be possible that two thinking substances may make but one person.[1] For the same consciousness being preserved, whether in the same or different substances, the personal identity is preserved.

14. As to the second part of the question, whether the same immaterial substance remaining, there may be two distinct persons; which question seems to me to be built on this, whether the same immaterial being, being conscious of the actions of its past duration, may be wholly stripped of all the consciousness of its past existence, and lose it beyond the power of ever retrieving again : and so, as it were, beginning a new account from a new period, have a consciousness that cannot reach beyond this new state. All those who hold pre-existence are evidently of this mind, since they allow the soul to have no remaining consciousness of what it did in that

---

[1] Kant, also arguing against the identification of the self with a metaphysical soul-substance, has the following illustration : ' An elastic ball which strikes full upon a similar one imparts to it all its motion or all its state (if we regard merely positions in space). Now let us assume substances after the analogy of such bodies, where each imparts ideas to the next, along with a consciousness of them. We might thus conceive a whole series, the first of which imparted its state and the consciousness thereof to the second ; this again its own state, along with that of the first, to the third ; this again its own and the states of all the previous ones, and so on. In such a case, the last substance would be conscious of all the states of the previously changed substances as its own, since those states were transferred to it along with the consciousness of them ; nevertheless it would not have been the very same person in all these states ' (*Critique of Pure Reason*, Transcendental Dialectic, Bk. II, Third Paralogism, in first edition).

pre-existent state, either wholly separate from body, or informing any other body. So that personal identity reaching no farther than consciousness reaches, a pre-existent spirit not having continued so many ages in a state of silence, must needs make different persons. Suppose a Christian Platonist or Pythagorean should, upon God's having ended all his works of creation the seventh day, think his soul hath existed ever since, and should imagine it has revolved in several human bodies; as I once met with one who was persuaded his had been the soul of Socrates (how reasonably I will not dispute: this I know, that in the post he filled, which was no inconsiderable one, he passed for a very rational man; and the press has shown that he wanted not parts or learning)—would any one say that he, being not conscious of any of Socrates' actions or thoughts, could be the same person with Socrates? Let any one reflect upon himself, and conclude, that he has in himself an immaterial spirit, which is that which thinks in him, and, in the constant change of his body, keeps him the same, and is that which he calls himself: let him also suppose it to be the same soul that was in Nestor or Thersites, at the siege of Troy (for souls being, as far as we know anything of them, in their nature indifferent to any parcel of matter, the supposition has no apparent absurdity in it), but he now having no consciousness of any of the actions either of Nestor or Thersites, does or can he conceive himself the same person with either of them? Can he be concerned in either of their actions, attribute them to himself, or think them his own, more than the actions of any other man that ever existed? So that this consciousness not reaching to any of the actions of either of those men, he is no more one *self* with either of them, than if the soul or immaterial spirit that now informs him had been created and began to exist when it began to inform his present body, though it were never so true that the same spirit that informed Nestor's or Thersites' body were numerically the same that now informs his. For this would no more make him the same person with Nestor, than if some of the particles of matter that were once a part of Nestor were now a part of this man; the same immaterial substance, without the same consciousness, no more making the same person by being united to any body, than the same particle of matter, without consciousness, united to any body, makes the same person. But let him once find himself conscious of any of the actions of Nestor, he then finds himself the same person with Nestor.

15. And thus we may be able, without any difficulty, to conceive the same person at the resurrection, though in a body not exactly in make or parts the same which he had here, the same consciousness going along with the soul that inhabits it. But yet the soul alone, in the change of bodies, would scarce to any one but to him that makes the soul the man, be enough to make the same man. For should the soul of a prince, carrying with it the consciousness of the prince's past life, enter and inform the body of a cobbler, as soon as deserted by his own soul, every one sees he would be the same person with the prince, accountable only for the prince's actions : but who would say it was the same man ? The body too goes to the making of the man, and would, I guess, to everybody determine the man in this case, wherein the soul, with all its princely thoughts about it, would not make another man ; but he would be the same cobbler to every one besides himself. I know that, in the ordinary way of speaking, the same person, and the same man, stand for one and the same thing. And indeed every one will always have a liberty to speak as he pleases, and to apply what articulate sounds to what ideas he thinks fit, and change them as often as he pleases. But yet, when we will enquire what makes the same *spirit, man,* or *person,* we must fix the ideas of spirit, man, or person, in our minds ; and having resolved with ourselves what we mean by them, it will not be hard to determine in either of them, or the like, when it is the same, and when not.

16. *Consciousness makes the same person.*—But though the same immaterial substance or soul does not alone, wherever it be, and in whatsoever state, make the same man; yet it is plain, consciousness, as far as ever it can be extended, should it be to ages past, unites existences and actions, very remote in time, into the same person, as well as it does the existence and actions of the immediately preceding moment : so that whatever has the consciousness of present and past actions is the same person to whom they both belong. Had I the same consciousness that I saw the ark and Noah's flood, as that I saw an overflowing of the Thames last winter, or as that I write now, I could no more doubt that I that write this now, that saw the Thames overflowed last winter, and that viewed the flood at the general deluge, was the same *self,* place that self

in what substance you please, than that I that write this am the same *myself* now whilst I write (whether I consist of all the same substance, material or immaterial, or no) that I was yesterday. For as to this point of being the same self, it matters not whether this present self be made up of the same or other substances, I being as much concerned and as justly accountable for any action was done a thousand years since, appropriated to me now by this self-consciousness, as I am for what I did the last moment.

17. *Self depends on consciousness.*—Self is that conscious thinking thing (whatever substance made up of, whether spiritual or material, simple or compounded, it matters not) which is sensible, or conscious of pleasure and pain, capable of happiness or misery, and so is concerned for itself, as far as that consciousness extends. Thus every one finds, that whilst comprehended under that consciousness, the little finger is as much a part of itself as what is most so. Upon separation of this little finger, should this consciousness go along with the little finger, and leave the rest of the body, it is evident the little finger would be the person, the same person; and self then would have nothing to do with the rest of the body. As in this case it is the consciousness that goes along with the substance, when one part is separate from another, which makes the same person, and constitutes this inseparable self: so it is in reference to substances remote in time. That with which the consciousness of this present thinking thing can join itself makes the same person, and is one self with it, and with nothing else; and so attributes to itself and owns all the actions of that thing as its own, as far as that consciousness reaches, and no farther; as every one who reflects will perceive.[1]

18. *Object of reward and punishment.*—In this personal

[1] It is in many ways undesirable to apply the term substance to the self at all, but if we are to continue to use it as an emphatic expression of the distinctive reality of the individual self, then, as Lotze says, ' the fact of the unity of consciousness is *eo ipso* at once the fact of the existence of a substance '. ' So far as, and so long as, the soul knows itself as this identical subject, it is, and is named, simply for that reason, substance. But the attempt to find its capacity of thus knowing itself in the numerical unity of another underlying substance is not a process of reasoning which merely fails to reach an admissible aim—it has no aim at all. That which is not only conceived by others as unity in multiplicity, but knows and makes itself good as such, is, simply on that account, the truest and most indivisible unity there can be' (*Metaphysic*, Bk III, ch. 1)

identity is founded all the right and justice of reward and punishment, happiness and misery being that for which every one is concerned for himself, not mattering what becomes of any substance not joined to or affected with that consciousness. For as is evident in the instance I gave but now, if the consciousness went along with the little finger when it was cut off, that would be the same self which was concerned for the whole body yesterday, as making a part of itself, whose actions then it cannot but admit as its own now. Though if the same body should still live, and immediately from the separation of the little finger have its own peculiar consciousness, whereof the little finger knew nothing, it would not at all be concerned for it, as a part of itself, or could own any of its actions, or have any of them imputed to him.

19. This may show us wherein personal identity consists, not in the identity of substance, but, as I have said, in the identity of consciousness, wherein if Socrates and the present mayor of Queenborough agree, they are the same person. If the same Socrates waking and sleeping do not partake of the same consciousness, Socrates waking and sleeping is not the same person ; and to punish Socrates waking for what sleeping Socrates thought, and waking Socrates was never conscious of, would be no more of right than to punish one twin for what his brother-twin did, whereof he knew nothing, because their outsides were so like that they could not be distinguished.

20. But yet possibly it will still be objected, Suppose I wholly lose the memory of some parts of my life, beyond the possibility of retrieving them, so that perhaps I shall never be conscious of them again ; yet am I not the same person that did those actions, had those thoughts, that I was once conscious of, though I have now forgot them ? To which I answer, That we must here take notice what the word *I* is applied to ; which in this case, is the man only. And the same man being presumed to be the same person, *I* is easily here supposed to stand also for the same person. But if it be possible for the same man to have distinct incommunicable consciousness at different times,[1] it is past doubt the same man would at

[1] The facts of secondary or ' split off ' consciousnesses (disclosed for example by automatic writing), and of ' multiple personality ' generally, have been carefully studied in recent psychology. The most celebrated case, that of ' Sally Beauchamp ', is recorded and analysed in Dr. Morton Prince's *Dissociation of a Personality.*

different times make different persons; which, we see, is the sense of mankind in the solemnest declaration of their opinions, human laws not punishing the mad man for the sober man's actions, nor the sober man for what the mad man did, thereby making them two persons; which is somewhat explained by our way of speaking in English, when we say, such an one is 'not himself', or is 'beside himself;' in which phrases it is insinuated as if those who now or, at least, first used them, thought that self was changed, the selfsame person was no longer in that man.

23. *Consciousness alone makes self.*—Nothing but consciousness can unite remote existences into the same person; the identity of substance will not do it. For whatever substance there is, however framed, without consciousness there is no person: and a carcase may be a person, as well as any sort of substance be so without consciousness.

Could we suppose two distinct incommunicable consciousnesses acting the same body, the one constantly by day, the other by night; and, on the other side, the same consciousness acting by intervals two distinct bodies: I ask, in the first case, whether the day and the night man would not be two as distinct persons as Socrates and Plato; and whether, in the second case, there would not be one person in two distinct bodies, as much as one man is the same in two distinct clothings. Nor is it at all material to say, that this same and this distinct consciousness, in the cases above mentioned, is owing to the same and distinct immaterial substances, bringing it with them to those bodies. For granting that the thinking substance in man must be necessarily supposed immaterial, it is evident that immaterial thinking thing may sometimes part with its past consciousness, and be restored to it again, as appears in the forgetfulness men often have of their past actions; and the mind many times recovers the memory of a past consciousness which it had lost for twenty years together. Make these intervals of memory and forgetfulness to take their turns regularly by day and night, and you have two persons with the same immaterial spirit, as much as in the former instance two persons with the same body. So that self is not determined by identity or diversity of substance, which it cannot be sure of, but only by identity of consciousness.[1]

[1] Cf. Butler's argument *per contra*: 'Though consciousness of what

24. Indeed it may conceive the substance whereof it is now made up to have existed formerly, united in the same conscious being : but, consciousness removed, that substance is no more itself, or makes no more a part of it, than any other substance ; as is evident in the instance we have already given of a limb cut off, of whose heat or cold or other affections having no longer any consciousness, it is no more of a man's self than any other matter of the universe. In like manner it will be in reference to any immaterial substance, which is void of that consciousness whereby I am myself to myself : if there be any part of its existence which I cannot upon recollection join with that present consciousness whereby I am now myself, it is in that part of its existence no more *myself* than any other immaterial being. For whatsoever any substance has thought or done, which I cannot recollect, and by my consciousness make my own thought and action, it will no more belong to me, whether a part of me thought or did it, than if it had been thought or done by any other immaterial being anywhere existing.

25. I agree, the more probable opinion is, that this consciousness is annexed to, and the affection of, one individual immaterial substance.[1]

But let men, according to their diverse hypotheses, resolve of that as they please. This every intelligent being, sensible of happiness or misery, must grant—that there is something that is *himself* that he is concerned for, and would have happy ;

is past does thus ascertain our personal identity to ourselves, yet to say that it makes personal identity, or is necessary to our being the same persons, is to say that a person has not existed a single moment, nor done one action, but what he can remember. . . . And one should really think it self-evident, that consciousness of personal identity presupposes, and therefore cannot constitute personal identity, any more than knowledge, in any other case, can constitute truth, which it presupposes.' So also John Sergeant (*Solid Philosophy*, p. 265) : ' A man must *be* the same, ere he can *know* or *be conscious* that he *is* the same.'

[1] It is characteristic of Locke that, after demonstrating the utter uselessness of the soul-substance to explain the unity of mental life (' it concerns not personal identity at all,' section 10), he still does not discard the conception. He treats the difficulties he has raised as proofs of our ignorance (see e. g. section 27) rather than of the ineptitude of the traditional idea of a substantial soul. Hume's celebrated account of Personal Identity (*Treatise*, Bk. I, part 4, section 6), though defective on its constructive side, owing to the psychological atomism on which Hume's whole philosophy is based, must be accepted as finally disposing of this metaphysical entity.

that this self has existed in a continued duration more than one instant, and therefore it is possible may exist, as it has done, months and years to come, without any certain bounds to be set to its duration ; and may be the same self, by the same consciousness, continued on for the future. And thus, by this consciousness, he finds himself to be the same self which did such or such an action some years since, by which he comes to be happy or miserable now. In all which account of self, the same numerical substance is not considered as making the same self : but the same continued consciousness, in which several substances may have been united, and again separated from it, which, whilst they continued in a vital union with that wherein this consciousness then resided, made a part of that same self. Thus any part of our bodies vitally united to that which is conscious in us, makes a part of ourselves ; but upon separation from the vital union by which that consciousness is communicated, that which a moment since was part of ourselves, is now no more so than a part of another man's self is a part of me ; and it is not impossible, but in a little time may become a real part of another person. And so we have the same numerical substance become a part of two different persons ; and the same person preserved under the change of various substances. Could we suppose any spirit wholly stripped of all its memory or consciousness of past actions, as we find our minds always are of a great part of ours, and sometimes of them all ;[1] the union or separation of such a spiritual substance would make no variation of personal identity, any more that that of any particle of matter does. Any substance vitally united to the present thinking being is a part of that very same self which now is : anything united to it by a consciousness of former actions makes also a part of the same self, which is the same both then and now.

26. *Person, a forensic term.*—*Person*, as I take it, is the name for this self. Wherever a man finds what he calls *himself*, there, I think, another may say is the same person. It is a forensic term appropriating actions and their merit ; and so belongs only to intelligent agents capable of a law, and happiness and misery. This personality extends itself beyond present existence to what is past, only by consciousness ; whereby it becomes concerned and accountable, owns and imputes to itself past actions, just upon the same ground and

[1] i.e. temporarily, as in sleep.

for the same reason that it does the present. All which is founded in a concern for happiness, the unavoidable concomitant of consciousness; that which is conscious of pleasure and pain desiring that that self that is conscious should be happy. And therefore whatever past actions it cannot reconcile or appropriate to that present self by consciousness, it can be no more concerned in, than if they had never been done: and to receive pleasure or pain, i.e., reward or punishment, on the account of any such action, is all one as to be made happy or miserable in its first being without any demerit at all. And therefore, conformable to this, the apostle tells us, that at the great day, when every one shall 'receive according to his doings, the secrets of all hearts shall be laid open'. The sentence shall be justified by the consciousness all persons shall have that they *themselves*, in what bodies soever they appear, or what substances soever that consciousness adheres to, are the *same* that committed those actions, and deserve that punishment for them.[1]

27. I am apt enough to think I have, in treating of this subject, made some suppositions that will look strange to some readers, and possibly they are so in themselves.[2] But yet, I think, they are such as are pardonable in this ignorance we are in of the nature of that thinking thing that is in us, and which we look on as *ourselves*. Did we know what it was, or how it was tied to a certain system of fleeting animal spirits; or whether it could or could not perform its operations of thinking and memory out of a body organized as ours is; and whether it has pleased God that no one such spirit shall ever be united to any but one such body, upon the right constitution of whose organs its memory should depend, we might see the absurdity of some of those suppositions I have made. But taking, as we

[1] Coleridge, in a well-known passage of the *Biographia Literaria*, has suggested that there are no depths of latency from which memories may not be recovered, and that under appropriate conditions there might thus be recalled to 'every human soul the collective experience of its whole first existence. And thus this, perchance, is the dread book of judgement in whose mysterious hieroglyphics every idle word is recorded' (*Biographia Literaria*, ch. 6 *ad finem*). John Sergeant expresses the same idea (*Solid Philosophy*, p. 266).

[2] Locke's doctrine of personal identity called forth much criticism. It was attacked by Stillingfleet as inconsistent with the Christian doctrine of the Resurrection. John Sergeant and other contemporary critics also condemned it. At a later date Clarke, Butler, Reid and Cousin criticized it adversely.

ordinarily now do (in the dark concerning these matters), the soul of a man for an immaterial substance, independent from matter, and indifferent alike to it all, there can from the nature of things be no absurdity at all to suppose that the same soul may, at different times, be united to different bodies, and with them make up, for that time, one man: as well as we suppose a part of a sheep's body yesterday, should be a part of a man's body to-morrow, and in that union make a vital part of Melibaeus himself, as well as it did of his ram.

28. *The difficulty from ill use of names.*—To conclude: Whatever substance begins to exist, it must, during its existence, necessarily be the same: whatever compositions of substances begin to exist, during the union of those substances, the concrete must be the same: whatsoever mode begins to exist, during its existence it is the same: and so if the composition be of distinct substances and different modes, the same rule holds. Whereby it will appear, that the difficulty or obscurity that has been about this matter rather rises from the names ill used, than from any obscurity in things themselves. For whatever makes the specific idea to which the name is applied, if that idea be steadily kept to, the distinction of anything into the same and diverse will easily be conceived, and there can arise no doubt about it.

29. *Continued existence makes identity.*—For supposing a rational spirit be the idea of a man, it is easy to know what is the same man; viz. the same spirit, whether separate or in a body, will be the same man. Supposing a rational spirit vitally united to a body of a certain conformation of parts to make a man, whilst that rational spirit, with that vital conformation of parts, though continued in a fleeting successive body, remains, it will be the same man. But if to any one the idea of a man be but the vital union of parts in a certain shape; as long as that vital union and shape remains, in a concrete no otherwise the same but by a continued succession of fleeting particles, it will be the same man. For whatever be the composition whereof the complex idea is made, whatever makes it one particular thing under any denomination, the same existence continued preserves it the same individual under the same denomination.

## CHAPTER XXVIII

### OF OTHER RELATIONS

1. *Proportional.*—Besides the before-mentioned occasions of time, place, and causality, of comparing, or referring things one to another, there are, as I have said, infinite others, some whereof I shall mention. The first I shall name, is some one simple idea, which being capable of parts or degrees, affords an occasion of comparing the subjects wherein it is to one another, in respect of that simple idea, v. g., whiter, sweeter, bigger, equal, more, &c. These may be called, if one will, proportional.

4. *Moral.*—There is another sort of relation, which is the conformity or disagreement men's voluntary actions have to a rule to which they are referred, and by which they are judged of; which, I think, may be called moral relation. [5.] Good and evil, as hath been shown (Bk. II, ch. 20, sect. 2, and ch. 21, sect. 42), are nothing but pleasure or pain, or that which occasions or procures pleasure or pain to us. *Morally good and evil*, then, is only the conformity or disagreement of our voluntary actions to some law, whereby good or evil is drawn on us from the will and power of the law-maker; which good and evil, pleasure or pain, attending our observance or breach of the law, by the decree of the law-maker, is that we call *reward* and *punishment*.

6. *Moral rules.*—Of these moral rules or laws, to which men generally refer, and by which they judge of the rectitude or pravity of their actions, there seem to me to be *three sorts*, with their three different enforcements, or rewards and punishments. For since it would be utterly in vain to suppose a rule set to the free actions of man, without annexing to it some enforcement of good and evil to determine his will, we must, wherever we suppose a law, suppose also some reward or punishment annexed to that law, some good and evil that is not the natural product and consequence of the action itself. For that, being a natural convenience or inconvenience, would operate of itself without a law. This, if I mistake not, is the true nature of all law, properly so called.

7. *Laws.*—The laws that men generally refer their actions to, to judge of their rectitude or obliquity, seem to me to be these

three: (1) The *divine* law. (2) The *civil* law. (3) The law of *opinion* or *reputation*, if I may so call it.[1] By the relation they bear to the first of these, men judge whether their actions are sins or duties; by the second, whether they be criminal or innocent; and by the third, whether they be virtues or vices.

8. *Divine law, the measure of sin and duty.*—First, The *divine law*, whether promulgated to them by the light of nature,[2] or the voice of revelation. That God has given a rule whereby men should govern themselves, I think there is nobody so brutish as to deny. He has a right to do it; we are his creatures. He has goodness and wisdom to direct our actions to that which is best; and he has power to enforce it by rewards and punishments, of infinite weight and duration, in another life: for nobody can take us out of his hands. This is the only true touchstone of moral rectitude.[3]

9. *Civil law, the measure of crimes and innocence.*—Secondly, The *civil law*. This law nobody overlooks; the rewards and punishments that enforce it being ready at hand, and suitable to the power that makes it; which is the force of the commonwealth, engaged to protect the lives, liberties, and possessions of those who live according to its laws, and has power to take away life, liberty, or goods from him who disobeys.

10. *Philosophical law, the measure of virtue and vice.*—Thirdly, The *law of opinion or reputation*. Virtue and vice are names pretended and supposed everywhere to stand for actions in their own nature right and wrong: and as far as they really are so applied, they so far are coincident with the divine law above mentioned. But yet, whatever is pretended, this is visible, that these names, virtue and vice, in the particular instances of their application, through the several nations and societies of men in the world, are constantly attributed only to such actions as in each country and society are in reputation or discredit. [11.] That this is the common *measure* of virtue and vice [4] will appear to any one who considers, that though

[1] This was called 'the philosophical law' in the first edition, and the name is retained in the summary of section 10. Locke explained in the first edition that he called it so, 'not because philosophers make it, but because they have most busied themselves to enquire after it, and talk about it': a rather odd reason.

[2] Elsewhere reason is called 'natural revelation' (IV. 19. 4).

[3] 'So Paley afterwards in his definitions of virtue' (Fraser).

[4] As he explained in his prefatory note to the second edition, in answer to a critic, Locke is here only reporting, 'as matters of fact,

that passes for vice in one country which is counted a virtue, or at least not vice, in another; yet everywhere virtue and praise, vice and blame, go together. Virtue is everywhere that which is thought praiseworthy; and nothing else but that which has the allowance of public esteem is called virtue.

12. *Its enforcements, commendation and discredit.*—If any one shall imagine that I have forgot my own notion of a law, when I make the law whereby men judge of virtue and vice to be nothing else but the consent of private men who have not authority enough to make a law : I think I may say, that he who imagines commendation and disgrace not to be strong motives on men to accommodate themselves to the opinions and rules of those with whom they converse, seems little skilled in the nature or history of mankind : the greatest part whereof he shall find to govern themselves chiefly, if not solely, by this law of fashion. The penalties that attend the breach of God's laws, some, nay, perhaps most, men seldom seriously reflect on ; and amongst those that do, many, whilst they break the law, entertain thoughts of future reconciliation, and making their peace for such breaches : and as to the punishments due from the laws of the commonwealth, they frequently flatter themselves with the hopes of impunity. But no man escapes the punishment of their censure and dislike who offends against the fashion and opinion of the company he keeps, and would recommend himself to. Nor is there one of ten thousand who is stiff and insensible enough to bear up under the constant dislike and condemnation of his own club. Solitude many men have sought, and been reconciled to; but nobody that has the least thought or sense of a man about him can live in society under the constant dislike and ill opinion of his familiars and those he converses with. This is a burden too heavy for human sufferance.

what others call virtue and vice', not what he himself thinks ' of the eternal and unalterable nature of right and wrong, and what [he calls] virtue and vice ' (Clarendon Press edition, vol. i, p. 18).

## CHAPTER XXIX

OF CLEAR AND OBSCURE, DISTINCT AND CONFUSED IDEAS

1. *Ideas, some clear and distinct, others obscure and confused.*—Having shown the original of our ideas, and taken a view of their several sorts; considered the difference between the simple and the complex, and observed how the complex ones are divided into those of modes, substances, and relations; it will, perhaps, be thought I have dwelt long enough upon the examination of ideas. I must, nevertheless, crave leave to offer some few other considerations concerning them.[1]

[1] As Locke here intimates, he has now completed his survey of the different classes of our ideas, and demonstrated, as he thinks, their origin in the facts of sensation and reflection, or at least their relation to these facts. The remaining chapters of Book II are, therefore, of the nature of an appendix. The topic of the present chapter—the obligation to ensure that our ideas are clear and distinct—belongs to the practical side of logic as the art of thinking and of improving the understanding. Locke would find several chapters on the subject in the Port Royal *Logic*, the most popular manual of the seventeenth century, published in 1662. The subject had also been dealt with by Leibniz in an essay *Meditationes de cognitione, veritate et ideis*, printed in 1684, but this was doubtless unknown to Locke. It was natural for Locke to employ Descartes's criteria of clearness and distinctness, seeing that for both thinkers explicit self-conscious thought is the only recognized operation of the mind. But if, as Locke teaches, ideas are 'nothing but actual perceptions in the mind' (II. 10. 2), and if, as he acknowledges in the present chapter, 'let any idea be as it will, it can be no other but such as the mind perceives it to be, and that very perception sufficiently distinguishes it from all other ideas' (section 5), then confusion between ideas is strictly impossible. This consequence is accepted by Locke in section 10, and the solution suggested there, and in section 6, is that the real source of confusion is in the reference of ideas to their names. He takes up the same position in a passage in his *Examination of Malebranche* (section 29), quoted by Professor Gibson: 'What it is to see any idea, to which I do not give a name, confusedly is what I do not well understand. What I see, I see, and the idea I see is distinct from all others that are not the same with it.' In a prefatory note to the fourth edition of the *Essay*, Locke intimated that he had 'in most places put *determinate* or *determined* instead of *clear* and *distinct* as most likely to direct men's thoughts to my meaning in this matter'. But here again the criterion cannot be applied except in reference to names, as appears in Locke's careful definition of his new term: 'This, I think, may fitly be called a determinate or determined idea, when such as it is objectively in the mind, and so determined there, it is annexed, and without variation determined, to a name or articulate sound, which is to

The first is, that some are *clear*, and others *obscure*; some *distinct*, and others *confused*.

2. *Clear and obscure explained by sight.*—The perception of the mind being most aptly explained by words relating to the sight, we shall best understand what is meant by *clear* and *obscure* in our ideas, by reflecting on what we call clear and obscure in the objects of sight. Light being that which discovers to us visible objects, we give the name of obscure to that which is not placed in a light sufficient to discover minutely to us the figure and colours which are observable in it, and which in a better light would be discernible. In like manner our simple ideas are clear, when they are such as the objects themselves, from whence they were taken, did or might, in a well-ordered sensation or perception, present them. Whilst the memory retains them thus, and can produce them to the mind whenever it has occasion to consider them, they are clear ideas. So far as they either want anything of that original exactness, or have lost any of their first freshness, and are, as it were, faded or tarnished by time, so far are they obscure. Complex ideas, as they are made up of simple ones, so they are clear when the ideas that go to their composition are clear, and the number and order of those simple ideas that are the ingredients of any complex one is determinate and certain.

4. *Distinct and confused, what.*—As a clear idea is that whereof the mind has such a full and evident perception as it does receive from an outward object operating duly on a well-disposed organ, so a *distinct* idea is that wherein the mind perceives a difference from all other, and a *confused* idea is such an one as is not sufficiently distinguishable from another from which it ought to be different.

5. *Objection.*—If no idea be confused, but such as is not sufficiently distinguishable from another, from which it should be different, it will be hard, may any one say, to find anywhere a *confused* idea. For let any idea be as it will, it can be no other but such as the mind perceives it to be; and that very perception sufficiently distinguishes it from all other ideas, which cannot be other, i.e. different, without being perceived to be so. No idea, therefore, can be undistinguishable

be steadily the sign of that very same object of the mind, or determinate idea' (Clarendon Press edition, vol. i, p. 22). Cf. Professor Gibson's statement, *Locke's Theory of Knowledge*, pp. 22–5. Berkeley takes up the same position (*Principles*, Introduction, section 22).

from another, from which it ought to be different, unless you would have it different from itself; for from all other it is evidently different.

6. *Confusion of ideas is in reference to their names.*—To remove this difficulty, and to help us to conceive aright what it is that makes the confusion ideas are at any time chargeable with, we must consider that things ranked under distinct names are supposed different enough to be distinguished, that so each sort, by its peculiar name, may be marked, and discoursed of apart upon any occasion. Now every idea a man has being visibly what it is, and distinct from all other ideas but itself, that which makes it confused is, when it is such that it may as well be called by another name as that which it is expressed by; the difference which keeps the things (to be ranked under those two different names) distinct, and makes some of them belong rather to the one, and some of them to the other, of those names, being left out; and so the distinction, which was intended to be kept up by those different names, is quite lost.

7. The defaults which usually occasion this confusion, I think, are chiefly these following :

First, when any complex idea is made up of too small a number of single ones. Thus he that has an idea made up of barely the simple ones of a beast with spots, has but a confused idea of a leopard, it not being thereby sufficiently distinguished from a lynx, and several other sorts of beasts that are spotted.

8. Secondly, when, though the particulars that make up any idea are in number enough, yet they are so jumbled together, that it is not easily discernible whether it more belongs to the name that is given it, than to any other. [9.] A third defect is when any one of [our ideas] is uncertain and undetermined. Thus we may observe men who, not forbearing to use the ordinary words of their language till they have learned their precise signification, change the idea they make this or that term stand for, almost as often as they use it.

10. By what has been said, we may observe how much names, as supposed steady signs of things, and by their difference to stand for and keep things distinct that in themselves are different, are the occasion of denominating ideas distinct or confused, by a secret and unobserved reference the mind makes of its ideas to such names. Without taking

notice of such a reference of ideas to distinct names, as the signs of distinct things, it will be hard to say what a confused idea is.[1]

13. *Complex ideas may be distinct in one part, and confused in another.*—Our complex ideas being made up of collections, and so variety of simple ones, may accordingly be very clear and distinct in one part, and very obscure and confused in another. In a man who speaks of a chiliaëdron, or a body of a thousand sides, the idea of the figure may be very confused, though that of the number be very distinct ; so that he being able to discourse and demonstrate concerning that part of his complex idea which depends upon the number of a thousand, he is apt to think he has a distinct idea of a chiliaëdron ; though it be plain he has no precise idea of its figure, so as to distinguish it by that from one that has but nine hundred and ninety-nine sides.[2]

16. *Divisibility of matter.*—In matter, we have no clear ideas of the smallness of parts much beyond the smallest that occur to any of our senses ; and therefore when we talk of the divisibility of matter *in infinitum*, though we have clear ideas of division and divisibility, and have also clear ideas of parts made out of a whole by division ; yet we have but very obscure and confused ideas of corpuscles, or minute bodies, so to be divided, when by former divisions they are reduced to a smallness much exceeding the perception of any of our senses ; and so all that we have clear and distinct ideas of, is of what division in general or abstractly is, and the relation of *totum* and *pars* : but of the bulk of the body, to be thus infinitely divided after certain progressions, I think we have no clear nor distinct idea at all.

[1] Remarking on Locke's failure to make an effective distinction between clear and distinct ideas, Leibniz points out that, according to the Cartesian terminology (which he adopts), an idea is distinct, when it not only serves to distinguish its object, but enables us to distinguish in the object the marks by which we recognize it. That is to say, we not only know it by an example ; we can give a definition of it. The distinction between a distinct and a confused idea lies therefore in the ideas themselves, and is not to be explained solely by reference to names.

[2] Locke fails to distinguish here between idea in the sense of notion or concept and idea as equivalent to an image or picture. We cannot picture to ourselves a figure of a thousand sides as distinguished from one of nine hundred and ninety-nine ; but it is plain that we have a perfectly precise conception of the figure, because we can define it and, as Leibniz says, discover and demonstrate all kinds of truths about it. Cf. Descartes's sixth *Meditation*, where he uses the same example to illustrate the difference between ' imagination ' and ' pure intellection '. The same confusion is observable in Locke's remarks on infinite divisibility.

## CHAPTER XXX

### OF REAL AND FANTASTICAL IDEAS [1]

1. *Real ideas are conformable to their archetypes.*—Besides what we have already mentioned concerning ideas, other considerations belong to them, in reference to things from whence they are taken, or which they may be supposed to represent; and thus, I think, they may come under a threefold distinction; and are,

First, either real or fantastical.

Secondly, adequate or inadequate.

Thirdly, true or false.

First, By *real ideas*, I mean such as have a foundation in nature; such as have a conformity with the real being and existence of things, or with their archetypes. *Fantastical* or *chimerical*, I call such as have no foundation in nature, nor have any conformity with that reality of being to which they are tacitly referred as to their archetypes. If we examine the several sorts of ideas before mentioned, we shall find that,

2. First, Our *simple ideas are all real*, all agree to the reality of things. Not that they are all of them the images or representations of what does exist; the contrary whereof, in all but the primary qualities of bodies, hath been already showed. But though whiteness and coldness are no more in snow than pain is; yet those ideas of whiteness and coldness, pain, &c., being in us the effects of powers in things without us, ordained by our Maker to produce in us such sensations; they are real ideas in us, whereby we distinguish the qualities that are really in things themselves. For these several appearances being designed to be the marks whereby we are to know and distinguish things which we have to do with; our ideas do as well serve us to that purpose, and are as real distinguishing characters, whether they be only constant effects or else exact resemblances of something in the things themselves: the reality lying in that steady correspondence they have with

[1] As the previous chapter dealt with ideas ' in reference to names ', this and the two following chapters consider them ' in reference to things ', which they are supposed to ' represent '. These chapters therefore anticipate the discussions and conclusions of Book IV, and involve a considerable amount of overlapping. Repetitions have been omitted as far as practicable.

# Of Real and Fantastical Ideas

the distinct constitutions of real beings. But whether they answer to those constitutions, as to causes or patterns, it matters not; it suffices that they are constantly produced by them.

4. *Mixed modes made of consistent ideas are real.*—Secondly, Mixed modes and relations having no other reality but what they have in the minds of men, there is nothing more required to those kinds of ideas to make them real but that they be so framed that there be a possibility of existing conformable to them. These ideas, being themselves archetypes, cannot differ from their archetypes, and so cannot be chimerical, unless any one will jumble together in them inconsistent ideas.[1]

5. *Ideas of substances are real, when they agree with the existence of things.*—Thirdly, Our complex ideas of substances, being made all of them in reference to things existing without us, and intended to be representations of substances as they really are, are no farther real than as they are such combinations of simple ideas as are really united, and coexist in things without us. On the contrary, those are fantastical which are made up of such collections of simple ideas as were really never united, never were found together in any substance; v.g., a rational creature, consisting of a horse's head, joined to a body of human shape, or such as the centaurs are described.


## CHAPTER XXXI

### OF ADEQUATE AND INADEQUATE IDEAS

1. *Adequate ideas are such as perfectly represent their archetypes.*—Of our real ideas, some are adequate, and some are inadequate. Those I call *adequate* which perfectly represent those archetypes which the mind supposes them taken from; which it intends them to stand for, and to which it refers them. *Inadequate* ideas are such which are but a partial or incomplete representation of those archetypes to which they are referred. Upon which account it is plain,

2. *Simple ideas all adequate.*—First, That all our simple ideas

[1] As Leibniz remarks, to speak of mixed modes as ' real ', is to use the term in quite a different sense from that in which we apply it to simple ideas and to our ideas of substances. The distinction between real and fantastical is in fact only applicable where there is a reference to ' the real being and existence of things '.

are adequate. Because being nothing but the effects of certain powers in things, fitted and ordained by God to produce such sensations in us, they cannot but be correspondent and adequate to those powers : and we are sure they agree to the reality of things.

3. *Modes are all adequate.*—Secondly, Our complex ideas of modes, being voluntary collections of simple ideas which the mind puts together, without reference to any real archetypes or standing patterns existing anywhere, are and cannot but be adequate ideas.[1] Because they, not being intended for copies of things really existing, but for archetypes made by the mind to rank and denominate things by, cannot want anything ; they having each of them that combination of ideas, and thereby that perfection, which the mind intended they should. Thus by having the idea of a figure with three sides meeting at three angles, I have a complete idea, wherein I require nothing else to make it perfect. But in our ideas of substances it is otherwise. For there, desiring to copy things as they really do exist, and to represent to ourselves that constitution on which all their properties depend, we perceive our ideas attain not that perfection we intend : we find they still want something we should be glad were in them ; and so are all inadequate. But mixed modes and relations, being archetypes without patterns, and so having nothing to represent but themselves, cannot but be adequate. [An] idea thus made, and laid up for a pattern, must necessarily be adequate, being referred to nothing else but itself, nor made by any other original but the good liking and will of him that first made [the] combination.

4. *Modes, in reference to settled names, may be inadequate.*— Another coming after, and in conversation learning from him the word courage, may make an idea, to which he gives that name courage, different from what the first author applied it to, and has in his mind when he uses it. And on this account, our ideas of mixed modes are the most liable to be faulty of any other ; but this refers more to proper speaking, than knowing right.

6. *Ideas of substances, as referred to real essences, not adequate.*

[1] ' What of the *simple modes*, e. g. of space and duration ', asks Professor Fraser, ' as in our ideas of Immensity and Eternity ? Are *they* adequate to the reality ? ' But here, as in the previous chapter, Locke is apparently thinking only of ' mixed modes ' and ' relations '.

## Ch. 31 *Of Adequate and Inadequate Ideas*

—Thirdly, What ideas we have of substances, I have above showed.[1] Now those ideas have in the mind a double reference: (1) Sometimes they are referred to a supposed real essence of each species of things. (2) Sometimes they are only designed to be pictures and representations in the mind of things that do exist, by ideas of those qualities that are discoverable in them. In both which ways, these copies of those originals and archetypes are imperfect and inadequate.

First, It is usual for men to make the names of substances stand for things, as supposed to have certain real essences, whereby they are of this or that species: and names standing for nothing but the ideas that are in men's minds, they must consequently refer their ideas to such real essences as to their archetypes. That men (especially such as have been bred up in the learning taught in this part of the world) do suppose certain specific essences of substances, which each individual, in its several kind, is made conformable to and partakes of,[2] is so far from needing proof, that it will be thought strange if any one should do otherwise. And yet if you demand what those real essences are, it is plain men are ignorant, and know them not. From whence it follows, that the ideas they have in their minds, being referred to real essences, as to archetypes which are unknown, must be so far from being adequate, that they cannot be supposed to be any representation of them at all. The complex ideas we have of substances are, as it has been shown, certain collections of simple ideas that have been observed or supposed constantly to exist together. But such a complex idea cannot be the real essence of any substance; for then the properties we discover in that body would depend on that complex idea, and be deducible from it, and their necessary connexion with it be known; as all properties of a triangle depend on, and, as far as they are discoverable, are deducible from, the complex idea of three lines, including a space.[3] But it is plain, that in our complex ideas of substances

[1] Ch. 23.
[2] The 'substantial forms' of the Scholastic philosophy. See note, p. 156. Cf. Bk. III. 3. 17.
[3] Cf. II. 32. 24: 'The essence of a triangle lies in a very little compass; ... three lines including a space make up that essence: but the properties that flow from this essence are more than can be easily known or enumerated. So I imagine it is in substance: their real essences lie in a little compass, though the properties flowing from that internal constitution are endless.' Cf. also IV. 6. 11.

are not contained such ideas on which all the other qualities that are to be found in them do depend. The common idea men have of iron, is a body of a certain colour, weight, and hardness; and a property that they look on as belonging to it is malleableness. But yet this property has no necessary connexion with that complex idea, or any part of it : and there is no more reason to think, that malleableness depends on that colour, weight, and hardness, than that that colour or that weight depends on its malleableness. And yet, though we know nothing of these real essences, there is nothing more ordinary than that men should attribute the sorts of things to such essences. The particular parcel of matter which makes the ring I have on my finger, is forwardly, by most men, supposed to have a real essence, whereby it is gold ; and from whence those qualities flow which I find in it. This essence, from which all these properties flow, when I enquire into it and search after it, I plainly perceive I cannot discover : the farthest I can go is only to presume, that, it being nothing but body, its real essence or internal constitution, on which these qualities depend, can be nothing but the figure, size, and connexion of its solid parts ; of neither of which having any distinct perception at all, I can have no idea of its essence. If any one will say that the real essence and internal constitution, on which these properties depend, is not the figure, size, and arrangement or connexion of its solid parts, but something else, called its particular *form* ; I am farther from having any idea of its real essence than I was before ; for I have an idea of figure, size, and situation of solid parts in general, though I have none of the particular figure, size, or putting together of parts, whereby the qualities above mentioned are produced. But when I am told that something besides the figure, size, and posture of the solid parts of that body is its essence, something called *substantial form* ; of that, I confess, I have no idea at all, but only of the sound, *form* ; which is far enough from an idea of its real essence or constitution.

8. *Ideas of substances, as collections of their qualities, are all inadequate.*—Secondly, Those who, neglecting that useless supposition of unknown real essences whereby they are distinguished, endeavour to copy the substances that exist in the world by putting together the ideas of those sensible qualities which are found coexisting in them, though they come much

nearer a likeness of them, than those who imagine they know not what real specific essences; yet they arrive not at perfectly adequate ideas of those substances they would thus copy into their minds; nor do those copies exactly and fully contain all that is to be found in their archetypes. Because those qualities and powers of substances, whereof we make their complex ideas, are so many and various that no man's complex idea contains them all. That our abstract ideas of substances do not contain in them all the simple ideas that are united in the things themselves, is evident, in that men do rarely put into their complex idea of any substance all the simple ideas they do know to exist in it. Because endeavouring to make the signification of their specific names as clear and as little cumbersome as they can, they make their specific ideas of the sorts of substances, for the most part, of a few of those simple ideas which are to be found in them: but these having no original precedency or right to be put in and make the specific idea, more than others that are left out, it is plain that, both these ways, our ideas of substances are deficient and inadequate. The simple ideas, whereof we make our complex ones of substances, are all of them (bating only the figure and bulk of some sorts [1]) powers; which being relations to other substances, we can never be sure that we know all the powers that are in any one body, till we have tried what changes it is fitted to give to, or receive from, other substances in their several ways of application: which being impossible to be tried upon any one body, much less upon all, it is impossible we should have adequate ideas of any substance made up of a collection of all its properties.[2]

11. *Ideas of substances, as collections of their qualities, are all inadequate.*—So that all our complex ideas of substances are imperfect and inadequate. Which would be so also in mathematical figures, if we were to have our complex ideas of them only by collecting their properties in reference to other figures. How uncertain and imperfect would our ideas be of an ellipse, if we had no other idea of it but some few of its properties! Whereas, having in our plain idea the whole essence of that figure, we from thence discover those properties, and demonstratively see how they flow and are inseparable from it.

[1] 'Some sorts', i.e. bodies, not spiritual substances.
[2] Cf. IV. 6. 11.

12. *Simple ideas ἔκτυπα, and adequate.*—Thus the mind has three sorts of abstract ideas, or nominal essences.[1]

First, *Simple* ideas which are ἔκτυπα, or copies; but yet certainly adequate. Because being intended to express nothing but the power in things to produce in the mind such a sensation, that sensation, when it is produced, cannot but be the effect of that power.

13. *Ideas of substances are ἔκτυπα, and inadequate.* Secondly, The complex ideas of substances are ectypes, copies too; but not perfect ones, not adequate. Not having tried all the operations of all other substances upon [any substance], and found all the alterations it would receive from, or cause in other substances, [the mind] cannot have an exact adequate collection of all its active and passive capacities : which is that sort of complex idea of substances we have. And after all, if we could have, and actually had, in our complex idea, an exact collection of all the secondary qualities or powers of any substance, we should not yet thereby have an idea of the essence of that thing. For since the powers or qualities that are observable by us are not the real essence of that substance, but depend on it, and flow from it, any collection whatsoever of these qualities cannot be the real essence of that thing. Whereby it is plain that our ideas of substances are not adequate; are not what the mind intends them to be. Besides, a man has no idea of substance in general, nor knows what substance is in itself.

14. *Ideas of modes and relations are archetypes, and cannot but be adequate.*—Thirdly, Complex ideas of modes and relations are originals and archetypes. Being such collections of simple ideas that the mind itself puts together, and such collections that each of them contains in it precisely all that the mind intends it should, they are archetypes and essences of modes that may exist ; and so are designed only for, and belong only to such modes as, when they do exist, have an exact conformity with those complex ideas. The ideas therefore of modes and relations cannot but be adequate.

[1] This term, introduced here without comment, is explained in Book III, ch. 3. 15, where the relation of nominal and real essences is again under discussion. Book III, ch. 6, on the ' Names of Substances ', is largely devoted to the same subject. Cf. also IV. 3. 9–14; 4. 11–13; 6. 4–15.

## CHAPTER XXXII

### OF TRUE AND FALSE IDEAS

1. *Truth and falsehood properly belong to propositions.*—Though truth and falsehood belong, in propriety of speech, only to propositions, yet ideas are oftentimes termed true or false, though I think that there is still some secret or tacit proposition which is the foundation of that denomination. For our ideas being nothing but bare appearances or perception in our minds, cannot properly and simply in themselves be said to be true or false, no more than a single name of anything can be said to be true or false.

4. *Ideas referred to anything may be true or false.*—Whenever the mind refers any of its ideas to anything extraneous to them, they are then capable to be called true or false. Because the mind in such a reference makes a tacit supposition of their conformity to that thing : which supposition, as it happens to be true or false, so the ideas themselves come to be denominated. The most usual cases wherein this happens are these following :
[5.] First, When the mind supposes any idea it has conformable to that in other men's minds, called by the same common name ; v. g., when the mind intends or judges its ideas of justice, temperance, religion, to be the same with what other men give those names to. Secondly, When the mind supposes any idea it has in itself to be conformable to some real existence. Thus the two ideas of a man and a centaur, supposed to be the ideas of real substances, are the one true and the other false. Thirdly, When the mind refers any of its ideas to that *real* constitution and essence of anything, whereon all its properties depend : and thus the greatest part, if not all our ideas of substances, are false.

6. *The cause of such references.*—These suppositions the mind is very apt tacitly to make concerning its own ideas. But yet, if we will examine it, we shall find it is chiefly, if not only, concerning its abstract complex ideas. For the natural tendency of the mind being towards knowledge, and finding that, if it should proceed by and dwell upon only particular things, its progress would be very slow, and its work endless : therefore to shorten its way to knowledge, and make each perception the more comprehensive, the first thing it does, as

the foundation of the easier enlarging its knowledge, is to bind them into bundles, and rank them so into sorts, that what knowledge it gets of any of them, it may thereby with assurance extend to all of that sort ; and so advance by larger steps in that which is its great business, knowledge. This, as I have elsewhere showed,[1] is the reason why we collect things under comprehensive ideas, with names annexed to them, into *genera* and *species*, i. e., into kinds and sorts. [7.] The mind having got any idea which it thinks it may have use of, either in contemplation or discourse, the first thing it does, is to abstract it, and then get a name to it; and so lay it up in its storehouse, the memory, as containing its essence of a sort of things, of which that name is always to be the mark. [8.] But this abstract idea being something in the mind between the thing that exists, and the name that is given to it, it is in our ideas that both the rightness of our knowledge, and the propriety or intelligibleness of our speaking, consists.

[9.] First then, I say, that when the truth of our ideas is judged of by the conformity they have to the ideas which other men have and commonly signify by the same name, they may be any of them false. [13.] Secondly, As to the truth and falsehood of our ideas, in reference to the real existence of things, when that is made the standard of their truth, none of them can be termed false, but only our complex ideas of substances.

26. *More properly to be called right or wrong.*—Upon the whole matter, I think, that our ideas, as they are considered by the mind, either in reference to the proper signification of their names, or in reference to the reality of things, may very fitly be called right or wrong ideas, according as they agree or disagree to those patterns to which they are referred. But if any one had rather call them true or false, it is fit he use a liberty which every one has to call things by those names he thinks best ; though, in propriety of speech, truth or falsehood will, I think, scarce agree to them, but as they, some way or other, virtually contain in them some mental proposition.

---

[1] Bk. III, ch. 3. The same theory of the origin of general names is stated, Bk. III. 1. 3, where see Leibniz's criticism, note p. 223.

## CHAPTER XXXIII

### OF THE ASSOCIATION OF IDEAS [1]

1. *Something unreasonable in most men.*—There is scarce any one that does not observe something that seems odd to him, and is in itself really extravagant, in the opinions, reasonings, and actions of other men. The least flaw of this kind, if at all different from his own, every one is quick-sighted enough to espy in another, and will by the authority of reason forwardly condemn, though he be guilty of much greater unreasonableness in his own tenets and conduct, which he never perceives, and will very hardly, if at all, be convinced of.

5. *From a wrong connexion of ideas.*—Some of our ideas have a natural correspondence and connexion one with another; it is the office and excellency of our reason to trace these, and hold them together in that union and correspondence which is founded in their peculiar beings. Besides this, there is another connexion of ideas wholly owing to chance or custom: ideas that in themselves are not at all of kin, come to be so united in some men's minds that it is very hard to separate them; they always keep in company, and the one no sooner at any time comes into the understanding, but its associate appears with it; and if they are more than two which are thus united, the whole gang, always inseparable, show themselves together.

6. *This connexion how made.*—This strong combination of ideas, not allied by nature, the mind makes in itself either

---

[1] This chapter first appeared in the fourth edition. Writing to Molyneux in 1695, Locke mentions his intention ' to make some additions to be put into your Latin translation, particularly concerning the *connexion of ideas* which has not that I know been hitherto considered'. The last statement is of course incorrect. The subject had been dealt with by a variety of writers from Aristotle downwards, and prominence had recently been given to it by Hobbes (*Human Nature*, ch. 4. 2; *Leviathan*, ch. 3). Half a century later, David Hartley in his *Observations on Man* (1749) worked out a scheme of physiological psychology, in which he made association the central principle by which mental action is explained. It had already been used in that sense philosophically in Hume's *Treatise* (1738). Under the combined influence of Hume and Hartley, an equally dominant place was assigned to the principle by James Mill and the English Associationist School in the nineteenth century. Far from viewing it in that light, Locke treats it, in this supplementary chapter, as an explanation of the ' wrong connexion of ideas ' which is the fertile source of ' false views ' and ' false consequences '.

voluntarily or by chance; and hence it comes in different men to be very different, according to their different inclinations, educations, interests, &c. Custom settles habits of thinking in the understanding,[1] as well as of determining in the will, and of motions in the body; all which seems to be but trains of motion in the animal spirits, which, once set agoing, continue in the same steps they have been used to, which, by often treading, are worn into a smooth path, and the motion in it becomes easy, and as it were natural. As far as we can comprehend thinking, thus ideas seem to be produced in our minds; or if they are not, this may serve to explain their following one another in an habitual train, when once they are put into that track, as well as it does to explain such motions of the body.[2] A musician used to any tune will find that, let it but once begin in his head, the ideas of the several notes of it will follow one another orderly in his understanding, without any care or attention, as regularly as his fingers move orderly over the keys of the organ to play out the tune he has begun, though his unattentive thoughts be elsewhere a-wandering. Whether the natural cause of these ideas, as well as of that regular dancing of his fingers, be the motion of his animal spirits, I will not determine, how probable soever by this instance it appears to be so: but this may help us a little to conceive of intellectual habits, and of the tying together of ideas.

7. *Some antipathies an effect of it.*—That there are such associations of them made by custom in the minds of most men, I think nobody will question who has well considered himself or others; and to this, perhaps, might be justly attributed most of the sympathies and antipathies observable in men, which work as strongly, and produce as regular effects, as if they were natural, and are therefore called so, though they at first had no other original but the accidental connexion of two ideas which either the strength of the first impression, or future indulgence so united, that they always afterwards kept company together in that man's mind, as if they were but one idea. I say, most of the antipathies, I do not say all; for some of them are truly natural, depend upon our original constitution, and are born with us.

[1] 'Custom', says Hume, 'is the great guide of human life.' 'All inferences from experience are effects of custom, not of reasoning' (*Enquiry*, section 5, part 1).

[2] This was the line of thought followed out by Hartley in his theory of 'vibrations' and 'vibratiuncles'.

8. I mention this not out of any great necessity there is, in this present argument, to distinguish nicely between natural and acquired antipathies; but I take notice of it for another purpose, viz., that those who have children, or the charge of their education, would think it worth their while diligently to watch, and carefully to prevent the undue connexion of ideas in the minds of young people. [9.] This wrong connexion in our minds of ideas, in themselves loose and independent one of another, is of so great force to set us awry in our actions, as well moral as natural, passions, reasonings, and notions themselves, that perhaps there is not any one thing that deserves more to be looked after. [10.] The ideas of goblins and sprites have really no more to do with darkness than light; yet let but a foolish maid inculcate these often on the mind of a child, and raise them there together, possibly he shall never be able to separate them again so long as he lives.

11. A man receives a sensible injury from another, thinks on the man and that action over and over, and by ruminating on them strongly or much in his mind, so cements those two ideas together, that he makes them almost one; never thinks on the man, but the pain and displeasure he suffered comes into his mind with it, so that he scarce distinguishes them, but has as much an aversion for the one as the other. Thus hatreds are often begotten from slight and almost innocent occasions, and quarrels propagated and continued in the world. [12.] A man has suffered pain or sickness in any place; he saw his friend die in such a room. Though these have in nature nothing to do with one another, yet when the idea of the place occurs to his mind, it brings that of the pain and displeasure with it; he confounds them in his mind, and can as little bear the one as the other.

13. *Why time cures some disorders in the mind which reason cannot.*—When this combination is settled, and whilst it lasts, it is not in the power of reason to help us, and relieve us from the effects of it. Ideas in our minds, when they are there, will operate according to their natures and circumstances: and here we see the cause why time cures certain affections, which reason, though in the right and allowed to be so, has not power over. The death of a child, that was the daily delight of his mother's eyes and joy of her soul, rends from her heart the whole comfort of her life. Use the consolations of reason in this case, and you were as good preach ease to one on the rack.

Till time has by disuse separated the sense of that enjoyment, and its loss, from the idea of the child returning to her memory, all representations, though never so reasonable, are in vain; and therefore some in whom the union between these ideas is never dissolved, spend their lives in mourning, and carry an incurable sorrow to their graves.

15. Many children, imputing the pain they endured at school to their books they were corrected for, so join those ideas together that a book becomes their aversion, and they are never reconciled to the study and use of them all their lives after; and thus reading becomes a torment to them, which otherwise possibly they might have made the great pleasure of their lives. There are rooms convenient enough that some men cannot study in, and fashions of vessels which, though never so clean and commodious, they cannot drink out of, and that by reason of some accidental ideas which are annexed to them, and make them offensive; and who is there that hath not observed some man to flag at the appearance or in the company of some certain person not otherwise superior to him, but because having once on some occasion got the ascendant, the idea of authority and distance goes along with that of the person, and he that has been thus subjected is not able to separate them.

16. Instances of this kind are so plentiful everywhere, that if I add one more, it is only for the pleasant oddness of it. It is of a young gentleman, who having learnt to dance, and that to great perfection, there happened to stand an old trunk in the room where he learnt. The idea of this remarkable piece of household stuff had so mixed itself with the turns and steps of all his dances, that though in that chamber he could dance excellently well, yet it was only whilst that trunk was there, nor could he perform well in any other place, unless that or some such other trunk had its due position in the room. If this story shall be suspected to be dressed up with some comical circumstances a little beyond precise nature, I answer for myself, that I had it some years since from a very sober and worthy man, upon his own knowledge, as I report it; and I dare say there are very few inquisitive persons, who read this, who have not met with accounts, if not examples, of this nature, that may parallel, or at least justify this.

17. *Its influence on intellectual habits.*—Intellectual habits and defects this way contracted, are not less frequent and

powerful, though less observed. Let the ideas of 'being' and 'matter' be strongly joined either by education or much thought; whilst these are still combined in the mind, what notions, what reasonings, will there be about separate spirits? Let custom from the very childhood have joined figure and shape to the idea of God, and what absurdities will that mind be liable to about the Deity?

18. *Observable in different sects.*—Some such wrong and unnatural combinations of ideas will be found to establish the irreconcilable opposition between different sects of philosophy and religion; for we cannot imagine every one of their followers to impose wilfully on himself, and knowingly refuse truth offered by plain reason. Interest, though it does a great deal in the case, yet cannot be thought to work whole societies of men to so universal a perverseness, as that every one of them to a man should knowingly maintain falsehood: some at least must be allowed to do what all pretend to, i.e., to pursue truth sincerely; and therefore there must be something that blinds their understandings, and makes them not see the falsehood of what they embrace for real truth. That which thus captivates their reasons, and leads men of sincerity blindfold from common sense, will, when examined, be found to be what we are speaking of; some independent ideas, of no alliance to one another, are by education, custom, and the constant din of their party, so coupled in their minds that they always appear there together, and they can no more separate them in their thoughts, than if they were but one idea, and they operate as if they were so. This gives sense to jargon, demonstration to absurdities, and consistency to nonsense, and is the foundation of the greatest, I had almost said of all the errors in the world; or if it does not reach so far, it is at least the most dangerous one, since, so far as it obtains, it hinders men from seeing and examining.

19. *Conclusion.*—Having thus given an account of the original, sorts, and extent of our *Ideas*, with several other considerations about these (I know not whether I may say) instruments, or materials of our knowledge, the method I at first proposed to myself would now require that I should immediately proceed to show, what use the understanding makes of them, and what *Knowledge* we have by them. This was that which, in the first general view I had of this subject, was all that I thought I should have to do: but upon

a nearer approach, I find that there is so close a connexion between ideas and *Words*, and our abstract ideas and general words have so constant a relation one to another, that it is impossible to speak clearly and distinctly of our knowledge, which all consists in propositions, without considering first the nature, use, and signification of Language; which therefore must be the business of the next Book.[1]

[1] This section gives the scheme of the *Essay*, as it existed in Locke's mind. Cf. Introduction, pp. xiv–xvii.

# BOOK III

## CHAPTER I

### OF WORDS OR LANGUAGE IN GENERAL

1. *Man fitted to form articulate sounds.*—God, having designed man for a sociable creature, made him not only with an inclination and under a necessity to have fellowship with those of his own kind, but furnished him also with language, which was to be the great instrument and common tie of society. Man therefore had by nature his organs so fashioned as to be fit to frame articulate sounds, which we call words. But this was not enough to produce language. [2.] It was farther necessary that he should be able to use these sounds as signs of internal conceptions, and to make them stand as marks for the ideas within his own mind, whereby they might be made known to others.

3. *To make general signs.*—But neither was this sufficient to make words so useful as they ought to be. For the multiplication of words would have perplexed their use, had every particular thing need of a distinct name to be signified by. To remedy this inconvenience, language had yet a farther improvement in the use of general terms, whereby one word was made to mark a multitude of particular existences.[1]

---

[1] ' General terms ', says Leibniz, ' serve not only for the perfection of language, but they are necessary even to their essential constitution. For if by " particular things " we mean individual things, it would be impossible to speak if there were only *proper* names and not *appellatives*, i. e. if there were words only for the individuals, since at every moment fresh ones present themselves, when it is a question of individuals, of qualities, and particularly of actions, which are what most frequently receive names. But if by particular things we understand the lowest species (*species infimae*), besides the fact that it is very often difficult to determine them, it is plain that they are already universals based upon similitude. Since the question, then, is only of a similitude more or less extended, according as one speaks of *genera* or of *species*, it is natural to indicate every sort of similitude or agreement, and consequently to employ general terms of all degrees. And indeed the most general ... were often the easiest to form and are the most useful. Thus you see that children, and those who know little of the language which they wish to

5. *Words ultimately derived from such as signify sensible ideas.*—It may also lead us a little towards the original of all our notions and knowledge, if we remark how great a dependence our words have on common sensible ideas; and how those which are made use of to stand for actions and notions quite removed from sense, have their rise from thence, and from obvious sensible ideas are transferred to more abstruse significations, and made to stand for ideas that come not under the cognizance of our senses: v. g., to *imagine, apprehend, comprehend, adhere, conceive, instil, disgust, disturbance, tranquillity*, &c., are all words taken from the operations of sensible things, and applied to certain modes of thinking. *Spirit*, in its primary signification, is breath; *angel*, a messenger: and I doubt not but, if we could trace them to their sources, we should find, in all languages, the names which stand for things that fall not under our senses to have had their first rise from sensible ideas.[1] By which we may give some kind of guess what kind of notions they were, and whence derived, which filled their minds who were the first beginners of languages; and how nature, even in the naming of things, unawares suggested to men the originals and principles of all their knowledge.

6. *Distribution.*—But to understand better the use and force of language as subservient to instruction and knowledge, it will be convenient to consider,

First, To what it is that names, in the use of language, are immediately applied.

Secondly, Since all (except proper) names are general, and so stand not particularly for this or that single thing, but for sorts and ranks of things, it will be necessary to consider, in the next place, what the sorts and kinds, or, if you rather like the Latin names, what the *species* and *genera* of things are, wherein they consist, and how they come to be made. These being (as they ought) well looked into, we shall the better come to find the right use of words, the natural advantages and defects of

speak, or of the subject about which they speak, avail themselves of general terms like "thing", "plant", "animal", instead of the proper terms which they lack. And it is certain that all *proper* or individual names were originally *appellative* or general.'

[1] Leibniz adds, as an example, the use of *prepositions*, such as *to, with, from, before, in, without, by, for, upon*, which are all derived from place, from distance, and from motion, and afterwards transferred to every sort of change, order, sequence, difference, agreement.

Ch. 1    *Of Words or Language in General*    225

language; and the remedies that ought to be used to avoid the inconveniences of obscurity or uncertainty in the signification of words.

These considerations therefore shall be the matter of the following chapters.

## CHAPTER II

### OF THE SIGNIFICATION OF WORDS

1. THE use of words is to be sensible marks of ideas, and the ideas they stand for are their proper and immediate signification. [2.] The use men have of these marks being either to record their own thoughts for the assistance of their own memory;[1] or, as it were, to bring out their ideas, and lay them before the view of others: words in their primary and immediate signification stand for nothing but *the ideas in the mind of him that uses them*, how imperfectly soever or carelessly those ideas are collected from the things which they are supposed to represent. [4.] But though words, as they are used by men, can properly and immediately signify nothing but the ideas that are in the mind of the speaker, yet they in their thoughts give them a secret reference to two other things. *First*, they suppose their words to be marks of the ideas in the minds also of other men with whom they communicate. [5.] *Secondly*, because men would not be thought to talk barely of their own imaginations, but of things as really they are, therefore they often suppose their words to stand also for the reality of things.

6. Concerning words also it is farther to be considered: *First*, that they being immediately the signs of men's ideas, and by that means the instruments whereby men communicate their conceptions, there comes by constant use to be such a connexion between certain sounds and the ideas they stand for, that the names heard almost as readily excite certain ideas, as if the objects themselves which are apt to produce them did actually affect the senses. [7.] *Secondly*, that though the proper and immediate signification of words are

[1] ' The concept formed by an abstraction of the resembling from the non-resembling qualities of objects, would again fall back into the confusion and infinitude from which it has been called out, were it not rendered permanent for consciousness by being fixed and ratified in a verbal sign ' (Hamilton, *Lectures on Logic*, vol. i, p. 137).

ideas in the mind of the speaker; yet because by familiar use from our cradles, we come to learn certain articulate sounds very perfectly, and have them readily on our tongues, and always at hand in our memories, but yet are not always careful to examine or settle their significations perfectly, it often happens that men, even when they would apply themselves to an attentive consideration, do set their thoughts more on words than things. Nay, because words are many of them learned before the ideas are known for which they stand: therefore some, not only children, but men, speak several words no otherwise than parrots do, only because they have learned them, and have been accustomed to those sounds.

## CHAPTER III

### OF GENERAL TERMS

1. *The greatest part of words general.*—All things that exist being particulars, it may perhaps be thought reasonable that words, which ought to be conformed to things, should be so too, I mean in their signification: but yet we find the quite contrary. The far greatest part of words, that make all languages, are general terms: which has not been the effect of neglect or chance, but of reason and necessity.[1]

[1] It cannot be said, however, that Locke has appreciated the true 'reason and necessity'. He represents general terms as a contrivance of the mind to 'abridge discourse'. But it is so far from being true that general terms or universals are only makeshifts for an infinite number of proper names, that even the possession of an infinite store of such names would not enable us to frame a single sentence. A proper name is an identification-mark put upon a particular object, and in a language limited to proper names, the very form of predication or judgement would be absent, for we do not predicate substances of one another, and there would be no adjectives. At most we could but say of each particular that it was itself—that it is it. This extreme nominalism thus refutes itself, as Plato sufficiently showed in the second part of the *Theaetetus*. A concrete individual is not a mere 'this', it is a definite *kind* of thing, i.e. it possesses a characteristic nature or set of qualities. Proper names apart, which are a special device (as Locke goes on to acknowledge in section 4), a name given to an individual object signifies some of its more striking attributes or qualities; and, just on that account, it is from the beginning capable of extension to other objects possessing the same qualities. In Mill's language it is potentially the name of a class, i.e. it is a universal. Language, in proceeding thus, simply reflects the concrete nature of existent fact.

2. *For every particular thing to have a name is impossible.*—First, It is impossible that every particular thing should have a distinct peculiar name. For the signification and use of words depending on that connexion which the mind makes between its ideas and the sounds it uses as signs of them, it is necessary, in the application of names to things, that the mind should have distinct ideas of the things, and retain also the particular name that belongs to every one, with its peculiar appropriation to that idea. But it is beyond the power of human capacity to frame and retain distinct ideas of all the particular things we meet with : every bird and beast men saw, every tree and plant that affected the senses, could not find a place in the most capacious understanding. If it be looked on as an instance of a prodigious memory, that some generals have been able to call every soldier in their army by his proper name : we may easily find a reason why men have never attempted to give names to each sheep in their flock, or crow that flies over their heads ; much less to call every leaf of plants or grain of sand that came in their way by a peculiar name.

3. *And useless.*—Secondly, If it were possible, it would yet be useless, because it would not serve to the chief end of language. Men would in vain heap up names of particular things, that would not serve them to communicate their thoughts. Men learn names, and use them in talk with others, only that they may be understood : which is then only done when by use or consent the sound I make by the organs of speech excites in another man's mind who hears it, the idea I apply it to in mine when I speak it. This cannot be done by names applied to particular things, whereof I alone having the ideas in my mind, the names of them could not be significant or intelligible to another who was not acquainted with all those very particular things which had fallen under my notice.

4. Thirdly, But yet granting this also feasible (which I think is not), yet a distinct name for every particular thing would not be of any great use for the improvement of knowledge : which though founded in particular things, enlarges itself by general views ; to which, things reduced into sorts under general names are properly subservient. And therefore in these, men have for the most part stopped : but yet not so as to hinder themselves from distinguishing

particular things by appropriated names, where convenience demands it: and therefore in their own species, which they have most to do with, and wherein they have often occasion to mention particular persons, they make use of proper names.

5. *What things have proper names.*—Besides persons, countries also, cities, rivers, mountains, and other the like distinctions of place, have usually found peculiar names, and that for the same reason; they being such as men have often an occasion to mark particularly, and, as it were, set before others in their discourses with them. And I doubt not but if we had reason to mention particular horses as often as we have to mention particular men, we should have proper names for the one as familiar as for the other; and Bucephalus would be a word as much in use as Alexander.

6. *How general words are made.*—The next thing to be considered is, how general words come to be made. For since all things that exist are only particulars,[1] how come we by general terms, or where find we those general natures they are supposed to stand for? Words become general by being made the signs of general ideas: and ideas become general by separating from them the circumstances of time and place, and any other ideas that may determine them to this or that particular existence. By this way of abstraction they are made capable of representing more individuals than one; each of which, having in it a conformity to that abstract idea, is (as we call it) of that sort.[2]

7. But to deduce this a little more distinctly, it will not perhaps be amiss to trace our notions and names from their beginning, and observe by what degrees we proceed, and by what steps we enlarge our ideas from our first infancy. There is nothing more evident than that the ideas of the persons children converse with are, like the persons themselves, only particular. The ideas of the nurse and the mother are well framed in their minds; and, like pictures of them there, represent only those individuals;[3] and the names of *nurse* and

[1] An individual thing, in virtue of the possession of *qualities*, is not a bare particular. Cf. note p. 226.

[2] 'Abstracting' was similarly defined in a previous chapter (II. 11. 9).

[3] The question of the *Primum Cognitum*—does language originate in general appellatives or in proper names?—has been much discussed. If children, as Aristotle already observed, at first call all men fathers, and only afterwards learn to discriminate one individual from another, can

*mamma* the child uses, determine themselves to those persons. Afterwards, when time and a larger acquaintance has made them observe that there are a great many other things in the world, that, in some common agreements of shape and several other qualities, resemble their father and mother and those persons they have been used to, they frame an idea which they find those many particulars do partake in; and to that they give, with others, the name *man*, for example. And thus they come to have a general name, and a general idea. Wherein they make nothing new, but only leave out of the complex idea they had of Peter and James, Mary and Jane, that which is peculiar to each, and retain only what is common to them all.

8. By the same way that they come by the general name and idea of man, they easily advance to more general names and notions. For observing that several things that differ from their idea of man, and cannot therefore be comprehended under that name, have yet certain qualities wherein they agree with man, by retaining only those qualities, and uniting them into one idea, they have again another and a more general idea; to which having given a name, they make a term of a more comprehensive extension : which new idea is made, not by any new addition but only, as before, by leaving out the shape and some other properties signified by the name man, and retaining only a body, with life, sense, and spontaneous motion, comprehended under the name animal.

9. *General natures are nothing but abstract ideas.*—He that thinks general natures or notions are anything else but such abstract and partial ideas of more complex ones, taken at first from particular existences, will, I fear, be at a loss where to find them. For let any one reflect, and then tell me wherein does his idea of man differ from that of Peter and Paul, or his idea of horse from that of Bucephalus, but in the leaving out something that is peculiar to each individual; and retaining so much of those particular complex ideas of several particular existences as they are found to agree in ? This whole mystery of *genera* and *species*, which make such a noise in the schools, and are, with justice, so little regarded out of them, is nothing else but abstract ideas, more or less comprehensive, with names annexed to them. In all which, this is constant and invariable,

the name father, in their mouth, be said to be in strictness a proper name ? See Hamilton's *Lectures on Metaphysics* (vol. ii, pp. 319–32) for a statement of opposing views.

that every more general term stands for such an idea as is but a part of any of those contained under it.

10. *Why the genus is ordinarily made use of in definitions.*—This may show us the reason why, in the defining of words, which is nothing but declaring their signification, we make use of the *genus*, or next general word that comprehends it. Which is not out of necessity, but only to save the labour of enumerating the several simple ideas which the next general word or *genus* stands for ; or perhaps sometimes the shame of not being able to do it.

11. *General and universal are creatures of the understanding.*—It is plain, by what has been said, that *general* and *universal* belong not to the real existence of things ; but are the inventions and creatures of the understanding, made by it for its own use, and concern only signs, whether words or ideas. Words are general, as has been said, when used for signs of general ideas; and so are applicable indifferently to many particular things : and ideas are general when they are set up as the representatives of many particular things : but universality belongs not to things themselves, which are all of them particular in their existence, even those words and ideas which in their signification are general.[1] When therefore we quit particulars, the generals that rest are only creatures of our own making, their general nature being nothing but the capacity they are put into by the understanding of signifying or representing many particulars. For the signification they have is nothing but a relation that by the mind of man is added to them.

12. *Abstract ideas are the essences of the genera and species.* The next thing therefore to be considered is, what kind of signification it is that general words have. For as it is evident that they do not signify barely one particular thing, for then they would not be general terms, but proper names ; so on the

[1] Ideas are ' particular in their existence ', i. e. as mental facts or occurrences, each at its own moment of time in the history of an individual mind. Cf. the account of ' abstracting' (II. 11. 9). The contrast between ideas as psychical states and ideas as meanings or symbols—' signs of an existence other than themselves '—is brilliantly stated by Mr. Bradley, *Principles of Logic*, ch. 1. But Locke introduces a fundamental confusion when he speaks as if the ideas as psychical states were the objects of the mind in reasoning and knowledge. (Cf. IV. 17. 8 and note 2, p. 352.) Clearly it is only as logical meanings or signs that ideas function in knowledge ; and, as meanings, they are all universals.

other side it is as evident they do not signify a plurality; for man and men would then signify the same; and the distinction of numbers (as grammarians call them) would be superfluous. That then which general words signify, is a sort of things; and each of them does that by being a sign of an abstract idea in the mind: to which idea as things existing are found to agree, so they come to be ranked under that name; or, which is all one, be of that sort. Whereby it is evident, that the essences of the sorts, or (if the Latin word pleases better) *species* of things, are nothing else but these abstract ideas.

13. *They are the workmanship of the understanding, but have their foundation in the similitude of things.*—I would not here be thought to forget, much less to deny, that nature, in the production of things, makes several of them alike: there is nothing more obvious, especially in the races of animals, and all things propagated by seed. But yet, I think, we may say, the sorting of them under names is the workmanship of the understanding, taking occasion, from the similitude it observes amongst them,[1] to make abstract general ideas, and set them up in the mind with names annexed to them, as patterns or forms (for in that sense the word form has a very proper signification), to which, as particular things existing are found to agree, so they come to be of that species, have that denomination, or are put into that *classis*. For when we say, this is a man, that a horse; this justice, that cruelty; what do we else but rank things under different specific names, as agreeing to those abstract ideas of which we have made those names the signs? And what are the essences of those species, set out and marked by names, but those abstract ideas in the mind; which are, as it were, the bonds between particular things that exist, and the names they are to be ranked under?[2] And therefore the

[1] This is obviously a fundamental modification of the nominalistic expressions he has hitherto used. In his *Third Letter* to Stillingfleet Locke appealed to this passage and to Bk. III, ch. 6 as evidence that he had not neglected to ' consider beings as God had ordered them in their several sorts and ranks '. Cf. Bosanquet's view : ' Knowledge is an essential form of the self-revelation of the universe. It is ... elicited from a relativity given by the forming and interpreting activity of mind, which in this activity is an organ of the universe itself ' (*Logic*, vol. ii, p. 322, second edition).

[2] The abstract idea or concept—Locke's ' nominal essence '—is here distinguished from the general name. It is the bond or intermediary between the name and ' the particular things that exist ', to which the name is applicable. Words and ideas are both ' signs ' (section 11). Words

supposed real essences of substances, if different from our abstract ideas, cannot be the essences of the species we rank things into. For I demand, what are the alterations [which] may or may not be in a horse or lead, without making either of them to be of another species? In determining the species of things by our abstract ideas, this is easy to resolve. But if any one will regulate himself herein by supposed real essences, he will, I suppose, be at a loss: and he will never be able to know when anything precisely ceases to be of the species of a horse or lead.

14. *Each distinct abstract idea is a distinct essence.*—Nor will any one wonder that I say these essences, or abstract ideas (which are the measures of names, and the boundaries of species), are the workmanship of the understanding, who considers that at least the complex ones are often, in several men, different collections of simple ideas: and therefore that is *covetousness* to one man, which is not so to another. Nay, even in substances, where their abstract ideas seem to be taken from the things themselves, they are not constantly the same; no, not in that species which is most familiar to us, and with which we have the most intimate acquaintance: it having been more than once doubted, whether the foetus born of a woman were a man, even so far as that it hath been debated whether it were or were not to be nourished and baptized: which could not be if the abstract idea or essence to which the name man belonged were of nature's making; and were not the uncertain and various collection of simple ideas, which the understanding puts together, and then abstracting it, affixed a name to it. So that in truth every distinct abstract idea is a distinct essence: and the names that stand for such distinct ideas, are the names of things essentially different. Thus a circle is as essentially different from an oval as a sheep from a goat: and rain is as essentially different from snow as water from earth; that abstract idea which is the essence of one, being impossible to be communicated to the other. And thus any two abstract ideas, that in any part vary one from another, with two distinct names annexed to them, constitute two distinct sorts, or, if you please, *species*, as essentially different as any two the most remote or opposite in the world.

are general when used for signs of general ideas, and general ideas are signs in so far as ' they are set up as the representatives of many particular things '.

## Of General Terms

15. *Real and nominal essence.*—But since the essences of things are thought, by some (and not without reason), to be wholly unknown; it may not be amiss to consider the several significations of the word *essence*.[1]

[1] The distinction between nominal and real essences is closely connected with several recurring theses in the *Essay*. The nominal essence is the connotation of the term, the collection of attributes whose presence we mean to assert in applying the name. The real essence, on the other hand, is, as he puts it here, ' the real internal constitution of things on which their discoverable qualities depend '. This internal constitution we have no means of ascertaining, and our ignorance of the real essence cuts off the possibility of a deductive or demonstrative science of nature. ' In the knowledge of bodies, we must be content to glean what we can from particular experiments, since we cannot, from a discovery of their real essences, grasp at a time whole sheaves, and in bundles comprehend the nature and properties of whole species together ' (IV. 12. 12). We have no certainty as to the necessary coexistence of the qualities we have been accustomed to include in the nominal essence. There is only an inductive probability based upon past experience; for ' experience (which way ever it prove in that particular body I examine) makes me not certain that it is so in any other bodies but that which I have tried ' (IV. 12. 9). Our assurance does not amount to ' knowledge ' or ' science ' in Locke's strict sense of these terms.

By this ' real but unknown ' internal constitution Locke might naturally be supposed to mean the ' substance ' or the *substratum* or support which he supposes to be ' always something besides ' the qualities, ' though we know not what it is ' (II. 23. 3). The assertion of our ignorance of the real essences of things would in this case be simply a reassertion of the essential unknowableness of substance, as laid down in chapter 23. The notion of a real essence on which the properties depend is, indeed, historically connected in the closest way with the scholastic conception of substance. But Locke plainly distinguishes the two, and teaches a twofold ignorance—in the first place, of the essence (' for the powers or qualities that are observable by us are not the real essence of that substance, but depend upon it or flow from it '), and in the second place, of the substance itself (' *Besides*, a man has no idea of substance in general, nor knows what substance is in itself.' Bk. II. 31. 13). A passage in his *First Letter* to Stillingfleet throws some light on his way of looking at the matter. He objects to a phrase of Stillingfleet's in which the internal frame and constitution of things is spoken of as ' flowing from the substance '. ' My notion of these essences differs a little from your Lordship's ; for I do not take them to flow from the substance in any created being, but to be in everything that internal constitution or frame or modification of the substance, which God in his wisdom and good pleasure thinks fit to give to every particular creature, when he gives a being.' And such essences, he adds, are not unchangeable ; ' they may be changed all as easily, by that hand that made them, as the internal frame of a watch.' The passage throws incidentally an instructive light on Locke's conception of ' naked substances ' to which

First, Essence may be taken for the being of anything, whereby it is what it is. And thus the real internal, but generally in substances unknown, constitution of things, whereon their discoverable qualities depend, may be called their essence. This is the proper original signification of the word, as is evident from the formation of it; *essentia*, in its primary notation, signifying properly being. And in this sense it is still used when we speak of the essence of particular things without giving them any name.[1]

Secondly, The learning and disputes of the schools having been much busied about *genus* and *species*, the word essence has almost lost its primary signification; and instead of the real constitution of things, has been almost wholly applied to the artificial constitution of *genus* and *species*. It is true, there is ordinarily supposed a real constitution of the sorts of things; and it is past doubt there must be some real constitution, on which any collection of simple ideas coexisting must depend. But it being evident that things are ranked under names into sorts or species only as they agree to certain abstract ideas to which we have annexed those names, the essence of each genus or sort comes to be nothing but that abstract idea, which the general or *sortal* (if I may have leave so to call it from sort, as I do general from *genus*) name stands for. And this we shall find to be that which the word essence imports in its most familiar use. These two sorts of essences, I suppose, may not unfitly be termed, the one the *real*, the other the *nominal*, essence.

any kind of qualities may be arbitrarily 'annexed'. / All substances, spiritual as well as material, are conceived by Locke as possessing such real essences (cf. III. 6. 3), but it is chiefly in the case of material substances that he dwells on the idea. ? In their case the real essence is 'the real constitution of their insensible parts', i.e. the ultimate molecular stracture on which its various 'powers' depend. It is unknown to us with our present senses, but might be knowable if we had 'microscopical eyes' (II. 23. 12), as it possibly is to angels and certainly is to God (III. 6. 3).

[1] In his *First Letter* to Stillingfleet, Locke says: 'The real constitutions or essences of particular things existing do not depend on the ideas of men, but on the will of the Creator; but their being ranked into sorts, under such and such names, does depend, and wholly depend, upon the ideas of men' (quoted by Fraser, Clarendon Press edition, vol. ii, p. 25). But according to the ordinary usage, he tells us (III. 6. 5), 'particular beings, considered barely in themselves, will be found to have all their qualities equally essential; and everything in each individual will be essential to it, or, which is more, nothing at all'.

17. *Supposition that species are distinguished by their real essences, useless.*—Concerning the real essences of corporeal substances (to mention those only), there are, if I mistake not, two opinions. The one is of those who, using the word essence for they know not what, suppose a certain number of those essences, according to which all natural things are made, and wherein they do exactly every one of them partake, and so become of this or that species. The other and more rational opinion is of those who look on all natural things to have a real but unknown constitution of their insensible parts, from which flow those sensible qualities which serve us to distinguish them one from another, according as we have occasion to rank them into sorts under common denominations. The former of these opinions, which supposes these essences as a certain number of forms or moulds [1] wherein all natural things that exist are cast and do equally partake, has, I imagine, very much perplexed the knowledge of natural things. The frequent productions of monsters, in all the species of animals, and of changelings, and other strange issues of human birth, carry with them difficulties not possible to consist with this hypothesis : since it is as impossible that two things, partaking exactly of the same real essence, should have different properties, as that two figures partaking in the same real essence of a circle should have different properties. But were there no other reason against it, yet the supposition of essences that cannot be known, and the making them nevertheless to be that which distinguishes the species of things, is so wholly useless and unserviceable to any part of our knowledge, that that alone were sufficient to make us lay it by, and content ourselves with such essences of the sorts or species of things as come within the reach of our knowledge : which, when seriously considered, will be found, as I have said, to be nothing else but those abstract complex ideas to which we have annexed distinct general names.

18. *Real and nominal essence the same in simple ideas and modes, different in substances.*—Essences being thus distinguished into nominal and real, we may farther observe, that in the species of simple ideas and modes, they are always the

[1] These are the 'substantial forms' already mentioned (II. 23. 3 ; 31. 6), and further criticized in ch. 6 of this book (sections 14-17). Locke repeatedly brings forward monstrous births to refute the hypothesis of a fixed number of species. See note p. 156.

same: but in substances, always quite different. Thus a figure including a space between three lines, is the real as well as nominal essence of a triangle; it being not only the abstract idea to which the general name is annexed, but the very *essentia*, or being of the thing itself, that foundation from which all its properties flow, and to which they are all inseparably annexed. But it is far otherwise concerning that parcel of matter which makes the ring on my finger, wherein these two essences are apparently different. For it is the real constitution of its insensible parts, on which depend all those properties of colour, weight, fusibility, fixedness, &c., which makes it to be gold, or gives it a right to that name, which is therefore its nominal essence. Since nothing can be called gold but what has a conformity of qualities to that abstract complex idea to which that name is annexed. But this distinction of essences, belonging particularly to substances, we shall, when we come to consider their names, have an occasion to treat of more fully.[1]

19. *Essences ingenerable and incorruptible.*—That such abstract ideas with names to them, as we have been speaking of, are essences, may farther appear by what we are told concerning essences; viz., that they are all ingenerable and incorruptible. Which cannot be true of the real constitutions of things, which begin and perish with them. Thus that which was grass to-day, is to-morrow the flesh of a sheep; and within few days after, becomes part of a man; in all which and the like changes, it is evident their real essence, i. e., that constitution whereon the properties of these several things depended, is destroyed, and perishes with them. But essences being taken for ideas established in the mind, with names annexed to them, they are supposed to remain steadily the same, whatever mutations the particular substances are liable to. For whatever becomes of Alexander and Bucephalus, the ideas to which man and horse are annexed, are supposed nevertheless to remain the same; and so the essences of those species are preserved whole and undestroyed, whatever changes happen to any or all of the individuals of those species. By this means the essence of a species rests safe and entire, without the existence of so much as one individual of that kind. For were there now no circle existing anywhere in the world (as, perhaps, that figure exists

---

[1] In chapter 6.

not anywhere exactly marked out), yet the idea annexed to that name would not cease to be what it is ; nor cease to be as a pattern, to determine which of the particular figures we meet with, have, or have not, a right to the name circle, and so to show which of them, by having that essence, was of that species. And though there neither were nor had been in nature such a beast as an unicorn, nor such a fish as a mermaid ; yet the essence of a mermaid is as intelligible as that of a man ; and the idea of an unicorn, as certain, steady, and permanent as that of a horse. From what has been said, it is evident, that the doctrine of the immutability of essences proves them to be only abstract ideas.[1]

20. *Recapitulation.*—To conclude: This is that which in short I would say, viz., that all the great business of *genera* and *species*, and their essences, amounts to no more but this, that men making abstract ideas, and settling them in their minds, with names annexed to them, do thereby enable themselves to consider things, and discourse of them, as it were in bundles, for the easier and readier improvement and communication of their knowledge, which would advance but slowly, were their words and thoughts confined only to particulars.


## CHAPTER IV

### OF THE NAMES OF SIMPLE IDEAS

1. *Names of simple ideas, modes, and substances, have each something peculiar.*—Though all words, as I have shown, signify nothing immediately but the ideas in the mind of the speaker; yet upon a nearer survey, we shall find that the names of simple ideas, mixed modes (under which I comprise relations too), and natural substances, have each of them something peculiar, and different from the other. For example :

2. First, The names of simple ideas and substances, with the abstract ideas in the mind which they immediately

---

[1] Cf. IV. 11. 14, on so-called 'eternal verities'. 'All general knowledge', Locke teaches, 'lies only in our own thoughts and consists in the contemplation of our own abstract ideas' (IV. 6. 13). Cf. Lotze's chapter on the changeless world of ideas as contrasted with the ever-changing world of real things and events (*Logic*, Bk. III, ch. 2).

signify, intimate also some real existence, from which was derived their original pattern. But the names of *mixed modes* terminate in the idea that is in the mind, and lead not the thoughts any farther, as we shall see more at large in the following chapter.

3. Secondly, The names of simple ideas and modes signify always the real as well as nominal essence of their species. But the names of natural substances signify rarely, if ever, anything but barely the nominal essences of those species, as we shall show in the chapter that treats of the names of substances in particular.

4. Thirdly, The names of simple ideas are not capable of any definitions; the names of all complex ideas are.

8. The not observing this difference in our ideas and their names has produced that eminent trifling in the schools, which is so easy to be observed in the definitions they give us of some few of these simple ideas. [10.] Those who tell us that light is a great number of little globules striking briskly on the bottom of the eye, speak more intelligibly than the schools: but yet these words, never so well understood, would make the idea the word light stands for, no more known to a man that understands it not before, than if one should tell him that light was nothing but a company of little tennis-balls, which fairies all day long struck with rackets against some men's foreheads, whilst they passed by others. For granting this explication of the thing to be true; yet the idea of the cause of light, if we had it never so exact, would no more give us the idea of light itself as it is such a particular perception in us, than the idea of the figure and motion of a sharp piece of steel would give us the idea of that pain which it is able to cause in us. For the cause of any sensation, and the sensation itself, in all the simple ideas of one sense, are two ideas; and two ideas so different and distant one from another, that no two can be more so.

11. Simple ideas are only to be got by those impressions objects themselves make on our minds by the proper inlets appointed to each sort. If they are not received this way, all the words in the world made use of to explain or define any of their names, will never be able to produce in us the idea it stands for. He that thinks otherwise, let him try if any words can give him the taste of a pine-apple, and make him have the true idea of the relish of that celebrated delicious fruit. So far as he is told

it has a resemblance with any tastes whereof he has the ideas already in his memory, imprinted there by sensible objects not strangers to his palate, so far may he approach that resemblance in his mind. But this is not giving us that idea by a definition, but exciting in us other simple ideas by their known names; which will be still very different from the true taste of that fruit itself. In light and colours, and all other simple ideas, it is the same thing. And therefore he that has not before received into his mind, by the proper inlet, the simple idea which any word stands for, can never come to know the signification of that word by any other words or sounds whatsoever, put together according to any rules of definition. The only way is by applying to his senses the proper object; and so producing that idea in him for which he has learned the name already. A studious blind man, who had mightily beat his head about visible objects, and made use of the explication of his books and friends to understand those names of light and colours which often came in his way, bragged one day, that he now understood what scarlet signified. Upon which his friend demanding, what scarlet was? The blind man answered, It was like the sound of a trumpet. Just such an understanding of the name of any other simple idea will he have who hopes to get it only from a definition, or other words made use of to explain it.

12. The case is quite otherwise in complex ideas, which consisting of several simple ones, it is in the power of words, standing for the several ideas that make that composition, to imprint complex ideas in the mind which were never there before, and so make their names be understood, provided that none of the terms of the definition stand for any such simple ideas which he to whom the explication is made has never yet had in his thoughts.

17. The names of *simple modes* differ little from those of simple ideas.[1]

---

[1] Fraser again calls attention to the ideas of 'immensity,' 'eternity', and 'infinity', which 'are not presented in the senses or in reflection', and 'are surely more apt to be obscure and ambiguous than *white* or *red*'.

## CHAPTER V

### OF THE NAMES OF MIXED MODES AND RELATIONS [1]

1. [*Mixed modes*] *stand for abstract ideas, as other general names.*
2. *The ideas they stand for are made by the understanding.*
3. *Made arbitrarily, and without patterns.*

5. *Evidently arbitrary, in that the idea is often before the existence.*—Who can doubt but the ideas of sacrilege or adultery might be framed in the mind of men, and have names given them, and so these species of mixed modes be constituted, before either of them was ever committed; and might be as well discoursed of and reasoned about, and as certain truths discovered of them, whilst yet they had no being but in the understanding, as well as now that they have but too frequently a real existence? [2]

10. *In mixed modes it is the name that ties the combination together, and makes it a species.*—For the connexion between the loose parts of those complex ideas being made by the mind, this union, which has no particular foundation in nature, would cease again, were there not something that did, as it were, hold it together, and keep the parts from scattering. Though therefore it be the mind that makes the collection, it is the name which is, as it were, the knot that ties them fast together. What a vast variety of different ideas does the word *triumphus* hold together, and deliver to us as one species! Had this name been never made, or quite lost, we might, no doubt, have had descriptions of what passed in that solemnity: but yet, I think, that which holds those different parts together in the unity of one complex idea, is that very word annexed to it: without which the several parts of that would no more be thought to make one thing than any other show, which having never been made but once, had never been united into one complex idea under one denomination. [12.] And hence I think it is, that these essences of the species of mixed modes are by a more particular name called *notions*; [3] as by a peculiar right appertaining to the understanding.

---

[1] Much of this chapter has been already anticipated in Bk. II, ch. 22, 'Of Mixed Modes', and ch. 31, 'Of Adequate and Inadequate Ideas'.

[2] Hence Locke considers 'morality' to be an abstract science, capable of demonstration like mathematics (Bk. IV. 3. 18).

[3] Locke repeats the suggestion he had already made, II. 22. 2, where see note (p. 151). Notion is of course popularly used in a very loose way

## 15. Why their names are usually got before their ideas.

—This also may show us the reason, why for the most part the names of mixed modes are got before the ideas they stand for are perfectly known. Because there being no species of these ordinarily taken notice of but what have names; and those species, or rather their essences, being abstract complex ideas made arbitrarily by the mind, it is convenient, if not necessary, to know the names before one endeavour to frame these complex ideas. I confess that, in the beginning of languages, it was necessary to have the idea before one gave it the name: and so it is still, where, making a new complex idea, one also, by giving it a new name, makes a new word. But this concerns not languages made, and in such, I ask, whether it be not the ordinary method, that children learn the names of mixed modes before they have their ideas? What one of a thousand ever frames the abstract idea of *glory* and *ambition* before he has heard the names of them? In simple ideas and substances, I grant it is otherwise; which being such ideas as have a real existence and union in nature, the ideas or names are got one before the other, as it happens.

## 16. Reason of my being so large on this subject.

—What has been said here of mixed modes is with very little difference applicable also to relations; which since every man himself may observe, I may spare myself the pains to enlarge on: especially since what I have here said concerning words in this Third Book, will possibly be thought by some to be much more than what so slight a subject required. I allow, it might be brought into a narrower compass: but I was willing to stay my reader on an argument that appears to me new, and a little out of the way (I am sure it is one I thought not of when I began to write). When it is considered what a pudder[1] is made about essences, and how much all sorts of knowledge, discourse, and conversation are pestered and disordered by the careless and confused use and application of words, it will, perhaps, be thought worth while thoroughly to lay

sometimes, for example, to indicate a baseless or whimsical idea, a subjective fancy. But if it is to be used as a technical term in philosophy, it is best restricted to the non-sensuous concept, as proposed by Berkeley, the *Begriff* as distinguished from the *Vorstellung*. This usage is prominent in Hegel and Hegelian writers.

[1] More usually 'pother', from F. *poudre*, dust. Locke uses 'pudder' as a verb (in the *Conduct of the Understanding*, section 13), 'to perplex and pudder him'.

it open. Men would often see what a small pittance of reason and truth, or possibly none at all, is mixed with those huffing opinions they are swelled with, if they would but look beyond fashionable sounds, and observe what ideas are or are not comprehended under those words with which they are so armed at all points, and with which they so confidently lay about them. I shall imagine I have done some service to truth, peace, and learning, if, by any enlargement on this subject, I can make men reflect on their own use of language; and give them reason to suspect, that since it is frequent for others, it may also be possible for them to have sometimes very good and approved words in their mouths and writings, with very uncertain, little, or no signification.

## CHAPTER VI

### OF THE NAMES OF SUBSTANCES

1. *The common names of substances stand for sorts.* The common names of substances, as well as other general terms, stand for *sorts* : which is nothing else but the being made signs of such complex ideas, wherein several particular substances do or might agree, by virtue of which they are capable of being comprehended in one common conception, and signified by one name. I say, do or might agree : for though there be but one sun existing in the world, yet the idea of it being abstracted, so that more substances (if there were several) might each agree in it; it is as much a sort, as if there were as many suns as there are stars.[1]

2. *The essence of each sort is the abstract idea.*—The measure and boundary of each sort or species whereby it is constituted that particular sort and distinguished from others, is that we call its *essence*, which is nothing but that abstract idea to which the name is annexed : so that everything contained in that idea is essential to that sort. This, though it be all the essence of natural substances that we know, or by which we distinguish them into sorts ; yet I call it by a peculiar name, the *nominal essence*, to distinguish it from that real constitution of substances upon which depends this nominal essence, and all

[1] So Mill (*Logic*, Bk. I. 7. 1): ' Every name, the signification of which is constituted by attributes, is potentially the name of an indefinite number of objects ; but it need not be actually the name of any [real object] ; and if of any, it may be the name of only one.'

the properties of that sort; which therefore, as has been said, may be called the *real essence*: v.g., the nominal essence of gold is that complex idea the word gold stands for, let it be, for instance, a body yellow, of a certain weight, malleable, fusible, and fixed. But the real essence is the constitution of the insensible parts of that body, on which those qualities and all the other properties of gold depend. How far these two are different, though they are both called essence, is obvious.[1]

3. *The nominal and real essence different.*—For though, perhaps, voluntary motion, with sense and reason, joined to a body of a certain shape, be the complex idea to which I and others annex the name man, and so be the nominal essence of the species so called; yet nobody will say that that complex idea is the real essence and source of all those operations which are to be found in any individual of that sort. The foundation of all those qualities which are the ingredients of our complex idea is something quite different: and had we such a knowledge of that constitution of man from which his faculties of moving, sensation, and reasoning, and other powers flow, and on which his so regular shape depends, as it is possible angels have, and it is certain his Maker has, we should have a quite other idea of his essence than what now is contained in our definition of that species, be it [2] what it will: and our idea of any individual man would be as far different from what it now is, as is his who knows all the springs and wheels, and other contrivances within, of the famous clock at Strasburg, from that which a gazing countryman has of it, who barely sees the motion of the hand, and hears the clock strike, and observes only some of the outward appearances.

4. *Nothing essential to individuals.*—That *essence*, in the ordinary use of the word, relates to sorts, and that it is considered in particular beings no farther than as they are ranked into sorts, appears from hence; that take but away the abstract ideas by which we sort individuals, and rank them under common names, and then the thought of anything essential to any of them instantly vanishes: we have no notion of the one without the other; which plainly shows their relation. It is necessary for me to be as I am: God and nature has made me so: but there is nothing I have is essential to me.

---

[1] The distinction was explained in ch. 3. 15–19.
[2] This is one of Locke's comparatively few references to the real essence of *immaterial* substances.

An accident or disease may very much alter my colour or shape; a fever or fall may take away my reason or memory, or both; and an apoplexy leave neither sense nor understanding, no, nor life. Other creatures of my shape may be made with more and better, or fewer and worse, faculties than I have; and others may have reason and sense in a shape and body very different from mine. None of these are essential to the one or the other, or to any individual whatsoever, till the mind refers it to some sort or species of things; and then presently, according to the abstract idea of that sort, something is found essential. Let any one examine his own thoughts, and he will find, that as soon as he supposes or speaks of essential, the consideration of some species, or the complex idea, signified by some general name, comes into his mind: and it is in reference to that, that this or that quality is said to be essential. So that if it be asked, whether it be essential to me or any other particular corporeal being to have reason, I say, No; no more than it is essential to this white thing I write on to have words in it. But if that particular being be to be counted of the sort man, and to have the name man given it, then reason is essential to it, supposing reason to be a part of the complex idea the name man stands for: as it is essential to this thing I write on to contain words, if I will give it the name treatise, and rank it under that species. So that essential and not essential relate only to our abstract ideas, and the names annexed to them; which amounts to no more but this, that whatever particular thing has not in it those qualities which are contained in the abstract idea which any general term stands for, cannot be ranked under that species, nor be called by that name, since that abstract idea is the very essence of that species.

5. Thus, if the idea of body, with some people,[1] be bare extension or space, then solidity is not essential to body; if others make the idea to which they give the name body, to be solidity and extension, then solidity is essential to body. Should there be found a parcel of matter that had all the other qualities that are in iron, but wanted obedience to the loadstone, would any one question whether it wanted anything essential? It would be absurd to ask, whether a thing really existing wanted anything essential to it. Or could it be demanded,

[1] Descartes and the Cartesians.

whether this made an essential or specific difference or no, since we have no other measure of essential or specific but our abstract ideas? And to talk of specific differences in nature, without reference to general ideas and names, is to talk unintelligibly. All such patterns and standards being quite laid aside, particular beings, considered barely in themselves, will be found to have all their qualities equally essential; and everything in each individual will be essential to it, or, which is more, nothing at all.[1] For though it may be reasonable to ask, whether obeying the magnet be essential to iron, yet, I think, it is very improper and insignificant to ask, whether it be essential to the particular parcel of matter I cut my pen with, without considering it under the name iron, or as being of a certain species.

6. It is true I have often mentioned a real essence, distinct in substances from those abstract ideas of them, which I call their nominal essence. By this real essence, I mean that real constitution of anything which is the foundation of all those properties that are combined in, and are constantly found to coexist with the nominal essence; that particular constitution which everything has within itself, without any relation to anything without it. But essence, even in this sense, relates to a sort, supposes a species: for, being that real constitution on which the properties depend, it necessarily supposes a sort of things, properties belonging only to species, and not to individuals; v. g., supposing the nominal essence of gold to be body of such a peculiar colour and weight, with malleability and fusibility, the real essence is that constitution of the parts of matter on which these qualities and their union depend; and is also the foundation of its solubility in *aqua regia*, and other properties accompanying that complex idea.

[1] Locke seems to forget here, what he freely acknowledges elsewhere, that although ' men determine the sorts ', ' nature makes the similitude ' —that ' the mind of man in making its complex ideas of substances never puts any together that do not really, or are not supposed to coexist, and so it truly borrows that union from nature ' (sections 28–9, 36, &c.). In sections 4 and 5 his language suggests a nominalism as extreme as that of Spinoza, who represents all our universal ideas of species or sorts as creatures of the ' imagination ', merely human norms or types. Men reckon perfection, goodness, or beauty by approximation to such types, whereas, he says, ' the perfection of things is to be reckoned only from *their own nature and power* ', and, so considered, each individual thing realizes its own nature, and is all that it has in it to be. Cf. *Ethics*, Part I, Appendix; Part II, Prop. 40, Sch. 1; Part IV, Preface, &c.

Here are essences and properties, but all upon supposition of a sort, or general abstract idea, which is considered as immutable: but there is no individual parcel of matter to which any of these qualities are so annexed as to be essential to it or inseparable from it. That which is essential belongs to it as a condition whereby it is of this or that sort: but take away the consideration of its being ranked under the name of some abstract idea, and then there is nothing necessary to it, nothing inseparable from it. Indeed, as to the real essences of substances, we only suppose their being, without precisely knowing what they are: but that which annexes them still to the species is the nominal essence, of which they are the supposed foundation and cause.

7. *The nominal essence bounds the species.*—The next thing to be considered is, by which of those essences it is that substances are determined into sorts or species; and that, it is evident, is by the nominal essence. For it is that alone that the name, which is the mark of the sort, signifies.

9. *Not the real essence, which we know not.*—Nor indeed can we rank and sort things, and consequently (which is the end of sorting) denominate them, by their real essences, because we know them not. Our faculties carry us no farther towards the knowledge and distinction of substances than a collection of those sensible ideas which we observe in them; which however made with the greatest diligence and exactness we are capable of, yet is more remote from the true internal constitution from which those qualities flow, than, as I said, a countryman's idea is from the inward contrivance of that famous clock at Strasburg, whereof he only sees the outward figure and motions. There is not so contemptible a plant or animal that does not confound the most enlarged understanding. Though the familiar use of things about us take off our wonder, yet it cures not our ignorance. When we come to examine the stones we tread on, or the iron we daily handle, we presently find we know not their make, and can give no reason of the different qualities we find in them. It is evident the internal constitution, whereon their properties depend, is unknown to us. For to go no farther than the grossest and most obvious we can imagine amongst them, what is that texture of parts, that real essence, that makes lead and antimony fusible; wood and stones, not? What makes lead and iron malleable; antimony and stones, not?

10. *Not substantial forms, which we know less.*

11. *That the nominal essence is that whereby we distinguish species, farther evident from spirits.*—Though we are told that there are different species of angels, yet we know not how to frame distinct specific ideas of them: not out of any conceit that the existence of more species than one of spirits is impossible, but because, having no more simple ideas (nor being able to frame more) applicable to such beings, but only those few taken from ourselves, and from the actions of our own minds in thinking and being delighted and moving several parts of our bodies, we can no otherwise distinguish in our conceptions the several species of spirits one from another, but by attributing those operations and powers we find in ourselves to them in a higher or lower degree.

12. *Whereof there are probably numberless species.*—It is not impossible to conceive, nor repugnant to reason, that there may be many species of spirits, as much separated and diversified one from another by distinct properties whereof we have no ideas, as the species of sensible things are distinguished one from another by qualities which we know and observe in them. That there should be more species of intelligent creatures above us than there are of sensible and material below us, is probable to me from hence, that in all the visible corporeal world, we see no chasms, or gaps.[1] All quite down from us the descent is by easy steps, and a continued series of things, that in each remove differ very little one from the other. There are fishes that have wings, and are not strangers to the airy region: and there are some birds that are inhabitants of the water, whose blood is cold as fishes, and their flesh so like in taste that the scrupulous are allowed them on fish-days. There are animals so near of kin both to birds and beasts, that they are in the middle between both: amphibious animals link the terrestrial and aquatic together; seals live at land and at sea, and porpoises have the warm blood and entrails of a hog, not to mention what is confidently reported of mermaids or sea-men. There are some brutes that seem to have as much knowledge and reason as some that are called men: and the animal and vegetable kingdoms are so nearly joined, that if you will take the lowest of one and the highest of the other,

[1] Cf. IV. 16. 12 for a similar insistence on the continuity of nature's processes and the imperceptible gradations by which we pass from one 'rank of beings' to another.

there will scarce be perceived any great difference between them; and so on till we come to the lowest and the most inorganical parts of matter, we shall find everywhere that the several species are linked together, and differ but in almost insensible degrees. And when we consider the infinite power and wisdom of the Maker, we have reason to think that it is suitable to the magnificent harmony of the universe, and the great design and infinite goodness of the Architect, that the species of creatures should also, by gentle degrees, ascend upward from us toward his infinite perfection, as we see they gradually descend from us downwards: which if it be probable, we have reason then to be persuaded that there are far more species of creatures above us than there are beneath; we being in degrees of perfection much more remote from the infinite being of God, than we are from the lowest state of being, and that which approaches nearest to nothing. And yet of all those distinct species, for the reasons above said, we have no clear distinct ideas.

14. *Difficulties against a certain number of real essences.*— To distinguish substantial beings into species, according to the usual supposition, that there are certain precise essences or forms of things, whereby all the individuals existing are by nature distinguished into species,[1] these things are necessary:

15. First, To be assured that nature, in the production of things, always designs them to partake of certain regulated, established essences, which are to be the models of all things to be produced. This, in that crude sense it is usually proposed, would need some better explication before it can fully be assented to.

16. Secondly, It would be necessary to know whether nature always attains that essence it designs in the production of things. The irregular and monstrous births that in divers sorts of animals have been observed, will always give us reason to doubt of one or both of these.

17. Thirdly, It ought to be determined whether those we call monsters be really a distinct species, according to the scholastic notion of the word species; since it is certain that everything that exists has its particular constitution: and yet we find, that some of these monstrous productions have few or

---

[1] i.e. a fixed number of *infimae species* or 'real kinds', according to the doctrine of 'substantial forms'.

none of those qualities which are supposed to result from and accompany the essence of that species from whence they derive their originals, and to which by their descent they seem to belong.

20. By all which it is clear, that our distinguishing substances into species by names, is not at all founded on their real essences; nor can we pretend to range and determine them exactly into species according to internal essential differences. [21.] All we can do is to collect such a number of simple ideas as by examination we find to be united together in things existing, and thereof to make one complex idea. The essence of anything, in respect of us, is the whole complex idea comprehended and marked by that name; and in substances, besides the several distinct simple ideas that make them up, the confused one of substance, or of an unknown support and cause of their union, is always a part.

25. *The specific essences are made by the mind.*

26. *Therefore very various and uncertain.*

28. But though these nominal essences of substances are made by the mind, they are not yet made so arbitrarily as those of mixed modes. The mind, in making its complex ideas of substances, puts none together, which are not supposed to have an union in nature. Men, observing certain qualities always joined and existing together, therein copied nature; and of ideas so united made their complex ones of substances. For though men may make what complex ideas they please, and give what names to them they will; yet, if they will be understood when they speak of things really existing, they must, in some degree, conform their ideas to the things they would speak of: or else men's language will be like that of Babel; if the ideas they stand for be not some way answering the common appearances and agreement of substances as they really exist.

29. Though the mind of man, in making its complex ideas of substances, never puts any together that do not really, or are not supposed to coexist; and so it truly borrows that union from nature; yet the number it combines depends upon the various care, industry, or fancy of him that makes it. Men generally content themselves with some few sensible obvious qualities; and often, if not always, leave out others as material, and as firmly united as those that they take. Of sensible substances there are two sorts; one of organized bodies, which are propagated by seed; and in these the shape is that

which to us is the leading quality, and most characteristical part, that determines the species. For, however some men seem to prize their definition of *animal rationale*, yet should there a creature be found that had language and reason, but partaked not of the usual shape of man, I believe it would hardly pass for a man, how much soever it were *animal rationale*. And if Balaam's ass had, all his life, discoursed as rationally as he did once with his master, I doubt yet whether any one would have thought him worthy the name man, or allowed him to be of the same species with himself. As in vegetables and animals it is the shape, so in most other bodies not propagated by seed it is the colour we most fix on, and are most led by. Thus where we find the colour of gold, we are apt to imagine all the other qualities comprehended in our complex idea to be there also : and we commonly take these two obvious qualities, viz., shape and colour, for so presumptive ideas of several species, that in a good picture we readily say, this is a lion, and that a rose ; this is a gold, and that a silver goblet, only by the different figures and colours represented to the eye by the pencil.

32. *The more general our ideas are, the more incomplete and partial they are.*—If the number of simple ideas that make the nominal essence of the lowest species or first sorting of individuals depends on the mind of man variously collecting them, it is much more evident that they do so in the more comprehensive classes, which by the masters of logic are called *genera*. These are complex ideas designedly imperfect : and it is visible at first sight that several of those qualities that are to be found in the things themselves, are purposely left out of generical ideas. So that in this whole business of *genera* and *species*, the genus, or more comprehensive, is but a partial conception of what is in the species, and the species but a partial idea of what is to be found in each individual. If, therefore, any one will think that a man, and a horse, and an animal, and a plant, &c., are distinguished by real essences made by nature, he must think nature to be very liberal of these real essences, making one for body, another for an animal, and another for a horse ; and all these essences liberally bestowed upon Bucephalus.

35. *Men determine the sorts.*

36. *Nature makes the similitude.* This then, in short, is the case : *nature makes many particular things which do agree* one

with another in many sensible qualities,[1] and probably, too, in their internal frame and constitution ; but it is not this real essence that distinguishes them into species ; it is men, who taking occasion from the qualities they find united in them, and wherein they observe often several individuals to agree, *range them into sorts in order to their naming*, for the convenience of comprehensive signs ; under which, individuals, according to their conformity to this or that abstract idea, come to be ranked as under ensigns ; so that this is of the blue, that the red regiment ; this is a man, that a drill ; and in this, I think, consists the whole business of *genus* and *species*. [37.] I do not deny but nature, in the constant production of particular beings, makes them not always new and various, but very much alike and of kin one to another ; but I think it nevertheless true, that the boundaries of the species, whereby men sort them, are made by men ; since the essences of the species, distinguished by different names, are, as has been proved, of man's making, and seldom adequate to the internal nature of the things they are taken from.

47. [For example, let us suppose] that the essence Adam made the name [gold] first stand for was nothing but a body hard, shining, yellow, and very heavy. The inquisitive mind of man, not content with the knowledge of these, as I may say, superficial qualities, puts Adam upon farther examination of this matter. He therefore knocks and beats it with flints to see what was discoverable in the inside : he finds it yield to blows, but not easily separate into pieces : he finds it will bend without breaking. Is not now ductility to be added to his former idea, and made part of the essence of the species that name [gold] stands for ? Farther trials discover fusibility and fixedness.

---

[1] Hence he says, in section 46, man ' has a standard made by nature ', and in section 51 he speaks of man's ' necessity of conforming his ideas of substances to things without him, as to archetypes made by nature '. (Cf. ch. 3, section 13.)  In a letter replying to certain difficulties raised by Molyneux, Locke thus restates his position in this chapter : ' This I dare say : that there are real constitutions in things, from whence those simple ideas flow which we observe in them. And this I farther say : that there are real distinctions and differences in those real constitutions, one from another, whereby they are distinguished one from another, *whether we think of them, or name them, or no* ; but that that whereby *we* distinguish and rank particular substances into sorts, is *not those real essences or inward constitutions*, but *such combinations of simple ideas as we observe in them*. This I designed to show in Lib. III, ch. 6.' (Quoted in Clarendon Press edition, vol. ii, p. 87.)

Are not they also, by the same reason that any of the others were, to be put into the complex idea? If not, what reason will there be shown more for the one than the other? If these must, then all the other properties which any farther trials shall discover in this matter ought, by the same reason, to make a part of the ingredients of the complex idea which the name stands for, and so be the essence of the species marked by that name. Which properties, because they are endless, it is plain that the idea made after this fashion, by this archetype, will be always inadequate.

48. *Men's ideas imperfect and therefore various.*—But this is not all: it would also follow that the names of substances would not only have (as in truth they have), but would also be supposed to have different significations, as used by different men, which would very much cumber the use of language. For if every distinct quality that were discovered in any matter by any one, were supposed to make a necessary part of the complex idea signified by the common name given it, it must follow that men must suppose the same word to signify different things in different men: since they cannot doubt but different men may have discovered several qualities in substances of the same denomination, which others know nothing of.[1]

49. *Therefore to fix their species, a real essence is supposed.*—To avoid this therefore, they have supposed a real essence belonging to every species from which these properties all flow, and would have their name of the species stand for that. But they not having any idea of that real essence in substances, and their words signifying nothing but the ideas they have, that which is done by this attempt is only to put the name

---

[1] Formal logicians have discussed the question whether the connotation of a term should be considered to include (1) a certain number of fundamental attributes on which the other attributes of the class in question depend, or (2) all the attributes which members of the class are known to possess in common, or (3) all the attributes which they actually do possess in common, many of which may remain to be disclosed by the progress of scientific research. The first is the traditional view, based on the Aristotelian distinction between essence and property. According to the second view, the connotation of a term would vary from man to man, and would be continually changing with the progress of discovery. According to the third, the knowledge of the real connotation would be reserved for omniscience. Dr. Keynes has proposed to distinguish the three as conventional intension, subjective intension, and objective intension (*Formal Logic*, ch. 2).

or sound in the place and stead of the thing having that real essence, without knowing what the real essence is; and this is that which men do when they speak of species of things, as supposing them made by nature and distinguished by real essences.

## [CHAPTER VII

### OF PARTICLES]

## CHAPTER VIII

### OF ABSTRACT AND CONCRETE TERMS

1. *Abstract terms not predicable one of another, and why.*—Each abstract idea being distinct, so that of any two the one can never be the other, the mind will, by its intuitive knowledge, perceive their difference; and therefore in propositions no two whole ideas can ever be affirmed one of another. This we see in the common use of language, which permits not any two abstract words, or names of abstract ideas, to be affirmed one of another. For how certain soever it is that man is an animal, or rational, or white, yet every one, at first hearing, perceives the falsehood of these propositions; *Humanity is animality*, or *rationality*, or *whiteness*: and this is as evident as any of the most allowed maxims. All our affirmations then are only in concrete, which is the affirming not one abstract idea to be another, but one abstract idea to be joined to another. V. g., A man is white, signifies that the thing that has the essence of a man has also in it the essence of whiteness.

2. *They show the difference of our ideas.*—This distinction of names shows us also the difference of our ideas: for if we observe them, we shall find that our *simple ideas have all abstract as well as concrete names*: the one whereof is (to speak the language of grammarians) a substantive, the other an adjective; as whiteness, white; sweetness, sweet. The like also holds in our ideas of modes and relations, as justice, just; equality, equal. But as to our ideas of substances, we have very few or no abstract names at all. For though the Schools have introduced *animalitas, humanitas, corporeitas*, and some others; yet they hold no proportion with that

infinite number of names of substances to which they never were ridiculous enough to attempt the coining of abstract ones. Which seems to me at least to intimate the confession of all mankind, that they have no ideas of the real essences of substances, since they have not names for such ideas : which no doubt they would have had, had not their consciousness to themselves of their ignorance of them kept them from so idle an attempt. And therefore though they had ideas enough to distinguish gold from a stone, and metal from wood ; yet they but timorously ventured on such terms as *aurietas* and *saxietas*, *metalleitas* and *ligneitas*, or the like. And indeed, it was only the doctrine of *substantial forms*, and the confidence of mistaken pretenders to a knowledge that they had not, which first coined and then introduced *animalitas*, and *humanitas*, and the like ; which yet went very little farther than their own schools, and could never get to be current amongst understanding men.

The remaining chapters of this Book, chapters 9, 10, 11 (Of the Imperfection of Words, Of the Abuse of Words, Of the Remedies of the Foregoing Imperfections and Abuses), are here omitted, as containing nothing of philosophical importance that does not occur elsewhere in the *Essay*.

# BOOK IV

## CHAPTER I

### OF KNOWLEDGE IN GENERAL

1. *Our knowledge conversant about our ideas.*—Since the mind, in all its thoughts and reasonings, hath no other immediate object but its own ideas, which it alone does or can contemplate, it is evident that our knowledge is only conversant about them.[1]

2. *Knowledge is the perception of the agreement or disagreement of two ideas.*—Knowledge then seems to me to be nothing but the perception of the connexion and agreement, or disagreement and repugnancy, of any of our ideas. In this alone it consists. Where this perception is, there is knowledge; and where it is not, there, though we may fancy, guess, or believe, yet we always come short of knowledge.[2] For when we know that white is not black, what do we else but perceive that these two ideas do not agree? When we possess ourselves with the utmost security of the demonstration that the three angles of a triangle are equal to two right ones, what do we more but perceive, that equality to two right ones does necessarily agree to, and is inseparable from, the three angles of a triangle?

3. *This agreement fourfold.*—But to understand a little more distinctly wherein this agreement or disagreement consists, I think we may reduce it all to these four sorts: (1) *Identity*, or *diversity*. (2) *Relation*. (3) *Coexistence*, or *necessary connexion*.[3] (4) *Real existence*.

4. *First, Of identity or diversity.*—As to the first sort of

---

[1] Cf. Introduction, p. xxxvi *et seq*.

[2] This implies—what is really the case—that the definition here given only covers 'knowledge' in Locke's restricted sense of the term, i.e., where we possess intuitive or demonstrative certainty. Strictly speaking, therefore, it would include only the first and second of the four sorts of agreement or disagreement which he goes on to enumerate.

[3] Coexistence, as Locke expounds it, is *de facto* concomitance, where we can see no necessary connexion (except in a few negligible instances). That is the whole point of his reiterated argument.

agreement or disagreement, viz., *identity, or diversity*. It is the first act of the mind, when it has any sentiments or ideas at all, to perceive its ideas, and, so far as it perceives them, to know each what it is, and thereby also to perceive their difference, and that one is not another. This is so absolutely necessary, that without it there could be no knowledge, no reasoning, no imagination, no distinct thoughts at all. By this the mind clearly and infallibly perceives each idea to agree with itself, and to be what it is; and all distinct ideas to disagree, i.e., the one not to be the other: and this it does without pains, labour, or deduction; but at first view, by its natural power of perception and distinction. And though men of art have reduced this into those general rules, *What is, is*; and, *It is impossible for the same thing to be and not to be,* for ready application in all cases wherein there may be occasion to reflect on it; yet it is certain that the first exercise of this faculty is about particular ideas. A man infallibly knows, as soon as ever he has them in his mind, that the ideas he calls white and round are the very ideas they are, and that they are not other ideas which he calls red or square. Nor can any maxim or proposition in the world make him know it clearer or surer than he did before, and without any such general rule.[1] This then is the first agreement or disagreement which the mind perceives in its ideas; which it always perceives at first sight; and if there ever happen any doubt about it, it will always be found to be about the names, and not the ideas themselves, whose identity and diversity will always be perceived as soon and as clearly as the ideas themselves are, nor can it possibly be otherwise.[2]

5. *Secondly, Relative.*—The next sort of agreement or disagreement the mind perceives in any of its ideas may, I think, be called *relative*, and is nothing but the perception of the *relation*[3] between any two ideas, of what kind soever, whether substances, modes, or any other. For, since all distinct ideas must eternally be known not to be the same, and so be

[1] This is the argument of Bk. I and of Bk. IV. ch. 7.
[2] Cf. II. 29. 6–10 on distinct ideas and confusion about their names.
[3] Relation, as here contemplated, refers to the necessary implications of abstract ideas which are exempt from change and have 'immutably the same habitudes one to another' (IV. 11. 14). Cf. the mathematical example given in section 7, and the treatment of demonstration in the following chapter.

universally and constantly denied one of another, there could be no room for any positive knowledge at all, if we could not perceive any relation between our ideas, and find out the agreement or disagreement they have one with another, in several ways the mind takes of comparing them.

6. *Thirdly, Of coexistence.*—The third sort of agreement or disagreement to be found in our ideas, which the perception of the mind is employed about, is *coexistence,* or *non-coexistence* in the same subject; and this belongs particularly to substances.[1] Thus when we pronounce concerning gold that it is fixed, our knowledge of this truth amounts to no more but this, that fixedness, or a power to remain in the fire unconsumed, is an idea that always accompanies and is joined with that particular sort of yellowness, weight, fusibility, malleableness, and solubility in *aqua regia,* which make our complex idea, signified by the word gold.

7. *Fourthly, Of real existence.*—The fourth and last sort is that of *actual real existence* agreeing to any idea.[2] Within these four sorts of agreement or disagreement is, I suppose, contained all the knowledge we have or are capable of; for all the enquiries that we can make concerning any of our ideas, all that we know or can affirm concerning any of them, is, that it is or is not the same with some other; that it does or does not always coexist with some other idea in the same subject; that it has this or that relation to some other idea; or that it has a real existence without the mind.[3] Thus, 'Blue is not yellow', is of identity. 'Two triangles upon equal bases between two parallels are equal', is of relation. 'Iron is susceptible of magnetical impressions', is of coexistence. 'God is', is of real existence. Though identity and coexistence are truly nothing but relations, yet they are

[1] Coexistence means for Locke the coexistence of qualities in the same substance, but practically includes the sequences usually spoken of as cause and effect.

[2] This relation is not in strictness a relation *between ideas* at all. Cf. Introduction, p. xl. Locke says (IV. 7. 7) that 'real existence has no connexion with any other of our ideas but that of ourselves and a First Being'. The connexion is intuitively perceived, he holds, in the case of our own existence, from which we may infer demonstratively the existence of God.

[3] A very loose form of expression. The 'idea' does not exist without the mind; the meaning of an existential judgement is that the idea in the mind is the idea of a real object, in other words, that there exists a real object to which the idea refers.

so peculiar ways of agreement or disagreement of our ideas, that they deserve well to be considered as distinct heads, and not under relation in general:[1] since they are so different grounds of affirmation and negation, as will easily appear to any one who will but reflect on what is said in several places of this *Essay*. I should now proceed to examine the several degrees of our knowledge, but that it is necessary first to consider the different acceptations of the word *knowledge*.

8. *Knowledge actual or habitual.*—There are several ways wherein the mind is possessed of truth, each of which is called knowledge.

(1) There is *actual knowledge*, which is the present view the mind has of the agreement or disagreement of any of its ideas, or of the relation they have one to another.

(2) A man is said to know any proposition which having been once laid before his thoughts, he evidently perceived the agreement or disagreement of the ideas whereof it consists; and so lodged it in his memory, that whenever that proposition comes again to be reflected on, he, without doubt or hesitation, embraces the right side, assents to and is certain of the truth of it. This, I think, one may call *habitual knowledge*. For our finite understandings being able to think clearly and distinctly but on one thing at once, if men had no knowledge of any more than what they actually thought on, he that knew most would know but one truth, that being all he was able to think on at one time.

9. *Habitual knowledge twofold.*—Of habitual knowledge there are also, vulgarly speaking, two degrees:—

First, The one is of such truths laid up in the memory as, whenever they occur to the mind, it *actually perceives the rela-*

---

[1] Clearly all the four 'sorts' might be described as relations, and the first three at all events as relations between ideas; but Locke's restricted use of the term is perpetuated in the famous distinction between 'relations of ideas' and 'matters of fact', with which Hume starts his *Enquiry* (section 4). 'Of the first kind are the Sciences of Geometry, Algebra, and Arithmetic, and in short every affirmation which is either intuitively or demonstratively certain. . . . Matters of fact are not ascertained in the same manner, nor is our evidence of their truth, however great, of a like nature.' As Locke's discussion of ideas of co-existence led him to regard these as entirely dependent on experience— on our *finding* two facts together, without being able to show any reason for the conjunction—Hume's sharp distinction between the two 'objects of human reason or enquiry' emerges naturally from Locke's fourfold classification here.

*tion is between those ideas.* And this is in all those truths whereof we have an intuitive knowledge, where the ideas themselves, by an immediate view, discover their agreement or disagreement one with another.

Secondly, The other is of such truths, whereof the mind having been convinced, it *retains the memory of the conviction without the proofs.* Thus a man that remembers certainly that he once perceived the demonstration that the three angles of a triangle are equal to two right ones, is certain that he knows it, because he cannot doubt of the truth of it. In his adherence to a truth where the demonstration by which it was at first known is forgot, though a man may be thought rather to believe his memory than really to know, and this way of entertaining a truth seemed formerly to me like something between opinion and knowledge, a sort of assurance which exceeds bare belief, for that relies on the testimony of another;[1] yet, upon a due examination, I find it comes not short of perfect certainty, and is, in effect, true knowledge. That which is apt to mislead our first thoughts into a mistake in this matter is, that the agreement or disagreement of the ideas in this case is not perceived, as it was at first, by an actual view of all the intermediate ideas whereby the agreement or disagreement of those in the proposition was at first perceived; but by other intermediate ideas, that show the agreement or disagreement of the ideas contained in the proposition whose certainty we remember. For example: in this proposition, that ' the three angles of a triangle are equal to two right ones ', one who has seen and clearly perceived the demonstration of this truth knows it to be true, when that demonstration is gone out of his mind, so that at present it is not actually in view, and possibly cannot be recollected; but he knows it in a different way from what he did before. The agreement of the two ideas joined in that proposition is perceived; but it is by the intervention of other ideas than those which at first produced that perception. He remembers, i.e., he knows (for remembrance is but the reviving of some past knowledge) that he was once certain of the truth of this proposition, that ' the three angles of a triangle are equal to two right ones '. The immutability of the same relations between the same immutable things is now

[1] This was the view accepted by Locke in the first edition: the man rather believes his memory than knows the thing'. The argument that follows in an opposite sense was inserted in the fourth edition.

the idea that shows him, that if the three angles of a triangle were once equal to two right ones, they will always be equal to two right ones. And hence he comes to be certain, that what was once true in the case is always true ; what ideas once agreed will always agree : and consequently, what he once knew to be true he will always know to be true, as long as he can remember that he once knew it. Upon this ground it is that particular demonstrations in mathematics afford general knowledge. If then the perception that the same ideas will eternally have the same habitudes and relations be not a sufficient ground of knowledge, there could be no knowledge of general propositions in mathematics ; for no mathematical demonstration would be any other than particular : and when a man had demonstrated any proposition concerning one triangle or circle, his knowledge would not reach beyond that particular diagram.[1] If he would extend it farther, he must renew his demonstration in another instance, before he could know it to be true in another like triangle, and so on : by which means one could never come to the knowledge of any general propositions. Nobody, I think, can deny that Mr. Newton certainly knows any proposition that he now at any time reads in his book to be true, though he has not in actual view that admirable chain of intermediate ideas whereby he at first discovered it to be true. Such a memory as that, able to retain such a train of particulars, may be well thought beyond the reach of human faculties, when the very discovery, perception, and laying together that wonderful connexion of ideas is found to surpass most readers' comprehension. But yet it is evident the author himself knows the proposition to be true, remembering he once saw the connexion of those ideas, as certainly as he knows such a man wounded another, remembering that he saw him run him through. But because

[1] ' It is not the figures which furnish the proofs with geometers. The force of the demonstration is independent of the figure drawn, which is drawn only to facilitate the knowledge of our meaning and to fix the attention ; it is the universal propositions, i.e. the definitions, axioms, and theorems already demonstrated, which make the reasoning, and which would sustain it, though the figure were not there ' (Leibniz). Locke himself seems to see this in his account of what he calls ' the reality of mathematical knowledge ' (IV. 4. 6) : ' The mathematician considers the truth and properties belonging to a rectangle or circle only as they are in idea in his own mind. For it is possible he never found either of them existing mathematically, i. e., precisely true, in his life.' They will not in fact be precisely true of any diagram he can draw.

the memory is not always so clear as actual perception, and does in all men more or less decay in length of time, this, amongst other differences, is one which shows that *demonstrative* knowledge is much more imperfect than *intuitive*, as we shall see in the following chapter.[1]

## CHAPTER II

### OF THE DEGREES OF OUR KNOWLEDGE

1. *Intuitive.*—All our knowledge consisting, as I have said, in the view the mind has of its own ideas, which is the utmost light and greatest certainty we, with our faculties and in our way of knowledge, are capable of, it may not be amiss to consider a little the degrees of its evidence. The different clearness of our knowledge seems to me to lie in the different way of perception the mind has of the agreement or disagreement of any of its ideas. For if we will reflect on our own ways of thinking, we shall find that sometimes the mind perceives the agreement or disagreement of two ideas immediately by themselves, without the intervention of any other: and this, I think, we may call *intuitive knowledge*. For in this the mind is at no pains of proving or examining, but perceives the truth, as the eye doth light, only by being directed towards it. Thus the mind perceives that white is not black, that a circle is not a triangle, that three are more than two, and equal to one and two. Such kind of truths the mind perceives at the first sight of the ideas together, by bare intuition, without the intervention of any other idea; and this kind of knowledge is the clearest and most certain that human frailty is capable of. This part of knowledge is irresistible, and like bright sunshine, forces itself immediately to be perceived as soon as ever the mind turns its view that way; and leaves no room for hesitation, doubt, or examination, but the mind is presently filled with the clear light of it. It is on this intuition that depends all the certainty and evidence of all our knowledge,[2] which certainty

[1] In so far as there must be intuitive evidence of every step in a demonstration, intuitive and demonstrative knowledge stand on the same level of certitude, and it is hardly correct to describe them as different 'degrees' of knowledge or evidence. The practical 'imperfection' or risk of error in the case of demonstration is due entirely (as Locke shows) to possible lapses of memory.

[2] Locke rejects innateness, as he understands the term, but he accepts self-evidence as the ultimate foundation of 'certainty and evidence'.

every one finds to be so great, that he cannot imagine, and therefore not require, a greater: for a man cannot conceive himself capable of a greater certainty, than to know that any idea in his mind is such as he perceives it to be ; and that two ideas wherein he perceives a difference, are different, and not precisely the same. He that demands a greater certainty than this demands he knows not what, and shows only that he has a mind to be a sceptic without being able to be so. Certainty depends so wholly on this intuition, that in the next degree of knowledge, which I call demonstrative, this intuition is necessary in all the connexions of the intermediate ideas, without which we cannot attain knowledge and certainty.

2. *Demonstrative.*—The next degree of knowledge is, where the mind perceives the agreement or disagreement of any ideas, but not immediately. In this case, when the mind cannot so bring its ideas together as, by their immediate comparison and, as it were, juxtaposition or application one to another, to perceive their agreement or disagreement, it is fain, by the intervention of other ideas (one or more, as it happens), to discover the agreement or disagreement which it searches ; and this is that which we call *reasoning*.[1] Thus the mind, being willing to know the agreement or disagreement in bigness between the three angles of a triangle and two right ones, cannot, by an immediate view and comparing them, do it : because the three angles of a triangle cannot be brought at once, and be compared with any other one or two angles ; and so of this the mind has no immediate, no intuitive knowledge. In this case the mind is fain to find out some other angles, to which the three angles of a triangle have an equality ; and finding those equal to two right ones, comes to know their equality to two right ones.

3. *Depends on proofs.*—Those intervening ideas which serve to show the agreement of any two others, are called *proofs* ; and where the agreement or disagreement is by this means plainly and clearly perceived, it is called *demonstration*, it being shown to the understanding, and the mind made to see that it is so. A quickness in the mind to find out these intermediate ideas (that shall discover the agreement or disagreement of any other), and to apply them right, is, I suppose, that which is called *sagacity*.

[1] Cf. chs. 7 and 17 on 'Maxims' and 'Reason', where this 'finding out intermediate ideas' is further emphasized as the characteristic feature of reasoning.

**4. *But not so easy.*—**This knowledge by intervening proofs, though it be certain, yet the evidence of it is not altogether so clear and bright, nor the assent so ready, as in intuitive knowledge. For though in demonstration the mind does at last perceive the agreement or disagreement of the ideas it considers, yet it is not without pains and attention: there must be more than one transient view to find it. A steady application and pursuit is required to this discovery: and there must be a progression by steps and degrees before the mind can in this way arrive at certainty.

**5. *Not without precedent doubt.*—**Another difference between intuitive and demonstrative knowledge is, that though in the latter all doubt be removed, when by the intervention of the intermediate ideas the agreement or disagreement is perceived; yet before the demonstration there was a doubt;[1] which in intuitive knowledge cannot happen to the mind that has its faculty of perception left to a degree capable of distinct ideas, no more than it can be a doubt to the eye (that can distinctly see white and black), whether this ink and this paper be all of a colour.

**6. *Not so clear.*—**It is true, the perception produced by demonstration is also very clear; yet it is often with a great abatement of that evident lustre and full assurance that always accompany that which I call intuitive; like a face reflected by several mirrors one to another, where, as long as it retains the similitude and agreement with the object, it produces a knowledge; but it is still, in every successive reflection, with a lessening of that perfect clearness and distinctness which is in the first, till at last, after many removes, it has a great mixture of dimness, and is not at first sight so knowable, especially to weak eyes. Thus it is with knowledge made out by a long train of proofs.

**7. *Each step must have intuitive evidence.*—**Now, in every step reason makes in demonstrative knowledge, there is an intuitive knowledge of that agreement or disagreement it seeks with the next intermediate idea, which it uses as a proof: for if it were not so, that yet would need a proof; since without the perception of such agreement or disagreement there is no

---

[1] 'The need for reasoning is thus a sign of our intellectual finitude, intermediate between animal sense and Omniscience. We cannot suppose that the Divine Mind is ratiocinative' (Fraser). Cf. IV. 17. 14 and note 2, p. 353.

knowledge produced. This intuitive perception of the agreement or disagreement of the intermediate ideas, in each step and progression of the demonstration, must also be carried exactly in the mind, and a man must be sure that no part is left out : which, because in long deductions, and the use of many proofs, the memory does not always so readily and exactly retain ; therefore it comes to pass, that this is more imperfect than intuitive knowledge, and men embrace often falsehood for demonstrations.

8. *Hence the mistake*, ex praecognitis et praeconcessis.—The necessity of this intuitive knowledge, in each step of scientifical or demonstrative reasoning, gave occasion, I imagine, to that mistaken axiom, that all reasoning was *ex praecognitis et praeconcessis* ; which how far it is mistaken, I shall have occasion to show more at large where I come to consider propositions, and particularly those propositions which are called ' maxims ' ; and to show that it is by a mistake that they are supposed to be the foundations of all our knowledge and reasonings.[1]

9. *Demonstration not limited to quantity.*—It has been generally taken for granted, that mathematics alone are capable of demonstrative certainty : but to have such an agreement or disagreement as may intuitively be perceived being, as I imagine, not the privilege of the ideas of number, extension, and figure alone,[2] it may possibly be the want of due method and application in us, and not of sufficient evidence in things, that demonstration has been thought to have so little to do in other parts of knowledge, and been scarce so much as aimed at by any but mathematicians.

10. *Why it has been so thought.*—The reason why it has been generally sought for and supposed to be only in those, I imagine, has been not only the general usefulness of those sciences, but because, in comparing their equality or excess, the modes of numbers have every the least difference very clear and perceivable : and though in extension every the least excess is not so perceptible, yet the mind has found out ways to examine and discover demonstratively the just equality of two angles, or extensions, or figures. [11.] But in other simple ideas, whose modes and differences are

[1] Cf. IV. 7. 8–10.
[2] He develops in the following chapter, sections 18–20, his favourite idea of a demonstrative science of morality.

made and counted by degrees, and not quantity, we have not so nice and accurate a distinction of their differences as to perceive or find ways to measure their just equality or the least differences. For those other simple ideas, being appearances or sensations produced in us by the size, figure, number, and motion of minute corpuscles singly insensible, their different degrees also depend upon the variation of some or all of those causes; which since it cannot be observed by us in particles of matter whereof each is too subtle to be perceived, it is impossible for us to have any exact measures of the different degrees of these simple ideas. [13.] Not knowing therefore what number of particles, nor what motion of them, is fit to produce any precise degree of whiteness, we cannot demonstrate the certain equality of any two degrees of whiteness; because we have no certain standard to measure them by, nor means to distinguish every the least real difference; the only help we have being from our senses, which in this point fail us. But where the difference is so great as to produce in the mind clearly distinct ideas, whose differences can be perfectly retained, there these ideas of colours, as we see in different kinds, as blue and red, are as capable of demonstration as ideas of number and extension.[1]

14. *Sensitive knowledge of particular existence.*—These two, viz., intuition and demonstration, are the degrees of our knowledge; whatever comes short of one of these, with what assurance soever embraced, is but *faith* or *opinion*, but not knowledge, at least in all general truths.[2] There is, indeed, another perception of the mind employed about *the particular existence of finite beings* without us; which, going beyond bare probability, and yet not reaching perfectly to either of the foregoing degrees of certainty, passes under the name of knowledge. There can be nothing more certain, than that the idea

[1] Experimental psychology has had, as one of its chief aims, the extension of definite measurement to the whole range of mental phenomena.

[2] ' All general knowledge ... consists barely in the contemplation of our own abstract ideas ' (IV. 6. 13). All our knowledge of real existence is particular: we have, according to Locke, an intuitive knowledge of our own existence, a demonstrative knowledge of the existence of God, and what he here calls sensitive knowledge of the existence of particular finite beings without us. The last is not correctly described as an inferior degree of ' knowledge ' in Locke's sense. Whatever ' assurance ' belongs to, it is altogether different in kind from the certainty which characterizes the intuitive apprehension of relations between ideas.

we receive from an external object is in our minds; this is intuitive knowledge.[1] But whether there be anything more than barely that idea in our minds, whether we can thence certainly infer the existence of anything without us which corresponds to that idea, is that whereof some men think there may be a question made;[2] because men may have such ideas in their minds when no such thing exists, no such object affects their senses. But yet here, I think, we are provided with an evidence that puts us past doubting; for I ask any one, whether he be not invincibly conscious to himself of a different perception when he looks on the sun by day, and thinks on it by night; when he actually tastes wormwood, or smells a rose, or only thinks on that savour or odour? We as plainly find the difference there is between any idea revived in our minds by our own memory, and actually coming into our minds by our senses, as we do between any two distinct ideas. If any one say, a dream may do the same thing, and all these ideas may be produced in us without any external objects; he may

---

[1] Here intuitive knowledge is used by Locke in the same sense in which he applies it to the knowledge of our own existence in ch. 9. It should be noted that the certainty here is not the same in kind as that which accompanies the intuitive apprehension of an intellectual truth. The certainty may be as absolute in the one case as in the other, but in the one case it is the apprehension of an intellectual relation, in the other the immediate assurance of a fact. Leibniz designates the latter a 'primitive truth of fact' as distinguished from the logical laws which he calls 'primitive truths of reason'. The former are 'expériences immédiates internes d'une immédiation de sentiment'.

[2] It is impossible to doubt the reality of the idea as a conscious experience; the existence of an object corresponding to it may be doubted, Locke says, though he proceeds to argue that the doubt is unreasonable. We must not press Locke's question-begging description of the idea as 'the idea we receive from an external object', for that of course is the point in debate. Locke's argument here for the reality of the object—and again in ch. 11, where our 'knowledge of the existence of other things' is more fully discussed—is an appeal to the difference between what Berkeley called ideas of sense and ideas of imagination or memory, and does not profess to reach more than *practical* certainty. Leibniz is not inclined to lay so much stress on the difference in vividness (which 'the sceptics will say is, after all, only a question of degree') as on the orderly connexion which characterizes our sense-experience (*la liaison des phénomènes*). 'It is not impossible, metaphysically speaking, that there should be a dream continuous and lasting, like the life of a man; but it is a thing as contrary to reason as the fiction of a book which should take shape by chance by throwing the type pell-mell. For the rest, provided the phenomena are connected, it does not matter whether they are called dreams or not.'

please to dream that I make him this answer: (1) That it is no great matter whether I remove his scruple or no: where all is but dream, reasoning and arguments are of no use, truth and knowledge nothing. (2) That I believe he will allow a very manifest difference between dreaming of being in the fire, and being actually in it. But yet if he be resolved to appear so sceptical as to maintain, that what I call being actually in the fire is nothing but a dream; and that we cannot thereby certainly know that any such thing as fire actually exists without us; I answer, that we certainly finding that pleasure or pain follows upon the application of certain objects to us, whose existence we perceive, or dream that we perceive, by our senses; this certainty is as great as our happiness or misery, beyond which we have no concernment to know or to be. So that, I think, we may add to the two former sorts of knowledge this also, of the existence of particular external objects by that perception and consciousness we have of the actual entrance of ideas from them, and allow these three degrees of knowledge, viz., *intuitive, demonstrative,* and *sensitive*: in each of which there are different degrees and ways of evidence and certainty.[1]

## CHAPTER III

### OF THE EXTENT OF HUMAN KNOWLEDGE

1. KNOWLEDGE, as has been said, lying in the perception of the agreement or disagreement of any of our ideas, it follows from hence that,

*First, No farther than we have ideas.*—First, We can have knowledge no farther than we have ideas.

2. *Secondly, No farther than we can perceive their agreement or disagreement.*—Secondly, That we can have no knowledge farther than we can have *perception* of that agreement or disagreement: which perception being, (1) Either by *intuition*, or the immediate comparing any two ideas; or, (2) By *reason*, examining the agreement or disagreement of two ideas by the

---

[1] If this sentence is to be intelligible and consistent with Locke's express statements, the last clause must be taken as equivalent to 'each of which constitutes a different degree and way of evidence and certainty'. There certainly cannot be different degrees of evidence in intuitive knowledge, and the same would seem to be true of demonstrative knowledge.

intervention of some others; or (3) By *sensation*, perceiving the existence of particular things; hence it also follows,

3. *Thirdly, Intuitive knowledge extends itself not to all the relations of all our ideas.*—Thirdly, that we cannot have an intuitive knowledge that shall extend itself to all our ideas, and all that we would know about them; because we cannot examine and perceive all the relations they have one to another by juxtaposition, or an immediate comparison one with another. Thus having the ideas of an obtuse and an acute angled triangle, both drawn from equal bases, and between parallels, I can by intuitive knowledge perceive the one not to be the other; but cannot that way know whether they be equal or no: because their agreement or disagreement in equality can never be perceived by an immediate comparing them; the difference of figure makes their parts incapable of an exact immediate application; and therefore there is need of some intervening quantities to measure them by, which is demonstration or rational knowledge.

4. *Fourthly, Nor demonstrative knowledge.*—Fourthly, It follows also, from what is above observed, that our rational[1] knowledge cannot reach to the whole extent of our ideas. Because between two different ideas we would examine, we cannot always find such mediums as we can connect one to another with an intuitive knowledge, in all the parts of the deduction; and wherever that fails, we come short of knowledge and demonstration.

5. *Fifthly, Sensitive knowledge narrower than either.*—Fifthly, Sensitive knowledge, reaching no farther than the existence of things actually present to our senses, is yet much narrower than either of the former.

6. *Sixthly, Our knowledge therefore narrower than our ideas.*—From all which it is evident, that the extent of our knowledge comes not only short of the reality of things, but even of the extent of our own ideas. We have the ideas of a square, a circle, and equality: and yet, perhaps, shall never be able to find a circle equal to a square, and certainly know that it is so. We have the ideas of matter and thinking, but possibly shall never be able to know whether any mere material being thinks or no;[2] it being impossible for us, by the contempla-

[1] Rational=demonstrative.
[2] Locke had already touched upon this subject in the chapter on the

tion of our own ideas without revelation, to discover whether Omnipotency has not given to some systems of matter, fitly disposed, a power to perceive and think, or else joined and fixed to matter, so disposed, a thinking immaterial substance : it being, in respect of our notions, not much more remote from our comprehension to conceive that God can, if he pleases, superadd to matter a faculty of thinking, than that he should superadd to it another substance with a faculty

idea of Substance (II. 23), and in the discussion of Personal Identity (II. 27), but this is the section which so exercised the orthodox theologians of his day. It is one of the speculative 'asides' which add so much to the interest of the *Essay*, and seem to bring us nearer to the personality of its author. The denial of an immaterial soul was not an article of his own creed. He agrees, for his own part, that ' the more probable opinion is ' that the consciousness of personal identity is ' annexed to, and the affection of, one individual immaterial substance' (II. 27. 25), and this is practically assumed in the doctrinal structure of the *Essay*. But it is characteristic of his revolt against dogmatism, that he refuses to allow that the belief reaches beyond ' faith and probability' ; and he has a mild enjoyment in ventilating the opposite possibility. The question may have arisen for him in connexion with his polemic against the Cartesian doctrine that the soul thinks always, deduced, as that seemed to be, from the previous definition of thought as the essence of the soul. When Locke maintained, on the contrary, that thinking was to be regarded, not as the essence of the soul but as one of its operations, the assertion meant for him doubtless, in that connexion, no more than that the operation was one which could be intermitted : it was not a function in which the very existence of the soul consisted. But Locke was also in revolt (for another reason) against the Cartesian doctrine of extension as the essence of matter ; and in his own doctrine of substance he departs altogether from the Cartesian equation (as we may say) of a substance with its fundamental attribute. According to Descartes or Spinoza, the attribute expresses the nature of the substance ; it is the substance functioning. In Descartes we have accordingly the two essentially disparate substances, the *res cogitans* and the *res extensa*. For Locke, on the contrary, substance is something purely indeterminate, and therefore finite substances have no intrinsic nature which they express in action. Any attributes or powers may be annexed to, or conferred upon any substance, according to ' the good pleasure' of their Maker. The section should be read in the light of Locke's emphatic assertions (in II. 23) of our complete ignorance of the substance either of spirit or of body. There can be no ' repugnancy ' therefore in the idea of the same substance acting as a support both of bodily and of mental phenomena. Locke's tendency, in reaction against rationalistic dogmatism, to fall back on ' the arbitrary will and good pleasure of the wise Architect ' is exemplified, in another connexion, in this chapter (sections 28–9). Like the Scotist resort to the divine will in the Middle Ages, the position contains in itself the germ of a scepticism which soon showed itself in the historical development.

of thinking;[1] since we know not wherein thinking consists, nor to what sort of substances the Almighty has been pleased to give that power, which cannot be in any created being, but merely by the good pleasure and bounty of the Creator. [For I see no contradiction in it, that the first eternal thinking Being or omnipotent Spirit should, if he pleased, give to certain systems of created senseless matter, put together as he thinks fit, some degrees of sense, perception, and thought: though, as I think I have proved (Bk. IV, ch. 10), it is no less than a contradiction to suppose matter (which is evidently in its own nature void of sense and thought) should be that eternal first thinking Being.][2] What certainty of knowledge can any one have that some perceptions, such as, v. g., pleasure and pain, should not be in some bodies themselves, after a certain manner modified and moved, as well as that they should be in an immaterial substance upon the motion of the parts of body? Body, as far as we can conceive, being able only to strike and affect body; and motion, according to the utmost reach of our ideas, being able to produce nothing but motion: so that when we allow it to produce pleasure or pain, or the idea of a colour or sound, we are fain to quit our reason, go beyond our ideas, and attribute it wholly to the good pleasure of our Maker. For since we must allow he has annexed effects to motion, which we can no way conceive motion able to produce, what reason have we to conclude that he could not order them as well to be produced in a subject we cannot conceive capable of them, as well as in a subject we cannot conceive the motion of matter can any way operate upon?[3] I say not this that I would any way lessen the belief of the soul's immateriality: I am not here speaking of probability, but knowledge; and I think not only that it becomes the modesty of philosophy

[1] 'The bald fact', says William James, 'is that *when the brain acts, a thought occurs*. The spiritualistic formulation says that the brain processes knock the thought, so to speak, out of a Soul which stands there to receive their influence. The simpler formulation says that the thought simply *comes*' (*Principles of Psychology*, i. 345). James's vivid statement looks like an unconscious reminiscence of this sentence of Locke's. [2] Inserted in the second edition.
[3] Cf. *Third Letter* to Stillingfleet: ' That Omnipotency cannot make a substance to be solid and not solid at the same time, I think, with due reverence, we may say; but that a solid substance may not have qualities and powers which have no natural, or visibly necessary, connexion with solidity, is too much for us (who are but of yesterday) to be positive in.'

not to pronounce magisterially, where we want that evidence that can produce knowledge ; but also, that it is of use to us to discern how far our knowledge does reach ; for the state we are at present in, not being that of vision, we must, in many things, content ourselves with faith and probability : and in the present question about the immateriality of the soul, if our faculties cannot arrive at demonstrative certainty, we need not think it strange. All the great ends of morality and religion are well enough secured, without philosophical proofs of the soul's immateriality ; since it is evident that he who made us at first begin to subsist here, sensible intelligent beings, and for several years continued us in such a state, can and will restore us to the like state of sensibility in another world, and make us capable there to receive the retribution he has designed to men according to their doings in this life.[1] [And therefore it is not of such mighty necessity to determine one way or the other, as some, over zealous for or against the immateriality of the soul, have been forward to make the world believe. Who, either on the one side, indulging too much their thoughts immersed altogether in matter, can allow no existence to what is not material : or who, on the other side, finding not cogitation within the natural powers of matter, examined over and over again by the utmost intention of mind, have the confidence to conclude that Omnipotency itself cannot give perception and thought to a substance which has the modification of solidity. He that considers how hardly sensation is, in our thoughts, reconcilable to extended matter, or existence to anything that hath no extension at all, will confess that he is very far from certainly knowing what his soul is. It is a point which seems to me to be put out of the reach of our knowledge : and he who will give himself leave to consider freely, and look into the dark and intricate part of each hypothesis, will scarce find his reason able to determine him fixedly for or against the soul's materiality. Since on which side soever he views it, either as an unextended substance, or as a thinking extended matter, the difficulty to conceive either will, whilst either alone is in his thoughts, still drive him to the contrary side. An unfair way which some men take with themselves ; who,

[1] In his *Reasonableness of Christianity* Locke makes man's immortality the gift of God, conditional upon faith. Annihilation is the lot of the rest of mankind.

because of the unconceivableness of something they find in one, throw themselves violently into the contrary hypothesis, though altogether as unintelligible to an unbiased understanding.

It is past controversy, that we have in us something that thinks; our very doubts about what it is confirm the certainty of its being, though we must content ourselves in the ignorance of what kind of being it is: and it is in vain to go about to be sceptical in this, as it is unreasonable in most other cases to be positive against the being of anything, because we cannot comprehend its nature. For I would fain know, what substance exists, that has not something in it which manifestly baffles our understandings. Other spirits,[1] who see and know the nature and inward constitution of things, how much must they exceed us in knowledge? To which if we add larger comprehension, which enables them at one glance to see the connexion and agreement of very many ideas, and readily supplies to them the intermediate proofs, which we, by single and slow steps, and long poring in the dark, hardly at last find out, and are often ready to forget one before we have hunted out another, we may guess at some part of the happiness of superior ranks of spirits, who have a quicker and more penetrating sight, as well as a larger field of knowledge.][2] But, to return to the argument in hand: our knowledge, I say, is not only limited to the paucity and imperfections of the ideas we have, and which we employ it about, but even comes short of that too; but how far it reaches, let us now enquire.

7. *How far our knowledge reaches.*—The affirmations or negations we make concerning the ideas we have, may, as I have before intimated in general, be reduced to these four sorts, viz., identity, coexistence, relation, and real existence. I shall examine how far our knowledge extends in each of these:

8. *First, Our knowledge of identity and diversity, as far as our ideas.*—First, As to identity and diversity, there can be no

[1] For Locke's ideas about the capacities of 'other spirits' see II. 10. 9; 23. 13 and 36; III. 6. 3; IV. 17. 14. In Bk. III. 11. 23 he repeats this particular point: it is 'not to be doubted that spirits of a higher rank than those immersed in flesh may have as clear ideas of the radical constitution of substances as we have of a triangle, and so perceive how all their properties and operations flow from thence: though the manner how they come by that knowledge exceeds our conceptions'.    [2] Added in fourth edition.

idea in the mind which it does not presently, by an intuitive knowledge, perceive to be what it is, and to be different from any other.

9. *Secondly, Of coexistence, a very little way.*—Secondly, As to *coexistence,* in this our knowledge is very short, though in this consists the greatest and most material part of our knowledge concerning substances. For our ideas of the species of substances being, as I have showed, nothing but certain collections of simple ideas united in one subject, and so coexisting together, when we would know anything farther concerning these, what do we enquire but what other qualities or powers these substances have or have not ? which is nothing else but to know what other simple ideas do or do not coexist with those that make up that complex idea.

10. *Because the connexion between most simple ideas is unknown.*—This, how weighty and considerable a part soever of human science, is yet very narrow, and scarce any at all. The reason whereof is, that the simple ideas whereof our complex ideas of substances are made up, are, for the most part, such as carry with them, in their own nature, no visible necessary connexion or inconsistency with any other simple ideas, whose coexistence with them we would inform ourselves about.

11. *Especially of secondary qualities.*—The ideas that our complex ones of substances are made up of, and about which our knowledge concerning substances is most employed, are those of their secondary qualities; which depending all (as has been shown) upon the primary qualities of their minute and insensible parts; or, if not upon them, upon something yet more remote from our comprehension,[1] it is impossible we should know which have a necessary union or inconsistency one with another : for not knowing the root they spring from, not knowing what size, figure, and texture of parts they are,

---

[1] The meaning of this alternative is not obvious. Professor Fraser considers that Locke simply intends, by introducing this qualification, to guard himself against a too dogmatic assumption that the secondary qualities and powers must be the effect of the hidden molecular constitution and nothing else. It might be taken as a reference to 'substance', which underlies both the primary and the secondary qualities, but Locke in his *First Letter* to Stillingfleet expressly repudiates the idea of making the qualities depend on the substance. Cf. note, p. 233.

on which depend, and from which result, those qualities which make our complex idea of gold, it is impossible we should know what other qualities result from, or are incompatible with, the same constitution of the insensible parts of gold ; and so, consequently, must always coexist with that complex idea we have of it, or else are inconsistent with it.

12. *Because all connexion between any secondary and primary qualities is undiscoverable.*—Besides this ignorance of the primary qualities of the insensible parts of bodies, on which depend all their secondary qualities, there is yet another and more incurable part of ignorance, which sets us more remote from a certain knowledge of the coexistence or in-coexistence (if I may so say) of different ideas in the same subject ; and that is, that there is no discoverable connexion between any secondary quality and those primary qualities that it depends on.

13. That the size, figure, and motion of one body should cause a change in the size, figure, and motion of another body, is not beyond our conception ; the separation of the parts of one body upon the intrusion of another ; and the change from rest to motion upon impulse ; these, and the like, seem to us to have some connexion one with another. And if we knew these primary qualities of bodies, we might have reason to hope we might be able to know a great deal more of these operations of them one upon another : but our minds not being able to discover any connexion betwixt these primary qualities of bodies and the sensations that are produced in us by them, we can never be able to establish certain and undoubted rules of the consequence or coexistence of any secondary qualities, though we could discover the size, figure, or motion of those invisible parts which immediately produce them. We are so far from knowing what figure, size, or motion of parts produce a yellow colour, a sweet taste, or a sharp sound, that we can by no means conceive how any size, figure, or motion of any particles can possibly produce in us the idea of any colour, taste, or sound whatsoever ; there is no conceivable connexion betwixt the one and the other.

14. In vain therefore shall we endeavour to discover by our ideas (the only true way of certain and universal knowledge [1]) what other ideas are to be found constantly joined with that of

[1] This conclusion is enforced at the close of the chapter and again at the close of ch. 6.

our complex idea of any substance : since we neither know the real constitution of the minute parts on which their qualities do depend ; nor, did we know them, could we discover any necessary connexion between them and any of the secondary qualities. So that, let our complex idea of any species of substances be what it will, we can hardly, from the simple ideas contained in it, certainly determine the necessary coexistence of any other quality whatsoever. Our knowledge in all these enquiries reaches very little farther than our experience. Indeed some few of the primary qualities have a necessary dependence and visible connexion one with another, as figure necessarily supposes extension, receiving or communicating motion by impulse supposes solidity. But though these and perhaps some others of our ideas have, yet there are so few of them that have a visible connexion one with another, that we can by intuition or demonstration discover the coexistence of very few of the qualities that are to be found united in substances : and we are left only to the assistance of our senses to make known to us what qualities they contain. For of all the qualities that are coexistent in any subject, without this dependence and evident connexion of their ideas one with another, we cannot know certainly any two to coexist any farther than experience, by our senses, informs us. Thus though we see the yellow colour, and upon trial find the weight, malleableness, fusibility, and fixedness that are united in a piece of gold ; yet because no one of these ideas has any evident dependence or necessary connexion with the other, we cannot certainly know that where any four of these are, the fifth will be there also, how highly probable soever it may be : because the highest probability amounts not to certainty ; without which there can be no true knowledge. For this coexistence can be no farther known than it is perceived ; and it cannot be perceived but either in particular subjects, by the observation of our senses, or in general, by the necessary connexion of the ideas themselves.

15. *Of repugnancy to coexist, larger.*—As to incompatibility or repugnancy to coexistence, we may know that any subject can have of each sort of primary qualities but one particular at once ; v. g., each particular extension, figure, number of parts, motion, excludes all other of each kind. The like also is certain of all sensible ideas peculiar to each sense ; for whatever of each kind is present in any subject, excludes all

other of that sort ; v. g., no one subject can have two smells or two colours at the same time.

16. *Of the coexistence of powers, a very little way.*—But as to the powers of substances to change the sensible qualities of other bodies, which makes a great part of our enquiries about them, and is no inconsiderable branch of our knowledge ; I doubt, as to these, whether our knowledge reaches much farther than our experience ; or whether we can come to the discovery of most of these powers, and be certain that they are in any subject, by the connexion with any of those ideas which to us make its essence.

17. *Of spirits yet narrower.*—If we are at a loss in respect of the powers and operations of bodies, I think it is easy to conclude we are much more in the dark in reference to spirits, whereof we naturally have no ideas but what we draw from that of our own, by reflecting on the operations of our own souls within us, as far as they can come within our observation. But how inconsiderable a rank the spirits that inhabit our bodies hold amongst those various, and possibly innumerable, kinds of nobler beings ; and how far short they come of the endowments and perfections of cherubims and seraphims, and infinite sorts of spirits above us, is what by a transient hint, in another place,[1] I have offered to my reader's consideration.

18. *Thirdly, Of other relations, it is not easy to say how far.*— As to the third sort of our knowledge, viz., the agreement or disagreement of any of our ideas in any other relation : this, as it is the largest field of our knowledge, so it is hard to determine how far it may extend : because the advances that are made in this part of knowledge, depending on our sagacity in finding intermediate ideas that may show the relations and habitudes of ideas, whose coexistence is not considered, it is a hard matter to tell when we are at an end of such discoveries ; and when reason has all the helps it is capable of, for the finding of proofs, or examining the agreement or disagreement of remote ideas. They that are ignorant of algebra cannot imagine the wonders in this kind are to be done by it ; and what farther improvements and helps, advantageous to other parts of knowledge, the sagacious mind of man may yet find out, it is not easy to determine. This at least I believe, that

[1] Cf. III. 6. 11–12.

the ideas of quantity are not those alone that are capable of demonstration and knowledge ; and that other, and perhaps more useful, parts of contemplation would afford us certainty, if vices, passions, and domineering interest did not oppose or menace such endeavours.

*Morality capable of demonstration.*—The idea of a Supreme Being, infinite in power, goodness, and wisdom, whose workmanship we are, and on whom we depend ; and the idea of ourselves, as understanding, rational beings, being such as are clear in us, would, I suppose, if duly considered and pursued, afford such foundations of our duty and rules of action as might place *morality amongst the sciences capable of demonstration* : wherein I doubt not, but from self-evident propositions, by necessary consequences, as incontestable as those in mathematics, the measures of right and wrong might be made out, to any one that will apply himself with the same indifferency and attention to the one as he does to the other of these sciences. The relation of other modes may certainly be perceived, as well as those of number and extension ; and I cannot see why they should not also be capable of demonstration, if due methods were thought on to examine or pursue their agreement or disagreement. ' Where there is no property, there is no injustice,' is a proposition as certain as any demonstration in Euclid : for the idea of property being a right to anything, and the idea to which the name injustice is given being the invasion or violation of that right ; it is evident that these ideas being thus established, and these names annexed to them, I can as certainly know this proposition to be true as that a triangle has three angles equal to two right ones. Again, ' No government allows absolute liberty '. The idea of government being the establishment of society upon certain rules or laws, which require conformity to them ; and the idea of absolute liberty being for any one to do whatever he pleases : I am as capable of being certain of the truth of this proposition as of any in mathematics.[1]

---

[1] This is another of Locke's favourite speculations, recurring at different points in the *Essay*. He was repeatedly urged by Molyneux and other friends to work out himself the desiderated science of morality, but declined on various grounds. Had he seriously made the attempt, he must soon have convinced himself of the illusory character of the undertaking. The examples which he gives are analytical judgements. If property is defined as a right to anything, and injustice as a

19. *Two things have made moral ideas thought incapable of demonstration. Their complexedness, and want of sensible representations.*—That which, in this respect, has given the advantage to the ideas of quantity, and made them thought more capable of certainty and demonstration, is,

First, That they can be set down and represented by sensible marks, which have a greater and nearer correspondence with them than any words or sounds whatsoever. Diagrams drawn on paper are copies of the ideas in the mind, and not liable to the uncertainty that words carry in their signification. An angle, circle, or square, drawn in lines, lies open to the view, and cannot be mistaken : it remains unchangeable, and may at leisure be considered and examined, and the demonstration be revised, and all the parts of it may be gone over more than once, without any danger of the least change in the ideas. This cannot be thus done in moral ideas : we have no sensible marks that resemble them, whereby we can set them down : we have nothing but words to express them by ; which though, when written, they remain the same, yet the ideas they stand for may change in the same man ; and it is very seldom that they are not different in different persons.

Secondly, Another thing that makes the greater difficulty in ethics is, that moral ideas are commonly more complex than those of the figures ordinarily considered in mathematics. From whence these two inconveniences follow : First, that their names are of more uncertain signification, the precise collection of simple ideas they stand for not being so easily agreed on, and so the sign that is used for them does not

violation of that right, the proposition ' Where there is no property there is no injustice ' is undoubtedly a proposition as certain as any demonstration in Euclid, but it is as obviously an example of those merely verbal or ' trifling ' propositions which (in his own words) ' though they be certainly true, yet they add no light to our understandings, bring no increase to our knowledge ' (IV. 8. 1). Although Locke, in an important passage (IV. 8. 8), differentiates between such ' verbal certainty ' and the ' instructive real knowledge ' contained in mathematical demonstrations, the examples he gives of a supposed demonstrative science of ethics show that, in practice, the distinction was not always clear to him, and that he did not realize (any more than Descartes) that the geometer arrives at his conclusions, not by manipulating abstract definitions, but by constructing a figure according to the definition. The construction brings to light the consequences necessitated by the concrete nature of space as a perceptive reality. Cf. Professor Kemp Smith's *Studies in the Cartesian Philosophy*, pp. 43-5.

steadily carry with it the same idea. Upon which the same disorder, confusion, and error follows, as would if a man, going to demonstrate something of an heptagon, should, in the diagram he took to do it, leave out one of the angles, or by oversight make the figure with one angle more than the name ordinarily imported, or he intended it should when at first he thought of his demonstration. Secondly, the mind cannot easily retain those precise combinations so exactly and perfectly as is necessary in the examination of the habitudes and correspondences, agreements or disagreements, of several of them one with another; especially where it is to be judged of by long deductions, and the intervention of several other complex ideas to show the agreement or disagreement of two remote ones.

The great help against this which mathematicians find in diagrams and figures, which remain unalterable in their drafts, is very apparent; and the memory would often have great difficulty otherwise to retain them so exactly, whilst the mind went over the parts of them, step by step, to examine their several correspondences. And though, in casting up a long sum, either in addition, multiplication, or division, every part be only a progression of the mind taking a view of its own ideas and considering their agreement or disagreement; and the resolution of the question be nothing but the result of the whole, made up of such particulars whereof the mind has a clear perception; yet without setting down the several parts by marks whose precise significations are known, and by marks that last and remain in view when the memory had let them go; it would be almost impossible to carry so many different ideas in mind, without confounding or letting slip some parts of the reckoning, and thereby making all our reasonings about it useless. In which case, the ciphers or marks help not the mind at all to perceive the agreement of any two or more numbers, their equalities or proportions: that the mind has only by intuition of its own ideas of the numbers themselves. But the numerical characters are helps to the memory to record and retain the several ideas about which the demonstration is made, whereby a man may know how far his intuitive knowledge in surveying several of the particulars has proceeded; that so he may, without confusion, go on to what is yet unknown; and, at last, have in one view before him the result of all his perceptions and reasonings.

20. *Remedies of those difficulties.*—One part of these disadvantages in moral ideas, which has made them be thought not capable of demonstration, may in a good measure be remedied by definitions, setting down that collection of simple ideas which every term shall stand for, and then using the terms steadily and constantly for that precise collection. And what methods algebra, or something of that kind, may hereafter suggest, to remove the other difficulties, is not easy to foretell. Confident I am, that if men would in the same method, and with the same indifferency, search after moral as they do mathematical truths, they would find them to have a stronger connexion one with another, and a more necessary consequence from our clear and distinct ideas, and to come nearer perfect demonstration, than is commonly imagined. But whilst the parties of men cram their tenets down all men's throats whom they can get into their power, without permitting them to examine their truth or falsehood; and will not let truth have fair play in the world, nor men the liberty to search after it; what improvements can be expected of this kind? What greater light can be hoped for in the moral sciences? The subject part of mankind in most places might, instead thereof, with Egyptian bondage, expect Egyptian darkness, were not the candle of the Lord set up by himself in men's minds, which it is impossible for the breath or power of man wholly to extinguish.

21. *Fourthly, Of real existence we have an* intuitive *knowledge of our own,* demonstrative *of God's,* sensible *of some few other things.*—As to the fourth sort of our knowledge, viz., of the real actual existence of things, we have an intuitive knowledge of our own existence; a demonstrative knowledge of the existence of a God; of the existence of anything else, we have no other but a sensitive knowledge, which extends not beyond the objects present to our senses.

22. *Our ignorance great.*—Our knowledge being so narrow, as I have showed, it will, perhaps, give us some light into the present state of our minds, if we look a little into the dark side, and take a view of our ignorance: which being infinitely larger than our knowledge, may serve much to the quieting of disputes, and improvement of useful knowledge, if, discovering how far we have clear and distinct ideas, we confine our thoughts within the contemplation of those things that are within the reach of our understandings. The causes of our

ignorance, I suppose, will be found to be chiefly these three :

First, Want of ideas.

Secondly, Want of a discoverable connexion between the ideas we have.

Thirdly, Want of tracing and examining our ideas.

23. *First, One cause of it, want of ideas, either such as we have no conception of.*—All the simple ideas we have are confined (as I have shown) to those we receive from corporeal objects by sensation, and from the operations of our own minds as the objects of reflection. But how much these few and narrow inlets are disproportionate to the vast whole extent of all beings, will not be hard to persuade those who are not so foolish as to think their span the measure of all things. He that will consider the infinite power, wisdom, and goodness of the Creator of all things, will find reason to think it was not all laid out upon so inconsiderable, mean, and impotent a creature as he will find man to be; who, in all probability, is one of the lowest of all intellectual beings.[1] We may be convinced that the ideas we can attain to by our faculties are very disproportionate to things themselves, when a positive, clear, distinct one of substance itself, which is the foundation of all the rest, is concealed from us. But want of ideas of this kind, being a part as well as cause of our ignorance, cannot be described. Only this, I think, I may confidently say of it, that the intellectual and sensible world are in this perfectly alike; that that part which we see of either of them holds no proportion with what we see not; and whatsoever we can reach with our eyes or our thoughts of either of them, is but a point, almost nothing, in comparison of the rest.

24. *Or such as particularly we have not, because of their remoteness.*—Another great cause of ignorance is the want of ideas we are capable of. Bulk, figure, and motion, we have ideas of. But though we are not without ideas of these primary qualities of bodies in general; yet not knowing what is the particular bulk, figure, and motion of the greatest part of the bodies of the universe, we are ignorant of the several powers, efficacies, and ways of operation, whereby the effects which we daily see are produced. These are hid from us in

[1] ' I do not know but that there are also some below us. Why should we degrade ourselves unnecessarily ? Perhaps we hold a sufficiently honourable rank among rational animals ' (Leibniz).

some things by being too remote; and, in others, by being too minute. What are the particular fabrics of the great masses of matter which make up the whole stupendous frame of corporeal beings; how far they are extended; what is their motion, and how continued or communicated; and what influence they have one upon another, are contemplations that, at first glimpse, our thoughts lose themselves in. If we narrow our contemplation, and confine our thoughts to this little canton, I mean this system of our sun, and the grosser masses of matter that visibly move about it, what several sorts of vegetables, animals, and intellectual corporeal beings, infinitely different from those of our little spot of earth, may there probably be in the other planets; to the knowledge of which, even of their outward figure and parts, we can no way attain whilst we are confined to this earth?

25. *Or because of their minuteness.*—If a great, nay, far the greatest part of the several ranks of bodies in the universe escape our notice by their remoteness, there are others that are no less concealed from us by their minuteness. These insensible corpuscles, being the active parts of matter, and the great instruments of nature, on which depend not only all their secondary qualities, but also most of their natural operations, our want of precise distinct ideas of their primary qualities keeps us in an incurable ignorance of what we desire to know about them. I doubt not but if we could discover the figure, size, texture, and motion of the minute constituent parts of any two bodies, we should know without trial several of their operations one upon another, as we do now the properties of a square or a triangle. Did we know the mechanical affections of the particles of rhubarb, hemlock, opium, and a man, as a watchmaker does those of a watch, whereby it performs its operations, and of a file, which by rubbing on them will alter the figure of any of the wheels, we should be able to tell beforehand that rhubarb will purge, hemlock kill, and opium make a man sleep, as well as a watchmaker can, that a little piece of paper laid on the balance will keep the watch from going, till it be removed; or that some small part of it being rubbed by a file, the machine would quite lose its motion, and the watch go no more. The dissolving of silver in *aqua fortis*, and gold in *aqua regia*, and not vice versa, would be then perhaps no more difficult to know, than it is to a smith to understand why the turning of one key will open a lock,

and not the turning of another. But whilst we are destitute of senses acute enough to discover the minute particles of bodies, and to give us ideas of their mechanical affections, we must be content to be ignorant of their properties and ways of operation; nor can we be assured about them any farther than some few trials we make are able to reach. But whether they will succeed again another time, we cannot be certain. This hinders our certain knowledge of universal truths concerning natural bodies: and our reason carries us herein very little beyond particular matter of fact.

26. *Hence no science of bodies.*—And therefore I am apt to doubt, that how far soever human industry may advance useful and experimental philosophy in physical things, *scientifical* will still be out of our reach; because we want perfect and adequate ideas of those very bodies which are nearest to us, and most under our command. Distinct ideas of the several sorts of bodies that fall under the examination of our senses perhaps we may have; but adequate ideas, I suspect, we have not of any one amongst them. And though the former of these will serve us for common use and discourse; yet whilst we want the latter, we are not capable of scientifical knowledge; nor shall ever be able to discover general, instructive, unquestionable truths concerning them. *Certainty* and *demonstration* are things we must not, in these matters, pretend to. By the colour, figure, taste, and smell, and other sensible qualities, we have as clear and distinct ideas of sage and hemlock, as we have of a circle and a triangle: but having no ideas of the particular primary qualities of the minute parts of either of these plants, nor of other bodies which we would apply them to, we cannot tell what effects they will produce; nor when we see those effects can we so much as guess, much less know, their manner of production.

27. *Much less of spirits.*—This, at first sight, will show us how disproportionate our knowledge is to the whole extent even of material beings; to which if we add the consideration of that infinite number of spirits that may be, and probably are, which are yet more remote from our knowledge, we shall find this cause of ignorance conceal from us, in an impenetrable obscurity, almost the whole intellectual world; a greater, certainly, and more beautiful world than the material. For, bating some very few, and those, if I may so call them, superficial, ideas of spirit, which by reflection we get of our own, and

from thence the best we can collect of the Father of all spirits, the eternal independent Author of them and us and all things, we have no certain information so much as of the existence of other spirits but by revelation. Angels of all sorts are naturally beyond our discovery; and all those intelligences, whereof it is likely there are more orders than of corporeal substances, are things whereof our natural faculties give us no certain account at all. That there are minds and thinking beings in other men, as well as himself, every man has a reason, from their words and actions, to be satisfied; and the knowledge of his own mind cannot suffer a man that considers, to be ignorant that there is a God.[1] But that there are degrees of spiritual beings between us and the great God, who is there that by his own search and ability can come to know? Much less have we distinct ideas of their different natures, conditions, states, powers, and several constitutions, wherein they agree or differ from one another and from us.

28. *Secondly, Want of a discoverable connexion between ideas we have.*—Another cause of ignorance of no less moment is a want of a discoverable connexion between those ideas which we have. For wherever we want that, we are utterly incapable of universal and certain knowledge; and are, as in the former case, left only to observation and experiment. I shall give some few instances of this cause of our ignorance, and so leave it. It is evident that the bulk, figure, and motion of several bodies about us, produce in us several sensations, as of colours, sounds, tastes, smells, pleasure and pain, &c. These mechanical affections of bodies having no affinity at all with those ideas they produce in us (there being no conceivable connexion between any impulse of any sort of body, and any perception of a colour or smell which we find in our minds), we can have no distinct knowledge of such operations beyond our experience; and can reason no otherwise about them than as effects produced by the appointment of an infinitely wise Agent, which perfectly surpass our comprehensions. As the ideas of sensible secondary qualities which we have in our minds, can by us be no way deduced from bodily causes, nor any correspondence or connexion be found between them and those primary qualities which (experience shows us) produce them in us; so, on the other side, the operation of our minds upon our bodies

---

[1] According to the argument of ch. 10.

is as inconceivable. How any thought should produce a motion in body, is as remote from the nature of our ideas, as how any body should produce any thought in the mind.[1] These and the like, though they have a constant and regular connexion in the ordinary course of things ; yet that connexion being not discoverable in the ideas themselves, which appearing to have no necessary dependence one on another, we can attribute their connexion to nothing else but the arbitrary determination of that all-wise Agent who has made them to be, and to operate as they do, in a way wholly above our weak understandings to conceive.

29. *Instances.*—In some of our ideas there are certain relations, habitudes, and connexions so visibly included in the nature of the ideas themselves, that we cannot conceive them separable from them by any power whatsoever. And in these only we are capable of certain and universal knowledge. Thus the idea of a right-lined triangle necessarily carries with it an equality of its angles to two right ones. Nor can we conceive this relation, this connexion of these two ideas, to be possibly mutable, or to depend on any arbitrary power, which of choice made it thus, or could make it otherwise. But the coherence and continuity of the parts of matter, the production of sensation in us of colours and sounds, &c., by impulse and motion ; nay, the original rules and communication of motion, being such wherein we can discover no natural connexion with any ideas we have, we cannot but ascribe them to the arbitrary will and good pleasure of the wise Architect.[2] The things

---

[1] Locke here recognizes the twin inconceivabilities that led so many Cartesians to adopt the theory of Occasionalism. Locke's solution at once resembles the Occasionalistic doctrine and differs from it. As Professor Gibson remarks, ' Although, like the Occasionalists, he makes his final appeal to the will of God, this is not represented as producing an appearance of interaction where there is none in reality, but as endowing body and mind with powers of operating upon each other which are to us incomprehensible ' (*op. cit.*, p. 165). Cf. II. 23. 27.

[2] The ' arbitrary ' character of nature's coexistences and sequences is Berkeley's constant argument for interpreting these relations as a divinely instituted system of signs and things signified. It is not ' any essential or necessary, but only a customary tie ', which we observe between the phenomena ; and this he ascribes, like Locke, to ' the arbitrary imposition of Providence '. (Cf. *New Theory of Vision*, section 62 ; *Alciphron*, Fourth Dialogue, section 10.) Stripped of this theistic presupposition, the contrast between reason and experience (or custom), which we find both in Locke and Berkeley, is simply

that, as far as our observation reaches, we constantly find to proceed regularly, we may conclude do act by a law set them; but yet by a law that we know not; whereby, though causes work steadily, and effects constantly flow from them, yet their connexions and dependences being not discoverable in our ideas, we can have but an experimental knowledge of them. We can go no farther than particular experience informs us of matter of fact, and by analogy to guess what effects the like bodies are, upon other trials, like to produce. But as to a perfect *science* of natural bodies (not to mention spiritual beings), we are, I think, so far from being capable of any such thing, that I conclude it lost labour to seek after it.

30. *Thirdly, Want of tracing our ideas.*—Thirdly, Where we have adequate ideas, and where there is a certain and discoverable connexion between them, yet we are often ignorant for want of tracing those ideas which we have or may have; and for want of finding out those intermediate ideas which may show us what habitude of agreement or disagreement they have one with another. And thus many are ignorant of mathematical truths, not out of any imperfection of their faculties, or uncertainty in the things themselves; but for want of application in acquiring, examining, and by due ways comparing those ideas.

31. *Extent in respect of universality.*—Hitherto we have examined the extent of our knowledge in respect of the several sorts of beings that are.[1] There is another extent of it, *in respect of universality*, which will also deserve to be considered: and in this regard our knowledge follows the nature of our ideas. If the ideas are abstract, whose agreement or disagreement we perceive, our knowledge is universal. For what is known of such general ideas will be true of every particular thing in whom that essence, i.e., that abstract idea, is to be found; and what is once known of such ideas will be per-

restated by Hume: 'One event follows another, but we can never observe any tie between them. They seem *conjoined*, but never *connected*' (*Enquiry*, section 7). Some of Locke's expressions here closely anticipate Hume's formulation of the position.

[1] As stated in the threefold classification of section 21 (self, God, and other things). The natural sequel of the present chapter would therefore be chs. 9–11, in which the nature of our knowledge of these three 'sorts of being' is analysed. The interpolated chapters, 4–8, involve a good deal of repetition, and have accordingly been curtailed in this edition.

petually and for ever true. So that as to all general knowledge, we must search and find it only in our own minds, and it is only the examining of our own ideas that furnisheth us with that. Truths belonging to essences of things (that is, to abstract ideas) are eternal, and are to be found out by the contemplation only of those essences; as the existence of things is to be known only from experience. But having more to say of this in the chapters where I shall speak of general and real knowledge, this may here suffice as to the universality of our knowledge in general.

## CHAPTER IV [1]

### OF THE REALITY OF OUR KNOWLEDGE

1. *Objection, Knowledge placed in ideas may be all bare vision.*—I doubt not but my reader by this time may be apt to think that I have been all this while only building a castle in the air; and be ready to say to me, ' To what purpose all this stir? Knowledge, say you, is only the perception of the agreement or disagreement of our own ideas; but who knows what those ideas may be? If it be true, that all knowledge lies only in the perception of the agreement or disagreement of our own ideas, the visions of an enthusiast and the reasonings of a sober man will be equally certain. It is no matter how things are: so a man observe but the agreement of his own imaginations, and talk conformably, it is all truth, all certainty. That an harpy is not a centaur, is by this way as certain knowledge, and as much a truth, as that a square is not a circle.

' But of what use is all this fine *knowledge of men's own imaginations* to a man that enquires after the reality of things? It matters not what men's fancies are, it is the knowledge of things that is only to be prized: it is this alone gives a value to our reasonings, and preference to one man's knowledge over another's, that it is of things as they really are, and not of dreams and fancies.'

2. *Answer, Not so, where ideas agree with things.*—To which I answer, That if our knowledge of our ideas terminate in them,[2]

---

[1] The contents of this chapter have been largely anticipated in Bk. II, ch. 30, ' Of Real and Fantastical Ideas ', and in Bk. III, ch. 6, ' Of the Names of Substances '.

[2] This phraseology is worthy of note. Though ideas are the only

and reach no farther, where there is something farther intended, our most serious thoughts will be of little more use than the reveries of a crazy brain; and the truths built thereon of no more weight than the discourses of a man who sees things clearly in a dream, and with great assurance utters them. But I hope before I have done to make it evident that this way of certainty, by the knowledge of our own ideas,[1] goes a little farther than bare imagination; and I believe it will appear, that all the certainty of general truths a man has lies in nothing else.

3. It is evident the mind knows not things immediately, but only by the intervention of the ideas it has of them.[2] Our knowledge, therefore, is real only so far as there is a conformity between our ideas and the reality of things. But what shall be here the criterion? How shall the mind, when it perceives nothing but its own ideas, know that they agree with things themselves? This, though it seems not to want difficulty, yet I think there be two sorts of ideas that we may be assured agree with things.

4. *As, First, all simple ideas do.*—The first are simple ideas, which since the mind, as has been showed, can by no means make to itself, must necessarily be the product of things operating on the mind in a natural way, and producing therein those perceptions which by the wisdom and will of our Maker they are ordained and adapted to. From whence it follows, that simple ideas are not fictions of our fancies, but the natural and regular productions of things without us, really operating upon us; and so carry with them all the conformity which is intended, or which our state requires; for they represent to us things under those appearances which they are fitted to produce in us: whereby we are enabled to distinguish the sorts of particular substances, to discern the states they are in, and so to take them for our necessities, and apply them to our uses. And this conformity between our simple ideas and the existence of things is sufficient for real knowledge.

---

'immediate object' of the mind, 'which it alone does or can contemplate' (IV. I. I), Locke does not regard our knowledge as 'terminating' in them. Except in the case of mixed modes there is 'something farther intended'.

[1] Stillingfleet plays upon this phrase and contrasts Locke's 'way of certainty by ideas' with 'the way of certainty by reason'.

[2] This is the fundamental tenet of the Representative theory of perception, which Reid traced back in modern philosophy to Descartes, and of which he held Hume's scepticism to be the inevitable outcome.

5. *Secondly, All complex ideas, except of substances.*—All our complex ideas except those of substances being archetypes of the mind's own making, not intended to be the copies of anything, nor referred to the existence of anything, as to their originals, cannot want any conformity necessary to real knowledge. So that we cannot but be infallibly certain, that all the knowledge we attain concerning these ideas is real, and reaches things themselves: because in all our thoughts, reasonings, and discourses of this kind, we intend things no farther than as they are conformable to our ideas. So that in these we cannot miss of a certain undoubted reality.

6. *Hence the reality of mathematical knowledge.*—I doubt not but it will be easily granted that the knowledge we have of mathematical truths, is not only certain but real knowledge,[1] and not the bare empty vision of vain, insignificant chimeras of the brain; and yet if we will consider, we shall find that it is only of our own ideas. The mathematician considers the truth and properties belonging to a rectangle or circle only as they are in idea in his own mind. For it is possible he never found either of them existing mathematically, i.e., precisely true, in his life. But yet the knowledge he has of any truths or properties belonging to a circle, or any other mathematical figure, are nevertheless true and certain, even of real things existing: because real things are no farther concerned, nor intended to be meant by any such propositions, than as things really agree to those archetypes in his mind. Is it true of the idea of a triangle, that its three angles are equal to two right ones? It is true also of a triangle, wherever it really exists. Whatever other figure exists, that is not exactly answerable to that idea of a triangle in his mind, is not at all concerned in that proposition.

7. *And of moral.*—And hence it follows that moral knowledge is as capable of real certainty as mathematics. [8.] All the discourses of the mathematicians concern not the existence of any of those figures. In the same manner, the truth and

---

[1] The reality of our knowledge in mathematics, and in mixed modes generally, is a somewhat misleading expression, although Locke's meaning is sufficiently plain. It would be more correct to say that the question of reality, or, as he also expresses it, of conformity, does not arise in this class of ideas. Kant's question as to our warrant for applying the *a priori* propositions of geometry to the objects of experience raises a different problem.

certainty of moral discourses abstracts from the lives of men, and the existence of those virtues in the world, whereof they treat : nor are Tully's *Offices* less true, because there is nobody in the world that exactly practises his rules, and lives up to that pattern of a virtuous man which he has given us, and which existed nowhere when he writ but in idea.

11. *Ideas of substances have their archetypes without us.*

12. *So far as they agree with those, so far our knowledge concerning them is real.*

13. *In our enquiries about substances we must consider ideas, and not confine our thoughts to names or species supposed set out by names.*—If we confine not our thoughts and abstract ideas to names, as if there were or could be no other sorts of things than what known names had already determined, and as it were set out, we should think of things with greater freedom and less confusion than perhaps we do. It would possibly be thought a bold paradox, if not a very dangerous falsehood, if I should say that some changelings who have lived forty years together without any appearance of reason, are something between a man and a beast : which prejudice is founded upon nothing else but a false supposition that these two names, man and beast, stand for distinct species so set out by real essences, that there can come no other species between them: whereas, if we would not fancy that there were a certain number of these essences, wherein all things, as in moulds, were cast and formed, we should find that the idea of the shape, motion, and life of a man without reason is as much a distinct idea, and makes as much a distinct sort of things from man and beast, as the idea of the shape of an ass with reason would be different from either that of man or beast, and be a species of an animal between, or distinct from both.

14. But I am not so unacquainted with the zeal of some men, which enables them to spin consequences, and to see religion threatened, whenever any one ventures to quit their forms of speaking, as not to foresee what names such a proposition as this is like to be charged with : and without doubt it will be asked, If changelings are something between man and beast, what will become of them in the other world ? To which I answer, It concerns me not to know or enquire. To their own Master they stand or fall. They are in the hands of a faithful Creator and a bountiful Father, who disposes not of his creatures according to our narrow thoughts or opinions,

Ch. 4       *Reality of our Knowledge*       291

nor distinguishes them according to names and species of our contrivance. And we that know so little of this present world we are in may, I think, content ourselves without being peremptory in defining the different states which creatures shall come into when they go off this stage. [15.] This or that outward make of our bodies no more carries with it the hope of an eternal duration, than the fashion of a man's suit gives him reasonable grounds to imagine it will never wear out.

## CHAPTER V

### OF TRUTH IN GENERAL

1. *What truth is.*—What is truth, was an enquiry many ages since ; and it being that which all mankind either do, or pretend to search after, it cannot but be worth our while carefully to examine wherein it consists ; and so acquaint ourselves with the nature of it, as to observe how the mind distinguishes it from falsehood.

2. *A right joining or separating of signs, i.e., ideas or words.*— Truth then seems to me, in the proper import of the word, to signify nothing but the joining or separating of signs, as the things signified by them do agree or disagree one with another. The joining or separating of signs here meant, is what by another name we call proposition. So that truth properly belongs only to propositions :[1] whereof there are two sorts, viz., mental and verbal ; as there are two sorts of signs commonly made use of, viz., ideas and words.

3. *Which make mental or verbal propositions.*—To form a clear notion of truth, it is very necessary to consider truth of thought, and truth of words, distinctly one from another : but yet it is very difficult to treat of them asunder. Because it is unavoidable, in treating of mental propositions, to make use of words ; and then the instances given of mental propositions cease immediately to be barely mental, and become verbal.

4. *Mental propositions are very hard to be treated of.*—And that which makes it yet harder to treat of mental and verbal propositions separately, is, that most men, if not all, in their thinking and reasonings within themselves, make use of

[1] Cf. II. 32. 1.

words instead of ideas, at least when the subject of their meditation contains in it complex ideas. When we make any propositions within our own thoughts about white or black, sweet or bitter, a triangle or a circle, we can, and often do, frame in our minds the ideas themselves without reflecting on the names. But when we would consider, or make propositions about the more complex ideas, as of a man, vitriol, fortitude, glory, we usually put the name for the idea:[1] because, the ideas these names stand for, being for the most part imperfect, confused, and undetermined, we reflect on the names themselves, because they are more clear, certain, and distinct, and readier occur to our thoughts than the pure ideas. In substances, as has been already noted, this is occasioned by the imperfection of our ideas: we making the name stand for the real essence, of which we have no idea at all. In modes, it is occasioned by the great number of simple ideas that go to the making them up.

5. But to return to the consideration of truth. We must, I say, observe two sorts of propositions that we are capable of making:

[1] This is what Leibniz called symbolical thinking. Thinking by means of mental images is called, by contrast, intuitive thinking, intuitive being used in that connexion in quite a different sense from that which it bears in Locke. Intuition, so applied, refers (as it does in Kant) to the concrete individual, as presented in sense or represented in imagination, contrasted with the general or abstract, the unpicturable. So space and time are according to Kant pure intuitions or *perceptions*, while the categories are pure *conceptions* of reason. In intuitive thinking, accordingly, the meaning of the words we use is realized in a series of images or pictures as we proceed. In symbolic thinking we do not pause to do so; for long stretches at a time we are content with the words alone, using them, it is suggested, much as we use signs in algebra, which we translate back into the concrete only at the close of our operation. But the analogy of algebraic signs (used by Berkeley, Introduction to *Principles*, section 19) does not exactly suit the case; for, as Hume points out, the customary associations of the words are still vaguely present to the mind, and check us when we are faced by some grotesque or impossible combination. Moreover, we do not concentrate our attention on the signs as we do in an algebraic operation; it is the meaning which we follow throughout, and when our attention to the train of thought is keenest, the verbal signs are least obtrusive. The whole question of the imagery which accompanies thinking is admirably discussed in Stout's *Analytical Psychology*, Bk. I, ch. 4. Stout maintains that images when present are 'mere accessories of imageless apprehension'. Imageless or 'implicit' apprehension is what is meant by '*understanding* a word'. This 'is certainly a state of cognitive consciousness', and we ought therefore 'frankly to affirm the existence of notions which are not images'.

First, *Mental*, wherein the ideas in our understandings are, without the use of words, put together or separated by the mind perceiving or judging of their agreement or disagreement.

Secondly, *Verbal* propositions, which are words, the signs of our ideas, put together or separated in affirmative or negative sentences. So that proposition consists in joining or separating signs, and truth consists in the putting together or separating these signs, according as the things which they stand for agree or disagree. [6.] When ideas are so put together or separated in the mind, as they or the things they stand for do agree or not, that is, as I may call it, mental truth. Truth of words is the affirming or denying of words one of another, as the ideas they stand for agree or disagree; and this again is twofold; either purely verbal and trifling, which I shall speak of (ch. 8), or real and instructive, which is the object of that real knowledge which we have spoken of already. [10.] But because words are looked on as the great conduits of truth and knowledge, I shall more at large enquire wherein the certainty of real truths, contained in propositions, consists, and where it is to be had; and endeavour to show in what sort of universal propositions we are capable of being certain of their real truth or falsehood.

## CHAPTER VI [1]

OF UNIVERSAL PROPOSITIONS, THEIR TRUTH AND CERTAINTY

6. *The truth of few universal propositions concerning substances is to be known.*

7. *Because coexistence of ideas in few cases is to be known.*— The complex ideas that our names of the species of substances properly stand for, are collections of such qualities as have been observed to coexist in an unknown substratum which we call substance; but what other qualities necessarily coexist with such combinations, we cannot certainly know, unless we can discover their natural dependence; which in their primary qualities we can go but a very little way in; and in all their secondary qualities we can discover no connexion at all, for the reasons mentioned (ch. 3), viz., (1) Because we know not the real constitutions of substances, on which each secondary quality particularly depends. (2) Did we know that, it would

[1] With the exception of one fine and very noteworthy section (11), the most of this chapter has been anticipated, and its framework is merely indicated here.

serve us only for experimental (not universal) knowledge; and reach with certainty no farther than that bare instance. Because our understandings can discover no conceivable connexion between any secondary quality and any modification whatsoever of any of the primary ones.

9. I would gladly meet with one general affirmation, concerning any quality of gold, that any one can certainly know is true. It will, no doubt, be presently objected, Is not this a universal certain proposition, 'All gold is malleable'? To which I answer, It is a very certain proposition, if malleableness be a part of the complex idea the word gold stands for. But then here is nothing affirmed of gold, but that that sound stands for an idea in which malleableness is contained: and such a sort of truth and certainty as this it is to say, 'A centaur is four-footed'. But if malleableness makes not a part of the specific essence the name gold stands for, it is plain 'All gold is malleable' is not a certain proposition; because, let the complex idea of gold be made up of whichsoever of its other qualities you please, malleableness will not appear to depend on that complex idea, nor follow from any simple one contained in it. The connexion that malleableness has (if it has any) with those other qualities, being only by the intervention of the real constitution of its insensible parts; which since we know not, it is impossible we should perceive that connexion, unless we could discover that which ties them together.

11. *The qualities which make our complex ideas of substances depend mostly on external, remote, and unperceived causes.*—Had we such ideas of substances as to know what real constitutions produce those sensible qualities we find in them, and how those qualities flowed from thence, we could, by the specific ideas of their real essences in our own minds, more certainly find out their properties, and discover what qualities they had or had not, than we can now by our senses: and to know the properties of gold, it would be no more necessary that gold should exist, and that we should make experiments upon it, than it is necessary for the knowing the properties of a triangle, that a triangle should exist in any matter; the idea in our minds would serve for the one as well as the other. But we are so far from being admitted into the secrets of nature, that we scarce so much as ever approach the first entrance towards them. For we are wont to consider the substances we meet with, each of them as an entire thing by itself, having

all its qualities in itself, and independent of other things;[1] overlooking, for the most part, the operations of those invisible fluids they are encompassed with, and upon whose motions and operations depend the greatest part of those qualities which are taken notice of in them, and are made by us the inherent marks of distinction whereby we know and denominate them. Put a piece of gold anywhere by itself, separate from the reach and influence of all other bodies, it will immediately lose all its colour and weight, and perhaps malleableness too; which, for aught I know, would be changed into a perfect friability. But if inanimate bodies owe so much of their present state to other bodies without them, that they would not be what they appear to us were those bodies that environ them removed, it is yet more so in vegetables, which are nourished, grow, and produce leaves, flowers, and seeds, in a constant succession. And if we look a little nearer into the state of animals, we shall find that their dependence, as to life, motion, and the most considerable qualities to be observed in them, is so wholly on extrinsical causes and qualities of

[1] Cf. note, p. 175. As there indicated, this section involves a complete departure from the doctrine of self-contained substances, each with its real essence from which all its qualities and powers might be seen to flow. It points to the modern scientific view which interprets the world through the notion of cause rather than of substance. A thing, from this point of view, is what it does; its nature is disclosed in its relations to other things, in its actions and reactions. Relations are thus knit up, so to speak, into the nature of the thing; for without them it would become a mere point or unit, of which no nature or essence could be predicated at all. The philosophical conception of universal interrelatedness finds expression in Tennyson's 'Flower in the crannied wall' and in Leibniz's saying—'Every body feels the effect of all that takes place in the universe, so that he who sees all might read in each what is happening everywhere, and even what has happened or shall happen' (*Monadology*, section 61).

The question of 'terms' and 'relations' is one which touches ultimate philosophical issues and is therefore continually open to re-discussion. Under the title of 'external' or 'internal' relations it has been recently much in debate between idealists and neo-realists. Idealists generally maintain that relations are grounded in the nature of their terms, and that all relations are therefore 'intrinsical'. The Realists, on the other hand, starting with a plurality of 'simple things', hold that many, if not all, relations are external. Cf. Bradley, *Appearance and Reality*, chs. 3 and 13; Bosanquet's *Logic* (2nd ed.), vol. ii, p. 276 *et seq.*; Joachim, *Nature of Truth*, ch. 2; Bertrand Russell, *Philosophical Essays*, Essay VI, 'The Monistic Theory of Truth'; G. E. Moore, 'External and Internal Relations', in *Proceedings of the Aristotelian Society*, 1919–20.

other bodies that make no part of them, that they cannot subsist a moment without them : though yet those bodies on which they depend are little taken notice of, and make no part of the complex ideas we frame of those animals. Take the air but a minute from the greatest part of living creatures, and they presently lose sense, life, and motion. This the necessity of breathing has forced into our knowledge. But how many other extrinsical, and possibly very remote, bodies do the springs of those admirable machines depend on which are not vulgarly observed, or so much as thought on ; and how many are there which the severest enquiry can never discover? The inhabitants of this spot of the universe, though removed so many millions of miles from the sun, yet depend so much on the duly tempered motion of particles coming from or agitated by it, that were this earth removed but a small part of that distance out of its present situation, and placed a little farther or nearer that source of heat, it is more than probable that the greatest part of the animals in it would immediately perish : since we find them so often destroyed by an excess or defect of the sun's warmth, which an accidental position in some parts of this our little globe exposes them to. The qualities observed in a loadstone must needs have their source far beyond the confines of that body ; and the ravage made often on several sorts of animals by invisible causes, the certain death (as we are told) of some of them by barely passing the line, or, as it is certain of others, by being removed into a neighbouring country, evidently show that the concurrence and operation of several bodies, with which they are seldom thought to have anything to do, is absolutely necessary to make them be what they appear to us, and to preserve those qualities by which we know and distinguish them. We are then quite out of the way, when we think that things contain within themselves the qualities that appear to us in them ; and we in vain search for that constitution within the body of a fly or an elephant, upon which depend those qualities and powers we observe in them. For which perhaps, to understand them aright, we ought to look not only beyond this our earth and atmosphere, but even beyond the sun or remotest star our eyes have yet discovered. For how much the being and operation of particular substances in this our globe depend on causes utterly beyond our view, is impossible for us to determine. We see and perceive some of the motions and grosser operations of things here about us; but whence the streams come that keep all these curious machines in motion and repair, how conveyed and modified, is beyond our notice and apprehension; and the great parts and wheels, as I may so say, of this stupendous structure of the universe, may, for aught we know, have such a connexion and dependence in their influences and operations one upon another, that perhaps things in this our mansion would put on quite another face, and cease to be what they are, if some one of the stars or great bodies incomprehensibly remote from us should cease to be or move as it does. This is certain, things, however absolute and entire they seem in themselves, are but retainers to other parts of nature for that which they are most taken notice of by us. Their observable qualities, actions, and powers are owing to something without them; and there is not so complete and perfect a part that we know of nature, which does not owe the being it has, and the excellences of it, to its neighbours; and we must not confine our thoughts within the surface of any body, but look a great deal farther, to comprehend perfectly those qualities that are in it.

12. If this be so, it is not to be wondered, that we have very imperfect ideas of substances; and that the real essences, on which depend their properties and operations, are unknown to us. We cannot discover so much as that size, figure, and texture of their minute and active parts, which is really in them; much less the different motions and impulses made in and upon them by bodies from without, upon which depends, and by which is formed, the greatest and most remarkable part of those qualities we observe in them, and of which our complex ideas of them are made up. This consideration alone is enough to put an end to all our hopes of ever having the ideas of their real essences; which whilst we want, the nominal essences, we make use of instead of them, will be able to furnish us but very sparingly with any general knowledge, or universal propositions capable of real certainty.

13. *Judgement may reach farther, but that is not knowledge.*— We are not therefore to wonder if certainty be to be found in very few general propositions made concerning substances: our knowledge of their qualities and properties goes very seldom farther than our senses reach and inform us. Possibly inquisitive and observing men may, by strength of judgement,[1] penetrate farther; and on probabilities taken from wary

[1] Judgement, in Locke's peculiar sense, as contrasted with knowledge.

observation, and hints well laid together, often guess right at what experience has not yet discovered to them. But this is but guessing still ; it amounts only to opinion, and has not that certainty which is requisite to knowledge. For all general knowledge lies only in our own thoughts, and consists barely in the contemplation of our own abstract ideas. Wherever we perceive any agreement or disagreement amongst them, there we have general knowledge ; and by putting the names of those ideas together accordingly in propositions, can with certainty pronounce general truths. But because the abstract ideas of substances have a discoverable connexion or inconsistency with but a very few other ideas, the certainty of universal propositions concerning substances is very narrow and scanty. [15.] We cannot with certainty affirm, that all men sleep by intervals, that no man can be nourished by wood or stones, that all men will be poisoned by hemlock ; because these ideas have no connexion nor repugnancy with our nominal essence of man, with the abstract idea that name stands for. We must, in these and the like, appeal to trial in particular subjects, which can reach but a little way. We must content ourselves with probability in the rest : but can have no general certainty, whilst our specific idea of man contains not that real constitution, which is the root wherein all his inseparable qualities are united, and from whence they flow. Those few ideas only which have a discernible connexion with our nominal essence, or any part of it, can afford us universal propositions. But these are so few and of so little moment,[1] that we may justly look on our certain general knowledge of substances as almost none at all.

16. *Wherein lies the general certainty of propositions.*—To conclude : general propositions, of what kind soever, are then only capable of certainty, when the terms used in them stand for such ideas whose agreement or disagreement, as there expressed, is capable to be discovered by us. And we are then certain of their truth or falsehood, when we perceive the ideas the terms stand for to agree or not agree, according as they are affirmed or denied one of another. Whence we may take notice, that *general certainty* is never to be found but in our ideas. Whenever we go to seek it elsewhere, in experiment or observations without us, our knowledge goes not beyond particulars. It is the contemplation of our own abstract ideas that alone is able to afford us *general knowledge.*

[1] He gives examples, IV. 3. 14 and 7. 5.

## CHAPTER VII[1]

### OF MAXIMS

1. *They are self-evident.*—There are a sort of propositions which, under the name of *maxims* and *axioms*, have passed for principles of science : and, because they are *self-evident*, have been supposed innate, without that anybody (that I know) ever went about to show the reason and foundation of their clearness or cogency. It may, however, be worth while to enquire into the reason of their evidence, and see whether it be peculiar to them alone, and also examine how far they influence and govern our other knowledge.

2. *Wherein that self-evidence consists.*—Knowledge, as has been shown, consists in the perception of the agreement or disagreement of ideas : now where that agreement or disagreement is perceived immediately by itself, without the intervention or help of any other, there our knowledge is self-evident.

3. *Self-evidence not peculiar to received axioms.*—This being so, in the next place let us consider whether this self-evidence be peculiar only to those propositions which commonly pass under the name of maxims, and have the dignity of axioms allowed them. And here it is plain that several other truths, not allowed to be axioms, partake equally with them in this self-evidence.

4. *First, As to identity and diversity, all propositions are equally self-evident.*—For the immediate perception of the agreement or disagreement of *identity* being founded in the mind's having distinct ideas, this affords us as many self-evident propositions as we have distinct ideas. Every one that has any knowledge at all, has, as the foundation of it, various and distinct ideas : and it is the first act of the mind (without which it can never be capable of any knowledge) to know every one of its ideas by itself, and distinguish it from others. It is not therefore alone to these two general propositions—' Whatsoever is, is ' ; and, ' It is impossible for the same thing to be, and not to be'—that this self-evidence belongs by any peculiar right. These two general maxims,

[1] This chapter should be studied in connexion with the attack on innate notions or principles in Bk. I. Cf. Introduction, pp. xxxi–vi.

amounting to no more, in short, but this, that *the same is the same*, and *the same is not different*, are truths known in more particular instances, as well as in these general maxims ; and known also in particular instances, before these general maxims are ever thought on ; and draw all their force from the discernment of the mind employed about particular ideas. There is nothing more visible than that the mind, without the help of any proof or reflection on either of these general propositions, perceives so clearly, and knows so certainly, that the idea of white is the idea of white, and not the idea of blue; and that the idea of white, when it is in the mind, is there, and is not absent, that the consideration of these axioms can add nothing to the evidence or certainty of its knowledge.

5. *Secondly, In coexistence we have few self-evident propositions.*—As to *coexistence*, or such necessary connexion between two ideas, that in the subject where one of them is supposed, there the other must necessarily be also ; of such agreement or disagreement as this, the mind has an immediate perception but in very few of them. And therefore in this sort we have but very little intuitive knowledge : nor are there to be found very many propositions that are self-evident, though some there are ; v. g., the idea of filling a place equal to the contents of its superficies, being annexed to our idea of body, I think it is a self-evident proposition, that ' two bodies cannot be in the same place '.

6. *Thirdly, In other relations we may have.*—As to the *relations of modes*, mathematicians have framed many axioms concerning that one relation of equality. As, ' Equals taken from equals, the remainder will be equals ' ; which, with the rest of that kind, however they are received for maxims by the mathematicians, and are unquestionable truths, yet I think that any one who considers them will not find that they have a clearer self-evidence than these, that ' one and one are equal to two ' ;[1] that ' if you take from the five fingers of one hand two, and from the five fingers of the other hand two, the remaining numbers will be equal '. These and a thousand other such propositions may be found in numbers, which at very first hearing force the assent, and carry with them an equal, if not greater clearness than those mathematical axioms.

7. *Fourthly, Concerning real existence we have none.*—As to

[1] This, Leibniz remarks, is not properly a truth ; it is the *definition* of two.

*real existence*, since that has no connexion with any other of our ideas, but that of ourselves, and of a First Being,[1] we have in that, concerning the real existence of all other beings, not so much as demonstrative, much less a self-evident, knowledge, and, therefore, concerning those there are no maxims.

8. *These axioms do not much influence our other knowledge.*—In the next place let us consider what influence these received maxims have upon the other parts of our knowledge. The rules established in the Schools, that all reasonings are *ex praecognitis et praeconcessis*, seem to lay the foundation of all other knowledge in these maxims, and to suppose them to be *praecognita*; whereby, I think, is meant these two things: First, That these axioms are those truths that are first known to the mind; and, Secondly, that upon them the other parts of our knowledge depend.

9. *Because they are not the truths we first knew.*—First, That they are not the truths first known to the mind is evident to experience, as we have shown in another place (Bk. I, ch. 2). Whereof the reason is very plain: such self-evident truths must be first known which consist of ideas that are first in the mind; and the ideas first in the mind, it is evident, are those of particular things, from whence, by slow degrees, the understanding proceeds to some few general ones; which being taken from the ordinary and familiar objects of sense, are settled in the mind with general names to them. Thus particular ideas are first received and distinguished; and next to them, the less general or specific, which are next to particular. For abstract ideas are not so obvious or easy to children, or the yet unexercised mind, as particular ones. If they seem so to grown men, it is only because by constant and familiar use they are made so. For when we nicely reflect upon them, we shall find that general ideas are fictions and contrivances of the mind, that carry difficulty with them, and do not so easily offer themselves as we are apt to imagine. For example, does it not require

---

[1] This statement is important as throwing light on Locke's fourth sort of agreement and disagreement—'actual real existence agreeing to any idea'. Cf. IV. 1. 7 and relative notes, also 9. 3 and 10. 1–3. See Introduction, pp. xli–ii. Even the *Cogito ergo sum*, Leibniz points out, is not a maxim, ' for it is a proposition of fact, based upon an immediate experience, not a necessary proposition whose necessity is seen in the immediate agreement of ideas. On the contrary, it is only God who sees how these two terms, *I* and *existence*, are united, i. e. why I exist.'

some pains and skill to form the general idea of a triangle (which is yet none of the most abstract, comprehensive, and difficult); for it must be neither oblique nor rectangle, neither equilateral, equicrural, nor scalenon; but all and none of these at once.[1] In effect, it is something imperfect, that cannot exist; an idea wherein some parts of several different and inconsistent ideas are put together. It is true, the mind in this imperfect state has need of such ideas, and makes all the haste to them it can, for the conveniency of communication and enlargement of knowledge; to both which it is naturally very much inclined. But yet one has reason to suspect such ideas are marks of our imperfection; at least, this is enough to show that the most abstract and general ideas are not those that the mind is first and most easily acquainted with.

10. *Because on them the other parts of our knowledge do not depend.*—Secondly, From what has been said, it plainly follows that these magnified maxims are not the principles and foundations of all our other knowledge. For if there be a great many other truths which have as much self-evidence as they, and a great many that we know before them, it is impossible they

---

[1] This passage was singled out for criticism by Berkeley in his polemic against 'abstract ideas' in the Introduction to his *Principles of Human Knowledge*. Berkeley, who understood by ideas only individual percepts or images, interpreted Locke's language here as an assertion of the possibility of framing a general *image* of a triangle, in which mutually exclusive characteristics should be co-present. It was easy for him to pour ridicule upon abstract ideas in this sense. But Locke, who uses 'idea' indifferently for the individual percept or image and the notion or concept (which is called 'abstract' just because it cannot be individualized or presented in sense), does not appear to make the claim which Berkeley reads into his language. The words here, 'In effect, it is something imperfect that cannot exist', might even be taken as repudiating such a claim; for what cannot exist as a concrete individual cannot be mirrored as an image in the mind. The words which follow, 'an idea wherein *some parts* of several inconsistent and different ideas are put together', must in fairness, Professor Fraser says, be taken to mean that the common elements of 'triangularity', abstracted from the mutually inconsistent features of the different species, constitute the general idea; and the mind is capable (as Berkeley acknowledges) of 'considering' these attributes apart, though not of envisaging them except in combination with the other attributes of one or other of the species. Berkeley, whose youthful philosophy was built upon the assumption that all ideas are 'particular', was fain, in the philosophy of his middle life, to reinstate the abstract idea or concept under the title of 'notion'. We cannot have an 'idea' of the self, he taught, but we have a 'notion' of it, and notions also of relations.

should be the principles from which we deduce all other truths. Is it impossible to know that one and two are equal to three, but by virtue of this, or some such axiom, viz., 'the whole is equal to all its parts taken together'? Many a one knows that one and two are equal to three, without having heard, or thought on, that or any other axiom, by which it might be proved ; and knows it as certainly as any other man knows that 'the whole is equal to all its parts',[1] or any other maxim ; and all from the same reason of self-evidence. Nor after the knowledge that the whole is equal to all its parts, does he know that one and two are equal to three better or more certainly than he did before.

11. *What use these general maxims have.*—What shall we then say? Are these general maxims of no use? [By no means; though perhaps their use is not that which it is commonly taken to be.

(1) It is evident from what has been already said, that they are of no use to prove or confirm less general self-evident propositions.

(2) It is as plain that they are not, nor have been, the foundations whereon any science hath been built. There is, I know, a great deal of talk, propagated from Scholastic men, of sciences and the maxims on which they are built : but it has been my ill luck never to meet with any such sciences ; much less any one built upon these two maxims, 'What is, is'; and, 'It is impossible for the same thing to be and not to be'. I ask, whether these general maxims have not the same use in the study of divinity, and in theological questions, that they have in the other sciences? They serve here, too, to silence wranglers, and put an end to dispute. But I think that nobody will therefore say, that the Christian religion is built on these maxims, or that the knowledge we have of it is derived from these principles.

(3) They are not of use to help men forward in the advance-

---

[1] Leibniz remarks again that 'one and two is three' is the definition of three. Moreover, the axiom 'the whole is equal to all its parts' requires qualification. It must be stipulated that the parts in question have no part in common : seven and eight are parts of twelve, but they make more than twelve. What Euclid says is that 'the whole is greater than its part'. The true way of looking at the matter, he adds, is not to oppose the axiom and the example as different truths, but to consider the axiom as embodied in the example and rendering it true.

ment of sciences, or new discoveries of yet unknown truths. Mr. Newton, in his never enough to be admired book,[1] has demonstrated several propositions, which are so many new truths, before unknown to the world, and are farther advances in mathematical knowledge : but for the discovery of these, it was not the general maxims ' What is, is ', or ' The whole is bigger than a part ', or the like, that helped him. Nor was it by them that he got the knowledge of those demonstrations ; but by finding out intermediate ideas, that showed the agreement or disagreement of the ideas, as expressed in the propositions he demonstrated. This is the great exercise and improvement of human understanding in the enlarging of knowledge, and advancing the sciences ; wherein they are far enough from receiving any help from the contemplation of these or the like magnified maxims. Would those who have this traditional admiration of these propositions, that they think no step can be made in knowledge without the support of an axiom, but distinguish between the method of acquiring knowledge, and of communicating it ; between the method of raising any science, and that of teaching it to others as far as it is advanced ; they would see that those general maxims were not the foundations on which the first discoverers raised their admirable structures, nor the keys that unlocked and opened those secrets of knowledge. Though afterwards, when Schools were erected, and sciences had their professors to teach what others had found out, they often made use of maxims, i. e., laid down certain propositions which were self-evident, or to be received for true, which being settled in the minds of their scholars as unquestionable verities, they on occasion made use of to convince them of truths in particular instances, that were not so familiar to their minds as those general axioms which had before been inculcated to them, and carefully settled in their minds. Though these particular instances, when well reflected on, are no less self-evident to the understanding, than the general maxims brought to confirm them : and it was in those particular instances that the first discoverer found the truth, without the help of the general maxims : and so may any one else do, who with attention considers them.

To come therefore to the use that is made of maxims.

(1) They are of use, as has been observed, in the ordinary

---

[1] The *Principia*, published in 1687.

methods of teaching sciences as far as they are advanced: but of little or none in advancing them farther.

(2) They are of use in disputes, for the silencing of obstinate wranglers, and bringing those contests to some conclusion. Whether a need of them to that end came not in, in the manner following, I crave leave to enquire. The Schools having made disputation the touchstone of men's abilities, and the criterion of knowledge, adjudged victory to him that kept the field; and he that had the last word was concluded to have the better of the argument, if not of the cause. But because by this means there was like to be no decision between skilful combatants, to prevent, as much as could be, the running out of disputes into an endless train of syllogisms, certain general propositions, most of them indeed self-evident, were introduced into the Schools; which being such as all men allowed and agreed in, were looked on as general measures of truth, and served instead of principles (where the disputants had not laid down any other between them), beyond which there was no going, and which must not be receded from by either side. And thus these maxims getting the name of 'principles', beyond which men in dispute could not retreat, were by mistake taken to be the originals and sources from whence all knowledge began, and the foundations whereon the sciences were built. This I think, that bating those places which brought the Peripatetic philosophy into their Schools, where it continued many ages, without teaching the world anything but the art of wrangling, these maxims were nowhere thought the foundations on which the sciences were built, nor the great helps to the advancement of knowledge.][1]

Before custom has settled methods of thinking and reasoning in our minds, I am apt to imagine, it is quite otherwise; and that the child, when a part of his apple is taken away, knows it better in that particular instance, than by this general proposition, 'The whole is equal to all its parts'; and that, if one of these have need to be confirmed to him by the other, the general has more need to be let into his mind by the particular, than the particular by the general. For in *particulars* our knowledge begins, and so spreads itself, by degrees, to *generals*; though afterwards the mind takes the quite contrary course, and having drawn its knowledge into as general propositions

[1] This long passage in brackets (pp. 303–5) was inserted by Locke in the fourth edition as a reasoned summary of his position.

as it can, makes those familiar to its thoughts, and accustoms itself to have recourse to them, as to the standards of truth and falsehood. By which familiar use of them as rules to measure the truth of other propositions, it comes in time to be thought, that more particular propositions have their truth and evidence from their conformity to these more general ones, which in discourse and argumentation are so frequently urged and constantly admitted. And this I think to be the reason why, amongst so many self-evident propositions, the most general only have had the title of maxims.

19. Intuitive knowledge neither requires nor admits any proof, one part of it more than another. He that will suppose it does, takes away the foundation of all knowledge and certainty: and he that needs any proof to make him certain, and give his assent to this proposition, that ' two are equal to two ', will also have need of a proof to make him admit that ' what is, is '.[1]

## CHAPTER VIII

### OF TRIFLING PROPOSITIONS

1. *Some propositions bring no increase to our knowledge.*—Whether the maxims treated of in the foregoing chapter be of that use to real knowledge as is generally supposed, I leave to be considered. This, I think, may confidently be affirmed, that there are universal propositions which, though they be certainly true, yet they add no light to our understandings, bring no increase to our knowledge. Such are,

2. First, All purely *identical* propositions. These obviously and at first blush appear to contain no instruction in them. For

[1] In the fourth edition Locke inserted the following passage (in section 14) in reply to the animadversions of his critics: ' It is to show men, that these maxims, however cried up for the great guards to truth, will not secure them from error in a careless, loose use of their words, that I have made this remark. In all that is here suggested concerning their little use for the improvement of knowledge, or dangerous use in undetermined ideas, I have been far enough from saying or intending they should be laid aside, as some have been too forward to charge me. I affirm them to be truths, self-evident truths; and so cannot be laid aside. As far as their influence will reach, it is in vain to endeavour, nor would I attempt to abridge it. But yet without any injury to truth or knowledge, I may have reason to think their use is not answerable to the great stress which seems to be laid on them, and I may warn men not to make an ill use of them for the confirming themselves in errors.'

## Of Trifling Propositions

when we affirm the said term of itself, whether it be barely verbal, or whether it contains any clear and real idea, it shows us nothing but what we must certainly know before. [3.] What is this more than trifling with words? It is but like a monkey shifting his oyster from one hand to the other; and had he had but words, might no doubt have said, ' Oyster in right hand is subject, and oyster in left hand is predicate '; and so might have made a self-evident proposition of oyster, i.e., ' Oyster is oyster '.

[I know there are some who, because identical propositions are self-evident, show a great concern for them, and think they do great service to philosophy by crying them up, as if in them was contained all knowledge, and the understanding were led into all truth by them only. I grant as forwardly as any one, that they are all true and self-evident. I grant farther, that the foundation of all our knowledge lies in the faculty we have of perceiving the same idea to be the same, and of discerning it from those that are different, as I have shown in the foregoing chapter. But how that vindicates the making use of identical propositions for the improvement of knowledge from the imputation of trifling, I do not see. Instruction lies in something very different, and he that would enlarge his own or another's mind to truths he does not yet know, must find out intermediate ideas, and then lay them in such order one by another, that the understanding may see the agreement or disagreement of those in question.][1]

4. Secondly, Another sort of trifling propositions is, *when a part of the complex idea is predicated of the name of the whole*; a part of the definition, of the word defined. Such are all propositions wherein the *genus* is predicated of the *species*; or more comprehensive of less comprehensive terms: for what information, what knowledge, carries this proposition in it, viz., ' Lead is a metal', to a man who knows the complex idea the name lead stands for? [5.] A like trifling it is to predicate any other part of the definition of the term defined; or to affirm any one of the simple ideas of a complex one, of the name of the whole complex idea; as, ' All gold is fusible '. For fusibility being one of the simple ideas that goes to the making up the complex one the sound gold stands for, what

---

[1] This paragraph was added in the fourth edition in reply to criticisms by Stillingfleet and others.

can it be but playing with sounds, to affirm that of the name gold which is comprehended in its received signification?
[6.] But he that shall tell me, that in whatever thing sense, motion, reason, and laughter were united, that thing had actually a notion of God, or would be cast into a sleep by opium, made indeed an instructive proposition: because neither 'having the notion of God', nor 'being cast into sleep by opium', being contained in the idea signified by the word man, we are by such propositions taught something more than barely what the word man stands for: and therefore the knowledge contained in it is more than verbal.[1]

7. Before a man makes any proposition, he is supposed to understand the terms he uses in it, or else he talks like a parrot, only making a noise by imitation, and framing certain sounds which he has learned of others; but not as a rational creature, using them for signs of ideas which he has in his mind. The hearer also is supposed to understand the terms as the speaker uses them. And therefore he trifles with words who makes such a proposition, which, when it is made, contains no more than one of the terms does; v. g., 'A triangle hath three sides', or, 'Saffron is yellow'. And this is no farther tolerable than where a man goes to explain his terms to one who is supposed or declares himself not to understand him.

8. We can know then the truth of two sorts of propositions with perfect certainty. The one is, of those trifling propositions which have a certainty in them, but it is but a verbal certainty, but not instructive. And, secondly, we can know the truth, and so may be certain in propositions which affirm something of another, which is a necessary consequence of its precise complex idea, but not contained in it: as that 'the external angle of all triangles is bigger than either of the opposite internal angles'; which relation of the outward angle to either of the opposite internal angles, making no part of the complex idea signified by the name triangle, this is a real truth, and conveys with it instructive real knowledge.[2]

---

[1] These are examples of Kant's 'synthetic judgements *a posteriori*'.

[2] In this section Locke clearly distinguishes between analytic judgements and those which Kant called 'synthetic judgements *a priori*'. But he was far from recognizing the philosophical importance of the distinction and (as we have seen from his remarks on a demonstrative science of morality) he did not always apply the distinction correctly. Cf. note, p. 277.

# CHAPTER IX

### OF OUR KNOWLEDGE OF EXISTENCE

1. *General certain propositions concern not existence.*—Hitherto we have only considered the essences of things, which being only abstract ideas, and thereby removed in our thoughts from particular existence (that being the proper operation of the mind in abstraction, to consider an idea under no other existence but what it has in the understanding), gives us no knowledge of real existence at all. Where, by the way, we may take notice, that universal propositions, of whose truth or falsehood we can have certain knowledge, concern not existence; and farther, that all particular affirmations or negations that would not be certain if they were made general, are only concerning existence; they declaring only the accidental union or separation of ideas in things existing, which, in their abstract natures, have no known necessary union or repugnancy.

2. *A threefold knowledge of existence.*—But leaving the nature of propositions, and different ways of predication, to be considered more at large in another place,[1] let us proceed now to enquire concerning our knowledge of the existence of things, and how we come by it. I say then, that we have the knowledge of *our own existence* by intuition; of the *existence of God* by demonstration; and of other things by sensation.

3. *Our knowledge of our own existence is intuitive.*—As for our own existence, we perceive it so plainly and so certainly that it neither needs nor is capable of any proof. For nothing can be more evident to us than our own existence. I think, I reason, I feel pleasure and pain: can any of these be more evident to me than my own existence? If I doubt of all other things, that very doubt makes me perceive my own existence, and will not suffer me to doubt of that. For if I know I feel pain, it is evident I have as certain perception of my own existence, as of the existence of the pain I feel: or if I know I doubt, I have as certain perception of the existence of the

---

[1] This would seem to imply that the chapters which follow concerning our knowledge of existence were written before chs. 5-8, and also perhaps before Bk. III. The threefold division of our knowledge of existence carries us back to ch. 3, section 21.

thing [1] doubting, as of that thought which I call doubt. Experience, then, convinces us that we have an *intuitive knowledge* [2] of our own existence, and an internal infallible perception that we are. In every act of sensation, reasoning, or thinking, we are conscious to ourselves of our own being; and in this matter, come not short of the highest degree of certainty.

## CHAPTER X

### OF OUR KNOWLEDGE OF THE EXISTENCE OF A GOD [3]

1. *We are capable of knowing certainly that there is a God.*—Though God has given us no innate ideas of himself; though he has stamped no original characters on our minds, wherein we may read his being; yet having furnished us with those faculties our minds are endowed with, he hath not left himself without witness; [4] since we have sense, perception, and reason, and cannot want a clear proof of him as long as we carry ourselves about us. Nor can we justly complain of our ignorance in this great point, since he has so plentifully provided us with the means to discover and know him, so far as is necessary to the end of our being, and the great concernment of our happiness. But though this be the most obvious truth that reason discovers, and though its evidence be (if I mistake not) equal to mathematical certainty; yet it requires thought and attention, and the mind must apply itself to a regular deduction of it from some part of our intuitive knowledge, or else we shall be as uncertain and ignorant of this as of other propositions which are in themselves capable of clear demonstration. To show, therefore, that we are capable of knowing, i.e., being

[1] Locke, like Descartes, interprets the immediately experienced certainty as proof of the existence of a 'thinking thing' or substance. Compare ch. 10, section 2, and relative note.

[2] On the difference between our certainty, in regard to a single contingent fact, and the intuitive certainty involved in the apprehension of necessary propositions, compare note, p. 301. Unlike 'other things', which are only mediately apprehended, the mind, Locke says, is immediately present 'to the understanding' (IV. 21. 4); hence every mental function involves an immediate knowledge of our own existence. As he says elsewhere (II. 27. 9), 'Consciousness always accompanies thinking'; 'when we see, hear, taste, feel, meditate, or will anything, we know that we do so.' Cf. Gibson, *op. cit.*, pp. 170–2.

[3] '"A God" instead of " God " suggests the inadequacy of Locke's idea of God' (Fraser). [4] Cf. I. 4. 8–16.

certain. that there is a God, and how we may come by this certainty, I think we need go no farther than ourselves, and that undoubted knowledge we have of our own existence.

2. *Man knows that he himself is.*—I think it is beyond question, that man has a clear perception of his own being; he knows certainly that he exists, and that he is something. He that can doubt whether he be anything or no, I speak not to, no more than I would argue with pure nothing, or endeavour to convince nonentity that it were something. If any one pretends to be so sceptical as to deny his own existence (for really to doubt of it is manifestly impossible), let him, for me, enjoy his beloved happiness of being nothing, until hunger or some other pain convince him of the contrary. This, then, I think I may take for a truth, which every one's certain knowledge assures him of, beyond the liberty of doubting, viz., that he is something that actually exists.[1]

3. *He knows also, that nothing cannot produce a being, therefore something eternal.*—In the next place, man knows by an intuitive certainty that bare *nothing can no more produce any real being, than it can be equal to two right angles.*[2] If a man

---

[1] The statement of the ultimate certainty in this form may be said to depend on the assumption that thought cannot exist except as a quality of a substance. Descartes states it in his *Principles* as a truth manifest by the natural light ' that to nothing no affections or qualities belong'. Cf. Kemp Smith, *Studies in the Cartesian Philosophy*, p. 50.

[2] The demonstration depends on the validity of the causal ' maxim ' that ' everything that has a beginning must have a cause '. Although Locke had spoken uncertainly about the origin of the idea of cause from experience, he appealed to this principle in his controversy with Stillingfleet as a true ' principle of reason '. Formally, Locke's statement in this section may be regarded as an argument to prove the principle by a *reductio ad absurdum* of the opposite alternative. As such, it is attacked by Hume, along with the similar argument of Samuel Clarke that, if anything had no cause, it must have produced itself and have existed, therefore, before it existed (*Treatise*, Bk. I, Part 3, section 3). 'When we exclude all causes,' says Hume, ' we really do exclude them, and neither suppose nothing nor the object itself to be the causes of the existence; and consequently can draw no argument from the absurdity of these suppositions to prove the absurdity of that exclusion. . . .'Tis the very point in question, whether everything must have a cause or not; and therefore, according to all just reasoning, it ought never to be taken for granted.' Locke's formulation corresponds with the third of the axioms or ' common notions ' which Descartes attributes to the 'lumen naturale ' : ' A thing or any perfection (i. e. quality) of a thing actually existing cannot have, as a cause of its existence, nothing or a thing which does not exist.'

knows not that nonentity, or the absence of all being, cannot be equal to two right angles, it is impossible he should know any demonstration in Euclid. If therefore we know there is some real being, and that nonentity cannot produce any real being, it is an evident demonstration that from eternity there has been something; since what was not from eternity had a beginning; and what had a beginning must be produced by something else.

4. *That eternal Being must be most powerful.*—Next, it is evident, that what had its being and beginning from another, must also have all that which is in and belongs to its being from another too. All the powers it has, must be owing to and received from the same source.[1] This eternal source, then, of all being, must also be the source and original of all power; and so this eternal Being must be also the most powerful.

5. *And most knowing.*—Again: a man finds in himself perception and knowledge. We have then got one step farther; and we are certain now that there is not only some being, but some knowing, intelligent being in the world.

There was a time, then, when there was no knowing being, and when knowledge began to be; or else there has been also *a knowing being from eternity.* If it be said, There was a time when no being had any knowledge, when that eternal being was void of all understanding; I reply, that then it was impossible there should ever have been any knowledge. It being as impossible that things wholly void of knowledge, and operating blindly and without any perception, should produce a knowing being, as it is impossible that a triangle should make itself three angles bigger than two right ones. For it is as repugnant to the idea of senseless matter that it should put into itself sense, perception, and knowledge, as it is repugnant to the idea of a triangle that it should put into itself greater angles than two right ones.[2]

---

[1] The argument in this and the following section depends on Descartes's fourth axiom: ' All the reality or perfection which is in a thing is to be found also, formally or eminently, in its first or complete cause.' In other words, the cause assumed must be at least sufficient to account for the observed facts; or, as Locke puts it himself (section 10), ' must necessarily contain in it, and actually have, at least all the perfections that can ever after exist'. The legitimate conclusion therefore is, as he puts it, most or very powerful, most or very knowing, not necessarily omnipotent and omniscient; though he uses the latter terms in the sequel, e. g. in section 13.

[2] Locke thus rejects Materialism as an ultimate theory of the cosmos,

6. *And therefore God.*—Thus from the consideration of ourselves, and what we infallibly find in our own constitutions, our reason leads us to the knowledge of this certain and evident truth, That *there is an eternal, most powerful, and most knowing Being*, which whether any one will please to call *God*, it matters not. The thing is evident; and from this idea duly considered, will easily be deduced all those other attributes which we ought to ascribe to this eternal Being. If, nevertheless, any one should be found so senselessly arrogant as to suppose man alone knowing and wise, but yet the product of mere ignorance and chance; and that all the rest of the universe acted only by that blind haphazard: I shall leave with him that very rational and emphatical rebuke of Tully, lib. ii, *De Leg.*, to be considered at his leisure: ' What can be more sillily arrogant and misbecoming than for a man to think that he has a mind and understanding in him, but yet in all the universe beside there is no such thing? Or that those things which, with the utmost stretch of his reason, he can scarce comprehend, should be moved and managed without any reason at all?'

From what has been said, it is plain to me we have a more certain knowledge of the existence of a God, than of anything our senses have not immediately discovered to us. Nay, I presume I may say, that we more certainly know that there is a God, than that there is anything else without us. When I say we *know*, I mean there is such a knowledge within our reach which we cannot miss, if we will but apply our minds to that, as we do to several other enquiries.

7. *Our idea of a most perfect being, not the sole proof of a God.*—How far *the idea of a most perfect being* which a man may frame in his mind, does or does not prove the existence of a God, I will not here examine.[1] For, in the different make of men's

although he was willing to consider the possibility of God's superadding to matter a faculty of thinking in the case of the human organism.

[1] This is the ontological or *a priori* argument, so prominent in Descartes's philosophy. Locke here leaves its validity an open question, only protesting against laying the whole stress upon it and disparaging other lines of proof. But it was explicitly rejected by him later. ' Real existence', he wrote in 1696, 'can be proved only by real existence; and therefore the real existence of a God can only be proved by the real existence of other things.' The connexion between the idea of God and real existence is mediated for him, accordingly, by the fact of his own existence. Cf. Introduction, p. xli. Locke's argument is a variety of what is known as the cosmological or the argument *a contingentia mundi*. It suffers in his hands from the deistic conception of God as a purely transcendent being. For a general criticism of the cosmological

tempers, and application of their thoughts, some arguments prevail more on one, and some on another, for the confirmation of the same truth. But yet, I think this I may say, that it is an ill way of establishing this truth and silencing atheists, to lay the whole stress of so important a point as this upon that sole foundation : and take some men's having that idea of God in their minds (for it is evident some men have none, and some worse than none, and the most very different) for the only proof of a Deity ; and out of an over-fondness of that darling invention, cashier, or at least endeavour to invalidate, all other arguments, and forbid us to hearken to those proofs, as being weak or fallacious, which our own existence and the sensible parts of the universe offer so clearly and cogently to our thoughts, that I deem it impossible for a considering man to withstand them. For I judge it as certain and clear a truth as can anywhere be delivered, that ' the invisible things of God are clearly seen from the creation of the world, being understood by the things that are made, even his eternal power and Godhead '.[1] Though our own being furnishes us, as I have shown, with an evident and incontestable proof of a Deity ; and I believe nobody can avoid the cogency of it, who will but as carefully attend to it as to any other demonstration of so many parts : yet this being so fundamental a truth, and of that consequence that all religion and genuine morality depend thereon, I doubt not but I shall be forgiven by my reader if I go over some parts of this argument again, and enlarge a little more upon them.

8. *Something from eternity.*—There is no truth more evident than that *something* must be *from eternity*. I never yet heard of any one so unreasonable, or that could suppose so manifest a contradiction, as a time wherein there was perfectly nothing. This being of all absurdities the greatest, to imagine that pure nothing, the perfect negation and absence of all beings, should ever produce any real existence.

It being then unavoidable for all rational creatures to conclude that something has existed from eternity, let us next see what kind of thing that must be.

9. *Two sorts of beings, cogitative and incogitative.*—There are but two sorts of beings in the world, that man knows or conceives :

argument in its traditional form see Kant's *Critique of Pure Reason*, Transcendental Dialectic, Bk. II, ch. 3, section 5. [1] Romans i. 20

First, Such as are purely material, without sense, perception, or thought, as the clippings of our beards, and paring of our nails.

Secondly, Sensible, thinking, perceiving beings, such as we find ourselves to be, which, if you please, we will hereafter call *cogitative* and *incogitative* beings; which, to our present purpose, if for nothing else, are perhaps better terms than material and immaterial.

10. *Incogitative being cannot produce a cogitative.*—If then there must be something eternal, let us see what sort of being it must be. And to that, it is very obvious to reason, that it must necessarily be a cogitative being. For it is as impossible to conceive that ever bare incogitative matter should produce a thinking intelligent being, as that nothing should of itself produce matter. Let us suppose any parcel of matter eternal, great or small, we shall find it in itself able to produce nothing. For example: Let us suppose the matter of the next pebble we meet with, eternal, closely united, and the parts firmly at rest together; if there were no other being in the world, must it not eternally remain so, a dead, inactive lump? Is it possible to conceive it can add motion to itself, being purely matter, or produce anything? Matter, then, by its own strength, cannot produce in itself so much as motion: the motion it has must also be from eternity, or else be produced and added to matter by some other being more powerful than matter. But let us suppose motion eternal too; yet matter, *incogitative* matter and motion, whatever changes it might produce of figure and bulk, could never produce thought. Knowledge will still be as far beyond the power of motion and matter to produce, as matter is beyond the power of nothing or nonentity to produce. And I appeal to every one's own thoughts, whether he cannot as easily conceive matter produced by nothing, as thought to be produced by pure matter, when before there was no such thing as thought or an intelligent being existing. Divide matter into as minute parts as you will (which we are apt to imagine a sort of spiritualizing or making a thinking thing of it); vary the figure and motion of it as much as you please; a globe, cube, cone, prism, cylinder, &c., whose diameters are but 1,000,000th part of a gry,[1] will operate no

---

[1] ' A gry is one-tenth of a line, a line one-tenth of an inch, an inch one-tenth of a philosophical foot. . . . I have affectedly made use of this measure here, and the parts of it, under a decimal division, because

otherwise upon other bodies of proportionable bulk than those of an inch or foot diameter. They knock, impel, and resist one another just as the greater do, and that is all they can do. So that, if we will suppose nothing first or eternal, matter can never begin to be: if we will suppose bare matter without motion eternal, motion can never begin to be: if we suppose only matter and motion first or eternal, thought can never begin to be. For it is impossible to conceive that matter, either with or without motion, could have, originally in and from itself, sense, perception, and knowledge; as is evident from hence, that then sense, perception, and knowledge must be a property eternally inseparable from matter and every particle of it. Not to add, that though our general or specific conception of matter makes us speak of it as one thing, yet really all matter is not one individual thing, neither is there any such thing existing as one material being, or one single body, that we know or can conceive. And therefore, if matter were the eternal first cogitative being, there would not be one eternal infinite cogitative being, but an infinite number of eternal finite cogitative beings independent one of another, of limited force and distinct thoughts, which could never produce that order, harmony, and beauty, which is to be found in nature. Since, therefore, whatsoever is the first eternal being must necessarily be cogitative; and whatsoever is first of all things must necessarily contain in it, and actually have, at least, all the perfections that can ever after exist; nor can it ever give to another any perfection that it hath not, either actually in itself or at least in a higher degree: it necessarily follows, that the first eternal being cannot be matter.

12. Though this discovery of the *necessary existence of an eternal Mind* does sufficiently lead us into the knowledge of God; since it will hence follow that all other knowing beings that have a beginning must depend on him, and have no other ways of knowledge or extent of power than what he gives them; and therefore, if he made those, he made also the less excellent pieces of this universe, all inanimate beings, whereby his omniscience, power, and providence will be established, and all his other attributes necessarily follow: yet, to clear up this a little farther, we will see what doubts can be raised against it.

I think it must be of general convenience that this should be the common measure in the Commonwealth of Letters' (Locke).

### Ch. 10 *Knowledge of the Existence of a God* 317

13. *Whether material or no.*—*First,* Perhaps it will be said, that though it be as clear as demonstration can make it, that there must be an eternal Being, and that Being must also be knowing; yet, it does not follow but that thinking Being may also be material. Let it be so; it equally still follows that there is a God. For if there be an eternal, omniscient, omnipotent Being, it is certain that there is a God, whether you imagine that Being to be material or no. But herein, I suppose, lies the danger and deceit of that supposition. There being no way to avoid the demonstration, that there is an eternal knowing Being, men devoted to matter would willingly have it granted that this knowing Being is material; and then, letting slide out of their minds, or the discourse, the demonstration whereby an eternal knowing Being was proved necessarily to exist, would argue all to be matter, and so deny a God, that is, an eternal cogitative Being.

14. *Not material: First, Because every particle of matter is not cogitative.*—But now let us see how they can satisfy themselves or others, that this eternal thinking Being is material.

First, I would ask them, whether they imagine that all matter, *every particle of matter*, thinks? This, I suppose, they will scarce say, since then there would be as many eternal thinking beings as there are particles of matter, and so an infinity of gods. And yet, if they will not allow matter as matter, that is, every particle of matter, to be as well cogitative as extended, they will have as hard a task to make out to their own reasons a cogitative being out of incogitative particles, as an extended being out of unextended parts, if I may so speak.

15. *Secondly, One particle alone of matter cannot be cogitative.*—If all matter does not think, I next ask, whether it be *only one atom* that does so? This has as many absurdities as the other; for then this atom of matter must be alone eternal or not. If this alone be eternal, then this alone, by its powerful thought or will, made all the rest of matter. And so we have the creation of matter by a powerful thought, which is that the materialists stick at. For if they suppose one single thinking atom to have produced all the rest of matter, they cannot ascribe that pre-eminency to it upon any other account than that of its thinking, the only supposed difference.

16. *Thirdly, A system of incogitative matter cannot be cogitative.*—If then neither one peculiar atom alone can be this eternal thinking Being, nor all matter, as matter, it only remains that it is some certain *system* of matter duly put together, that is this thinking eternal Being. This is that which, I imagine, is that notion which men are aptest to have of God; who would have him a material being, as most readily suggested to them by the ordinary conceit they have of themselves and other men, which they take to be material thinking beings. But this imagination, however more natural, is no less absurd than the other : for to suppose the eternal thinking Being to be nothing else but a composition of particles of matter, each whereof is incogitative, is to ascribe all the wisdom and knowledge of that eternal Being only to the juxtaposition of parts; than which nothing can be more absurd. For unthinking particles of matter, however put together, can have nothing thereby added to them but a new relation of position, which it is impossible should give thought and knowledge to them.

18. *Matter not coeternal with an eternal Mind.*—Others would have matter to be eternal,[1] notwithstanding that they allow an eternal, cogitative, immaterial Being. This, though it take not away the being of a God, yet since it denies one and the first great piece of his workmanship, the creation, let us consider it a little. Matter must be allowed eternal : why ? Because you cannot conceive how it can be made out of nothing: why do you not also think yourself eternal ? You will answer, perhaps, Because about twenty or forty years since you began to be. But if I ask you what that ' you ' is, which began then to be, you can scarce tell me. The matter whereof you are made began not then to be : for if it did, then it is not eternal. But it began to be put together in such a fashion and frame as

---

[1] ' The eternity of matter has been held by ancient and modern philosophers, in consistency with faith in supreme, all-governing Mind. ... To hold that the sensible world is an eternal manifestation of active Reason—" an eternal poem of spirit "—is very different from the hypothesis that resolves all at last into blind atoms, divorced from intelligence. That God should be immanent and eternally manifested in the sensible universe, or in a succession of waxing and waning sensible worlds, in which every event is regulated by active Reason, implies what is virtually a *constant* creation, instead of creation as a " singular effect "; and to some minds presents a more impressive idea of the Eternal Mind than the vulgar conception does ' (Fraser).

makes up your body; but yet that frame of particles is not you, it makes not that thinking thing you are; therefore when did that thinking thing begin to be? If it did never begin to be, then have you always been a thinking thing from eternity; the absurdity whereof I need not confute till I meet with one who is so void of understanding as to own it. If, therefore, you can allow a thinking thing to be made out of nothing (as all things that are not eternal must be), why also can you not allow it possible for a material being to be made out of nothing by an equal power, but that you have the experience of the one in view, and not of the other? Though, when well considered, creation [of a spirit will be found to require no less power than the creation of matter. Nay, possibly, if we would emancipate ourselves from vulgar notions, and raise our thoughts, as far as they would reach, to a closer contemplation of things, we might be able to aim at some dim and seeming conception how matter might at first be made, and begin to exist, by the power of that eternal first Being:[1] but to give beginning and being to a spirit would be found a more inconceivable effect of omnipotent power.[2] But this being what would, perhaps, lead us too far from the notions on which the philosophy now in the world is built, it would not be pardonable to deviate so far from them: especially in this place, where the received doctrine serves well enough to our present purpose, and leaves this past doubt, that][3], the creation or beginning of any one *Substance*

---

[1] This somewhat cryptic passage occasioned much conjecture as to what the 'dim conception' might be. From a note in the second edition of Coste's French translation of the *Essay*, it appears that the conception was suggested to Locke by Newton in conversation. We may have some rude idea, Newton said, that God, by his *power*, had (at a certain time) *prevented the entrance of anything into a certain portion of space*—space being in its own nature penetrable. Henceforward *this portion of space* would be endowed with *impenetrability*, one of the essential qualities of matter; and we have only again to suppose that God communicated the same impenetrability to *another portion of space*, and we should then obtain an idea of the *mobility* of matter, another of its essential qualities.' See relative note in Clarendon Press edition, vol. ii, p. 321.

[2] The origination of a being possessing moral independence or freedom remains the crux of philosophical speculation. Locke says in a letter to Molyneux: 'I own freely to you the weakness of my understanding, that though it be unquestionable that there is omnipotence and omniscience in God our Maker, yet I cannot make freedom in man consistent with omnipotence or omniscience in God—though I am as fully persuaded of both as of any truths I most freely assent to.'

[3] Inserted in the second edition.

out of nothing being once admitted, the creation of all other, but the *Creator* himself, may with the same ease, be supposed.

19. But you will say, Is it not impossible to admit of the making anything out of nothing, since we cannot possibly conceive it ? I answer, No : (1) Because it is not reasonable to deny the power of an infinite Being, because we cannot comprehend its operations. We do not deny other effects upon this ground, because we cannot possibly conceive the manner of their production. We cannot conceive how anything but impulse of body can move body ; and yet that is not a reason sufficient to make us deny it possible, against the constant experience we have of it in ourselves, in all our voluntary motions; which are produced in us only by the free action or thought of our own minds, and are not, nor can be, the effects of the impulse or determination of the motion of blind matter, in or upon our bodies ; for then it could not be in our power or choice to alter it. For example : my right hand writes whilst my left hand is still ; what causes rest in one and motion in the other ? Nothing but my will, a thought of my mind ; my thought only changing, the right hand rests, and the left hand moves. This is matter of fact which cannot be denied : explain this, and make it intelligible, and then the next step will be to understand creation. [For the giving a new determination to the motion of the animal spirits (which some[1] make use of to explain voluntary motion) clears not the difficulty one jot. To alter the determination of motion being in this case no easier nor less, than to give motion itself ; since the new determination given to the animal spirits must be either immediately by thought, or by some other body put in their way by thought, which was not in their way before, and so must owe its motion to thought ; either of which leaves voluntary motion as unintelligible as it was before.][2] In the meantime, it is an overvaluing ourselves, to reduce all to the narrow measure of our capacities, and to conclude all things impossible to be done, whose manner of doing exceeds our comprehension. This is to make our comprehension infinite, or God finite, when what he can do is limited to what we can conceive of it. If

---

[1] ' some ' = the Cartesians. The futility of the makeshift theory here referred to led to the development of Occasionalism within the Cartesian school. For Locke's own position cf. **IV.** 3. 28 and note 1, p. 285.

[2] Added in second edition.

Ch. 10 *Knowledge of the Existence of a God* 321

you do not understand the operations of your own finite mind, that thinking thing within you, do not deem it strange that you cannot comprehend the operations of that eternal, infinite Mind who made and governs all things, and whom the heaven of heavens cannot contain.[1]

## CHAPTER XI

OF OUR KNOWLEDGE OF THE EXISTENCE OF OTHER THINGS

1. *It is to be had only by sensation.*—The knowledge of our own being we have by intuition. The existence of a God reason [2] clearly makes known to us, as has been shown.

The knowledge of the existence of any other thing we can have only by sensation: for there being no necessary connexion of real existence with any idea a man hath in his memory; nor of any other existence but that of God with the existence of any particular man: no particular man can know the existence of any other being, but only when, by actual operating upon him, it makes itself perceived by him. For the having the idea of anything in our mind no more proves the existence of that thing than the picture of a man evidences his being in the world, or the visions of a dream make thereby a true history.

2. It is therefore the actual receiving of ideas from without that gives us notice of the existence of other things, and makes us know that something doth exist at that time without us which causes that idea in us, though perhaps we neither know nor consider how it does it. For it takes not from the certainty of our senses, and the ideas we receive by them, that we know not the manner wherein they are produced: v. g., whilst I write this, I have, by the paper affecting my eyes, that idea produced in my mind, which whatever object causes, I call white; by which I know that that quality or accident (i. e., whose appearance before my eyes always causes that idea) doth really exist, and hath a being without me. And of this, the greatest assurance I can possibly have, and to which my faculties can attain, is the testimony of my eyes, which are the proper and sole judges of this thing;

[1] Some further criticism of Locke's method of argument in this chapter will be found in the Editor's *Idea of God*, pp. 249 et seq.
[2] Reason, i. e. reasoning, demonstration.

whose testimony I have reason to rely on as so certain, that I can no more doubt, whilst I write this, that I see white and black, and that something really exists that causes that sensation in me, than that I write or move my hand; which is a certainty as great as human nature is capable of, concerning the existence of anything but a man's self alone, and of God.

3. *This, though not so certain as demonstration, yet may be called knowledge, and proves the existence of things without us.*—The notice we have by our senses of the existing of things without us, though it be not altogether so certain as our intuitive knowledge, or the deductions of our reason employed about the clear abstract ideas of our own minds; yet it is an assurance that deserves the name of *knowledge*. If we persuade ourselves that our faculties act and inform us right concerning the existence of those objects that affect them, it cannot pass for an ill-grounded confidence: for I think nobody can, in earnest, be so sceptical as to be uncertain of the existence of those things which he sees and feels.[1] At least, he that can doubt so far (whatever he may have with his own thoughts) will never have any controversy with me; since he can never be sure I say anything contrary to his opinion.[2] As to myself, I think God has given me assurance enough of the existence of things without me; since by their different application I can produce in myself both pleasure and pain, which is one great concernment of my present state. This is certain, the confidence that our faculties do not herein deceive us is the greatest assurance we are capable of concerning the existence of material beings. For we cannot act anything but by our faculties, nor talk of knowledge itself, but by the help of those faculties which are fitted to apprehend even what knowledge is. But besides the assurance we have from our senses themselves, that they do not err in the information they give us of the existence of things without us, when they are affected by them, we are farther confirmed in this assurance by other concurrent reasons.

---

[1] This form of words might be criticized as question-begging. It recalls the expressions in which Berkeley frequently assures us that the ideas of sense *are* the real world, the only real world with which we have any practical concern. But of course Locke only means 'the things which he knows through sight and touch', i.e. through the ideas which reach the mind by these channels.

[2] Because Locke and his arguments are only known to this sceptic through the facts of sense, and therefore subject to the same doubt.

## Ch. 11 *Knowledge of Existence of other Things* 323

4. *Because we cannot have them but by the inlet of the senses.*—First, It is plain those perceptions are produced in us by exterior causes affecting our senses, because those that want the organs [1] of any sense never can have the ideas belonging to that sense produced in their minds. The organs themselves, it is plain, do not produce them; [2] for then the eyes of a man in the dark would produce colours, and his nose smell roses in the winter: but we see nobody gets the relish of a pine-apple till he goes to the Indies where it is, and tastes it.

5. *Because an idea from actual sensation and another from memory are very distinct perceptions.*—Secondly, Because sometimes I find that I cannot avoid the having those ideas produced in my mind. For though when my eyes are shut, or windows fast, I can at pleasure recall to my mind the ideas of light or the sun, which former sensations had lodged in my memory; so I can at pleasure lay by that idea, and take into my view that of the smell of a rose, or taste of sugar. But if I turn my eyes at noon towards the sun, I cannot avoid the ideas which the light or sun then produces in me. So that there is a manifest difference between the ideas laid up in my memory, and those which force themselves upon me, and I cannot avoid having. And therefore it must needs be some exterior cause, and the brisk acting of some objects without me, whose efficacy I cannot resist, that produces those ideas in my mind, whether I will or no. Besides, there is nobody who doth not perceive the difference in himself between contemplating the sun as he hath the idea of it in his memory, and actually looking upon it: of which two, his perception is so distinct, that few of his ideas are more distinguishable one from another. And therefore he hath certain knowledge that they are not both memory, or the actions of his mind, and fancies only within him; but that actual seeing hath a cause without.

6. *Pleasure or pain, which accompanies actual sensation, accompanies not the returning of those ideas without the external objects.*—Thirdly, Add to this, that many of those ideas are produced in us with pain, which afterwards we remember without the least offence. Thus the pain of heat or

[1] The organs are, however, part of the sense-world just as much as the exterior causes.
[2] Abnormal conditions of the sense-organs may give rise to illusions and hallucinations.

cold, when the idea of it is revived in our minds, gives us no disturbance; which, when felt, was very troublesome, and is again, when actually repeated: which is occasioned by the disorder the external object causes in our bodies when applied to it. And we remember the pain of hunger, thirst, or the headache, without any pain at all; which would either never disturb us, or else constantly do it as often as we thought of it, were there nothing more but ideas floating in our minds, and appearances entertaining our fancies, without the real existence of things affecting us from abroad. The same may be said of pleasure accompanying several actual sensations; and though mathematical demonstration depends not upon sense, yet the examining them by diagrams gives great credit to the evidence of our sight, and seems to give it a certainty approaching to that of the demonstration itself. For it would be very strange that a man should allow it for an undeniable truth, that two angles of a figure which he measures by lines and angles of a diagram, should be bigger one than the other, and yet doubt of the existence of those lines and angles which, by looking on, he makes use of to measure that by.

*7. Our senses assist one another's testimony of the existence of outward things.*—Fourthly, Our senses, in many cases, bear witness to the truth of each other's report concerning the existence of sensible things without us. He that sees a fire may, if he doubt whether it be anything more than a bare fancy, feel it too, and be convinced by putting his hand in it; which certainly could never be put into such exquisite pain by a bare idea or phantom, unless that the pain be a fancy too; which yet he cannot, when the burn is well, by raising the idea of it, bring upon himself again.

Thus I see, whilst I write this, I can change the appearance of the paper; and by designing the letters, tell beforehand what new idea it shall exhibit the very next moment, barely by drawing my pen over it: which will neither appear (let me fancy as much as I will) if my hand stand still, or though I move my pen, if my eyes be shut; nor, when those characters are once made on the paper, can I choose afterwards but see them as they are; that is, have the ideas of such letters as I have made. Whence it is manifest that they are not barely the sport and play of my own imagination, when I find that the characters that were made at the pleasure of my own thoughts do not obey them; nor yet cease to be, whenever I shall fancy it, but continue to affect my senses constantly and regularly, according to the figures I made them. To which if we will add, that the sight of those shall, from another man, draw such sounds as I beforehand design they shall stand for, there will be little reason left to doubt that those words I write do really exist without me, when they cause a long series of regular sounds to affect my ears, which could not be the effect of my imagination, nor could my memory retain them in that order.

8. *This certainty is as great as our condition needs.*—But yet, if after all this any one will be so sceptical as to distrust his senses, and to affirm that all we see and hear, feel and taste, think and do, during our whole being, is but the series and deluding appearances of a long dream whereof there is no reality; and therefore will question the existence of all things or our knowledge of anything : I must desire him to consider, that if all be a dream, then he doth but dream that he makes the question ; and so it is not much matter that a waking man should answer him. But yet, if he pleases, he may dream that I make him this answer, that the certainty of things existing *in rerum natura*, when we have the testimony of our senses for it, is not only as great as our frame can attain to, but as our condition needs. For our faculties being suited not to the full extent of being, nor to a perfect, clear, comprehensive knowledge of things free from all doubt and scruple ; but to the preservation of us, in whom they are; and accommodated to the use of life : they serve to our purpose well enough, if they will but give us certain notice of those things which are convenient or inconvenient to us. For he that sees a candle burning, and hath experimented the force of its flame by putting his finger in it, will little doubt that this is something existing without him, which does him harm and puts him to great pain. And if our dreamer pleases to try whether the glowing heat of a glass furnace be barely a wandering imagination in a drowsy man's fancy, by putting his hand into it, he may perhaps be awakened into a certainty, greater than he could wish, that it is something more than bare imagination. So that this evidence is as great as we can desire, being as certain to us as our pleasure or pain, i.e., happiness or misery ; beyond which we have no concernment, either of knowing or being. Such an assurance of the existence of things without us is sufficient to direct us in the attaining the good and avoiding the evil

which is caused by them, which is the important concernment we have of being made acquainted with them.

9. *But reaches no farther than actual sensation.*—In fine, then, when our senses do actually convey into our understandings any idea, we cannot but be satisfied that there doth something at that time really exist without us, which doth affect our senses,[1] and by them give notice of itself to our apprehensive faculties, and actually produce that idea which we then perceive: and we cannot so far distrust their testimony as to doubt that such collections of simple ideas as we have observed by our senses to be united together,[2] do really exist together. But this knowledge extends as far as the present testimony of our senses,[3] employed about particular objects that do then affect them, and no farther. For if I saw such a collection of simple ideas as is wont to be called man, existing together one minute since, and am now alone, I cannot be certain that the same man exists now, since there is no necessary connexion of his existence a minute since with his existence now: by a thousand ways he may cease to be, since I had the testimony of my senses for his existence. And if I cannot be certain that the man I saw last to-day is now in being, I can less be certain that he is so who hath been longer removed from my senses, and I have not seen since yesterday, or since the last year; and much less can I be certain of the existence of men that I never saw. And therefore, though it be highly probable that

---

[1] This is the meagre result which Locke arrives at when he investigates our knowledge of the external world from the point of view of the subject or knower. In Book II, ch. 8 (and generally), he had assumed the reality of a world of material substances with primary and secondary qualities, to which our ideas correspond, either in the way of direct resemblance or as effect to cause. But when he starts in Book IV from the experiences of the individual mind, he gets no farther than the practical assurance of 'some cause' operating at any given moment to produce our involuntary sense-experiences. Berkeley may be said to start from this result. Admitting the necessity of postulating 'some cause', and taking strictly Locke's suggestion that matter may be 'wholly destitute of active power', he proceeds to substitute for Locke's independent world of material things the causal activity of a divine Spirit, operating according to self-imposed rules which we call laws of nature. Cf. Introduction, pp. xliii–iv.

[2] Complex ideas of particular substances.

[3] These are the very words afterwards used by Hume. His whole enquiry is into 'the nature of that evidence which assures us of any real existence and matter of fact beyond the present testimony of our senses or the records of our memory' (*Enquiry*, section 4).

millions of men do now exist, yet whilst I am alone writing this, I have not that certainty of it which we strictly call knowledge; though the great likelihood of it puts me past doubt, and it be reasonable for me to do several things upon the confidence that there are men (and men also of my acquaintance, with whom I have to do) now in the world : but this is but probability, not knowledge.

10. *Folly to expect demonstration in everything.*—Whereby yet we may observe how vain it is to expect demonstration and certainty in things not capable of it, and refuse assent to very rational propositions, and act contrary to very plain and clear truths, because they cannot be made out so evident as to surmount every the least (I will not say reason, but) pretence of doubting. He that, in the ordinary affairs of life, would admit of nothing but direct plain demonstration, would be sure of nothing in this world but of perishing quickly.

11. *Past existence is known by memory.*—As, when our senses are actually employed about any object, we do know that it does exist, so by our memory we may be assured that heretofore things that affected our senses have existed. And thus we have knowledge of the past existence of several things, whereof our senses having informed us, our memories still retain the ideas; and of this we are past all doubt, so long as we remember well. But this knowledge also reaches no farther than our senses have formerly assured us. Thus, seeing water at this instant, it is an unquestionable truth to me that water doth exist; and remembering that I saw it yesterday, it will also be always true, and as long as my memory retains it, always an undoubted proposition to me, that water did exist 10th July 1688; as it will also be equally true that a certain number of very fine colours did exist, which at the same time I saw upon a bubble of that water. But being now quite out of the sight both of the water and bubbles too, it is no more certainly known to me that the water doth now exist than that the bubbles or colours therein do so: it being no more necessary that water should exist to-day because it existed yesterday, than that the colours or bubbles exist to-day because they existed yesterday, though it be exceedingly much more probable; because water hath been observed to continue long in existence, but bubbles and the colours on them quickly cease to be.

12. *The existence of spirits not knowable.*—What ideas we

have of spirits, and how we come by them, I have already shown.[1] But the having the ideas of spirits does not make us know that any such things do exist without us, or that there are any finite spirits,[2] or any other spiritual beings but the eternal God. We have ground from revelation, and several other reasons, to believe with assurance that there are such creatures; but our senses not being able to discover them, we want the means of knowing their particular existences. For we can no more know that there are finite spirits really existing, by the idea we have of such beings in our minds, than by the ideas any one has of fairies or centaurs, he can come to know that things answering those ideas do really exist.

13. *Particular propositions concerning existence are knowable.*—By which it appears that there are two sorts of propositions.[3] (1) There is one sort of propositions concerning the existence of anything answerable to such an idea : as having the idea of an elephant, phoenix, motion, or an angel, in my mind, the first and natural enquiry is, whether such a thing does anywhere exist. And this knowledge is only of particulars. No existence of anything without us, but only of God, can certainly be known farther than our senses inform us. (2) There is another sort of propositions, wherein is expressed the agreement or disagreement of our abstract ideas, and their dependence one on another. Such propositions may be universal and certain. So, having the idea of God and myself, of fear and obedience, I cannot but be sure that God is to be feared and obeyed by me : and this proposition will be certain concerning man in general, if I have made an abstract idea of such a species, whereof I am one particular. But yet this proposition, how certain soever, that men ought to fear and obey God, proves not to me the existence of men in the world, but will be true of all such creatures, whenever they do exist : which certainty of such general propositions depends on the agreement or disagreement to be discovered in those abstract ideas.

14. *And general propositions concerning abstract ideas.*— In the former case, our knowledge is the consequence of the

[1] e. g., Bk. II, ch. 23, sections 5, 15, 19-22 ; Bk. IV. 3. 27.

[2] Locke is here referring not to his own existence or the existence of other men, but to that of angels or other unembodied spirits.

[3] These ' two sorts of propositions ' are precisely Hume's ' relations of ideas ' and ' matters of facts '.

existence of things, producing ideas in our minds by our senses: in the latter, knowledge is the consequence of the ideas (be they what they will) that are in our minds, producing there general certain propositions. Many of these are called *aeternae veritates*, and all of them indeed are so; not from being written, all or any of them, in the minds of all men; or that they were any of them propositions in any one's mind till he, having got the abstract ideas, joined or separated them by affirmation or negation: but because, being once made about abstract ideas so as to be true, they will, whenever they can be supposed to be made again at any time, past or to come, by a mind having those ideas, always actually be true. For names being supposed to stand perpetually for the same ideas, and the same ideas having immutably the same habitudes one to another, propositions concerning any abstract ideas that are once true must needs be eternal verities.

## CHAPTER XII

#### OF THE IMPROVEMENT OF OUR KNOWLEDGE

1. *Knowledge is not from maxims.*—It having been the common received opinion amongst men of letters, that *maxims*[1] were the foundation of all knowledge; and that the sciences were each of them built upon certain *praecognita*, the beaten road of the Schools has been, to lay down in the beginning one or more general propositions, as foundations whereon to build the knowledge that was to be had of that subject. These doctrines thus laid down for foundations of any science were called *principles*, as the beginnings from which we must set out. [2.] One thing which might probably give an occasion to this way of proceeding in other sciences was, as I suppose, the good success it seemed to have in mathematics, wherein men being observed to attain a great certainty of knowledge, these sciences came by pre-eminence to be called μαθήματα and μάθησις, learning, or things learned, as having, of all others, the greatest certainty, clearness, and evidence in them.

3. *But from the comparing clear and distinct ideas.*—But if any one will consider, he will (I guess) find that the great

[1] In the opening sections of this chapter he recurs to the theme of ch. 7.

advancement and certainty of real knowledge which men arrived to in these sciences, was not owing to the influence of these principles, nor derived from any peculiar advantage they received from two or three general maxims laid down in the beginning ; but from the clear, distinct, complete ideas their thoughts were employed about, and the relation of equality and excess so clear between some of them, that they had an intuitive knowledge, and by that, a way to discover it in others, and this without the help of those maxims.

7. *The true method of advancing knowledge is by considering our abstract ideas.*—We must therefore, if we will proceed as reason advises, *adapt our methods of enquiry to the nature of the ideas we examine,* and the truth we search after. General and certain truths are only founded in the habitudes and relations of abstract ideas. A sagacious and methodical application of our thoughts, for the finding out these relations, is the only way to discover all that can be put, with truth and certainty concerning them, into general propositions. By what steps we are to proceed in these, is to be learned in the schools of the mathematicians, who, from very plain and easy beginnings, by gentle degrees, and a continued chain of reasonings, proceed to the discovery and demonstration of truths that appear at first sight beyond human capacity. The art of finding proofs, and the admirable methods they have invented for the singling out and laying in order those intermediate ideas that demonstratively show the equality or inequality of unapplicable quantities, is that which has carried them so far, and produced such wonderful and unexpected discoveries.

9. *But knowledge of bodies is to be improved only by experience.*—In our search after the knowledge of *substances* [1] our want of ideas that are suitable to such a way of proceeding obliges us to a quite different method. We advance not here, as in the other (where our abstract ideas are real as well as nominal essences), by contemplating our ideas, and considering their relations and correspondences. The want of ideas of their real essences sends us from our own thoughts to the things themselves as they exist. *Experience here must teach*

[1] Our knowledge of substances has been repeatedly discussed before, notably in chapters 3 and 6 of this Book and in chapter 6 of Bk. III, but some of Locke's phrases in the sections which follow are specially happy expressions of his position and have become historical.

*me* what reason cannot : and it is by trying alone that I can certainly know what other qualities coexist with those of my complex idea, v. g., whether that yellow, heavy, fusible body I call gold be malleable or no ; which experience (which way ever it prove in that particular body I examine) makes me not certain that it is so in all, or any other yellow, heavy, fusible bodies, but that which I have tried.

10. *This may procure us convenience, not science.*—I deny not but a man accustomed to rational and regular experiments shall be able to see farther into the nature of bodies, and guess righter at their yet unknown properties, than one that is a stranger to them : but yet, as I have said, this is but judgement and opinion, not knowledge and certainty. This way of getting and improving our knowledge in substances only by experience and history, which is all that the weakness of our faculties in this state of mediocrity [1] which we are in in this world can attain to, makes me suspect that natural philosophy is not capable of being made a science.[2] We are able, I imagine, to reach very little general knowledge concerning the species of bodies and their several properties. Experiments and historical observations we may have, from which we may draw advantages of ease and health, and thereby increase our stock of conveniences for this life ; but beyond this I fear our talents reach not, nor are our faculties, as I guess, able to advance.

11. *We are fitted for moral knowledge and natural improvements.*—From whence it is obvious to conclude, that since our faculties are not fitted to penetrate into the internal fabric and real essences of bodies; but yet plainly discover to us the being of a God, and the knowledge of ourselves, enough to lead us into a full and clear discovery of our duty and great concernment; it will become us, as rational creatures, to employ those faculties we have about what they are most adapted to, and follow the direction of nature, where it seems to point us out the way. For it is rational to conclude that our proper employment lies in those enquiries, and in that sort of knowledge which is most suited to our natural capacities, and carries

---

[1] Mediocrity—a state intermediate between the animals and angelic intelligences. So again, ch. 14. 2, ' that state of mediocrity and probationership he has been pleased to place us in here '. Cf. Pope :
  Placed on this isthmus of a middle state,
  A Being darkly wise and rudely great.
[2] Cf. IV. 3. 26.

in it our greatest interest, i.e., the condition of our eternal estate. Hence I think I may conclude, that *morality is the proper science and business of mankind in general.*[1]

12. *But must beware of hypotheses and wrong principles.*—I would not therefore be thought to disesteem or dissuade the study of *nature*. I readily agree, the contemplation of his works gives us occasion to admire, revere, and glorify their Author : and if rightly directed, may be of greater benefit to mankind than the monuments of exemplary charity that have, at so great charge, been raised by the founders of hospitals and almshouses. He that first invented printing, discovered the use of the compass, or made public the virtue and right use of *kin-kina*,[2] did more for the propagation of knowledge, for the supplying and increase of useful commodities, and saved more from the grave, than those who built colleges, workhouses, and hospitals. All that I would say is, that we should not be too forwardly possessed with the opinion or expectation of knowledge where it is not to be had, or by ways that will not attain it ; that we should not take doubtful systems for complete sciences, nor unintelligible notions for scientifical demonstrations. In the knowledge of bodies, we must be content to glean what we can from particular experiments ; since we cannot, from a discovery of their real essences, grasp at a time whole sheaves, and in bundles comprehend the nature and properties of whole species together.

13. *The true use of hypotheses.*—Not that we may not, to explain any phenomena of nature, make use of any probable hypothesis whatsoever. Hypotheses, if they are well made, are at least great helps to the memory, and often direct us to new discoveries. But my meaning is, that we should not take up any one too hastily (which the mind, that would always penetrate into the causes of things, and have principles to rest on, is very apt to do), till we have very well examined particulars, and made several experiments in that thing which we would explain by our hypothesis, and see whether it will agree to them all ; whether our principles will carry us quite through, and not be as inconsistent with one phenomenon of nature as they seem to accommodate and explain another.

---

[1] Cf. Pope, *Essay on Man* :
   Know then thyself, presume not God to scan :
   The proper study of mankind is man.

[2] Quinine.

And at least that we take care that the name of *principles* deceive us not, nor impose on us, by making us receive that for an unquestionable truth which is really, at best, but a very doubtful conjecture, such as are most (I had almost said all) of the hypotheses in natural philosophy.[1]

## [CHAPTER XIII

### SOME FARTHER CONSIDERATIONS CONCERNING OUR KNOWLEDGE]

## CHAPTER XIV

### OF JUDGEMENT

1. *Our knowledge being short, we want something else.*—The understanding faculties being given to man, not barely for speculation, but also for the conduct of his life, man would be at a great loss if he had nothing to direct him but what has the certainty of true *knowledge*. [2.] Therefore, as God has set some things in broad daylight; as he has given us some certain knowledge, though limited to a few things in comparison, probably, as a taste of what intellectual creatures are capable of, to excite in us a desire and endeavour after a better state: so in the greatest part of our concernment, he has afforded us only the twilight, as I may so say, of *probability*, suitable, I presume, to that state of mediocrity and probationership he has been pleased to place us in here.

3. *Judgement supplies the want of knowledge.*—The faculty which God has given man to supply the want of clear and certain knowledge, in cases where that cannot be had, is *judgement*: whereby the mind takes its ideas to agree or disagree; or, which is the same, any proposition to be true or false, without perceiving a demonstrative evidence in the proofs. The mind sometimes exercises this judgement out of necessity,

---

[1] Hypothesis is of the very essence of scientific method, yet we find Newton (whose discovery of gravitation is the classical example of hypothesis and verification) saying in the *Principia*, '*Hypotheses non fingo*'. He defines hypothesis as 'whatever is not deduced from the phenomenon', and speaks of 'metaphysical hypotheses' and 'occult causes'. Evidently, therefore, in the language of the time, the term was in bad repute, being associated with speculative and unverifiable theories of a quasi-metaphysical nature.

where demonstrative proofs and certain knowledge are not to be had; and sometimes out of laziness, unskilfulness, or haste, even where demonstrative and certain proofs are to be had. This faculty of the mind, when it is exercised immediately about things, is called *judgement*; when about truths delivered in words, is most commonly called *assent* or *dissent*: which being the most usual way wherein the mind has occasion to employ this faculty, I shall, under these terms, treat of it, as least liable in our language to equivocation.

4. *Judgement is the presuming things to be so without perceiving it.*—Thus the mind has two faculties conversant about truth and falsehood:

First, *Knowledge*, whereby it certainly perceives, and is undoubtedly satisfied of the agreement or disagreement of any ideas.

Secondly, *Judgement*, which is the putting ideas together, or separating them from one another in the mind, when their certain agreement or disagreement is not perceived, but *presumed* to be so; which is, as the word imports, taken to be so before it certainly appears. And if it so unites or separates them as in reality things are, it is right judgement.

## CHAPTER XV

### OF PROBABILITY

1. *Probability is the appearance of agreement upon fallible proofs.*—As demonstration is the showing the agreement or disagreement of two ideas by the intervention of one or more proofs, which have a constant, immutable, and visible connexion one with another; so probability is nothing but the appearance of such an agreement or disagreement by the intervention of proofs, whose connexion is not constant and immutable, or at least is not perceived to be so; but is, or appears for the most part to be so, and is enough to induce the mind to judge the proposition to be true or false, rather than the contrary. For example: In the demonstration of it, a man perceives the certain immutable connexion there is of equality between the three angles of a triangle, and those intermediate ones which are made use of to show their equality to two right ones. But another man, who never took the pains to observe the demonstration, hearing a mathematician, a man

of credit, affirm 'the three angles of a triangle to be equal to two right ones', assents to it, i.e., receives it for true. In which case the foundation of his assent is the probability of the thing, the man on whose testimony he receives it not being wont to affirm anything contrary to, or besides his knowledge, especially in matters of this kind.

2. *It is to supply the want of knowledge.*—Our knowledge, as has been shown, being very narrow, most of the propositions we think, reason, discourse, nay, act upon, are such as we cannot have undoubted knowledge of their truth: yet some of them border so near upon certainty, that we make no doubt at all about them, but assent to them as firmly, and act according to that assent as resolutely, as if they were infallibly demonstrated, and that our knowledge of them was perfect and certain. But, there being degrees herein, from the very neighbourhood of certainty and demonstration, quite down to improbability and unlikeliness, even to the confines of impossibility; and also degrees of assent from full assurance and confidence, quite down to conjecture, doubt, and distrust; I shall come now (having, as I think, found out the bounds of human knowledge and certainty), in the next place, to consider *the several degrees and grounds of probability, and assent or faith.*

3. *Being that which makes us presume things to be true, before we know them to be so.*—Probability is likeliness to be true; the very notation of the word signifying such a proposition, for which there be arguments or proofs to make it pass, or be received for true. The entertainment the mind gives this sort of propositions is called *belief, assent,* or *opinion,* which is the admitting or receiving any proposition for true, upon arguments or proofs that are found to persuade us to receive it as true, without certain knowledge that it is so. Herein lies the difference between probability and certainty, faith and knowledge, that in all the parts of knowledge there is intuition; each immediate idea, each step has its visible and certain connexion; in belief not so. That which makes me believe, is something extraneous to the thing I believe; something not evidently joined on both sides to, and so not manifestly showing the agreement or disagreement, of those ideas that are under consideration.

4. Probability then being to supply the defect of our knowledge, the grounds of it are these two following:

First, The conformity of anything with our own knowledge, observation, and experience.

Secondly, The testimony of others, vouching their observation and experience. In the testimony of others is to be considered: (1) The number. (2) The integrity. (3) The skill of the witnesses. (4) The design of the author, where it is a testimony out of a book cited. (5) The consistency of the parts and circumstances of the relation. (6) Contrary testimonies.

5. The mind, if it will proceed rationally, ought to examine all the grounds of probability, and see how they make more or less for or against any proposition, before it assents to or dissents from it; and upon a due balancing the whole, reject or receive it with a more or less firm assent proportionably to the preponderancy of the greater grounds of probability on one side or the other. For example: If I myself see a man walk on the ice, it is past probability; it is knowledge. But if another tells me, he saw a man in England, in the midst of a sharp winter, walk upon water hardened with cold, this has so great conformity with what is usually observed to happen, that I am disposed, by the nature of the thing itself, to assent to it, unless some manifest suspicion attend the relation of that matter of fact. But if the same thing be told to one born between the tropics, who never saw nor heard of any such thing before, there the whole probability relies on testimony; and as the relators are more in number, and of more credit, and have no interest to speak contrary to the truth; so that matter of fact is like to find more or less belief. Though to a man, whose experience has been always quite contrary, and who has never heard of anything like it, the most untainted credit of a witness will scarcely be able to find belief. As it happened to a Dutch ambassador, who entertaining the King of Siam [1] with the particularities of Holland, which he was inquisitive after, amongst other things, told him, that the water in his country would sometimes, in cold weather, be so hard, that men walked upon it, and that it would bear an elephant, if he were there. To which the king replied, ' Hitherto I have believed the strange things you have told me, because I look upon you as a sober fair man; but now I am sure you lie'.

---

[1] Presumably this King of Siam is the ' Indian prince ' mentioned by Hume in his argument on Miracles (*Enquiry*, section 10).

## CHAPTER XVI

### OF THE DEGREES OF ASSENT

1. *Our assent ought to be regulated by the grounds of probability.*

2. *These cannot always be all actually in view, and then we must content ourselves with the remembrance that we once saw ground for such a degree of assent.*

3. *The ill consequence of this, if our former judgement were not rightly made.*—I cannot but own that men's sticking to their past judgement, and adhering firmly to conclusions formerly made, is often the cause of great obstinacy in error and mistake. But the fault is not, that they rely on their memories for what they have before well judged, but because they judged before they had well examined. May we not find a great number (not to say the greatest part) of men that think they have formed right judgements of several matters, and that for no other reason but because they never thought otherwise? who imagine themselves to have judged right, only because they never questioned, never examined their own opinions? Which is indeed to think they judged right, because they never judged at all. And yet these, of all men, hold their opinions with the greatest stiffness; those being generally the most fierce and firm in their tenets, who have least examined them. What we once know, we are certain is so; and we may be secure that there are no latent proofs undiscovered which may overturn our knowledge, or bring it in doubt. But in matters of probability, it is not in every case we can be sure that we have all the particulars before us, that any way concern the question; and that there is no evidence behind, and yet unseen, which may cast the probability on the other side, and outweigh all that at present seems to preponderate with us. And yet we are forced to determine ourselves on the one side or other. The conduct of our lives, and the management of our great concerns, will not bear delay.

4. *The right use of it, mutual charity and forbearance.*—Since therefore it is unavoidable to the greatest part of men, if not all, to have several *opinions*, without certain and indubitable proofs of their truths; it would, methinks, become

all men to maintain peace and the common offices of humanity and friendship in the diversity of opinions. We should do well to commiserate our mutual ignorance, and endeavour to remove it in all the gentle and fair ways of information; and not instantly treat others ill, as obstinate and perverse, because they will not renounce their own. and receive our opinions.[1]

5. *Probability is either of matter of fact or speculation.*—But, to return to the grounds of assent, and the several degrees of it: we are to take notice that the propositions we receive upon inducements of probability are of two sorts; either concerning some particular existence, or, as it is usually termed, matter of fact, which falling under observation, is capable of human testimony; or else concerning things which being beyond the discovery of our senses, are not capable of any such testimony.

6. The first and *highest degree of probability* is, when the general consent of all men in all ages, as far as it can be known, concurs with a man's constant and never-failing experience in like cases, to confirm the truth of any particular matter of fact attested by fair witnesses : such are all the stated constitutions and properties of bodies, and the regular proceedings of causes and effects in the ordinary course of nature. This we call an argument from the nature of things themselves. For what our own and other men's constant observation has found always to be after the same manner, that we with reason conclude to be the effects of steady and regular causes, though they come not within the reach of our knowledge. These *probabilities* rise so near to *certainty*, that they govern our thoughts as absolutely, and influence all our actions as fully, as the most evident demonstration ; and in what concerns us, we make little or no difference between them and certain knowledge. Our belief thus grounded rises to *assurance*.

---

[1] Locke's argument here is the same as in his *Letters on Toleration*. ' The toleration for which Locke argued, and which was one of his leading ideas, implied a revolution in the mediaeval conception of human life. It expressed the revolt from dogmatic authority, in favour of a critical treatment of beliefs, that was becoming a characteristic of the modern spirit. . . . In religion it implied a protest against those who in theology assume absolute certainty in questions which must be determined by balanced probabilities, and by the moral evidence that appeals to faith. The enforcement of a general toleration, amidst increasing religious differences, . . . is the most important practical application of Locke's answer in the *Essay* to his own memorable question about the nature and extent of a human understanding of the universe and of God' (Fraser).

7. Secondly, The next degree of probability is, when I find by my own experience, and the agreement of all others that mention it, a thing to be for the most part so, and that the particular instance of it is attested by many and undoubted witnesses: v.g., history giving us such an account of men in all ages, and my own experience, as far as I had an opportunity to observe, confirming it, that most men prefer their private advantage to the public. If all historians that write of Tiberius, say that Tiberius did so, it is extremely probable. And in this case, our assent has a sufficient foundation to raise itself to a degree which we may call *confidence*.

8. Thirdly, In things that happen indifferently, as that a bird should fly this or that way; that it should thunder on a man's right or left hand, &c., when any particular matter of fact is vouched by the concurrent testimony of unsuspected witnesses, there our assent is also unavoidable.

9. *Experience and testimonies clashing, infinitely vary the degrees of probability.*—Thus far the matter goes easy enough. Probability upon such grounds carries so much evidence with it, that it naturally determines the judgement, and leaves us as little liberty to believe or disbelieve, as a demonstration does whether we will know or be ignorant. The difficulty is, when testimonies contradict common experience, and the reports of history and witnesses clash with the ordinary course of nature, or with one another. This only may be said in general, that as the arguments and proofs, *pro* and *con*, upon due examination, nicely weighing every particular circumstance, shall to any one appear upon the whole matter, in a greater or less degree, to preponderate on either side; so they are fitted to produce in the mind such different entertainment as we call *belief, conjecture, guess, doubt, wavering, distrust, disbelief*, &c.

10. *Traditional testimonies, the farther removed the less their proof.*—This is what concerns assent in matters wherein testimony is made use of; concerning which, I think it may not be amiss to take notice of a rule observed in the law of England, which is, That though the attested copy of a record be good proof, yet the copy of a copy never so well attested, and by never so credible witnesses, will not be admitted as a proof in judicature. This practice, if it be allowable in the decisions of right and wrong, carries this observation along with it, viz., That any testimony, the farther off it is from the original truth,

the less force and proof it has. The being and existence of the thing itself, is what I call the original truth. A credible man vouching his knowledge of it, is a good proof : but if another equally credible do witness it from his report, the testimony is weaker ; and a third that attests the hearsay of an hearsay, is yet less considerable. So that, in traditional truths, each remove weakens the force of the proof. This I thought necessary to be taken notice of : because I find amongst some men the quite contrary commonly practised, who look on opinions to gain force by growing older ; and what a thousand years since would not, to a rational man, contemporary with the first voucher, have appeared at all probable, is now urged as certain beyond all question, only because several have since, from him, said it one after another. Upon this ground, propositions, evidently false or doubtful enough in their first beginning, come, by an inverted rule of probability, to pass for authentic truths.

11. *Yet history is of great use.*—I would not be thought here to lessen the credit and use of history : it is all the light we have in many cases ; and we receive from it a great part of the useful truths we have, with a convincing evidence. But this truth itself forces me to say, That no probability can arise higher than its first original. What has no other evidence than the single testimony of one only witness, must stand or fall by his only testimony, whether good, bad, or indifferent ; and though cited afterwards by hundreds of others, one after another, is so far from receiving any strength thereby, that it is only the weaker. Passion, interest, inadvertency, mistake of his meaning, and a thousand odd reasons or capricios men's minds are acted by (impossible to be discovered), may make one man quote another man's words or meaning wrong. He that has but ever so little examined the citations of writers, cannot doubt how little credit the quotations deserve, where the originals are wanting ; and consequently how much less quotations of quotations can be relied on. This is certain, that what in one age was affirmed upon slight grounds, can never after come to be more valid in future ages by being often repeated.

12. *In things which sense cannot discover, analogy is the great rule of probability.*—The probabilities we have hitherto mentioned are only such as concern matter of fact, and such things as are capable of observation and testimony. There

remains that other sort, concerning which men entertain opinions with variety of assent, though the things be such that, falling not under the reach of our senses, they are not capable of testimony. Such are, (1) The existence, nature, and operations of finite immaterial beings without us, as spirits, angels, devils, &c., or the existence of material beings, which, either for their smallness in themselves, or remoteness from us, our senses cannot take notice of : as whether there be any plants, animals, and intelligent inhabitants in the planets, and other mansions of the vast universe. (2) Concerning the manner of operation in most parts of the works of nature ; wherein, though we see the sensible effects, yet their causes are unknown, and we perceive not the ways and manner how they are produced. We see animals are generated, nourished and move ; the loadstone draws iron ; and the parts of a candle, successively melting, turn into flame, and give us both light and heat. These and the like effects we see and know ; but the causes that operate, and the manner they are produced in, we can only guess and probably conjecture. *Analogy* in these matters is the only help we have, and it is from that alone we draw all our grounds of probability. Thus observing that the bare rubbing of two bodies violently one upon another produces heat, and very often fire itself, we have reason to think that what we call heat and fire consists in a violent agitation of the imperceptible minute parts of the burning matter. Observing likewise that the different refractions of pellucid bodies produce in our eyes the different appearances of several colours; and also that the different ranging and laying the superficial parts of several bodies, as of velvet, watered silk, &c., does the like, we think it probable that the colour and shining of bodies is in them nothing but the different arrangement and refraction of their minute and insensible parts. Thus finding in all parts of the creation that fall under human observation, that there is a gradual connexion of one with another, without any great or discernible gaps between, in all that great variety of things we see in the world, which are so closely linked together that, in the several ranks of beings, it is not easy to discover the bounds betwixt them, we have reason to be persuaded that by such gentle steps things ascend upwards in degrees of perfection.[1] It is a hard matter to say where sensible and

[1] Locke develops here a speculative idea already broached in Book III. 6. 12, that of a continuous evolution and a graded hierarchy of

rational begin, and where insensible and irrational end; and who is there quick-sighted enough to determine precisely which is the lowest species of living things, and which the first of those which have no life? Things, as far as we can observe, lessen and augment, as the quantity does in a regular cone; where, though there be a manifest odds betwixt the bigness of the diameter at a remote distance, yet the difference between the upper and the under, where they touch one another, is hardly discernible. The difference is exceeding great between some men and some animals : but if we will compare the understanding and abilities of some men and some brutes, we shall find so little difference that it will be hard to say, that that of the man is either clearer or larger. Observing, I say, such gradual and gentle descents downwards in those parts of the creation that are beneath men, the rule of analogy may make it probable that it is so also in things above us and our observation ; and that there are several ranks of intelligent beings, excelling us in several degrees of perfection, ascending upwards towards the infinite perfection of the Creator, by gentle steps and differences, that are every one at no great distance from the next to it.

13. *One case where contrary experience lessens not the testimony.*—Though the common experience and the ordinary course of things have justly a mighty influence on the minds of men, to make them give or refuse credit to anything proposed to their belief ; yet there is one case wherein the strangeness of the fact lessens not the assent to a fair testimony given of it. For where such supernatural events are suitable to ends aimed at by him who has the power to change the course of nature, there, under such circumstances, they may be the fitter to procure belief, by how much the more they are beyond or contrary to ordinary observation. This is the proper case of *miracles*, which, well attested, do not only find credit them-

beings. Berkeley quotes the Neoplatonists : ' Iamblichus teacheth, what is also a received notion of the Pythagoreans and Platonists, that there is no chasm in nature, but a *chain* or *scale* of beings, rising by gentle uninterrupted graduations from the lowest to the highest, each nature being perfected by participation in a higher ' (*Siris*, section 274). *Siris*, the title of his latest work, is meant by Berkeley to express this conception of a chain (σειρά). It is the central idea of Leibniz's Monadology, and it is congenial to modern thought, dominated by the general conception of evolution.

selves, but give it also to other truths which need such confirmation.

14. *The bare testimony of revelation is the highest certainty.*—Besides those we have hitherto mentioned, there is one sort of propositions that challenge the highest degree of our assent, upon bare testimony, whether the thing proposed agree or disagree with common experience and the ordinary course of things or no. The reason whereof is, because the testimony is of such an one as cannot deceive nor be deceived, and that is of God himself. This carries with it assurance beyond doubt, evidence beyond exception. This is called by a peculiar name *revelation*, and our assent to it, *faith*; which as absolutely determines our minds and as perfectly excludes all wavering, as our knowledge itself; and we may as well doubt of our own being, as we can whether any revelation from God be true. So that faith is a settled and sure principle of assent and assurance, and leaves no manner of room for doubt or hesitation. Only we must be sure that it be a divine revelation, and that we understand it right: else we shall expose ourselves to all the extravagancy of enthusiasm, and all the error of wrong principles, if we have faith and assurance in what is not divine revelation. And therefore in those cases, our assent can be rationally no higher than the evidence of its being a revelation, and that this is the meaning of the expressions it is delivered in. If the evidence of its being a revelation, or that this is its true sense, be only on probable proofs, our assent can reach no higher than an assurance or diffidence, arising from the more or less apparent probability of the proofs. But of faith, and the precedency it ought to have before other arguments of persuasion, I shall speak more hereafter,[1] where I treat of it as it is ordinarily placed, in contradistinction to reason; though, in truth, it be nothing else but an assent founded on the highest reason.

[1] Ch. 18.

## CHAPTER XVII

### OF REASON

1. *Various significations of the word reason.*—The word *reason*, in the English language, has different significations : [1] sometimes it is taken for true and clear principles ; sometimes for clear and fair deductions from those principles ; and sometimes for the cause,[2] and particularly the final cause. But the consideration I shall have of it here is in a signification different from all these ; and that is, as it stands for a faculty in man, that faculty whereby man is supposed to be distinguished from beasts, and wherein it is evident he much surpasses them.

2. *Wherein reasoning consists.*—If general knowledge, as has been shown, consists in a perception of the agreement or disagreement of our own ideas; and the knowledge of the existence of all things without us (except only of a God) be had only by our senses ; what room then is there for the exercise of any

---

[1] 'Reason' with Locke generally means 'reasoning' or the discursive faculty, a usage common throughout the eighteenth century. Thus Reid (*Inquiry*, 2. 6) says, 'First principles fall not within the province of reason, but of common sense'. The same usage is revived in Lord Balfour's *Foundations of Belief*, when he opposes Authority to Reason, and insists on ' the comparative pettiness of the rôle played by reasoning in human affairs'. Reason is used throughout Lord Balfour's argument as interchangeable with reasoning or conscious logical ratiocination, the 'intellect', or ' discursive reason', which is only permitted, he says, to have a hand in the simplest jobs. But at other times he speaks of Reason as ' the roof and crown of things ', of Naturalism as deposing ' Reason from its ancient position as the ground of all existence ', and of all things as working together ' towards a reasonable end '. This larger sense of the term, in which Reason is opposed to the understanding or calculating intellect, is more usual among idealist writers of the nineteenth century, partly due to the influence of Coleridge, following German precedents. But Reid himself restores the larger sense. Reason, he says, has two offices or degrees. ' The first is to judge of things self-evident ; the second to draw conclusions that are not self-evident from those that are. The first of these is the province and sole province of common sense.' Common sense, in his meaning of the term—the intuitive intelligence, the source of the principles on which our thinking and our action depend—is therefore no longer distinguished from reason, but identified with one branch of it, and that the highest.

[2] In a loose and popular sense we might say, for example, that the reason ( = the cause) of a fire was a match dropped among the straw. We talk more legitimately of the ' reason ' of any arrangement, meaning the purpose it is intended to serve.

other faculty but outward sense and inward perception? What need is there of reason? Very much; both for the enlargement of our knowledge and regulating our assent: for it hath to do both in knowledge and opinion, and is necessary and assisting to all our other intellectual faculties, and indeed contains two of them, viz., *sagacity* and *illation*. By the one it finds out, and by the other it so orders, the intermediate ideas as to discover what connexion there is in each link of the chain, whereby the extremes are held together; and thereby, as it were, to draw into view the truth sought for, which is that we call *illation*[1] or *inference*, and consists in nothing but the perception of the connexion there is between the ideas in each step of the deduction; whereby the mind comes to see either the certain agreement or disagreement of any two ideas, as in demonstration, in which it arrives at knowledge, or their probable connexion, on which it gives or withholds its assent, as in opinion. Sense and intuition reach but a very little way. The greatest part of our knowledge depends upon deductions and intermediate ideas: and in those cases where we are fain to substitute assent instead of knowledge, and take propositions for true without being certain they are so, we have need to find out, examine, and compare the grounds of their probability. In both these cases the faculty which finds out the means, and rightly applies them to discover certainty in the one, and probability in the other, is that which we call reason.

3. So that we may in reason consider these *four degrees*: The first and highest is the discovering and finding out of proofs; the second, the regular and methodical disposition of them, and laying them in a clear and fit order, to make their connexion and force be plainly and easily perceived; the third is the perceiving their connexion; and the fourth, the making a right conclusion. These several degrees may be observed in any mathematical demonstration: it being one thing, to perceive the connexion of each part, as the demonstration is made by another; another, to perceive the dependence of the conclusion on all the parts; a third, to make out a demonstration clearly and neatly one's self; and something different from all these, to have first found out those intermediate ideas or proofs by which it is made.

4. *Syllogism not the great instrument of reason.*—There is one

[1] 'Illation' has quite gone out of use, but Newman uses the adjectival form in a chapter on 'the illative sense' in his *Grammar of Assent*.

thing more which I shall desire to be considered concerning reason; and that is, whether *syllogism*, as is generally thought, be the proper instrument of it, and the usefullest way of exercising this faculty. The causes I have to doubt are these :

Because syllogism serves our reason but in one only of the fore-mentioned parts of it ; and that is, to show the connexion of the proofs in any one instance, and no more ; but in this it is of no great use, since the mind can perceive such connexion where it really is, as easily, nay perhaps better, without it.

If we will observe the actings of our own minds, we shall find that we reason best and clearest, when we only observe the connexion of the proof, without reducing our thoughts to any rule of syllogism.[1] And therefore we may take notice that there are many men that reason exceeding clear and rightly, who know not how to make a syllogism ; and I believe scarce any one ever makes syllogisms in reasoning within himself. Indeed, syllogism is made use of, on occasion, to discover a fallacy hid in a rhetorical flourish, or cunningly wrapped up in a smooth period ; and stripping an absurdity of the cover of wit and good language, show it in its naked deformity. [[2] But the weakness or fallacy of such a loose discourse it shows, by the artificial form it is put into, only to those who have thoroughly studied *mode* and *figure*, and have so examined the many ways that three propositions may be put together, as to know which of them does certainly conclude right, and which not, and upon what grounds it is that they do so. If syllogisms must be taken for the only proper instrument of reason and

---

[1] There runs through Locke's attack on syllogism in this chapter the same misconception which characterizes his polemic against ' principles ' and ' maxims '. He supposes the defenders of syllogism to allege that, wherever the reasoning process takes place, the steps are consciously thrown into syllogistic form with all the apparatus of mood and figure. But it is obvious that what logic gives us is the reflective analysis of a process which went on spontaneously without reflection long before the science of logic was dreamt of. It brings to light and formulates the principles on which men had all along been unconsciously proceeding, and to which our reasonings must knowingly or unknowingly conform, if they are to be valid ; but for the ordinary business of thinking there is little virtue in a knowledge of the abstract formulae. In spite of this radical misconception, some of Locke's remarks on the actual process of reasoning are both shrewd and fresh.

[2] This long passage, enclosed in brackets, was introduced in the fourth edition, taking the place of a single sentence in the previous editions

means of knowledge, it will follow that before Aristotle there was not one man that did or could know anything by reason ; and that, since the invention of syllogisms, there is not one of ten thousand that doth.

But God has not been so sparing to men to make them barely two-legged creatures, and left it to Aristotle to make them rational. God has been more bountiful to mankind than so. He has given them a mind that can reason, without being instructed in methods of syllogizing. The understanding is not taught to reason by these rules ; it has a native faculty to perceive the coherence or incoherence of its ideas, and can range them right, without any such perplexing repetitions. I say not this any way to lessen Aristotle, whom I look on as one of the greatest men amongst the ancients ; whose large views, acuteness and penetration of thought, and strength of judgement, few have equalled ; and who, in this very invention of forms of argumentation, wherein the conclusion may be shown to be rightly inferred, did great service against those who were not ashamed to deny anything.[1] And I readily own that all right reasoning may be reduced to his forms of syllogism.[2] But yet I think, without any diminution to him, I may truly say, that they are not the only, nor the best way of reasoning, for the leading of those into truth who are willing to find it. And he himself, it is plain, found out some forms to be conclusive and others not, not by the forms themselves, but by the original way of knowledge, i.e., by the visible agreement of ideas.] Tell a country gentlewoman that the wind is southwest, and the weather louring and like to rain, and she will easily understand it is not safe for her to go abroad thin clad in such a day, after a fever : she clearly sees the probable connexion of all these, viz., south-west wind, and clouds, rain, wetting, taking cold, relapse, and danger of death, without

[1] The science of logic did actually take its rise in the analysis and exposure of the tricks and quibbles of sophistical reasoners, as we see in the *Euthydemus* and other dialogues of Plato, and in Aristotle's *De sophisticis elenchis*, which, though it now appears at the end of the *Organon* (like an appendix on Fallacies in a modern logic-book), was really the starting-point of the whole. From the study of fallacious reasonings, Aristotle was led back to formulate, in the syllogism, the laws of valid or conclusive reasoning, and, in the so-called laws of thought, the fundamental conditions of intelligible affirmation and denial.

[2] This grants all that any intelligent defender of the syllogism would claim for it—more, indeed, than would be conceded by many modern logicians.

tying them together in those artificial and cumbersome fetters of several syllogisms, that clog and hinder the mind, which proceeds from one part to another quicker and clearer without them. And I think every one will perceive in mathematical demonstrations, that the knowledge gained thereby comes shortest and clearest without syllogism.[1]

[[2] To infer is nothing but by virtue of one proposition laid down as true, to draw in another as true; v.g., let this be the proposition laid down, 'Men shall be punished in another world', and from thence be inferred this other, 'Then men can determine themselves'. The question now is, to know whether the mind has made this inference right or no; if it has made it by finding out the intermediate ideas, and taking a view of the connexion of them, placed in a due order, it has proceeded rationally, and made a right inference. If it has done it without such a view, it has not so much made an inference that will hold, as shown a willingness to have it be, or be taken for such. But in neither case is it syllogism that discovered those ideas, or showed the connexion of them; for they must be both found out, and the connexion everywhere perceived, before they can rationally be made use of in syllogism: unless it can be said that any idea, without considering what connexion it hath with the two other, whose agreement should be shown by it, will do well enough in a syllogism, and may be taken at a venture for the *medius terminus* to prove any conclusion.[3] But this nobody

---

[1] Recent logicians very generally reject the claim of syllogism to be the exclusive form of deductive reasoning. It is a natural form, they hold, only within the relation of subject and predicate; and the reduction to syllogistic form of reasonings dealing with other relations (such as those of space, time, degree, &c.) is illusory, seeing that the major premiss (which it is necessary to construct) simply restates in an abstract form the principle intuitively apprehended in the original argument. We may construct the major, 'Things which are equal to the same thing are equal to one another', and conclude that as A and C are equal to the same thing (B), therefore they are equal to one another. But unless the truth of the equation ' $A = B = C$ ' was intuitively apprehended, there would be no warrant for the major premiss with which we artificially head the new argument. Direct non-syllogistic reasonings of the type exemplified are sometimes spoken of as 'systematic' or 'constructional' inferences; and in text-books on formal logic the title 'logic of relations' is given to this extension of logical theory.

[2] What follows, as far as the middle of p. 350, was introduced in the fourth edition. It may be compared with the long passage (pp. 303–5) inserted at the same time in the chapter on Maxims.

[3] For precisely the same reasons Spencer pronounces the syllogism, in the logical order of its premisses, to be 'a psychological impossi-

will say; because it is by virtue of the perceived agreement of the intermediate idea with the extremes, that the extremes are concluded to agree; and therefore each intermediate idea must be such as, in the whole chain, hath a visible connexion with those two it is placed between. In the instance above mentioned the mind, seeing the connexion there is between the idea of men's punishment in the other world and the idea of God punishing, between God punishing and the justice of the punishment, between justice of punishment and guilt, between guilt and a power to do otherwise, between a power to do otherwise and freedom, and between freedom and self-determination, sees the connexion between men and self-determination.

Now I ask whether the connexion of the extremes be not more clearly seen in this simple and natural disposition than in the perplexed repetitions and jumble of five or six syllogisms. For the natural order of the connecting ideas must direct the order of the syllogisms, and a man must see the connexion of each intermediate idea with those that it connects, before he can with reason make use of it in a syllogism. And when all those syllogisms are made, neither those that are nor those that are not logicians will see the force of the argumentation, i.e., the connexion of the extremes, one jot the better.

Of what use, then, are syllogisms? I answer, Their chief and main use is in the Schools, where men are allowed without shame to deny the agreement of ideas that do manifestly agree; or out of the Schools, to those who from thence have learned without shame to deny the connexion of ideas, which even to themselves is visible. But to an ingenuous searcher after truth, who has no other aim but to find it, there is no need of any such form to force the allowing of the inference; the truth and reasonableness of it is better seen in ranging of the ideas in a simple and plain order. And hence it is that men, in their own enquiries after truth, never use syllogisms to convince themselves, because, before they can put them into a syllogism, they must see the connexion that is between the

bility'. The connexion of subject and predicate affirmed in the conclusion must be present in the first instance to the mind, as a suggestion, before we proceed to think of this or the other middle term, which may prove it or disprove it. Hence, as he says, 'the process of thought which the syllogism seeks to describe is *not that by which the inference is reached, but that by which it is justified*; and in its totality it is not gone through at all, unless the need for justification is suggested' (*Principles of Psychology*, ii. 97–8).

intermediate idea and the two other ideas it is set between and applied to, to show their agreement ; and when they see that, they see whether the inference be good or no ; and so syllogism comes too late to settle it.

I have had experience how ready some men are, when all the use which they have been wont to ascribe to anything is not allowed, to cry out, that I am for laying it wholly aside. But to prevent such unjust and groundless imputations, I tell them, that I am not for taking away any helps to the understanding in the attainment of knowledge. And if men skilled in and used to syllogisms find them assisting to their reason in the discovery of truth, I think they ought to make use of them. All that I aim at is, that they should not ascribe more to these forms than belongs to them. Some eyes want spectacles to see things clearly and distinctly ; but let not those that use them therefore say, nobody can see clearly without them.]

6. *Serves not to increase our knowledge, but fence with it.*—But let it help us (as perhaps may be said) in convincing men of their errors and mistakes ; (and yet I would fain see the man that was forced out of his opinion by dint of syllogism) yet still it fails our reason in that part which, if not its highest perfection, is yet certainly its hardest task, and that which we most need its help in ; and that is, *the finding out of proofs, and making new discoveries.*[1] The rules of syllogism serve not to furnish the mind with those intermediate ideas that may show the connexion of remote ones. This way of reasoning discovers no new proofs, but is the art of marshalling and ranging the old ones we have already. The forty-seventh proposition of the First Book of Euclid is very true ; but the discovery of it, I think, not owing to any rules of common logic. A man knows first, and then he is able to prove syllogistically.

[1] If logic did this, it would include all the sciences in itself. All that logic can teach us is the nature of evidence or conclusive proof. In all that concerns discovery—the formation of hypotheses and the devising of experiments—we are irretrievably dependent upon what Locke calls the 'sagacity' of the individual investigator, or to put it higher, upon his imagination, nourished by long familiarity with the range of facts in which his work lies. Bacon brought the same accusation against the old logic, and dreamt of a new logic as an *ars inveniendi*, which would equalize all intellects and yield us an uninterrupted harvest of discoveries and inventions. But the method he devised is not the method by which science has actually advanced.

So that syllogism comes after knowledge, and then a man has little or no need of it. But it is chiefly by the finding out those ideas that show the connexion of distant ones, that our stock of knowledge is increased, and that useful arts and sciences are advanced. Syllogism, at best, is but the art of fencing with the little knowledge we have, without making any addition to it. And if a man should employ his reason all this way, he will not do much otherwise than he who, having got some iron out of the bowels of the earth, should have it beaten up all into swords, and put it into his servants' hands to fence with and bang one another. And I am apt to think, that he who shall employ all the force of his reason only in brandishing of syllogisms, will discover very little of that mass of knowledge which lies yet concealed in the secret recesses of nature; and which, I am apt to think, native rustic reason (as it formerly has done) is likelier to open a way to, and add to the common stock of mankind.

7. *Other helps should be sought.*—I doubt not, nevertheless, but there are ways to be found to assist our reason in this most useful part; and this the judicious Hooker [1] encourages me to say, who, in his *Eccl. Pol.* lib. i. sec. 6, speaks thus: 'If there might be added the right helps of true art and learning, (which helps, I must plainly confess, this age of the world, carrying the name of a learned age, doth neither much know nor generally regard,) there would undoubtedly be almost as much difference in maturity of judgement between men therewith inured, and that which now men are, as between men that are now, and innocents.' I do not pretend to have found or discovered here any of those 'right helps of art' this great man of deep thought mentions: but this is plain, that syllogism, and the logic now in use, which were as well known in his days, can be none of those he means. It is sufficient for me, if by a discourse perhaps something out of the way, I am sure, as to me, wholly new and unborrowed, I shall have given an occasion to others to cast about for new discoveries, and to seek in their own thoughts for those right helps of art, which will scarce be found, I fear, by those who servilely confine themselves to the rules and dictates of others. But I can be bold to say, that this age is adorned with some men of that strength of

---

[1] Richard Hooker, whom Locke greatly admired, died in 1600. The first four books of his *Ecclesiastical Polity* were published in 1594.

judgement and largeness of comprehension, that if they would employ their thoughts on this subject, could open new and undiscovered ways to the advancement of knowledge.[1]

8. *We reason about particulars.*—It is fit, before I leave this subject, to take notice of one manifest mistake in the rules of syllogism ; viz., ' that no syllogistical reasoning can be right and conclusive, but what has, at least, one general proposition in it '. As if we could not reason and have knowledge about particulars : whereas, in truth, the matter rightly considered, the immediate object of all our reasoning and knowledge is nothing but particulars. Every man's reasoning and knowledge is only about the ideas existing in his own mind, which are truly, every one of them, particular existences ;[2] and our knowledge and reasoning about other things is only as they correspond with those our particular ideas. So that the perception of the agreement or disagreement of our particular ideas, is the whole and utmost of all our knowledge. Universality is but accidental to it, and consists only in this, that the particular ideas about which it is, are such as more than one particular thing can correspond with and be represented by. But the perception of the agreement or disagreement of any two ideas, and consequently our knowledge, is equally clear and certain, whether either, or both, or neither of those ideas be capable of representing more real beings than one, or no. [[3] One thing more I crave leave to offer about syllogism, before

---

[1] This section recalls the tone of the ' Epistle to the Reader ' with its reference to various 'master-builders' of the age, and Locke's own modest ambition ' to be employed as an under-labourer in clearing the ground a little and removing some of the rubbish that lies in the way to knowledge '.

[2] Cf. III. 3. 11 and relative note. Our ideas or images, as psychical states, are particular (full, it may be added, of irrelevant particularity), but the idea, as it functions in knowledge—what we 'mean' or 'intend', when we affirm or deny—is always general. Locke's language here and elsewhere is the basis of Berkeley's doctrine that we have ' no other but particular ideas', treated by Hume as ' one of the greatest and most valuable discoveries that has been made of late years in the republic of letters' (*Treatise*, Bk. I. 1. 7). But Berkeley admits that he can abstract, in so far as he can 'consider' a figure merely as triangular, and leave out of account in the demonstration the irrelevant particularities of the illustrative diagram (*Principles*, Introduction, sections 10 and 16). What we thus 'consider', 'intend', or 'mean' is the concept, the general or abstract idea which his argument ostensibly denies.

[3] Added in fourth edition.

I leave it, viz., May one not upon just ground enquire whether the form syllogism now has, is that which in reason it ought to have? For the *medius terminus* being to join the extremes, i.e., by its intervention to show the agreement or disagreement of the two in question, would not the position of the *medius terminus* be more natural, and show the agreement or disagreement of the extremes clearer and better, if it were placed in the middle between them?[1] which might be easily done by transposing the propositions, and making the *medius terminus* the predicate of the first, and the subject of the second. As thus:

> *Omnis homo est animal,*
> *Omne animal est vivens,*
> *Ergo omnis homo est vivens.*]

14. *Our highest degree of knowledge is intuitive, without reasoning.*—Some of the ideas that are in the mind, are so there, that they can be by themselves immediately compared one with another: and in these the mind is able to perceive, that they agree or disagree, as clearly as that it has them. This, therefore, as has been said, I call intuitive knowledge; which is certain, beyond all doubt, and needs no probation, nor can have any; this being the highest of all human certainty. In this consists the evidence of all those maxims which nobody has any doubt about, but every man (does not, as is said, only assent to, but) knows to be true, as soon as ever they are proposed to his understanding. In the discovery of, and assent to, these truths, there is no use of the discursive faculty, no need of reasoning, but they are known by a superior and higher degree of evidence. And such, if I may guess at things unknown, I am apt to think that angels have now, and the spirits of just men made perfect shall have, in a future state, of thousands of things, which now either wholly escape our apprehensions, or which our short-sighted reason having got some faint glimpse of, we, in the dark, grope after.[2]

---

[1] The order given by Locke is that assumed when the propositions are read in Intension or Comprehension. As a matter of fact, the middle term did stand *between* the two extremes in Aristotle's usual formulation: 'P is predicated of M; M is predicated of S; therefore P is predicated of S.'

[2] God alone, says Leibniz, has the advantage of having only intuitive knowledge. So Locke in his *Examination of Malebranche*, section 52: 'I think we cannot say God reasons at all; for he has at once a view of all things. But reason is very far from such an intuition; it is a laborious

15. *The next is demonstration by reasoning.*—But though we have, here and there, a little of this clear light, some sparks of bright knowledge; yet the greatest part of our ideas are such, that we cannot discern their agreement or disagreement by an immediate comparing them. And in all these we have need of reasoning, and must, by discourse and inference, make our discoveries.

23. *Above, contrary, and according to reason.*—By what has been before said of reason, we may be able to make some guess at the distinction of things, into those that are according to, above, and contrary to reason. (1) *According to reason* are such propositions whose truth we can discover by examining and tracing those ideas we have from sensation and reflection, and by natural deduction find to be true or probable. (2) *Above reason* are such propositions whose truth or probability we cannot by reason derive from those principles. (3) *Contrary to reason* are such propositions as are inconsistent with or irreconcilable to our clear and distinct ideas. Thus the existence of one God is according to reason; the existence of more than one God is contrary to reason; the resurrection of the dead above reason.

24. *Reason and faith not opposite.*—There is another use of the word *reason*, wherein it is *opposed to faith*; which, though it be in itself a very improper way of speaking, yet common use has so authorized it, that it would be folly either to oppose or hope to remedy it. Only I think it may not be amiss to take notice that however faith be opposed to reason, faith is nothing but a firm assent of the mind; which if it be regulated, as is our duty, cannot be afforded to anything but upon good reason, and so cannot be opposite to it. He that believes, without having any reason for believing, may be in love with his own fancies; but neither seeks truth as he ought, nor pays the obedience due to his Maker, who would have him use those discerning faculties he has given him, to keep him out of mistake and error. He that does not this to the best of his power, however he sometimes lights on truth, is in the right but by

and gradual progress in the knowledge of things by comparing one idea with a second, and a second with a third, and that with a fourth, to find the relation between the first and last in this train. . . . This way therefore of finding truth, so painful, uncertain, and limited, is proper only to men of finite understandings, but can by no means be supposed in God.'

chance; and I know not whether the luckiness of the accident will excuse the irregularity of his proceeding. This at least is certain, that he must be accountable for whatever mistakes he runs into: whereas he that makes use of the light and faculties God has given him, and seeks sincerely to discover truth by those helps and abilities he has, may have this satisfaction in doing his duty as a rational creature, that though he should miss truth, he will not miss the reward of it. For he governs his assent right, and places it as he should, who, in any case or matter whatsoever, believes or disbelieves according as reason directs him. He that does otherwise, transgresses against his own light, and misuses those faculties which were given him to no other end, but to search and follow the clearer evidence and greater probability. But since reason and faith are by some men opposed, we will so consider them in the following chapter.

## CHAPTER XVIII

### OF FAITH AND REASON, AND THEIR DISTINCT PROVINCES

2. I find every sect, as far as reason will help them, make use of it gladly; and, where it fails them, they cry out, It is matter of faith, and above reason.

*Reason* therefore here, as contradistinguished to faith, I take to be the discovery of the certainty or probability of such propositions or truths, which the mind arrives at by deductions made from such ideas which it has got by the use of its natural faculties, viz., by sensation or reflection.

*Faith*, on the other side, is the assent to any proposition, not thus made out by the deductions of reason, but upon the credit of the proposer, as coming from God in some extraordinary way of communication. This way of discovering truths to men we call *revelation*.

3. First, then, I say, that *no man inspired by God can, by any revelation, communicate to others any new simple ideas* which they had not before from sensation or reflection. For whatsoever impressions he himself may have from the immediate hand of God, this revelation, if it be of new simple ideas, cannot be conveyed to another, either by words or any other signs. Thus, whatever things were discovered to St. Paul when he was rapt up into the third heaven; whatever new ideas his

mind there received, all the description he can make to others of that place is only this, that there are such things as 'eye hath not seen, nor ear heard, nor hath it entered into the heart of man to conceive'. And supposing God should discover to any one, supernaturally, a species of creatures inhabiting, for example, Jupiter or Saturn (for that it is possible there may be such, nobody can deny), which had six senses; and imprint on his mind the ideas conveyed to theirs by that sixth sense: he could no more by words produce in the minds of other men those ideas imprinted by that sixth sense, than one of us could convey the idea of any colour by the sounds of words into a man who, having the other four senses perfect, had always totally wanted the fifth, of seeing. For our simple ideas, then, which are the foundation and sole matter of all our notions and knowledge, we must depend wholly on our reason, I mean, our natural faculties, and can by no means receive them, or any of them, from traditional revelation.

4. Secondly, I say, that *the same truths may be discovered and conveyed down from revelation, which are discoverable to us by reason* and by those ideas we naturally may have. So God might, by revelation, discover the truth of any proposition in Euclid. In all things of this kind there is little need or use of revelation, God having furnished us with natural and surer means to arrive at the knowledge of them. For the knowledge we have that this revelation came at first from God, can never be so sure as the knowledge we have from the clear and distinct perception of the agreement or disagreement of our own ideas. The like holds in matter of fact, knowable by our senses: v.g., the history of the deluge is conveyed to us by writings which had their original from revelation; and yet nobody, I think, will say he has as certain and clear a knowledge of the flood as Noah, that saw it: or that he himself would have had, had he then been alive and seen it.

5. *Revelation cannot be admitted against the clear evidence of reason.*—Since no evidence of our faculties by which we receive such revelations can exceed, if equal, the certainty of our intuitive knowledge, we can never receive for a truth anything that is directly contrary to our clear and distinct knowledge: v.g., the ideas of one body and one place do so clearly agree, and the mind has so evident a perception of their agreement, that we can never assent to a proposition that affirms the same body to be in two distant places at once,

however it should pretend to the authority of a divine revelation: since the evidence, first, that we deceive not ourselves in ascribing it to God, secondly, that we understand it right, can never be so great as the evidence of our own intuitive knowledge, whereby we discern it impossible for the same body to be in two places at once.[1] And therefore *no proposition can be received for divine revelation*, or obtain the assent due to all such, *if it be contradictory to our clear intuitive knowledge*, because this would be to subvert the principles and foundations of all knowledge, evidence, and assent whatsoever.

7. But, Thirdly, there being many things wherein we have very imperfect notions, or none at all; and other things, of whose past, present, or future existence, by the natural use of our faculties, we can have no knowledge at all: these, as being beyond the discovery of our natural faculties and above reason, are, when revealed, *the proper matter of faith*. Thus, that part of the angels rebelled against God, and thereby lost their first happy state: and that [the dead shall rise[2]] and live again: these, and the like, being beyond the discovery of reason, are purely matters of faith, with which reason has, directly, nothing to do. [8.] *Revelation*, where God has been pleased to give it, *must carry it against the probable conjectures of reason*. But yet it still belongs to reason to judge of the truth of its being a revelation, and of the signification of the words wherein it is delivered.

10. Thus far the dominion of faith reaches, and that without any violence or hindrance to reason; which is not injured or disturbed, but assisted and improved, by new discoveries of truth, coming from the eternal Fountain of all knowledge. Whatever God hath revealed is certainly true; no doubt can be made of it. This is the proper object of faith: but whether it be a divine revelation or no, reason must judge;

---

[1] This is adduced by Locke in connexion with the dogma of transubstantiation.

[2] In the first three editions this stood 'the bodies of men shall rise'. After the controversy with Stillingfleet the above was substituted. In his *Reply to Second Letter* he writes that he had originally taken it for granted 'that the Scriptures had mentioned in express terms the resurrection of the *body*. But upon the occasion your Lordship has given me to look more narrowly into what revelation has declared concerning the resurrection, and finding no such express words in the Scripture as that "the body shall rise" or " be raised ", I shall in the next edition change these words of my book—" the dead *bodies* of men shall rise ", into these of the Scripture—" the *dead* shall rise " (pp. 209-10).

which can never permit the mind to reject a greater evidence to embrace what is less evident, nor allow it to entertain probability in opposition to knowledge and certainty. There can be no evidence that any traditional revelation is of divine original, in the words we receive it, and in the sense we understand it, so clear and so certain as that of the principles of reason. And therefore *nothing that is contrary to, and inconsistent with, the clear and self-evident dictates of reason, has a right to be urged or assented to, as a matter of faith, wherein reason hath nothing to do.*

11. *If the provinces of faith and reason are not kept distinct by these boundaries*, there will, in matter of religion, be no room for reason at all; and those extravagant opinions and ceremonies that are to be found in the several religions of the world will not deserve to be blamed. For to this crying up of faith in opposition to reason, we may, I think, in good measure, ascribe those absurdities that fill almost all the religions which possess and divide mankind. For men, having been principled with an opinion that they must not consult reason in the things of religion, however apparently contradictory to common sense and the very principles of all their knowledge, have let loose their fancies and natural superstition; and have been by them led into so strange opinions and extravagant practices in religion, that a considerate man cannot but stand amazed at their follies, and judge them so far from being acceptable to the great and wise God, that he cannot avoid thinking them ridiculous and offensive to a sober, good man. So that, in effect, religion, which should most distinguish us from beasts, and ought most peculiarly to elevate us as rational creatures above brutes, is that wherein men often appear most irrational, and more senseless than beasts themselves. *Credo quia impossibile est*: ' I believe because it is impossible ', might, in a good man, pass for a sally of zeal, but would prove a very ill rule for men to choose their opinions or religion by.

## CHAPTER XIX[1]

#### OF ENTHUSIASM

1. HE that would seriously set upon the search of truth ought, in the first place, to prepare his mind with a love of it. For he that loves it not, will not take much pains to get it; nor be much concerned when he misses it. There is nobody in the commonwealth of learning who does not profess himself a lover of truth; and there is not a rational creature that would not take it amiss to be thought otherwise of. And yet, for all this, one may truly say, there are very few lovers of truth for truth's sake,[2] even amongst those who persuade themselves that they are so. How a man may know whether he be so in earnest, is worth enquiry: and I think there is this one unerring mark of it, viz., the not entertaining any proposition with greater assurance than the proofs it is built upon will warrant. Whoever goes beyond this measure of assent, it is plain, receives not truth in the love of it; loves not truth for truth's sake, but for some other by-end. For the evidence that any proposition is true (except such as are self-evident) lying only in the proofs a man has of it, whatsoever degrees of assent he affords it beyond the degrees of that evidence, it is plain all that surplusage of assurance is owing to some other affection, and not to the love of truth.

3. Upon this occasion I shall take the liberty to consider a third ground of assent,[3] which, with some men, has the same authority and is as confidently relied on, as either faith

---

[1] Added in the fourth edition.

[2] 'To love truth for truth's sake is the principal part of human perfection in this world, and the seed-plot of all the other virtues.' So Locke wrote to Anthony Collins, 29 October 1703. Lady Masham, in her letter to Le Clerc after Locke's death, wrote of him: 'He was always, in the greatest and in the smallest affairs of human life, as well as in speculative opinions, disposed to follow reason, whosoever suggested it; he being ever a faithful servant, I had almost said a slave, to truth; never abandoning her for anything else, and following her for her own sake purely.' This is very fitly prefixed by Mr. Fox Bourne as a motto to his *Life* of the philosopher.

[3] The other two grounds were reason and revelation.

or reason: I mean *enthusiasm*,[1] which, laying by reason, would set up revelation without it. Whereby in effect it takes away both reason and revelation, and substitutes in the room of it the ungrounded fancies of a man's own brain, and assumes them for a foundation both of opinion and conduct.

4. *Reason* is natural *revelation*, whereby the eternal Father of light, and Fountain of all knowledge, communicates to mankind that portion of truth which he has laid within the reach of their natural faculties. *Revelation* is natural *reason* enlarged by a new set of discoveries communicated by God immediately, which reason vouches the truth of, by the testimony and proofs it gives that they come from God. So that he that takes away reason to make way for revelation, puts out the light of both; and does much-what the same as if he would persuade a man to put out his eyes, the better to receive the remote light of an invisible star by a telescope.

5. Immediate revelation being a much easier way for men to establish their opinions and regulate their conduct than the tedious and not always successful labour of strict reasoning, it is no wonder that some have been very apt to pretend to revelation, and to persuade themselves that they are under the peculiar guidance of heaven in their actions and opinions, especially in those of them which they cannot account for by the ordinary methods of knowledge and principles of reason. Hence we see that in all ages men, in whom melancholy has mixed with devotion, or whose conceit of themselves has raised them into an opinion of a greater familiarity with God, and a nearer admittance to his favour, than is afforded to others, have often flattered themselves with a persuasion of an immediate intercourse with the Deity, and frequent communications from the Divine Spirit.

---

[1] 'Enthusiasm', says Leibniz, 'was originally a good term. Just as "sophism" properly indicates an exercise of wisdom, so enthusiasm signifies that there is a divinity in us (*Est deus in nobis*). But men having consecrated their passions, fancies, dreams, and even their anger, as something divine, enthusiasm began to signify a mental disturbance attributed to the influence of some divinity.... Since then, we attribute it to those who believe without foundation that their impulses come from God.' The term is similarly defined by Henry More in his *Enthusiasmus Triumphatus* (1662). Enthusiasm, in this sense, is satirized by Butler, Swift, Bishop Warburton, and in innumerable pamphlets throughout the eighteenth century.

6. Their minds being thus prepared, whatever groundless opinion comes to settle itself strongly upon their fancies, is an illumination from the Spirit of God, and presently of divine authority: and whatsoever odd action they find in themselves a strong inclination to do, that impulse is concluded to be a call or direction from heaven, and must be obeyed; it is a commission from above, and they cannot err in executing it. [7.] This I take to be properly enthusiasm, which, though founded neither on reason nor divine revelation, but rising from the conceits of a warmed or overweening brain, works yet, where it once gets footing, more powerfully on the persuasions and actions of men than either of those two, or both together: men being most forwardly obedient to the impulses they receive from themselves.

8. When once [men] are got into this way of immediate revelation, of illumination without search, and of certainty without proof and without examination, it is a hard matter to get them out of it. Reason is lost upon them, they are above it; they see the light infused into their understandings, and cannot be mistaken; it is clear and visible there, like the light of bright sunshine; shows itself, and needs no other proof but its own evidence; they feel the hand of God moving them within, and the impulses of the Spirit, and cannot be mistaken in what they feel. [9.] This is the way of talking of these men: they are sure, because they are sure: and their persuasions are right, only because they are strong in them. For when what they say is stripped of the metaphor of seeing and feeling, this is all it amounts to: and yet these similes so impose on them, that they serve them for certainty in themselves, and demonstration to others.

10. But to examine a little soberly this internal light and this feeling on which they build so much: The question here is, How do I know that God is the revealer of this to me; that this impression is made upon my mind by his Holy Spirit, and that therefore I ought to obey it? If I know not this, how great soever the assurance is, that I am possessed with, it is groundless; whatever light I pretend to, it is but *enthusiasm.* Does it not then stand them upon, to examine upon what grounds they presume it to be a revelation from God? Or else all their confidence is mere presumption; and this light they are so dazzled with, is nothing but an *ignis fatuus*, that

leads them continually round in this circle : *It is a revelation, because they firmly believe it ; and they believe it, because it is a revelation.*

13. Light, true light in the mind, is or can be nothing else but the evidence of the truth of any proposition ; and if it be not a self-evident proposition, all the light it has, or can have, is from the clearness and validity of those proofs upon which it is received. To talk of any other light in the understanding, is to put ourselves in the dark, or in the power of the Prince of Darkness, and by our own consent, to give ourselves up to delusion, to believe a lie. For if strength of persuasion be the light which must guide us, I ask, how shall any one distinguish between the delusions of Satan, and the inspirations of the Holy Ghost ?

14. He therefore that will not give himself up to all the extravagances of delusion and error, must bring this guide of his *light within* to the trial. God, when he makes the prophet, does not unmake the man. He leaves all his faculties in their natural state, to enable him to judge of his inspirations, whether they be of divine original or no. When he illuminates the mind with supernatural light, he does not extinguish that which is natural. If he would have us assent to the truth of any proposition, he either evidences that truth by the usual methods of natural reason, or else makes it known to be a truth which he would have us assent to by his authority, and convinces us that it is from him, by some marks which reason cannot be mistaken in. Reason must be our last judge and guide in everything.[1] I do not mean that we must consult reason, and examine whether a proposition revealed from God can be made out by natural principles, and if it cannot, that then we may reject it. But consult it we must, and by it examine whether it be a revelation from God or no : and if reason finds it to be revealed from God, reason then declares for it as much as for any other truth, and makes it one of her dictates. Every conceit that thoroughly warms our fancies must pass for an inspiration, if there be nothing but the strength of our persuasions, whereby to judge of our persuasions. If reason must not examine their truth by something extrinsical to the persuasions themselves, inspirations and delusions, truth and falsehood, will have the same measure, and

[1] This might be taken as the motto of the century of rationalism, which Locke did so much to inaugurate. Cf. Introduction, p. x.

will not be possible to be distinguished. [15.] Thus we see, the holy men of old, who had revelations from God, had something else besides that internal light of assurance in their own minds to testify to them that it was from God. They were not left to their own persuasions alone, that those persuasions were from God, but had outward signs to convince them of the Author of those revelations.

16. In what I have said, I am far from denying that God can or doth sometimes enlighten men's minds in the apprehending of certain truths, or excite them to good actions by the immediate influence and assistance of the Holy Spirit, without any extraordinary signs accompanying it. But in such cases too we have reason and the Scripture, unerring rules, to know whether it be from God or no. Where the truth embraced is consonant to the revelation in the written word of God, or the action conformable to the dictates of right reason or Holy Writ, we may be assured that we run no risk in entertaining it as such; because, though perhaps it be not an immediate revelation from God, extraordinarily operating on our minds, yet we are sure it is warranted by that revelation which he has given us of truth.

## CHAPTER XX

### OF WRONG ASSENT, OR ERROR

1. *Causes of error.*—Knowledge being to be had only of visible certain truth, *error* is not a fault of our knowledge, but a mistake of our judgement, giving assent to that which is not true.

But if assent be grounded on likelihood, if the proper object and motive of our assent be probability, and that probability consists in what is laid down in the foregoing chapters, it will be demanded, how men come to give their assents contrary to probability. For there is nothing more common than contrariety of opinions; nothing more obvious than that one man wholly disbelieves what another only doubts of, and a third steadfastly believes and firmly adheres to. The reasons whereof, though they may be very various, yet, I suppose, may all be reduced to these four: (1) *Want of proofs.* (2) *Want of ability to use them.* (3) *Want of will to use them.* (4) *Wrong measures of probability.*

2. First, By *want of proofs*, I do not mean only the want of those proofs which are nowhere extant, and so are no-

where to be had; but the want even of those proofs which are in being, or might be procured. And thus men want proofs, who have not the convenience or opportunity to make experiments and observations themselves, tending to the proof of any proposition; nor likewise the convenience to enquire into and collect the testimonies of others. And in this state are the greatest part of mankind who are given up to labour, and enslaved to the necessity of their mean condition, whose lives are worn out only in the provisions for living. These men's opportunities of knowledge and enquiry are commonly as narrow as their fortunes; and their understandings are but little instructed, when all their whole time and pains is laid out to still the croaking of their own bellies, or the cries of their children. It is not to be expected that a man who drudges on all his life in a laborious trade, should be more knowing in the variety of things done in the world, than a pack-horse, who is driven constantly forwards and backwards in a narrow lane and dirty road, only to market, should be skilled in the geography of the country. So that a great part of mankind are, by the natural and unalterable state of things in this world, and the constitution of human affairs, unavoidably given over to invincible ignorance of those proofs on which others build, and which are necessary to establish those opinions. [3.] [Nevertheless] no man is so wholly taken up with the attendance on the means of living as to have no spare time at all to think of his soul, and inform himself in matters of religion. Were men as intent upon this as they are on things of lower concernment, there are none so enslaved to the necessities of life, who might not find many vacancies that might be husbanded to this advantage of their knowledge.

5. Secondly, Those who *want skill to use those evidences they have* of probabilities, who cannot carry a train of consequences in their heads, nor weigh exactly the preponderancy of contrary proofs and testimonies, making every circumstance its due allowance, may be easily misled to assent to positions that are not probable. There are some men of one, some but of two syllogisms, and no more; and others that can but advance one step farther. Which great difference in men's intellectuals, whether it rises from any defect in the organs of the body particularly adapted to thinking; or in the dullness or untractableness of those faculties for want of use; or, as some think, in the natural

differences of men's souls themselves ; or some, or all of these together, it matters not here to examine : only this is evident, that there is a difference of degrees in men's understandings, apprehensions, and reasonings, to so great a latitude, that one may, without doing injury to mankind, affirm that there is a greater distance between some men and others in this respect than between some men and some beasts.[1]

6. Thirdly, There are another sort of people that want proofs, not because they are out of their reach, but *because they will not use them* : who, though they have riches and leisure enough, and want neither parts nor other helps, are yet never the better for them. Their hot pursuit of pleasure, or constant drudgery in business, engages some men's thoughts elsewhere ; laziness and oscitancy [2] in general, or a particular aversion for books, study, and meditation, keep others from any serious thoughts at all. And some, out of fear that an impartial enquiry would not favour those opinions which best suit their prejudices, lives, and designs, content themselves, without examination, to take upon trust what they find convenient and in fashion. We know some men will not read a letter which is supposed to bring ill news ; and many men forbear to cast up their accounts, or so much as think upon their estates, who have reason to fear their affairs are in no very good posture. How men whose plentiful fortunes allow them leisure to improve their understandings, can satisfy themselves with a lazy ignorance, I cannot tell : but methinks they have a low opinion of their souls, who lay out all their incomes in provisions for the body, and employ none of it to procure the means and helps of knowledge ; who take great care to appear always in a neat and splendid outside, and would think themselves miser-

---

[1] Commenting on this statement of Locke's, several times repeated (e. g. III. 6. 12, IV. 16. 12), Leibniz remarks that, in the case of such men, ' this is apparently not a defect of faculty but a hindrance to its exercise ; so that I think that the most stupid of men is incomparably more rational and more teachable than the cleverest of animals, although the contrary is sometimes said as a witticism '. ' As for those who lack capacity,' he says in the present context, ' they are fewer perhaps in number than you think ; I believe that good sense with application can suffice for everything which does not demand promptness. . . . It is certain that one soul might go as far as another (but not perhaps so rapidly) if it were led as it should be.'

[2] Oscitancy, from *oscitare*, to gape or yawn ; indolence, negligence.

able in coarse clothes, or a patched coat, and yet contentedly suffer their minds to appear abroad in a piebald livery of coarse patches and borrowed shreds, such as it has pleased chance or their country tailor (I mean the common opinion of those they have conversed with) to clothe them in.

7. Fourthly, There remains yet the last sort, who, even where the real probabilities appear, and are plainly laid before them, do not admit of the conviction, nor yield unto manifest reasons, but do either ἐπέχειν, suspend their assent,[1] or give it to the less probable opinion. And to this danger are those exposed who have taken up wrong *measures of probability*, which are, (1) *Propositions that are not in themselves certain and evident, but doubtful and false, taken up for principles.* (2) *Received hypotheses.* (3) *Predominant passions or inclinations.* (4) *Authority.*

8. *First, Doubtful propositions taken for principles.*

9. There is nothing more ordinary than that children should receive into their minds propositions (especially about matters of religion) from their parents, nurses, or those about them; which, being insinuated into their unwary as well as unbiased understandings, and fastened by degrees, are at last (equally, whether true or false) riveted there by long custom and education, beyond all possibility of being pulled out again. For men, when they are grown up, reflecting upon their opinions, and finding those of this sort to be as ancient in their minds as their very memories, not having observed their early insinuation, nor by what means they got them, they are apt to reverence them as sacred things, and not to suffer them to be profaned, touched, or questioned: they look on them as the *urim* and *thummim* set up in their minds immediately by God himself, to be the great and unerring deciders of truth and falsehood, and the judges to which they are to appeal in all manner of controversies.

11. *Secondly, Received hypotheses.*—Next to these are men whose understandings are cast into a mould, and fashioned just to the size of a received hypothesis. Would it not be an insufferable thing for a learned professor, and that which his scarlet would blush at, to have his authority of forty years' standing, wrought out of hardrock Greek and Latin,

---

[1] Ἐποχή, or suspense of judgement on all possible questions, the ideal of Pyrrhonian scepticism and the means of attaining mental imperturbability (ἀταραξία).

with no small expense of time and candle, and confirmed by general tradition and a reverend beard, in an instant overturned by an upstart novelist? Can any one expect that he should be made to confess, that what he taught his scholars thirty years ago was all error and mistake, and that he sold them hard words and ignorance at a very dear rate? What probabilities, I say, are sufficient to prevail in such a case? And who ever, by the most cogent arguments, will be prevailed with to disrobe himself at once of all his old opinions, and pretences to knowledge and learning, which, with hard study, he hath all his time been labouring for; and turn himself out stark naked, in quest afresh of new notions? All the arguments can be used will be as little able to prevail, as the wind did with the traveller to part with his cloak, which he held only the faster.

12. *Thirdly, Predominant passions.*—Probabilities which cross men's appetites and prevailing passions run the same fate. Let never so much probability hang on one side of a covetous man's reasoning, and money on the other; and it is easy to foresee which will outweigh. Earthly minds, like mud walls, resist the strongest batteries; and though, perhaps, sometimes the force of a clear argument may make some impression, yet they nevertheless stand firm, keep out the enemy truth that would captivate or disturb them. Tell a man passionately in love, that he is jilted; bring a score of witnesses of the falsehood of his mistress; it is ten to one but three kind words of hers shall invalidate all their testimonies. *Quod volumus, facile credimus*; 'What suits our wishes is forwardly believed', is, I suppose, what every one hath more than once experimented.

15. But yet there is some end of it, and a man, having carefully enquired into all the grounds of probability and unlikeliness; done his utmost to inform himself in all particulars fairly; and cast up the sum total on both sides, may in most cases come to acknowledge, upon the whole matter, on which side the probability rests. Where the proofs are such as make it highly probable, and there is not sufficient ground to suspect that there is either fallacy of words, nor equally valid proofs yet undiscovered, latent on the other side, there, I think, a man who has weighed them can scarce refuse his assent to the side on which the greater probability appears. In other less clear cases, I think

it is in a man's power to suspend his assent; and perhaps content himself with the proofs he has, if they favour the opinion that suits with his inclination or interest, and so stop from farther search. But that a man should afford his assent to that side on which the less probability appears to him, seems to me utterly impracticable, and as impossible as it is to believe the same thing probable and improbable at the same time. [16.] As knowledge is no more arbitrary than perception, so, I think, assent is no more in our power than knowledge. When the agreement of any two ideas appears to our minds, whether immediately or by the assistance of reason, I can no more refuse to perceive, no more avoid knowing it, than I can avoid seeing those objects which I turn my eyes to, and look on in daylight; and what, upon full examination, I find the most probable, I cannot deny my assent to. But though we cannot hinder our knowledge where the agreement is once perceived; nor our assent, where the probability manifestly appears upon due consideration of all the measures of it: yet *we can hinder both knowledge and assent* by *stopping our enquiry*, and not employing our faculties in the search of any truth.

17. *Fourthly, Authority.*—The fourth and last *wrong measure of probability* I shall take notice of, and which keeps in ignorance or error more people than all the other together, is that which I have mentioned in the foregoing chapter: I mean the *giving up our assent to the common received opinions*, either of our friends or party, neighbourhood or country. There is not an opinion so absurd which a man may not receive upon this ground. There is no error to be named which has not had its professors: and a man shall never want crooked paths to walk in, if he thinks that he is in the right way, wherever he has the footsteps of others to follow.[1]

18. But, notwithstanding the great noise is made in the world about errors and opinions, I must do mankind that right[2] as to say, *There are not so many men in errors and wrong opinions as is*

---

[1] With this section on Authority, as one of the chief sources of ignorance and error, the *Essay* closes on the same note with which it began.

[2] 'The justice you would herein do to men', says Leibniz, ' does not after all redound much to their credit. . . . Perhaps, however, there is among men more sincerity than you seem to allow, and without under-

*commonly supposed.* Not that I think they embrace the truth; but indeed, because, concerning those doctrines they keep such a stir about, they have no thought, no opinion at all. For if any one should a little catechize the greatest part of the partisans of most of the sects in the world, he would not find, concerning those matters they are so zealous for, that they have any opinions of their own: much less would he have reason to think that they took them upon the examination of arguments and appearance of probability. They are resolved to stick to a party that education or interest has engaged them in; and there, like the common soldiers of an army, show their courage and warmth as their leaders direct, without ever examining, or so much as knowing, the cause they contend for. If a man's life shows that he has no serious regard for religion, for what reason should we think that he beats his head about the opinions of his church, and troubles himself to examine the grounds of this or that doctrine? It is enough for him to obey his leaders, to have his hand and his tongue ready for the support of the common cause, and thereby approve himself to those who can give him credit, preferment, or protection in that society. Thus though one cannot say there are fewer improbable or erroneous opinions in the world than there are; yet this is certain, there are fewer that actually assent to them, and mistake them for truths, than is imagined.

## CHAPTER XXI

### OF THE DIVISION OF THE SCIENCES

1. *Three sorts.*—All that can fall within the compass of human understanding being either, *First*, the nature of things as they are in themselves, their relations, and their manner of operation: or, *Secondly*, That which man himself ought to do, as a rational and voluntary agent, for the attainment of any end, especially happiness: or, *Thirdly*, The ways and means whereby the knowledge of both the one and the other of these are attained and communicated; I think science[1] may be divided properly into these three sorts:

standing fully the cause which they support, men may submit themselves, often blindly but still in good faith, to the judgement of those whose authority they have once recognized.'

[1] 'Science' is used here in a wider sense than that in which Locke suspected that 'natural philosophy is not capable of being made a

2. *First*, Physica.—The knowledge of things as they are in their own proper beings, their constitutions, properties, and operations, whereby I mean not only matter and body, but spirits also, which have their proper natures, constitutions, and operations, as well as bodies. This, in a little more enlarged sense of the word, I call φυσική, or *natural philosophy*. The end of this is bare speculative truth : and whatsoever can afford the mind of man any such, falls under this branch, whether it be God himself, angels, spirits, bodies, or any of their affections, as number, and figure, &c.

3. *Secondly*, Practica.—Πρακτική, the skill of right applying our own powers and actions, for the attainment of things good and useful. The most considerable under this head is *ethics*, which is the seeking out those rules and measures of human actions which lead to happiness, and the means to practise them. The end of this is not bare speculation and the knowledge of truth ; but right, and a conduct suitable to it.

4. *Thirdly*, Σημειωτική.—The third branch may be called Σημειωτική, or *the doctrine of signs*, the most usual whereof being words, it is aptly enough termed also Λογική, *logic* ; the business whereof is to consider the nature of signs the mind makes use of for the understanding of things, or conveying its knowledge to others. For since the things the mind contemplates are none of them, besides itself,[1] present to the understanding, it is necessary that something else, as a sign or representation of the thing it considers, should be present to it : and these are *ideas*. And because the scene of ideas that makes one man's thoughts cannot be laid open to the immediate view of another, nor laid up anywhere but in the memory, a no very sure repository : therefore, to communicate our thoughts to one another, as well as record them for our own use, signs of our ideas are also necessary. Those which men have found most convenient, and therefore generally make use of, are articulate sounds. The consideration, then, of *ideas* and *words*, as the great instruments of knowledge, makes no despicable

science ' (IV. 12. 10). Locke's division reproduces the well-known threefold division by the Stoics. Logic, with the Stoics, included an inquiry into the standard of truth and other questions belonging to the theory of knowledge. The only importance of this chapter consists in Locke's remarks under the third head.

[1] An important statement both as regards our mediate knowledge of ' other things ' and the immediate or ' intuitive ' knowledge of our own existence. Cf. Introduction, pp. xxxvi–xli.

part of their contemplation who would take a view of human knowledge in the whole extent of it. And perhaps, if they were distinctly weighed and duly considered, they would afford us another sort of logic and critic than what we have been hitherto acquainted with.[1]

5. *This is the first division of the objects of knowledge.*—This seems to me the first and most general, as well as natural division of the objects of our understanding. For a man can employ his thoughts about nothing but, either the contemplation of things themselves, for the discovery of truth; or about the things in his own power, which are his own actions, for the attainment of his own ends; or the signs the mind makes use of, both in the one and the other, and the right ordering of them for its clearer information. All which three, viz., *things*, as they are in themselves knowable; *actions*, as they depend on us in order to happiness; and the right use of *signs* in order to knowledge, being *toto caelo* different, they seemed to me to be the three great provinces of the intellectual world, wholly separate and distinct one from another.

[1] Cf. Introduction, p. xiv.

# INDEX

Where the reference is to the Introduction or the Notes the page-numbers are printed in italics.

Absolute terms, contain relations, 177.
Abstract or general ideas, *xxii*, 87–90, *151*, 228–37, 301–2, *352*. See General ideas.
Abstract terms, not predicable of one another, 253.
Abstraction, 88–90, 93; puts a perfect distinction betwixt man and brutes, 89.
Acquired perceptions, 74–7.
Action, two sorts of, motion and thinking, 137, 148.
Active and passive powers, characterize spirit and matter respectively, 136–7, 148, 170.
Activity of mind, in attention, 73; in remembering, 82; in framing complex ideas, 92, 93; volition, 138.
Adam and Eve, 108.
Adamson, R., *16*, *19*.
Adequate and inadequate ideas, 209–14, 297.
Agreement and disagreement of ideas, knowledge consists in perception of, 255; four sorts, 255–8.
Alexander, Professor, *xxxvi*, *xxxix*, *111*, *121*.
Analogy, use of, 341–2.
Angelic and other intelligences, 84, 163–4, 173–4, 243, 272, 276, 284, 353.
Aquinas, *31*.
Archetypes and ectypes, ideas as, 214, 290.
Aristotle and Aristotelianism, *ix*, *xxxiii*, *xxxv*, 24, 27, 40, 82, *136*, *156*, 217, 228, 347 and note, *353*.
Arnauld, *15–16*.
Assent, or faith, 335; degrees of, 337–43; power to suspend, 368.
Association of ideas, *xxviii*; due to chance or custom, 217; its ill effects, 218–21.
Attention, 46, 133–4; present in perception, 73, in memory, 80; change necessary to sustain attention, 110.
Augustine, St., 106.
Authority, Locke's attitude to, *ix*, 40–1; one great cause of error, 368.
Axioms, see Maxims.

Bacon, *ix–x*, *350*.
Balaam's ass, 250, 290.
Balfour, Lord, *344*.
Belief, as distinguished from knowledge, *xv*, 9, 335. See Assent, Faith, Opinion.
Bergson, *106*.
Berkeley, *xiii*, *xxv*, *xxxix*, *xliv–vi*, 77, *154*, *173*, 205, *266*, *292*, *322*; abstract ideas, *xxii*, *352*; ideas and notions, *151*; primary qualities, *69*, *70*, *160*; Molyneux's problem, *75*; *minima sensibilia*, *120*; unity, *xxii*, *63*; power in matter, *66*; soul and thinking, *48*; activity of spirit, *xlii*, *136*, *326*; causation, *153*, *285*; visual language, *74*; *Siris*, *342*.
Bernoulli, J., *168*.
Blind; the born-blind, if made to see, 75–6; the 'studious blind man', *60*, 239.
Bodley's library, 97.
Body and extension not the same, 98–103; the primary ideas of body, 166; ultimate nature and behaviour of body and of soul equally incomprehensible, 168–70. See Matter.
Bosanquet, B., *231*, *295*.

# 374 Index

Boyle, 6, *67*, *168*.
Bradley, F. H., *230*, *295*.
Brutes and men, 84–5, 87–90, 247, 342, 365.
Butler, Bishop, *185*, *188*, *196*, *199*, *360*.

Candle of the Lord, 13, 280.
Capacities, our, suited to our state and concerns, 12 ; useful to know their extent, 13–14 ; not to be made judges of possibility and impossibility, 272, 320. *See* Faculties.
Cause and effect, ideas how got, 180; often tell us nothing of the *modus operandi*, 153. *See* Power.
Certainty belongs to ' knowledge ' and depends on intuition, 255, 261–5, 353 ; general certainty to be found only in our ideas, 298 ; certainty of senses and memory, 324–8.
Changelings, 235, 290–1.
Clarke, Samuel, *199*, *311*.
Clear and obscure ideas, 204–5.
Coexistence, of qualities in the same subject, 257; our knowledge of, ' very narrow and scarce any at all ', 273–6, 282–6, 293–8, 330–2.
Cohesion, 168–9.
Coleridge, *199*, *344*.
Collective substances, 94 ; ideas of, are artificial, 175.
Common Sense, Philosophy of, *xxii*, *32*, *54*.
Comparing, 86–7.
Complex ideas, their different kinds, how formed, 92–5.
Compounding, 87, 92.
Condillac, *xviii*, *42*.
Confused ideas, 205–7.
Conscience, 30.
Consciousness, ' the perception of what passes in a man's own mind ', 49–50 ; makes personal identity, 188–200.
Consent, argument from universal, 17–34.
Contemplation, 79, 133.

Coste, his French edition of the *Essay*, *8*, *9*, *51*, *118*, *319*.
Cousin, Victor, *xix*, *199*.
Creation, 180, 319–21.
Cudworth, *45*.
Culverwell, *31*.
Custom, a greater power than nature, 35 ; association of ideas due to, 218.

Definition, what it is, 230.
Democritus, *67*.
Demonstration, by intermediate ideas, 262, 276, 304 ; each step must have intuitive evidence, 263 ; a demonstrative science of ethics, 264–5, 277–80 ; demonstrative knowledge of the existence of a God, 280, 310–21.
Descartes and Cartesians, *ix–xiii*, *xxxiii*, *xlvii*, *135*, *207*, *278*; nature of ideas, *15* ; innate ideas, *xxxi*, *19*, *20* ; primary and secondary qualities, *67* ; hardness, *99* ; extension and body, *98*, *244*, *269* ; thinking and soul, *269* ; imagination and intellection, *207* ; *lumen naturale*, *311* ; infinity and continuity of matter, *103*, *168* ; Representative perception, *xxxix*, *xliv*, *288* ; existence, of self, *xli–ii*, *310–11*, of God, *xli*, *312–13*; Occasionalism, *170*, *285*, *320*.
Desire, to be distinguished from volition, 142–3 ; an uneasiness of the mind, 143 ; moved only by happiness, 145 ; mind's power to suspend execution of any desire, 146.
Discerning and distinguishing between ideas, 85–6, 256, 261, 353.
Disputation ; logic as the art of wrangling, 305 ; use of maxims and syllogisms in disputes, 305, 347, 349.
Distinct ideas, 205–7.
Divisibility, infinite, of time, space and matter, 119, 129, 207.
Dreaming, 49–51, 133–4.
Dualism, *xii–xiii*, *xxxviii–xl*.

Duns Scotus, *269*.
Duration, idea of, from reflection on the train of ideas in the mind, 106–11; measures of duration, 111–14; all parts of, are duration, 118–19; eternity, 115–16.

Ecstasy, 133.
Empiricism, *xvii–xxxi*, *xlvii*, *42*.
Enthusiasm, 359–63.
Error, causes of, 363–9.
Essence, real and nominal, 214, 230–7, 242–53; real, unknown, 173, 240, &c.; nominal, made by the mind, 230–1; each distinct abstract idea a distinct essence, 232; nothing essential to individuals, 243–5.
Eternal verities, 287, 329.
Eternity, idea of, how got, 114–15, 126.
Evolution, 53.
Existence, an idea of both sensation and reflection, 63; our knowledge of real existence, 257, 265–7, 280, 309–29.
Expansion, Locke's use of the term, 105, 115.
Experience, the source of all our knowledge, 42; experience and history distinguished from reason, 330–1.
Extension, Locke's use of the term, 96; extension and body, 98–105; all the parts of extension are extension, 118–19. *See* Space.

Faculties are powers of mind, not distinct agents, 139; our faculties suited to our state, 161–2; 'bare faculties', *48*, *80*.
Fairy money, 40.
Faith or opinion, as distinguished from knowledge, *xv*, 11, 335; faith in revelation, 343, 355; not opposed to reason, 343, 354; faith and reason, their distinct provinces, 355–8.
Fantastical ideas, 208–9.
Figure, 96–7, 275.

Forms, Scholastic doctrine of substantial, 156, 211, 231, 235, 248.
Fraser, A. Campbell, *xix*, *xxxiv*, *xlv*, *9*, *202*; Locke and authority, *39*; Locke on simple modes, *114*, *126*, *210*, *239*; Locke on secondary qualities, *273*; Locke on abstract ideas, *302*; Locke's idea of God, *310*; Divine mind not ratiocinative, *263*; Creation and eternity of matter, *318*; Locke on toleration, *338*.
Freedom, not of the will, but of the agent, 140–2; what it consists in, 146–7.

Galileo, 67.
Gassendi, *xviii*, 67.
Genera and species, nothing but abstract ideas, 229.
General ideas, made by the mind, but not arbitrarily, 230–2; fictions and contrivances that carry difficulty with them, 301–2; the more general our ideas, the more incomplete and partial, 250.
General knowledge, only of the relations of our abstract ideas, 286–7, 293–8, 328–30.
General terms, indispensable, 223, 226–8, and relative notes.
Gibson, Professor J., *xii*, *xix*, *xxxi–iii*, *xli*, *16*, *27*, *99*, *204*; Locke on complex ideas, *92*; nature of matter, *168*; Locke's doctrine of signs, *10*; Locke and Occasionalism, *285*; evolution and composition, *53*.
Glanville, *xxxiii*, *168*.
God, idea of, not innate, 37; how formed, 172–3; demonstrative knowledge of the existence of, 280, 310–21.
Good and evil, definition of, 145; moral good and evil, 201.
Green, T. H., *xviii–xix*, *178*.
Grotius, *31*.

Habitual knowledge, two degrees of, 258–60.

# Index

Hamilton, Sir W., *xviii–xix*, 55, 75, *83*, 225, 228.
Happiness alone moves desire, 145.
Hardness, distinguished from solidity, 59, 99.
Hartley, 217, 218.
Hegel, *241*.
Herbert of Cherbury, Lord, *xxxi*, 32–4.
Hobbes, Hobbist, *x–xi*, 29, 67, *82*, 217.
Hooker, *31*, 351.
Hume, *xiii–xiv*, *xviii–xx*, *xxxix–xl*, *xliv*, *xlvi–vii*, *42*, 217, *336*; abstract ideas, *xxii*, *352*; infinite divisibility, *120*; idea of existence, *xxii*, *63*; causation, *170*, *180*, *311*; 'secret tie', *153*, *285*; custom, *218*; 'relations of ideas' and 'matters of fact', *258*, *328*; real existence, *326*; personal identity, *197*; reason, *168*; Kant and Hume, *14*.
Huygenius, 6.
Hypotheses, use and dangers of, 332–3.

Idea, Locke's use of the term, *xxxvii*, 15 and note.
Ideas, without names, 56; positive, from privative causes, 64–5; truth or falsehood of, 215–16.
Identical propositions not instructive, 306–7.
Identity, idea of, not innate, 36; identity of plants and animals, 185–6; personal identity, 186–200; identity or diversity of ideas, immediately perceived, 255–6.
Idiots, 18, 27.
Ignorance, extent of our, 280; its causes, 281–7.
Illation, 345.
Imagination, limited by previous sense-experience, 54; use of images in thinking, 292; abstract ideas (concepts) cannot be imaged, 302 and note.
Immateriality of soul, not essential to morality or religion, 271.
Immensity, idea of, 96, 117, 126.
Immortality, 271 and note, 290–1.
Impenetrability = solidity, 57.
Impression, 'on the body made by an external object', 133. *Cf. 43²*, 73.
*Individuationis, principium*, *182*, 184, and Book II, ch. 27 *passim*.
Inference, reason, or reasoning, necessary to supplement 'sense and intuition', 345, 354; in what it consists, 344–53.
Infinity, idea of, from numbers, 124; has its origin in sensation and reflection, 132; a quantitative idea, 127; infinity of time and of space compared, 115–17; no positive idea of infinity, 129–32; infinite divisibility, 119, 129, 207.
Innate principles and innate ideas, *see* Book I *passim* and Introduction, pp. *xxxi–vi*.
Instant, defined, 109.
Internal sense, reflections compared to, 44 and note.
Intuitive knowledge, 21, 261–2, 266, 353; of our own existence, 280, 309, *310*.

James, William, 7, *106*, *110*, *270*.
Judgement, contrasted with knowledge, *12*, 297–8, 333–4; and wit, 85–6.

Kant, *xiii–xiv*, *xix*, *xxii*, *xxv*, *xxvii*, *xxx*, *xxxvi*, *xlvii*, *42*, *154*, *289*, *314*; on Locke's psychological method, *10*; extent of knowledge, *14*; intuition, *292*; synthetic judgements *a priori* and *a posteriori*, *308*; space, *100*, *119*, *128*; motion and change, *111*; soul-substance, *191*.
Keynes, J. N., *252*.
Knowledge, defined, 255; four sorts, 255–8; its degrees, intuitive, 261, 353, demonstrative, 262–5, 354, sensitive, 265–7, 321–8; its extent, 267–87;

knowledge of 'coexistence', 273–6; of our own existence, 280, 309–10; of the existence of God, 280, 310–21; knowledge or science distinguished from judgement, opinion, or probability, 9, 11, 254, 265, 334; general knowledge restricted to the relations of our own abstract ideas, 298; no science of physical nature, 282–3, 293–8, 330–1; nor of spirit, 283; knowledge of reality, how far attainable, 287–91.

Law, of nature, 31 and note; laws, divine, civil, and of opinion or reputation, 201–3.
Lee, Henry, *39*, *47*.
Leibniz, *xxxv–vi*, *100*, *204*, *207*, *209*, *281*, *295*, *342*, *369*; innate ideas, *18*, *19*, *20*, *26*; *perceptions petites*, *18*; Locke's ideas of Reflection, *44*; general terms, *223*; 'clear' and 'distinct', *207*; intuitive knowledge, *266*, *353*; 'cogito ergo sum', *301*; axioms, *303*; symbolical thinking, *292*; men and brutes, *365*; prepositions, *224*; indiscernibles, *184*; the senses, *58*, *63*; sense and imagination, *266*; Molyneux's problem, *75*; 'bare faculties', *48*, *80*; infinite, *103*, *114*, *125*; substance, *154*, *165*; *concretum*, *155*; enthusiasm, *360*.
Leviathan, 29.
Liberty and Necessity, 139–40. *See* Freedom.
Locke, his revolt against authority, *ix*; relation to Descartes, *x–xiii*; the second founder of modern philosophy, *xiv*; affinities with Kant, *xiv*, *xxx*; his 'historical plain method', *xv*; attack upon innate notions and maxims, *xvi*, *xxxi–vi*; founder of English Empirical philosophy, *xvii*; starts with simple ideas, *xx–iii*; equivocal analysis of ideas of Substance and Cause, *xxiii–vi*; his Empiricism part of his polemic against innate ideas, *xxix–xxx*; analysis of sense-perception, ideas and qualities, *xxxvii–viii*; Representative Perception and Cartesian dualism, *xxxviii–xl*; knowledge of real existence, the self and God, *xli–ii*; sensitive knowledge, *xliii*; Locke's realistic assumptions, *xxxvii*, *xlvi*; the sequel in Berkeley and Hume, *xliv–vi*, in Reid and Kant, *xlvii*, in recent discussion, *xlviii*.
Logic (of the schools), Locke's criticism of, 304–6, 346–51; the art of wrangling, 305; useless in the finding out of proofs and making new discoveries, 350.
Lotze, *48*, *194*, *237*.
*Lumen naturale*, light of nature, light of reason, 13 and note, 31–2, 37 and note, *311*.

Malebranche, *xii*, *xiii*, *15–16*, *168*.
Manna, 70.
Mathematics, Locke's ideal of knowledge, 262–5, 276–80, 329–30; 'reality' of mathematical knowledge, 289 and note.
Matter, *168*; cannot produce a thinking being, 315; not coeternal with an eternal Mind, 318. *See* Body.
Masham, Lady, *xi*, *359*.
Maxims, not the truths first known, 301–2; not the foundations of all other knowledge, 302–3, 329–30. *See* Book I, chs. 2–4, and Book IV, ch. 7 *passim*.
Memory, 79–85; activity of will in remembering, 82; defects of memory, 83; marks of a good memory, *83*.
Method, Locke's 'historical plain method', 10 and note.
Microscopical eyes, *71*, 162.
Mill, James, *xviii*, *42*, *217*.
Mill, J. S., *75*, *226*, *242*.
Mind, an empty cabinet, 22; white paper, 42; a dark room, 91;

necessary existence of an eternal Mind, 315-16. *See* Spirit.
Miracles, credibility of, 342-3.
Modes, simple and mixed, 94; simple, *xxvi–vii*, 95-150, 210; mixed, made by the mind, 150-3, their names usually learned before their ideas, 241.
Molyneux, 75, *182*, *217*, *251*, *277*, *319*.
Monkey and oyster, 307.
Monsters, 235, 248-9.
Morality, a demonstrative science of, 277-80, 289-90; the proper science and business of mankind, 331-2; moral rules or laws, of three sorts, 201-3.
More, Henry, *98*, *168*, *360*.
Motion, slow or very swift, why not perceived, 108; spirits capable of motion, 166-7; its communication incomprehensible, 169-71; matter not capable of originating, 315.

Names, use of, 88, 225 and note; necessary to numbers, 122-3; often got before the ideas they stand for, 241.
Natural philosophy, 65, 71, *149*, 331, 370.
Neo-Platonists, 341.
Nestor and Thersites, 192.
Newman, Cardinal, *345*.
Newton, 6, *68*, *98*, *100-1*, 260, 304, *319*, *333*.
Nominalism, *226*, *231*, 245; *cf.* *234*, *251*.
Norris, John, *79*.
Notions, 151, 240, and relative notes.
Number, 121-4; clearest idea of infinity from, 124.

Obscure ideas, 204-5.
Occasionalism, *170*, *285*, *320*.
Ontological argument, *xli*, 313 and note.
Opinion, as distinguished from knowledge, 9, 11, 265, 331, 337. *See* Assent, Faith, Judgement, Probability.

Paley, *202*.
Particular truths, known before general, 24-6, 305; possess the same self-evidence, 23, 300, 304, 306; particular ideas first received, 22, 301; things, ideas, and words, all particular in their existence, 220, 230 and note; only particular propositions about existence knowable, 328.
Pascal, 84.
Passive powers or capacities, 136 and note, 158; mind passive in reception of simple ideas, 92.
Perception, an operation of the mind, 43, 61; the first idea from reflection, 73; nature of, 73-9; other senses of perception, 138-9.
Person, a forensic term, 198-9; personal identity depends on consciousness, not on identity of substance, 188-200.
Place, 97-8.
Plato and Platonists, *20*, *178*, *226*, *347*.
Pleasure and pain, 61-3, 145-6.
Pope, *162*, *331*, *332*.
Power, idea of, *xxiii–iv*; how got, 63, 135; active or passive, 136, 148-9; active power and spirit, 137-8.
Powers, a great part of our ideas of substances, 158-61; secondary qualities, powers to produce certain ideas in us, 71-2, 158-9; powers to produce changes in some other substance, 71-2, 159; active powers and passive capacities, 148.
*Praecognita*, 264, 301.
Prince, Dr. Morton, *195*.
Probability, its degrees, 334-43. *See* Assent, Belief, Faith, Judgement.
Proof, depends on the discovery and proper arrangement of intermediate ideas, 262-4, 276, 330, 350.
Proper names, 228.
Propositions, truth belongs only

to, 215; mental and verbal, 291–3. *See* General, Particular.
Pythagoras, Pythagorean, 36, 192, *342*.

Qualities, *xxxvii*; primary and secondary, 63–73; how related to one another, 156–64; no necessary connexion discoverable between them, 274–5; sensible qualities and their causes, 294–7.
Real and fantastical ideas, 208–9.
Realism, *xvii*; Natural R., *xlvii*; New R., *xlviii*.
Reason, *21*, *37*, 344–55; distinct provinces of reason and faith, 354–8; reason and revelation, 362.
Reflection, ideas of, 44, 46, 51, 61–4, 91.
Reid, *xiii*, *xix*, *xxii*, *xlvii*, *199*, *288*, *344*.
Relation, ideas of, 86, 93, 95, 175–82; relation something extraneous and superinduced, 178; moral relations, 201–3.
Representative Perception, theory of, *xii*–*xiii*, *xxxix*, *xliv*–*vii*, *288*.
Retention, 79–85.
Revelation, grounds of our assent to, 343; revelation and reason, 360, 362.
*Rêverie*, 133–4.
Reward and punishment, 31, 198–9, 201–3.

Sagacity, in finding out intermediate ideas, 262, 276.
Scepticism, 13–14, *366*.
Schools and Scholastic men, *ix*, *xxxiii*, *xli*, *xlvi*, *167*, *211*, 303–5.
Science, none of bodies, 283, 331; none of spirits, 283.
Sciences, threefold division of, 369–71.
Self, knowledge of existence of, 309–10.
Self-evidence, *21*; not limited to maxims, 299, 304–5. *See* Certainty.
Sensation, definition of, 43, 51, 133; the source of all knowledge of reality except of self and God, 321; sensations often changed by the judgement, 74–7.
Sensationalism, *xviii*, *xliv*–*vi*, *42*.
Sense-datum or sensum, *xlviii*.
Sensible point = *minimum sensibile*, 120 and note.
Sensitive knowledge, 265–7; the nature of the certainty belonging to it, 322, 325; its extent, 326–7.
Sergeaunt, John, *197*, *199*.
Shaftesbury, Lord, *xxxiv*.
Siam, King of, 336.
Signs, doctrine of, *10*, 370–1.
Simple ideas, *43*, 53–5, 64, 92; names of, indefinable, 238.
Smith, Professor N. Kemp, *xii*, *xxi*, *176*, *278*, *311*.
Solidity, idea of, 57–60; not to be identified with extension, 99.
Sorley, Professor, *149*.
Space, idea of, *xxvii*, 96; space and body not the same, 98–105.
Spencer, Herbert, *154*, *348*.
Spinoza, *ix*, *xi*, *245*, *269*.
Spirit, thinking and motivity the primary ideas of, 166; idea of spirit as clear and distinct as that of body, 164–5, 168–72; spirits capable of motion, 166–7.
Stewart, Dugald, *45*.
Stillingfleet, *xxiv*, *xxv*, *xli*, *164*, *180*, *199*, *231*, *233*–*4*, *270*, *273*, *288*, *307*, *357*.
Stoics, *370*.
Stout, Professor, *80*, *83*, *292*.
Strasburg clock, 243, 246.
Substance, idea of, *xxiv*–*vi*; not innate, 39; idea of substance in general, 154–7; complex ideas of specific substances, 156–8, 164; ambiguity of the term, 101; substance and accidents, 102; substances, single or collective, 94, 175.
Succession, idea of, 63; how derived, 108–9; sense of, dependent on rate of movement, 109.
Sydenham, 6.
Syllogism, criticism of the, 346–53.
Synthetic judgements *a priori*, *308*.

Tennyson, *295*.

Terms, absolute and relative, 175–9; abstract and concrete, 253–4.

Testimony, how it is to be estimated, 339–41.

Thinking, the action and not the essence of the soul, 48–51, 134–5; faculty of thinking might be superadded to matter, 269–72.

Time = 'duration set out by measures', 111; natural measures of time, 111–12; mutual implication of time and space, *111*, 120–1, *121*.

Tolerance, 337–8.

Trifling propositions, 306–8.

Truth defined, 291; truth and falsehood properly belong to propositions, 215; truth either verbal or real, 295; truths of reason and truths of fact, *xxxv*, *328*.

Understanding, 3, 9, 14, 61, 138–9.

Unity, idea of, *xxii*, 63, 121–2.

Universal propositions, *see* General knowledge.

Urim and Thummim, 366.

Vacuum, distinct idea of, 102–4; its existence, 103–4.

Virtue and vice, 202–3.

Voltaire, 55.

Ward, Professor, *80*, *109*.

Webb, T. E., *xix*, *xxii*.

Whichcote, *13*.

Will and volition, 61; definition of, 138; to be distinguished from desire, 142; determined not by the greatest good but by the most pressing uneasiness, 143–5.

Worcester, Bishop of, *see* Stillingfleet.

Words, the signs or sensible marks of ideas, 223, 225. *See* Book III *passim.*

PRINTED IN GREAT BRITAIN
AT THE UNIVERSITY PRESS, OXFORD
BY VIVIAN RIDLER
PRINTER TO THE UNIVERSITY